WELDING SKILLS AND PRACTICES

J. W. GIACHINO, Head and
Professor Emeritus of Engineering and Technology
Western Michigan University
Kalamazoo, Michigan

WILLIAM WEEKS, Associate Professor
Welding and Metallurgy
Western Michigan University
Kalamazoo, Michigan

ELMER BRUNE, Associate Professor
Welding
Western Michigan University
Kalamazoo, Michigan

1971

American Technical Society **Chicago, Illinois 60637**

LIBRARY OF CONGRESS CATALOG CARD NUMBER 77-123471

ISBN: 0-8269-3042-5

PRINTED IN THE UNITED STATES OF AMERICA

PREFACE TO FOURTH EDITION

The original intent of *Welding Skills and Practices* was to provide current and authoritative welding information and techniques to those who are preparing for gainful employment in the field of welding as well as for the individuals who wished to upgrade their welding skills. The wide and continuous acceptance of this welding text has repeatedly demonstrated that its basic function is being fulfilled. Nevertheless, if a text is to remain authentic it must be subjected periodically to a critical analysis and then revised to reflect up-to-date practices. For this reason a fourth edition of Welding Skills and Practices was deemed necessary.

The new edition not only incorporates additional technical information and welding practices but some of its content has been reorganized for better understanding. The use of color will be found particularly attractive and far more stimulating for learning purposes.

Of special significance is the expansion of the units dealing with Gas-Tungsten Arc Welding and Gas Metal-Arc Welding. Since these areas of welding are more predominately used today, a more comprehensive coverage of them became advisable.

A new chapter on Underwater Cutting and Welding has also been included for those who have from time to time requested such information.

Incidentally, we are very grateful to Mr. Richard C. Kandel, President of Craftsweld Equipment Corporation, for his contribution to the revised text.

In the preparation of the original edition, considerable assistance was received from C. W. Sparrow, welding engineer, Purity Cylinder Gases, Inc.; Kenneth Nyhuis, District Manager, Purity Cylinder Gases, Inc.; and W. W. McClellan, former Manager of Acme Welding Supply. They all contributed valuable time in proofreading the manuscript and providing many helpful suggestions in describing welding techniques.

We hope that the new edition of *Welding Skills and Practices* will be found even more useful as a valuable teaching medium.

The Authors

Contents

Contents

Supplementary Welding Data

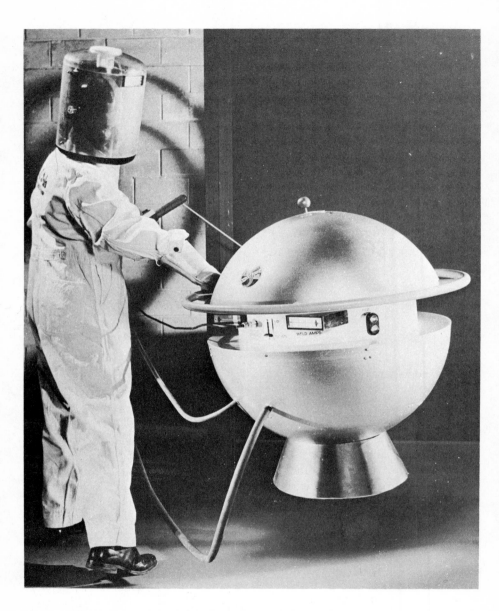

WELDING OF THE FUTURE?

This futuristic anti-gravity welder, the VEGA, would repeal the "law of gravity" by the flick of a lever. Still a gleam in the eye of researchers, the VEGA would have sufficient gravity-cancelling capacity to take care of its own weight, permitting an operator to pull it effortlessly up a ladder, over floor obstructions, etc. However, present plans do not include the operator going along for a free ride. The VEGA would also have a self-contained power supply. The operator is wearing a REGULUS helmet, which is said to provide maximum visibility and protection from welding flashes. (A. O. Smith Corp.)

CHAPTER 1

Welding

An Essential Skill

Welding is playing an important role in the expansion and production of our industries. Welding has become one of the principal means of fabricating and repairing metal products. It is almost impossible to name an industry, large or small, that does not employ some type of welding. Industry has found that welding is an efficient, dependable, and economical means of joining metal in practically all metal fabricating operations.

Where Welding is Used

In tooling-up for a new model automobile, a manufacturer may spend upward of a million dollars on welding equipment. Many buildings, bridges, and ships are fabricated by welding; and where construction noise must be kept at a minimum, such as in the building of hospital additions, the value of welding as the chief means of joining steel sections is particularly significant.

Without welding, the aircraft indus-

Fig. 1. Fabrication of metal structures is simplified by automatic welding techniques. (Bell Aircraft Corp.)

1

Fig. 2. Many parts of airplanes are joined by some welding process. (Douglas Aircraft Co.)

tries would never be able to meet the enormous demands for planes, rockets, and missiles. Rapid progress in the exploration of outer space has been made possible by new methods and knowledge of welding metallurgy.

Probably the most sizeable contribution welding has made to society is the manufacture of special products for household use. Welding processes are employed in the construction of such items as television sets, refrigera-

Fig. 3. Welding made possible the fabrication of this section of a missile.

Fig. 4. The metallic arc is used here to weld an industrial fan structure. (Clarage Fan Co.)

tors, kitchen cabinets, dishwashers, and other similar products. As a

Fig. 5. Welding plays an important role in the construction of heavy machinery, trucks, and armored military vehicles. (Borg-Warner Corp.)

means of fabrication, welding has proved fast, dependable, and flexible. It lowers production costs by simplifying design and eliminates costly patterns and machining operations.

Welding is used extensively for the manufacture and repair of farm equipment, mining and oil machinery, machine tools, jigs and fixtures, and in the construction of boilers, furnaces, and railway cars. With improved techniques for adding new metal to worn parts, welding has also resulted in economy for highly competitive industries.

Types of Welding Processes

Of the many methods of welding in use today, gas, arc, and resistance dominate the field. We can best explain these processes from the standpoint of the operator's duties.

The principal duty of the operator employing gas welding equipment is to control and direct the heat on the edges of metal to be joined, while ap-

Fig. 6. Welding is often indispensable in assembling the steel structure of a building.

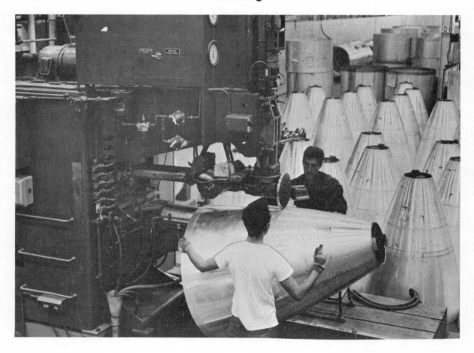

Fig. 7. Seam welding is being used here to weld aircraft tail sections. (Aluminum Company of America.)

Fig. 8. This refrigerator evaporator unit is being assembled by Tig welding. (Linde Co.)

plying a suitable metal filler to the molten pool. The intense heat is obtained from the combustion of gas, usually acetylene and oxygen. For this reason this process is also called *oxyacetylene welding*. The skills required for this job are adjustment of the regulators, selection of proper tips and rod, preparation of the metal edges to be joined, and the technique of flame and rod manipulation. The gas welder may also be called upon to do flame cutting with a cutting attachment and extra oxygen pressure. Flame or oxygen cutting is employed to cut various metals to a desired size or shape, or to remove excess metal from castings.

The arc welder performs his skill by first striking an arc at the starting point of a weld and maintaining this electric arc to fuse the metal joints. The molten metal from the tip of the electrode is then deposited in the joint and, together with the molten metal of the edges, solidifies to form a sound and uniform connection. The arc welding operator is expected to select the proper electrodes for the job and to be able to weld any type seam using the technique required due to the position of the work, i.e., overhead, horizontal, etc.

In the field of arc welding, the gas-shielded arc processes are rapidly gaining recognition as being superior to the standard metallic arc. With gas-shielded arc both the arc and molten puddle are covered by a shield of gas. The shield of gas prevents atmospheric contamination, thereby producing a sounder weld. The processes

Fig. 10. A stainless steel restaurant kettle is being completed by means of an inert-gas-shielded arc spot welder. (Linde Co.)

known as Tig and Mig welding are either manually or automatically operated.

Resistance welding operators are responsible for the control of machines which fuse metals together by heat and pressure. If two pieces of metal are placed between electrodes which become conductors for a low voltage and high amperage current, the materials will, because of their own resistance, become heated to a plastic, or semi-solid, state. To complete the weld, the current is interrupted before pressure is released, thereby allowing the weld metal to cool for solid strength. The operator's duty is to properly adjust the machine current, pressure, and feed settings suitable for the material to be welded. He usually will be responsible for the alignment of parts to be assembled and for controlling the passage of parts through the welding machine.

Fig. 9. Manually operated inert-gas-shielded arc welding equipment is being used to weld this fuel tank assembly. (Douglas Aircraft Co.)

Fig. 11. To attain the required welding skills, a person usually has to complete a formal course of instruction under a competent instructor.

Selection of the Proper Welding Process

There are no hard and fast rules which govern the type of welding that is to be used for a particular job. In general, the controlling factors are kind of metals to be joined, costs involved, nature of products to be fabricated, and production techniques. Some jobs are more easily accomplished by the oxyacetylene welding process whereas others are more easily done by means of arc welding.

Gas welding is used in all metal working industries and in the field as well as for plant maintenance. Because of its flexibility and mobility, it is widely used in maintenance and repair work. The welding unit can be moved on a two wheel cart or transported by truck to any field job where breakdowns occur. Its adaptability

Fig. 12. Job opportunities are available in the aerospace industries if you have the required technical skills and knowledge. (NASA)

makes the oxyacetylene process usually suitable for welding, brazing, cutting, and heat treating.

The chief advantage of arc welding is the rapidity with which a high quality weld can be made at a relatively low cost. Specific applications of this process are found in the manufacture of structural steel for buildings, bridges, and machinery. Arc welding is considered ideal for making storage and pressure tanks as well as for production line products using standard commercial metals.

Since the development of gas-shielded arc processes, there are indications that they will be used extensively in the future in welding all types of ferrous and nonferrous metals in both gage or plate thickness.

Resistance welding is primarily a production welding process. It is especially designed for the mass production of domestic goods, automobile bodies, electrical equipment, hardware, etc. Probably the outstanding characteristic of this type of welding is its adaptability to rapid fusion of seams.

Occupational Opportunities in Welding

The widespread use of welding in American industry provides a constant source of employment for both skilled and semi-skilled operators. Consequently job opportunities will continue to increase in this field.

Learning the essential skills required in order to fulfill the many welding job requirements varies from a few months of on-the-job training to several years of formal training. A knowledge of the properties of metals, blueprint reading, welding symbols, and the mastery of welding techniques are generally required.

A course in welding followed by several years of experience is the usual procedure by which a welder learns the trade. A beginner starts on simple production jobs and gradually works up to higher levels of skill as his experience and ability improve. Before being assigned to work where the quality and strength of the weld are critical, a welder may be required to pass a certification test given by the employer or some other inspection authority.

Skilled welders may, by promotion, become inspectors, foremen, or supervisors. There are unlimited opportunities for advancement in industry for those who become thoroughly acquainted with the techniques, materials, designs, and new applications of welding processes.

Welding is an important process in missile fabrication. (U.S. Army)

CHAPTER 2

Welding
Metallurgy

~~~~~~

In preparing yourself to become a skillful welder you should become familiar with the effects of heat on the grain structure of metal and with what happens to metal when certain alloying elements are added to it. You also need to know what safeguards must be followed in welding metals because application of heat during the welding process may destroy the very elements which were originally added to improve the structure of the metal. For example, metals expand and contract, thereby setting up great stresses which often result in severe distortions. Improper welding of stainless steel may result in a complete loss of its corrosion-resistant qualities, and welding high carbon steel in the same manner as low carbon steel may produce such a brittle weld as to make the welded piece unusable.

This chapter, then, deals with the metallurgy of welding; that is, the for- mation of impurities and the effects of heat on the chemical, physical, and mechanical properties of metals.

Mechanical Properties of Metals

Mechanical properties are measures of how materials behave under applied loads. Another way of saying this is how strong is a metal when it comes in contact with one or more forces. If you know the strength properties of a metal, you can build a structure that is safe and sound. Likewise, when a welder knows the strength of his weld as compared with the base metal, he can produce a weldment that is strong enough to do the job. Hence strength is the ability of a metal to withstand loads (forces) without breaking down.

Strength properties are commonly referred to as tensile strength, bending strength, compressive strength, torsional strength, shear strength, fatigue

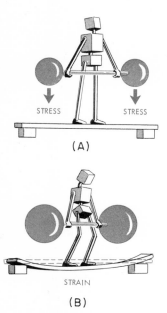

Fig. 2. A metal having elastic properties returns to its original shape after the load is removed.

Fig. 1. Example of stress and strain.

strength and impact strength. An explanation of these terms as well as other terms that are associated with mechanical properties are included in the following paragraphs.

1. *Stress* is the internal resistance a material offers to being deformed and is measured in terms of the applied load. See Fig. 1A.

2. *Strain* is the deformation that results from a stress and is expressed in terms of the amount of deformation per inch. See Fig. 1B.

3. *Elasticity* is the ability of a metal to return to its original shape after being elongated or distorted, when the forces are released. See Fig. 2. A rubber band is a good example of what is meant by elasticity. If the rubber is stretched, it will return to its original

shape after you let it go. However, if the rubber is pulled beyond a certain point, it will break. Metals with elastic properties react in the same way.

4. *Elastic limit* is the last point at which a material may be stretched and still return to its undeformed condition upon release of the stress.

5. *Modulus of elasticity* is the ratio of stress to strain within the elastic limit. The less a material deforms under a given stress the higher the modulus of elasticity. By checking the modulus of elasticity the comparative stiffness of different materials can readily be ascertained. Rigidity or stiffness is very important for many machine and structural applications.

6. *Tensile strength* is that property

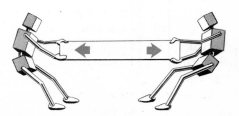

Fig. 3. A metal with tensile strength resists pulling forces.

which resists forces acting to pull the metal apart. See Fig. 3. It is one of the more important factors in the evaluation of a metal.

7. *Compressive strength* is the ability of a material to resist being crushed. See Fig. 4. Compression is the opposite of tension with respect to the direction of the applied load. Most metals have high tensile strength and high com-

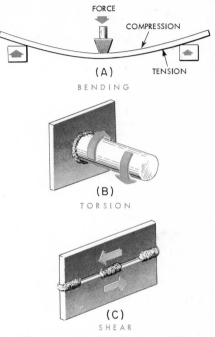

Fig. 5. Examples of bending, torsion, and shearing stresses.

Fig. 4. Compressive strength refers to the property of metal to resist crushing forces.

pressive strength. However, brittle materials such as cast iron have high compressive strength but only a moderate tensile strength.

8. *Bending strength* is that quality which resists forces from causing a member to bend or deflect in the direction in which the load is applied. Actually a bending stress is a combination of tensile and compressive stresses. See Fig. 5A.

9. *Torsional strength* is the ability of a metal to withstand forces that cause a member to twist. See Fig. 5B.

10. *Shear strength* refers to how well a member can withstand two equal forces acting in opposite directions. See Fig. 5C.

11. *Fatigue strength* is the property of a material to resist various kinds of rapidly alternating stresses. For example, a piston rod or an axle undergoes complete reversal of stresses from tension to compression. Bending a piece of wire back and forth until it breaks is another example of fatigue strength.

12. *Impact strength* is the ability of a metal to resist loads that are applied suddenly and often at high velocity. The higher the impact strength of a metal the greater the energy required to break it. Impact strength

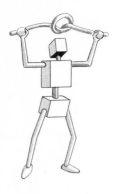

Fig. 6. A ductile metal can easily be shaped.

may be seriously affected by welding since it is one of the most structure sensitive properties.

13. *Ductility* refers to the ability of metal to stretch, bend, or twist without breaking or cracking. See Fig. 6. A metal having high ductility, such as copper or soft iron, will fail or break gradually as the load on it is increased. A metal of low ductility, such as cast iron, fails suddenly by cracking when subjected to a heavy load.

14. *Hardness* is that property in steel which resists indentation or penetration. See Fig. 7. Hardness is usually

Fig. 7. Hardness resists penetration.

expressed in terms of the area of an indentation made by a special ball under a standard load, or the depth of a special indenter under a specific load.

15. *Cryogenic properties* of metals represent behavior characteristics under stress in environments of very low temperatures. In addition to being sensitive to crystal structure and processing conditions, metals are also sensitive to low and high temperatures. Some alloys which perform satisfactorily at room temperatures may fail completely at low or high temperatures. The changes from ductile to brittle failure occurs rather suddenly at low temperatures.

Classification of Carbon Steels

A plain carbon steel is one in which carbon is the only alloying element. The amount of carbon in the steel controls its hardness, strength, and ductility. The higher the carbon content, the harder the steel. Conversely, the less the carbon the greater the ductility of the steel.

Carbon steels are classified according to the percentage of carbon they contain. They are referred to as low, medium, high, and very high carbon steels.

Low carbon steels. Steels with a carbon range of 0.05 to 0.30 per cent are called low carbon steels. Steels in this class are tough, ductile, and easily machined, formed, and welded. Most of them do not respond to any heat treating process except case hardening. Low carbon steel, when subjected to the spark test, will throw off

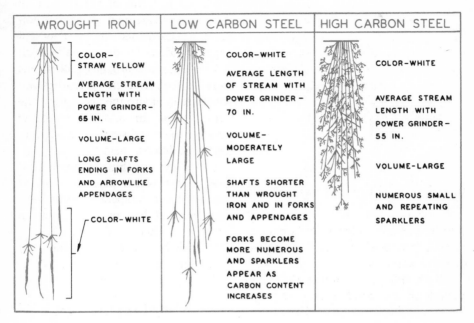

WROUGHT IRON	LOW CARBON STEEL	HIGH CARBON STEEL
COLOR— STRAW YELLOW AVERAGE STREAM LENGTH WITH POWER GRINDER— 65 IN. VOLUME—LARGE LONG SHAFTS ENDING IN FORKS AND ARROWLIKE APPENDAGES COLOR—WHITE	COLOR—WHITE AVERAGE LENGTH OF STREAM WITH POWER GRINDER— 70 IN. VOLUME— MODERATELY LARGE SHAFTS SHORTER THAN WROUGHT IRON AND IN FORKS AND APPENDAGES FORKS BECOME MORE NUMEROUS AND SPARKLERS APPEAR AS CARBON CONTENT INCREASES	COLOR—WHITE AVERAGE STREAM LENGTH WITH POWER GRINDER— 55 IN. VOLUME-LARGE NUMEROUS SMALL AND REPEATING SPARKLERS

Fig. 8. Spark characteristics of carbon steels.

long, white-colored streamers with very little or no sparklers. See Fig. 8.

Medium carbon steels. These steels have a carbon range from 0.30 to 0.45 per cent. They are strong and hard but cannot be worked or welded as easily as low carbon steels. Because of their higher carbon content, they can be heat treated. Successful welding of these steels often requires special electrodes, but even then greater care must be taken to prevent formation of cracks around the weld area.

The spark test will show more numerous sparklers, beginning closer to the wheel, with the streamers much lighter in color.

High and very high carbon steels. Steels with a carbon range of 0.45 to 0.75 per cent are classified as high

carbon and those with 0.75 to 1.7 per cent carbon as very high carbon steels. Both of these steels respond well to heat treatment. As a rule, steels up to 0.65 per cent carbon can be welded with special electrodes, although pre-heating and stress relieving techniques must often be used after the welding is completed. Usually it is not practical to weld steels in the very high carbon range.

The spark test for high carbon steels can easily be recognized by the numerous explosions or sparklers given off, which are practically white in color. See Fig. 8.

Alloy Steels

An alloy steel is a steel to which one or more of such elements as nickel, chromium, manganese, molybdenum, titanium, cobalt, tungsten, or vanadium have been added. The addition of these elements gives steel greater toughness, strength, resistance to wear, and resistance to corrosion.

Alloy steels are called by the predominating element which has been added. Most of them can be welded, provided special electrodes are used. The more common elements added to steel are:

1. *Chromium*—When quantities of chromium are added to steel the resulting product is a metal having extreme hardness and resistance to wear without making it brittle. Chromium also tends to refine the grain structure of steel, thereby increasing its toughness. It is used either alone in carbon steel or in combination with other elements such as nickel, vanadium, molybdenum, or tungsten.

2. *Manganese* — The addition of manganese to steel produces a fine grain structure which has greater toughness and ductility.

3. *Molybdenum* — This element produces the greatest hardening effect of any element except carbon and at the same time it reduces the enlargement of the grain structure. The result is a strong, tough steel. Although molybdenum is used alone in some alloys, often it is supplemented by other elements, particularly nickel or chromium or both.

4. *Nickel*—The addition of nickel to steel tends to increase its strength without decreasing its toughness or ductility. When large quantities of nickel are added (25 to 35 per cent),

the steels not only become tough but develop high resistance to corrosion and shock.

5. *Vanadium* — Addition of this element to steel inhibits grain growth when the steel is heated above its critical range for heat treatment. It also imparts toughness and strength to the metal.

6. *Tungsten*—This element is used mostly in steels designed for metal cutting tools. Tungsten steels are tough, hard, and very resistant to wear.

7. *Cobalt* — The chief function of cobalt is to strengthen the ferrite. It is used in combination with tungsten to develop red hardness; that is, the ability to remain hard when red hot.

Steel Code Classifying Systems

The two main systems used for classifying steels are known as the S.A.E. code (Society of Automotive Engineers) and the A.I.S.I. code (American Iron and Steel Institute).

The S.A.E. system is based on the chemical analysis of steel. The numbers of the code classifies the type of steel as follows: *1* represents carbon steel, *2* nickel, *3* nickel chromium, etc. In the case of alloy steels the second number of the series indicates the approximate amount of the predominating alloying element. The last two or three digits refer to the carbon content and are expressed in hundredths of 1 per cent. For example, a *2335 S.A.E.* steel indicates nickel steel of about 3 per cent nickel and 0.35 per cent carbon.

The following are the basic numerals for various S.A.E. steels:

TYPE OF STEEL	NUMERAL
Carbon Steels	1 xxx
Plain carbon	10 xx
Free cutting (screw stock) . .	11 xx
Free cutting, manganese	x13 xx
High manganese	T13 xx
Nickel Steels	2 xxx
.50% nickel	20 xx
1.50% nickel	21 xx
3.50% nickel	23 xx
5.00% nickel	25 xx
Nickel Chromium Steel	3 xxx
1.25% nickel; .60% chromium	31 xx
1.75% nickel; 1.00% chrom.	32 xx
3.50% nickel; 1.50% chrom.	33 xx
3.00% nickel; .80% chromium	34 xx
Corrosion and Heat-resisting Steels .	30 xxx
Molybdenum Steels	4 xxx
Chromium	41 xx
Chromium nickel	43 xx
Nickel . . . . 46 xx and 48 xx	
Chromium Steel	5 xxx
Low chromium	51 xx
Medium chromium	52 xxx
Corrosion and heat resisting .	51 xxx
Chromium Vanadium Steel	6 xxx
Tungsten Steel . . . . 7 xxx and 7 xxxx	
Silicon Manganese Steel	9 xxx

The A.I.S.I. code is a refinement of the S.A.E. code. This code consists of letter prefixes and number designations. The prefix letters indicate the basic process used in making the steel. They are:

A—Open-hearth alloy steel.

B—Acid Bessemer carbon steel.

C—Basic open-hearth carbon steel.

D—Acid open-hearth carbon steel.

E—Electric furnace steel of both carbon and alloy steels.

The number designation classifies the kind of steel, the alloying elements, and range of carbon content. The first number indicates the type of steel, and the second number in the series shows the amount of the predominating alloying element. The last two or three digits refer to the approximate permissible range of carbon content.

The following are the basic number designations:

TYPE OF STEEL	NUMERAL
Basic and acid open-hearth and acid Bessemer carbon steel grades, nonsulfurized and nonphosphorized . . .	10 xx
Basic open-hearth and acid Bessemer carbon steel grades, sulfurized but not phosphorized	11 xx
Basic open-hearth carbon steel grades, phosphorized	12 xx
Manganese 1.60 to 1.90%	13 xx
Nickel 3.50%	23 xx
Nickel 5.00%	25 xx
Nickel 1.25%—chromium 0.60% .	31 xx
Nickel 1.75%—chromium 1.00% .	32 xx
Nickel 3.50%—chromium 1.50% .	33 xx
Molybdenum	40 xx
Chromium-molybdenum	41 xx
Nickel-chromium-molybdenum . . .	43 xx
Nickel 1.65%—molybdenum 0.25%	46 xx
Nickel 3.25%—molybdenum 0.25%	48 xx
Low-chromium	50 xx
Medium-chromium	51 xx
Chromium-high carbon	52 xx
Chromium-vanadium	61 xx
Nickel-chromium-molybdenum . . .	86 xx
Manganese-silicon	92 xx

Examples of Steels With Codes

C1078—Basic open-hearth carbon steel; carbon 0.72-0.85%.

E50100 — Electric furnace chromium steel 0.40-0.60%; chromium, 0.95-1.10% carbon.

E2512 — Electric furnace nickel steel, 4.75-5.25% nickel; 0.09-0.14%

carbon. This can be shown diagrammatically as follows:

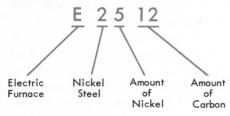

| Electric Furnace | Nickel Steel | Amount of Nickel | Amount of Carbon |

Structure of Metal

When you examine a polished piece of metal under a microscope, you will see small grains. Each of these grains is made up of smaller particles, called atoms, of which all matter is composed.

The grains, or crystals as they are often called, vary in shape and size. The arrangement of the atoms determines the shape of the crystalline structure. In general, the crystals of the more common types of metals arrange themselves in three patterns known as *space-lattices*. A space-lat-

tice is a graphical representation of the orderly geometric pattern into which the atoms of all metals arrange themselves upon cooling from a liquid to a solid state.

The first type of space-lattice, illustrated in Fig. 9, is the *body-centered cube*. Here you will find nine atoms—one at each corner of the cube and one in the center. This crystal pattern is found in such metals as iron, molybdenum, chromium, columbium, tungsten, and vanadium.

The second crystal pattern is the *face-centered cube*. Notice in Fig. 10 how the atoms are arranged. Metals having this space-lattice pattern are aluminum, nickel, copper, lead, platinum, gold, and silver.

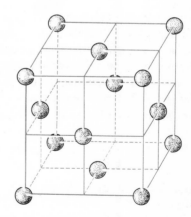

Fig. 10. The atoms in a face-centered cube crystal assume this arrangement.

The third space-lattice is called the *close packed hexagonal* form. See Fig. 11. Among the metals having this type of crystalline structure are cadmium, bismuth, cobalt, magnesium, titanium, and zinc.

Metals with the face-centered lattice

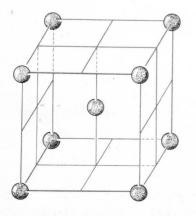

Fig. 9. Here is the arrangement of atoms in a body-centered cube crystal.

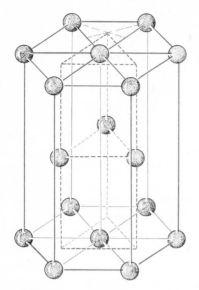

Fig. 11. This is the arrangement of the atoms in a hexagonal close packed crystal.

cubic structure at a temperature of 1670°F.

As liquid metal is cooled it loses thermal energy (heat) to the air and walls of the container. At the solidification temperature the atoms of the metal assume their characteristic crystal structure. Crystals begin growing at random in the melt at points of lowest energy. If the rate of cooling is fast, more crystals will form instantaneously than at slow rates of cooling. The more crystals that are growing simultaneously the finer will be the grain size of the metal.

Grain size is important since fine-grained steels have far superior mechanical properties than coarse-grained steels. Hence, it is important for a welder to preserve the grain size of the parent metal. The use of excessive heat leads to a slow rate of cooling, thus producing coarse grains and brittleness in a weldment.

generally are ductile; that is, plastic and workable. Metals with close packed hexagonal lattice lack plasticity and cannot be cold worked. Metals with body-centered crystals have higher strength but lower cold working properties than those with the face-centered pattern.

Solidification or Crystallization of Metals

All metals solidify in the form of crystals. As mentioned previously, each metal has its own characteristic geometric pattern. Some metals may change from one crystal structure to another crystal structure at a definite temperature. For example, iron when heated changes to a face-centered

Importance of Carbon in Steel

In carbon steel, at normal room temperature, the atoms are arranged in a body-centered lattice. This is known as *alpha iron.* Each grain of the structure is made up of layers of pure iron (ferrite) and a combination of iron and carbon. The compound of iron and carbon or iron carbide is called *cementite.* The cementite is very hard and has practically no ductility.

In a steel with 0.83 per cent carbon, the grains are *pearlitic,* meaning that all the carbon is combined with iron to form iron carbide. This is

Fig. 12. Here is how the pearlite grains arrange themselves in a eutectoid mixture.

known as a *eutectoid mixture* of carbon and iron. See Fig. 12. If there is less than 0.83 per cent carbon, the mixture of pearlite and ferrite is referred to as *hypoeutectoid*. An examination of such a mixture would show grains of pure iron and grains of pearlite as shown in Fig. 13. When the metal contains more than 0.83 per cent carbon, the mixture consists of pearlite and iron carbide and is called *hypereutectoid*. Notice in Fig. 14 how the grains of pearlite are surrounded by iron carbide. In general, the greatest percentage of steel used is of the hypoeutectoid type.

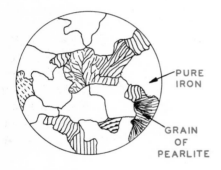

PURE
IRON

GRAIN
OF
PEARLITE

Fig. 13. An example of hypoeutectoid grain structure.

How Heating Affects the Grain Structure

When steel is heated from room temperature to above 1333° F, the pearlite grains change from a body-centered lattice to a face-centered structure. Such an arrangement of iron atoms is known as *gamma iron*. What has happened is that while the steel went through its *critical temperature* (temperature above which steel must be heated so it will harden when quenched), the iron carbide separated into carbon and iron, with the carbon distributing itself evenly in the iron. The material is now called *austenite*. If the heating is continued beyond the critical point, the grains grow larger or coarser until the melting point is reached. When the steel melts, the crystal structure is completely broken and the atoms float about without any definite relationship to one another.

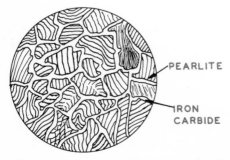

PEARLITE

IRON
CARBIDE

Fig. 14. This is an example of a hypereutectoid structure.

How the Rate of Cooling Affects the Grain Structure

If you cool a metal from a molten state to room temperature, the transformation that takes place, under proper conditions, is exactly the opposite of that which occurs while the metal is heating. As the metal begins to cool, the crystals of pure iron start to solidify. This is followed by a crystallization of the austenitic grains and eventually the entire mass becomes solid. During the range of temperatures at which various stages of solidification takes place, the metal passes from a "mushy" condition to a solid solution. While in a "mushy" stage the metal can be shaped easily. After it has reached a solid state, even though the alloy is still hot, it can be formed only by applying heavy pressure or blows.

With continued cooling of the solid metal, the austenite contracts evenly as the temperature falls. When it reaches its transformation temperature, the temperature drop stops for a time. At this point there occurs a rearrangement of gamma iron to alpha iron as well as a separation of iron carbide and pure iron into pearlite grains.

The transformation of the metal from a liquid to a solid is important because the proper rearrangement of the atoms depends on the rate of cooling. If, for example, a piece of 0.83 per cent carbon steel is cooled rapidly after its critical temperature is reached, certain actions are arrested before the pearlitic structure can be formed. The result is a metal that is hard, but very brittle, known as *martensite*. See Fig. 15. Martensite is the constituent found in fully hardened steel which is hard and brittle. On the other hand, if the rate of quenching (cooling) is somewhat slower, the structure will blend in a form to produce a much more ductile metal.

Fig. 15. Structure of Martensite.

Factors Altering Strength and Structure

When a metal is cold worked (that is; hammered, rolled or drawn through a die) the ferrite and pearlite grains are made smaller and the metal becomes stronger and harder. If after cold working, the metal is heated and allowed to cool, the grain size is again increased and the metal softened.

The grain size of some metals is reduced and the strength improved through a heating and quenching process. Thus if a high carbon steel

is heated to a prescribed temperature and then immediately quenched in oil or water, followed by a tempering process, the grain size remains fine. But if you allow the same metal to heat for a long time or if you subject it to temperatures beyond the critical range, then the grain size increases and the metal is weakened. This point is particularly important to remember in welding various steel alloys. The problem of structural change is not too serious in welding mild steel. On the other hand, alloy steels are greatly dependent on space-lattice formation and grain size for their strength. Therefore, you must take extreme care during welding to avoid seriously altering their space-lattice pattern through excessive application of heat or improper treatment of the weld during its cooling stages.

Effects of Heat During the Welding Process

In welding you must realize, too, that one edge of the metal may cool rapidly, thereby resulting in the formation of hard spots which cause cracks or failure in the weld. Also, there will be conditions where the metal is in a molten state at one point while the surrounding areas may have a temperature ranging from near the molten point down to room temperature. This means that in some areas the crystal structure is completely broken down while elsewhere recrystallization is taking place.

Keep in mind that when hardenable steels are being fused, and you make

no effort to control the structural changes either through preheating or by slowing down the cooling rate, the completed weld will be too brittle to be of any value. If a piece of steel, such as an automobile spring, is welded, the heat will remove the springiness from the metal. Moreover, you must remember that if a weld is made on a hardened structure, the act of welding will usually soften the steel and lower its strength. It is evident then, that in welding any alloy steel, an understanding of the effects of heating and cooling is important.

Heat Treating Metals

Heat treatment is used to soften metal and relieve internal stresses (annealing), harden metal, and temper metal (to toughen certain parts).

Annealing allows metal to be more readily machined and also eliminates stresses in metal after it has been welded. The steel is heated to a certain temperature and held at this temperature to allow the carbon to become evenly distributed throughout the steel. The degree of annealing temperature varies with different kinds of steel. After the metal has been heated for a sufficient period, it is allowed to cool slowly either in the furnace or by burying it in ashes, lime, or in some other insulating material. For some metals, the *normalizing* treatment is used. It differs from the standard annealing process in that the steel is heated to a higher temperature for shorter periods and then cooled in air.

Stress relieving is a means of removing the internal stresses which develop during the welding operation. The process consists of heating the structure to a temperature below the critical range (approximately 1100° F) and allowing it to cool slowly. Another method of relieving stresses is *peening* (hammering). However, peening must be undertaken with considerable care because there is always danger of weakening the physical strength of the metal.

Stress relieving should be done only if there is a possibility that the structure will crack upon cooling and no other means can be used to eliminate expansion and contraction forces.

Hardening increases the strength of pieces after they are fabricated. It is accomplishd by heating the steel to some temperature above the critical point and then cooling it rapidly in air, oil, water, or brine. Only medium, high, and very high carbon steels can be hardened by this method. The temperature at which the steel must be heated varies with the steel used.

The tendency of a steel to harden may or may not be desirable depending upon how it is going to be processed. For example, if it is to be welded, a strong tendency to harden will make a steel brittle and susceptible to cracking during the welding process. Special precautions such as preheating and a very careful control of heat input and cooling will be necessary to minimize this condition. During welding, an extremely high localized temperature differential exists between the molten metal of the weld and the solid,

much colder metal being welded. The cold parent metal acts as a quenchant to the weld metal and the metal nearby which has been heated above the upper critical temperature. The resulting structure of these areas is hard, brittle martensite. The greater the hardenability of a steel, the less severe the rate of heat extraction necessary to cause it to harden. This is one of the reasons that alloy and high carbon steels have to be welded with greater care than ordinary low carbon steels.

Case Hardening

Case hardening is a process of hardening low-carbon or mild steels by adding carbon, nitrogen, or a combination of carbon and nitrogen to the outer surface forming a hard, thin outer shell. The three principal case hardening techniques are known as carburizing, cyaniding, and nitriding.

Carburizing consists of heating low-carbon steel in a furnace containing a gas atmosphere with the desired amount of carbon monoxide. An alternate method is to heat the steel in contact with a carbonaceous material such as charcoal, coal, nuts, beans, bone, leather or a combination of these, however, modern methods of carburizing use gas atmosphere almost exclusively. The piece is heated to a temperature between 1650° and 1700°F where the steel in the austenitic condition readily absorbs carbon. The length of the heating period depends on the thickness of the hardened case desired. After heating, the steel is quenched, which produces a material with a hard surface and a relatively tough inner core.

Cyaniding involves heating a low-carbon steel in sodium cyanide or potassium cyanide. The cyanide is heated until it reaches a temperature of 1500°F and then the steel is placed in the liquid bath. This produces a very thin outer case which is harder than that obtained by the carburizing process.

Nitriding is a case hardening method which produces the hardest surface of any hardening process. Hardness is obtained by the formation of hard, wear-resistant nitrogen compounds in certain alloy steels where distortion must be kept to a minimum. The alloy is heated to about 900° to 1000°F in an atmosphere of dissociated ammonia gas.

Welding Defects

In the process of welding various materials precautions must be taken to prevent the development of certain defects in the weld metal otherwise these defects will severely weaken the weld. The following are some of the principal defects that are significant in any welding process.

Grain Growth. A wide temperature differential will exist between the molten metal of the actual weld and the edges of the heat-affected zone of the base metal. This temperature may range from a point far above the critical temperature down to an area unaffected by the heat. Thus the grain size can be expected to be large at the molten zone of the weld puddle and gradually reducing in size until recrystallization is reached. Grain growth can be kept to a minimum by effective control of preheating and postheating. Where heavy sections require successive passes, it is possible to use the heat of each successive pass to refine the grain of the previous pass. This can be done only if the metal is allowed to cool below the lower critical temperature between each pass. High carbon and alloy steels are especially vulnerable to coarse growth if cooled rapidly. These metals usually require a certain amount of preheating before welding and then allowed to cool slowly after the weld is completed.

Blowholes. Blowholes are cavities caused by gas entrapment during the solidification of the weld metal. They usually develop because of improper manipulation of the electrode and failure to maintain the molten pool long enough to float out the entrapped gas, slag, and other foreign matter. When gas and other matter become trapped in the grains of the solid metal, small holes are left in the weld after the metal cools.

Blowholes can be avoided by keeping the molten pool at a uniform temperature throughout the welding operation. This can be done by using a constant welding speed so the metal solidifies evenly. The possibility of blowholes is particularly prevalent during the stopping and starting of the weld along the seam, especially when the electrode must be changed.

Inclusions. Inclusions are impurities or foreign substances which are forced in a molten puddle during the welding process. Any inclusion tends to weaken a weld because it has the same effects as a crack. A typical example of an inclusion is slag which normally forms over a deposited weld. If the electrode is not manipulated correctly, the force of the arc causes some of the slag particles to be blown into the molten pool. When the molten metal freezes before these inclusions can float to the top, they become lodged in the metal, producing a defective weld. Inclusions are more likely to occur in overhead welding, since the tendency is not to keep the molten pool too long to prevent it from dripping off the seam. However, if the electrode is manipulated correctly and the right electrodes are used with proper current settings, inclusion can be avoided, or at least kept to a minimum.

Segregation. Segregation is a condition where some regions of the metal are enriched with an alloy ingredient while surrounding areas are actually impoverished. For example, when metal begins to solidify, tiny crystals form along grain boundaries. These so-called crystals or dendrites tend to exclude alloying elements. As other crystals form, they become progressively richer in alloying elements leaving other regions without the benefits of the alloying ingredients. Segregation can be remedied by proper heat treating or slow cooling.

Porosity. Porosity refers to the formation of tiny pinholes generated by atmospheric contamination. Some metals have a high affinity for oxygen and nitrogen when in a molten state. Unless an adequate protective shield is provided over the molten metal, gas will enter the metal and weaken it.

Residual Stresses

The strength of a welded joint depends a great deal on the way you control the expansion and contraction of the metal during the welding operation. Whenever heat is applied to a piece of metal, expansion forces are liberated which tend to change the dimensions of the piece. Upon cooling, the metal undergoes a change again as it attempts to resume its original shape. No serious consideration must be given these factors when there are no restricting forces to prevent the free movements of the expansion and contraction forces or when welding ductile metal, because the flow of metal will usually relieve the stresses. When free movement is restricted there is likely to occur a warping or distortion if the metal is malleable or ductile, and a fracture if the metal is brittle, as with cast iron.

To better understand the effects of expansion and contraction, assume that the bar shown in Fig. 16 is thoroughly and uniformly heated. Since the bar is not restricted in its movements, expansion is free to take place in all directions. Consequently, the

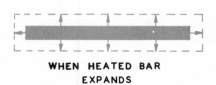

**WHEN HEATED BAR
EXPANDS**

Fig. 16. This is what happens when a bar is heated.

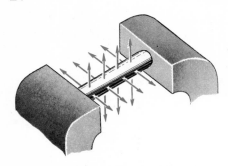

Fig. 17. The expansion forces are hindered when the bar has restricting forces like this.

nently distorted as illustrated in Fig. 18.

To show just how the expansion and contraction forces affect metal, study the results of welding two different pieces. In the first case, assume a break has occurred in the middle of a bar, as in Fig. 19. Upon welding the break, the heat naturally will cause the

Fig. 19. In welding this break, expansion forces are free to move.

overall size of the bar is increased. If the bar is allowed to cool without restraint of any kind, it will contract to its original shape.

Suppose now that this same bar is clamped in a vise, as shown in Fig. 17, and heated. Because the ends of the bar cannot move, expansion must take place in another direction. In this case the expansion occurs laterally.

If instead of heating the bar uniformly, the heat is applied only to one section, the expansion becomes localized and uneven. The surrounding cold metal prevents free expansion and the displacement of metal takes place in the heated area. When this area starts to cool, contraction will be uneven and some of the original displaced metal will become perma-

metal to expand. Since there are no obstructions on the ends of the bar the metal is permitted to move to whatever limits it desires. When the piece begins to cool, there are still no forces to prevent the metal from assuming its original shape.

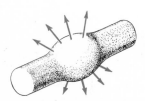

Fig. 18. This piece has been distorted because expansion forces were restricted.

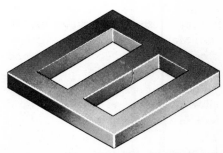

Fig. 20. Welding the frame in this portion will cause it to crack.

Suppose the break was in a center section as shown in Fig. 20. Note that in this case the ends of the bar are rigidly fastened to a solid frame. If the same procedure is used to weld the fracture as in the first case, it becomes evident that something is bound to happen to the casting if no provisions are made for expansion and contraction. Since the vertical and horizontal sections of the frame will prevent expanding the ends of the center piece, there is only one direction in which this movement can go while the metal is being heated, and that is at the point where fusion takes place. Now consider what will happen when the section begins to cool. The frame around the center section has not moved and, when contraction sets in, the center piece will be shortened. When the rigid frame resists this pull, a fracture or deformation at the line of weld or in some other place is bound to occur.

Controlling Residual Stresses

The following are a few simple procedures which will help control the forces caused by expansion and contraction.

Proper edge preparation and fit-up. Make certain that the edges are correctly beveled. Provide a space between the edges of the pieces to be joined. The common practice is to allow about ⅛″ at the end for each foot in length of the weld. See Fig. 21.

On long seams it is often advisable to use tack welds as shown in Fig. 22.

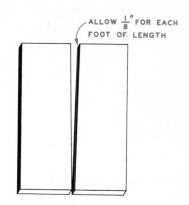

Fig. 21. Provide a space between the edges to be welded.

Fig. 22. Tacking the plates will hold them in position.

Space the tack welds about 12″ apart and run them approximately twice as long as the thickness of the weld. When tack welds are used, progressive spacing is not necessary. The plates are simply spaced an equal amount throughout the seam. Joints of maximum fixity should be welded first. Also, a long longitudinal seam is welded before a short transverse seam. See Fig. 23.

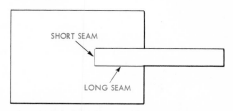

Fig. 23. Weld long longitudinal seam first.

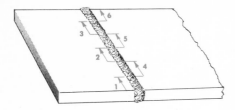

Fig. 24. The intermittent weld, sometimes referred to as the skip weld, will prevent distortion.

Minimizing heat input. Controlling the amount of heat input is somewhat more difficult for the beginner. An experienced welder is able to join a seam with the minimum amount of heat by rapid welding.

A technique often employed to minimize the heat input is the *intermittent, or skip, weld.* Instead of making one continuous weld, a short weld is made at the beginning of the joint; next a few inches is welded at the center of the seam, and then a short length is welded at the end of the joint. Finally you return to where the first weld ended and proceed in the same manner, repeating the cycle until the weld is completed. See Fig. 24.

The use of the *back-step,* or *step-back,* welding method also minimizes distortion. With this technique, instead of laying a continuous bead from left

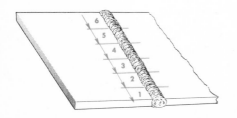

Fig. 25. This is how the back-step welding technique is done.

to right, you deposit short sections of the beads from right to left as illustrated in Fig. 25.

Preheating. On many pieces, particularly alloy steels and cast iron, expansion and contraction forces can be better controlled if the entire structure is preheated before the welding is started. To be effective, preheating must be kept uniform throughout the welding operation, and after the weld is completed the piece must be allowed to cool slowly. Preheating can be done with an oxyacetylene or carbon flame. Usually for work of this kind a second operator manipulates the preheating torch.

Fig. 26. Peening a weld helps to release locked-up stresses.

Peening. To help the metal stretch as it cools, a common practice is to peen it lightly with the round end of a ball peen hammer. However, peening should be done with care because too much hammering will impart stresses to the weld or cause the weld to work-harden and become brittle. See Fig. 26.

Heat Treatment. A common stress relieving method is heat treating. The welded component is placed in a furnace capable of uniform heating and temperature control. The metal must be kept in a soaking temperature until it is heated throughout. Correct temperatures are important to prevent injury to the metal being treated. For example, mild steels require temperatures of 1100° to 1200°F while other alloy steels must be heated to temperatures of 1600°F or more.

After the proper soaking period the heat must be reduced gradually to atmospheric temperature.

Jigs and fixtures. The use of jigs and fixtures will help prevent distortion, since holding the metal in a fixed position prevents excessive movements. A jig or a fixture is any device that holds the metal rigidly in position during the welding operation. Fig. 27 illustrates a simple way to hold pieces firmly in a flat position. These heavy plates not only prevent distortion but they also serve as *chill blocks* to avoid excessive heat building up in the work. Special chill plates made of copper or other metal having good conductivity are particularly effective in dissipating heat away from the weld area. See Fig. 28.

Jigs and fixtures are used extensively in production welding since they permit greater welding speed while reducing to a minimum any form of distortion. By and large, industrial

Fig. 27. Clamping pieces between heavy blocks will keep them straight.

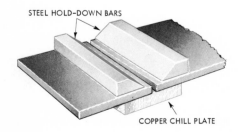

STEEL HOLD-DOWN BARS

COPPER CHILL PLATE

Fig. 28. Chill plates help to reduce heat and warpage in the weld area: (Republic Steel Corp.)

Fig. 29. Examples of industrial types of welding jigs. (Lincoln Electric Co.)

jigs and fixtures are designed to accommodate the specific production work being done. Fig. 29 shows a few such devices.

Number of passes. Distortion can be kept to a minimum by using as few passes as possible over the seam. Two passes made with large electrodes are often better than three or four with smaller electrodes. See Fig. 30.

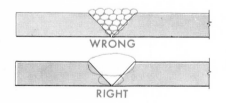

Fig. 30. Use few passes to reduce distortion.

Parts out of position. When a single vee butt joint is welded, the greater amount of hot metal at the top than at the root of the vee will cause more contraction across the top of the welded joint. The result is a distortion of the plate as shown in Fig. 31.

Fig. 31. Unless the plates are clamped, a butt joint will be distorted when welded.

In a T-joint, the weld along the seam will bend both the upright and flat piece. See Fig. 32.

To minimize these distortions, the simplest thing to do is to angle the pieces slightly in the opposite direction in which contraction is to take

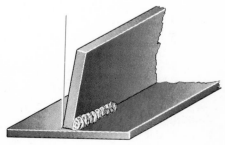

Fig. 32. A T-joint is likely to be distorted in this manner.

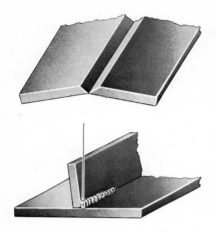

Fig. 33. To minimize distortion, set the pieces of the joint slightly out of alignment.

place. Then, upon cooling, the contraction forces will pull the pieces back into position. Thus, the distortion shown in Figs. 31 and 32 can be prevented by placing the pieces out of alignment as illustrated in Fig. 33.

Points to Remember

1. Be sure you know the kind of metal you are welding and the effects heat may have on the welded structure.

2. When welding alloy steels make certain that the piece is not subjected to prolonged periods of heat that are beyond the critical point.

3. The greater the carbon content in steel, the more difficult it is to weld.

4. Be sure provisions are made for expansion and contraction forces in any welding job.

5. For most butt welds, allow about ⅛" space at the end of the joint for each foot in length of the weld.

6. Keep the heat as low as possible on a piece being welded.

7. Heat can be controlled on a weld by using intermittent or back-step welding techniques.

8. Use as few passes as possible to minimize distortion.

9. Always guard against blowholes and inclusions in a weld.

10. Select the type of joint that best meets the load requirements of the welded structure.

QUESTIONS FOR STUDY AND DISCUSSION

1. What is the difference between a stress and a strain?

2. Why is elasticity an important property in metals?

3. How does tensile strength differ from compressive strength?

4. What is meant by torsional strength?

5. What is shear strength?

6. Why is fatigue strength in some structures very important?

7. Impact strength refers to what particular quality in metals?

8. What do cryogenic properties refer to?

9. Why is ductility important in some metals?

10. How are carbon steels classified?

11. What is meant by an alloy steel?

12. What are some of the alloying elements that are added to steel?

13. How would you identify a steel labeled C1024?

14. Why are space-lattice formations important in steels?

15. Ductile metals have what kind of space-lattice pattern?

16. How does grain size affect the strength of steel?

17. What is alpha iron?

18. What is meant by cementite?

19. What is meant by pearlite?

20. What is gamma iron?

21. What effects does heating beyond the critical range have on the grain size?

22. What is martensite?

23. What may cause brittleness in a weld area?

24. What are the principal functions of the annealing process?

25. What is stress relieving?

26. What is the difference between hardening and tempering?

27. Why are some metals case hardened?

28. What are the principal case hardening processes?

29. How can grain growth in a weld be controlled?

30. What are blowholes?

31. What causes inclusions in a weld?

32. How can porosity in a weld be prevented?

33. Why must a welder take into account expansion and contraction forces.

34. What means can be used to minimize distortion?

35. What is meant by an intermittent weld?

CHAPTER 3

Shielded Metal—Arc Welding

Machines and Accessories

~~~~~~

Shielded metal-arc welding, sometimes referred to as metallic-arc welding, or just arc welding, is widely used in the construction of many products, ranging from steamships, tanks, locomotives, and automobiles to small household appliances. Arc welding machines today are designed to join light and heavy gage metals of all kinds. The process of arc welding not only simplifies the maintenance and manufacture of goods and machines, but it permits the skilled operator to perform welding operations quickly and easily.

Welding Current

When an electrical current moves through a wire, heat is generated by the resistance of the wire to the flow of electricity. The greater the current flow the greater the resistance and the more intense the heat.

The heat generated for welding comes from an arc which develops when electricity jumps across an air gap between the end of an electrode and the base metal. The air gap produces a high resistance to the flow of current and this resistance generates an intense arc heat which may be anywhere from 6000°F to 10,000°F.

Welding current is provided by an AC or DC machine. The primary current (input) to a welding machine is either 220 or 440 volts. Since voltage of this magnitude is always dangerous, extreme care must be taken to ensure that the motor and frame are well grounded.

The actual voltage used to provide welding current is low (18-36) whereas high amperage is necessary to produce the heat required for welding. However, low voltage and high amperage for welding are not particularly dangerous if there is adequate grounding and proper insulation. Although they need not be feared, both should be treated with care to avoid any electrical accident.

Electrical Terms

To understand the correct operation of an electric arc welding machine, you must know something about a few basic electrical terms and principles. The following are especially important:

Alternating current (AC). An electrical current having alternating positive and negative values. In the first half cycle the current flows in one direction then reverses direction and for the next half cycle flows the opposite way. See Fig. 1. The rate of change is referred to as frequency.

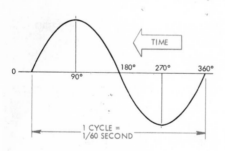

Fig. 1. Alternating current has alternating positive and negative values. (Miller Electric Manufacturing Co.)

This frequency is indicated as 25, 40, 50 and 60 cycles per second. In the United States, alternating current is usually established at 60 cycles per second.

Direct current (DC). Electrical current which flows in one direction only.

Conductor. A conductor is any material in the form of a wire, cable or bus which allows a free passage of an electrical current.

Electrical circuit. Path taken by an electric current in flowing through a conductor from one terminal of the source of supply to the other. It starts from the negative terminal of the power supply where the current is produced, moves along the wire or cable to the load or working source, and then returns to the positive terminal. See Fig. 2.

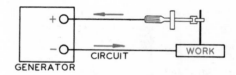

Fig. 2. An example of a simple electrical circuit.

Ampere.   Amperes (abbreviated amp. or amps.) or amperage refers to the amount or rate of current that flows in a circuit. The instrument that measures this rate is called an ammeter as shown in Fig. 3.

Fig. 3. An ammeter shows the amount of current that is flowing. (Weston Electrical Instrument Corp.)

Volt. The force (emf, or electromotive force) that causes current to flow in a circuit is known as voltage. This force is similar to the pressure used to make water flow in pipes. In a water system, the pump provides the pressure, whereas in an electrical circuit the power supply produces the force that pushes the current through the wires. Voltage does not flow; only current flows. The force is measured in volts and the instrument used to measure voltage is called a voltmeter. See Fig. 4.

Fig. 4. A voltmeter measures the force of electricity flowing in a circuit. (Weston Electrical Instrument Corp.)

Resistance. Resistance is the opposition of the material in a conductor to the passage of an electric current causing electrical energy to be transformed into heat.

Static electricity. Static electricity refers to electricity at rest or electricity that is not moving.

Dynamic electricity. Dynamic electricity is electricity in motion in an electrical current.

Constant potential. Potential is synonymous with voltage. It refers to the generation of a stable voltage regardless of the amperage output produced by the welding power supply. This characteristic is particularly important in Mig welding. See Chapter 16.

Variable voltage. A control used to set the open circuit voltage on a welding machine.

Voltage drop. Just as the pressure in a water system drops as the distance increases from the water pump, so does the voltage lessen as the distance increases from the generator. This fact is important to remember in using a welding machine because if the cable is too long, there will be too great a voltage drop. When there is too much drop, the welding machine cannot supply enough current for welding.

Open-circuit voltage and arc voltage. Open-circuit voltage is the voltage produced by the welder when the

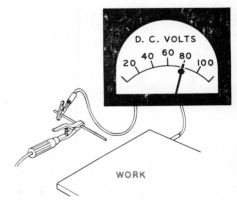

Fig. 5. When the machine is running and no welding is being done, you have an open circuit voltage.

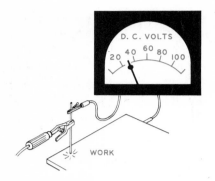

Fig. 6. Arc voltage is the voltage used when welding is in process.

more commonly referred to as *straight polarity*. See Fig. 7. If the electrode cable is attached to the positive pole of the generator and the cable leading to the work to the negative pole, the circuit is called *reversed polarity*. See Fig. 8.

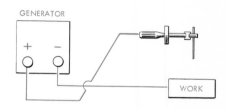

Fig. 8. This is how the cables are connected for reversed polarity.

machine is running and no welding is being done. This voltage varies from 50 to 100. After the arc is struck, the voltage drops to what is known as the arc or working voltage, which is between 18 and 36. An adjustment is provided to vary the open circuit voltage so welding can be done in different positions. See Figs. 5 and 6.

Polarity. Polarity indicates the direction of the current in that circuit. Since the current moves in one direction only in *DC welders,* polarity is important because for some welding operations the flow of current must be changed. When the electrode cable is fastened to the negative pole of the generator and the work to the positive pole, the polarity is negative, or

Polarity has a direct relationship to the location of the liberated heat since it is possible to control the amount of heat going into the base metal. By changing polarity the greatest heat can be concentrated where it is most needed. Usually for some types of welding situations, it is preferable to have more heat at the workpiece because the area of the work is greater and more heat is required to melt the metal than the electrode. Thus, if large, heavy deposits are to be made, the work should be hotter than the electrode. For this purpose, straight polarity would be more effective. On the other hand, in overhead welding it is necessary to quickly freeze the filler metal to help hold the molten metal in position against the force of gravity. By using reverse polarity, less heat is generated at the workpiece thereby giving the filler metal greater holding power for out of position welding. In

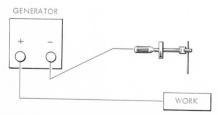

Fig. 7. This is how the circuit is arranged for straight polarity.

other situations, it may be more expedient to keep the workpiece as cool as possible such as in repairing a cast iron casting. With reverse polarity less heat is produced in the base metal and more heat at the electrode. The result is that the deposits can be applied rapidly while the base metal is prevented from overheating.

On early DC welders, the change of polarity involved reversing the cables. Modern machines equipped with a *polarity switch* eliminate disconnecting the cables. Moving the switch to straight or reverse, see Fig. 13, changes the polarity.

Inasmuch as the current is constantly reversing in AC welders, polarity is of no consequence.

Welding Machines

To supply the current for welding, three types of power sources are available: transformers, motor generators, and rectifiers.

Sizes of welding machines are rated according to their approximate amperage capacity at 60 per cent duty cycle, such as 150, 200, 250, 300, 400, 500 or 600. This amperage is the rated current output at the working terminal. Thus a machine rated at 150 amperes can be adjusted to produce a range of power up to 150 amperes. Duty cycle for most welding machines is based on a ten minute period of time. Every welding machine is rated at a certain amperage output and voltage output for a given period of time. The National Electrical Manufacturers Association (NEMA) has set a standard

based on the ten-minute period. Thus a welder rated at 300 amperes, 32 volts, 60 per cent duty cycle will put out the rated amperage at the rated voltage for six minutes out of every ten. The machine must idle and cool the other four of every ten. Duty cycle

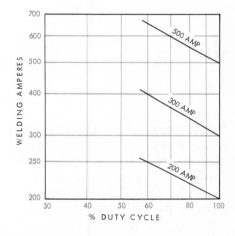

Fig. 9. Duty cycle chart. (Miller Electric Manufacturing Co.)

time is not accumulative over ten minutes. See Fig. 9.

The size of the welding machine to be used is governed largely by the kind of welding that is to be done. The following serves as a general guide.

150-200 Ampere—For light to medium duty welding. Excellent for all fabrication purposes, and rugged enough for continuous operation on light or medium production work.

250-300 Ampere — For average welding requirements. Used in plants for production, maintenance, repair, tool room work and all general shop welding.

400-600 Ampere—For heavy duty welding and specially for large capacity and a wide range of purposes. Used extensively in heavy structural work, fabricating heavy machine parts, heavy pipe and tank welding, and, in some cases, for cutting scrap and cast iron.

Transformers. The transformer type of welding machine produces AC current and is considered to be the least expensive, lightest, and smallest machine. It takes power directly from a power supply line and transforms it to the voltage required for welding.

Fig. 10. Welding current output on some AC machines is regulated by plugging leads into sockets. (Marquette Corp.)

The welding current output may be adjusted by plugging leads of the electrode holder into sockets on the front of the machine in various location, (Fig. 10) or by tapping the coil in the reactor (Fig. 11A), or by moving an iron block in and out of the reactor coil (Fig. 11B), or by saturating the magnetic circuit with a direct current supplied by a rectifier unit (Fig. 11C). Where the adjustment is made in

the reactance of the transformer, the output current is regulated by altering the position of the primary and secondary coil (Fig. 11D), or by having a movable iron member between the primary and secondary coils (Fig. 11E). The tap switch and movable shunt usually consists of a handwheel or crank which can be turned to the desired amperage setting. See Fig. 12.

Some AC transformers also have an arc booster switch which supplies a burst of current for easy arc starting as soon as the electrode comes in contact with the work. After the arc is struck, the current automatically returns to the amount set for the job. See Fig. 12. The arc booster switch has several settings to permit quick arc starting for welding either thin sheets or heavy plates.

One outstanding advantage of the AC welder is the freedom from *magnetic arc blow* which often occurs when welding with DC machines. Arc blow is a condition that causes the arc to wander while welding in corners on heavy metal or if using large electrodes. Since the current in a DC welder flows in one direction, metal being welded becomes magnetized. When this happens, the arc is often deflected, resulting in excessive spatter. Moreover, arc blow breaks the continuity of the deposited metal, usually referred to as the bead, making it necessary to refill the crater, or concave surface, which results from this arc blow. The process of refilling the crater not only slows down the welding but very often leaves weak spots in the weld.

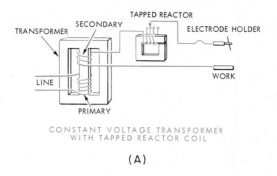

CONSTANT VOLTAGE TRANSFORMER
WITH TAPPED REACTOR COIL

(A)

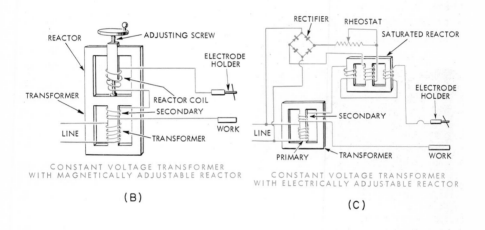

CONSTANT VOLTAGE TRANSFORMER
WITH MAGNETICALLY ADJUSTABLE REACTOR

(B)

CONSTANT VOLTAGE TRANSFORMER
WITH ELECTRICALLY ADJUSTABLE REACTOR

(C)

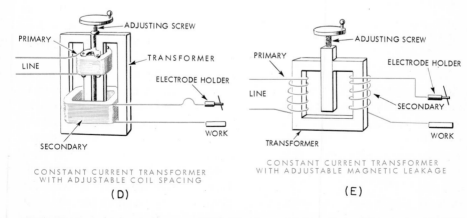

CONSTANT CURRENT TRANSFORMER
WITH ADJUSTABLE COIL SPACING

(D)

CONSTANT CURRENT TRANSFORMER
WITH ADJUSTABLE MAGNETIC LEAKAGE

(E)

Fig. 11. Welding current output on some AC machines is regulated by a tap switch or a movable shunt. (Hobart Brothers Co.)

CURRENT ADJUSTER
ARC BOOSTER SWITCH

Fig. 12. AC transformer type of welding unit. (Hobart Brothers Co.)

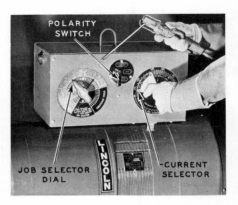

POLARITY SWITCH

JOB SELECTOR DIAL

CURRENT SELECTOR

Fig. 13. DC motor generator type.

Another feature of the AC welder is its low operating and maintenance cost, its high overall electrical efficiency, and noiseless operation.

Transformer types of welding machines are particularly adaptable for metallic arc (stick) welding. However, they do not, as a rule, have as much flexibility as the dual controlled generator to meet different welding requirements.

Motor generators. Motor generators are designed to produce DC current in either straight or reverse

polarity. The polarity selected for welding depends on the kind of electrode used and the material to be welded. A switch on the machine can be turned for straight or reverse polarity. See Fig. 13.

Present day motor generators are usually of the constant current, dual control type. Constant current simply means that a steady supply of current is produced over a wide range of welding voltages. Without a steady flow of current, it would be virtually impossible to produce consistently uniform welds with proper penetration.

Constant current motor generators have a sloping volt-amp characteristic. The volt-amp characteristic is actually a curve which shows how the voltage varies in its relationship to amperage between the open-circuit (where there is static electrical potential but no current is flowing) and short circuit (when the electrode touches the work). See Fig. 14.

Under normal welding operations, the open-circuit is between 50 and 100 volts where the output voltage is

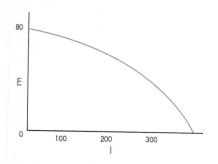

Fig. 14. The conventional DC generator has a sloping volt-amp curve.

control is usually a rheostat that can be turned to provide a fine adjustment of the welding current, that is, increase or decrease the heat. See Fig. 13.

On dual control machines the slope of the output current can be varied to produce a soft or harsh arc. By flatting the volt-amp curve (increasing the amperage) a digging arc can be obtained for a deeper penetration. With a steeper curve (reduced amperage in relation to voltage) a soft or quiet arc results which is useful for welding light gage materials. In other words, a machine with dual control allows the greatest flexibility for welding materials of different thicknesses.

The conventional DC motor generator has its widest usage in metallic arc (stick welding).

Rectifiers. Rectifiers are essentially transformers containing an electrical device which changes alternating current into direct current. Some types are designed to provide a choice of low voltage for metal inert gas welding and submerged arc welding, or a high open circuit with drooping voltage characteristics for tungsten inert gas welding and metallic arc (stick) electrode welding.

Rectifier welding machines are also available to produce both DC as well as AC current. By turning a switch the output terminals can be changed to the transformer or to the rectifier and produce either AC or DC straight or reverse polarity current.

The transformer rectifier is usually considered more efficient electrically than the generator and provides quiet operation. Current control is achieved

between 18 to 36 volts. By having a high open-circuit voltage easier arc starting is possible with all types of electrodes. As the welding proceeds, the high voltage drops to the arc (welding) voltage but regardless of the arc length, due to raising or lowering the electrode, the current output will not fluctuate appreciably. The actual arc voltage will vary, depending on the length of the arc. Thus to strike an arc, the electrode must be shorted to the work. At the moment of contact (short circuit) the amperage shoots up while the voltage drops. Then, as the electrode moves away from the work, the voltage rises to maintain the arc while the amperage drops to the required working level.

During welding if the arc length increases, the voltage increases. Conversely, if the arc length decreases the arc voltage decreases. This enables the operator to vary the heat by lengthening or shortening the arc.

With a dual control machine welding current is adjusted by two controls. One control provides an approximate or coarse setting. The second

by a switching arrangement where one switch can be set for the desired current range and a second dial for securing the fine adjustment desired for welding. See Fig. 15.

Constant potential (voltage) welding machine. This machine is either a rectifier or motor generator designed especially for Mig welding. It provides practically a constant voltage to the arc regardless of the arc length. Since in Mig welding a continuous wire electrode is fed into the arc, any variation in arc length will automatically bring about an adjustment in arc voltage. Thus the machine is inherently self-regulating. See Chapter 16.

Personal Equipment

Helmet and hand shield. An electric arc not only produces a brilliant light but it also gives off invisible ultraviolet and infrared rays which are extremely dangerous to the eyes and skin. *For this reason, you should never look at an arc with the naked eye within a distance of 50 feet.* To pro-

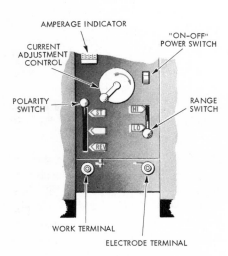

Fig. 15. DC/AC rectifier type adaptable to variety of welding applications. (Airco)

Fig. 16. The two types of head shields used for arc welding are the helmet (left) and the hand shield (right). (Purity Cylinder Gases Inc.)

tect yourself from harmful rays, you must use either a helmet or hand shield as illustrated in Fig. 16.

The *helmet* fits over the head and can be swung upward when you are not welding. The chief advantage of the helmet is that it leaves both hands free, thereby making it possible to hold the work and weld at the same time.

The *hand shield* provides the same protection as the helmet except that it is held in position by a handle. This shield is frequently used by an observer or a person who welds for only a short period. Both types of shields are equipped with special colored lenses that reduce the brilliancy of the light and screen out the infrared and ultraviolet rays. Lenses come in different shades, and the type used depends on the kind of welding done. In general, the recommended practice is as follows:

Shade 5 for light spot welding.

Shade 6 and 7 for arc welding up to 30 amperes.

Shade 8 for arc welding beyond 30 amperes and up to 75 amperes.

Shade 10 for arc welding beyond 75 amperes and up to 200 amperes.

Shade 12 for arc welding beyond 200 amperes and up to 400 amperes.

Shade 14 for arc welding over 400 amperes.

During the welding process, small particles of metal fly upward from the work and may lodge on the lens. Colored lenses are protected by use of *clear glass or plastic cover plates.* Although the methods of inserting the cover plates vary on different makes

of shields, you will find that the change can be made easily and quickly.

These clear glasses are inexpensive and can be purchased from any welding supply dealer. *Since you must have clear vision at all times during welding, always replace the cover glass when enough spatter has accumulated on them to interfere with your vision.*

Goggles. Goggles, as shown in Fig. 17, are worn when chipping slag from a weld. In arc welding a thin crust forms on the deposited bead. This substance, known as slag, must be removed. While removing slag, tiny particles are often deflected upward. Without proper eye protection, these particles may cause a serious eye in-

Fig. 17. Goggles must always be used when removing slag from a weld. (Purity Cylinder Gases Inc.)

jury. Therefore, *always wear goggles when removing slag from a weld.*

Gloves. Another important item you will need for arc welding is a pair of gloves. *You must wear gloves to protect your hands from the ultraviolet rays and spattering hot metal.*

Several different kinds of gloves are available. As a rule, the leather gaunt-

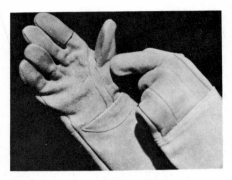

Fig. 18. Always wear gloves when arc welding. (The Lincoln Electric Co.)

let gloves shown in Fig. 18 provide ample protection. Regardless of the type used, they should be flexible enough to permit proper hand movement, yet not so thin as to allow the heat to penetrate easily.

Fig. 19. An apron provides protection for your clothes. (The Lincoln Electric Co.)

Apron. It is a good idea to wear an apron when learning to arc weld. Otherwise, spattering metal might r,in your clothes. Since the spattering particles are hot, a leather apron offers the best protection. A typical welding apron is illustrated in Fig. 19.

Most experienced welders seldom wear an apron on the job except in situations where there may be an excessive amount of metal spatter resulting from awkward welding positions. Usually they wear suitable coveralls to protect their clothing.

Shop Equipment

Electrode holder. To do a good welding job, a properly designed electrode holder is essential. The holder is a handle-like tool attached to the cable that holds the electrode during welding. See Fig. 20. You can generally identify a well designed holder by these features:

1. It is reasonably light, to reduce excessive fatigue while welding.

2. It does not heat too rapidly.

3. It is well balanced.

4. It receives and ejects the electrodes easily.

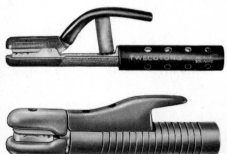

Fig. 20. Two common insulated electrode holders. (Purity Cylinder Gases Inc.)

5. All exposed surfaces, including the jaws, are protected by insulation. The jaws of some holders are not insulated. *When using a holder with uninsulated jaws, never lay it on the bench plate while the machine is running because it will cause a flash.*

Cleaning tools. To produce a strong welded joint, the surface of the metal must be free of all foreign matter such as rust, oil, and paint. A steel brush is used for cleaning purposes.

After a bead is deposited on the metal, the slag which covers the weld is removed with a chipping hammer, which is pictured in Fig. 21. The chipping operation is followed by additional wire brushing. Complete removal of slag is especially important when several passes must be made over a joint. Otherwise, gas holes will form in the bead, resulting in porosity which weakens the weld.

Fig. 21. To clean a weld, chipping hammers and wire brushes are used. (Hobart Brothers Co.)

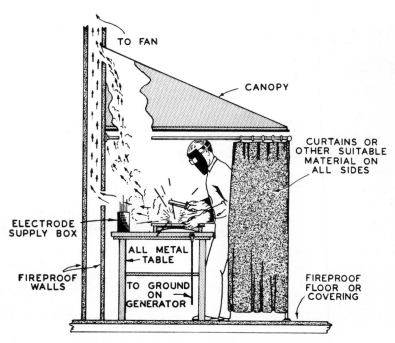

Fig. 22. A permanent welding booth provides a safe work area.

Welding screen. Whenever welding is done in areas where other people may be working, enclose the welding operation with screens so the ultraviolet rays will not injure those nearby. These screens can easily be constructed from heavy fire-resistant canvas painted with ultraviolet, black or gray protective paint.

Where the welding is to be done in a permanent location, a booth is desirable as illustrated in Fig. 22.

Providing ventilation. Electrodes used in arc welding give off a great deal of smoke and fumes. These fumes are not harmful if the welding area is properly ventilated. *Unless there is sufficient movement of air in the room, arc welding should not be done.* There should be either a suction fan or other good fresh air circulation.

Permanent welding booths should be equipped with a sheet metal hood mounted directly above the welding table, and a suction fan to draw out the smoke and fumes, as illustrated in Fig. 22.

Cables and ground clamp. The cables carry the current to and from the work. One cable runs from the welding machine to the holder and the other cable is attached to the work bench. The cable connected to the bench is called the *ground cable.* Thus when the welding machine is turned on and the electrode in the holder comes in contact with the work, a circuit is formed, allowing electricity to flow.

It is important to use the correct diameter cable specified for the welding machine. If the cable is too small

for the current, it overheats and a lot of power is lost. Furthermore, a larger cable is necessary to carry a required voltage any distance from the machine. Otherwise, there will be an excessive voltage drop. Even with larger diameter cables, you must take precaution not to exceed the recommended lengths, because the voltage drop will lower the efficiency of your welding.

Another important point is to have a *good ground connection.* Proper

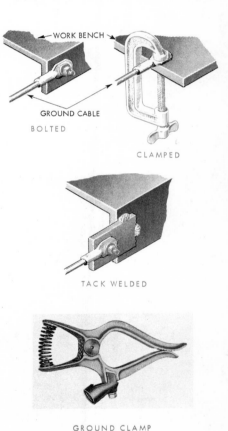

Fig. 23. Several connections can be used to provide a proper ground.

ground connections can be made in several ways. The ground cable can be fastened to the work bench by a *C* clamp, a special ground clamp, or by bolting or welding the lug on the end of the cable to the bench. See Fig. 23. All cable connections should be tight

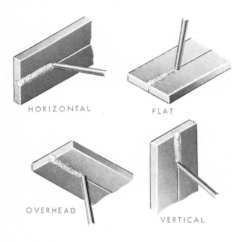

HORIZONTAL   FLAT

OVERHEAD   VERTICAL

Fig. 24. There are four main welding positions.

Fig. 25. These three electrodes are coated except for small portions at the lower right, where they are gripped by the electrode holder.

because any loose connection will cause the cable or clamp to overheat. A loose connection may even produce arcing at the connection.

Basic Welding Terms

Before continuing with various welding operations, you should understand the following terms:

Welding position—location of the piece to be welded. The four main positions are horizontal, flat, overhead, and vertical as shown in Fig. 24.

Electrode — thin metal rod, as shown in Fig. 25, coated with a special substance and used as a filler to join the metal to be welded.

Base metal or parent metal—metal to be welded. See Fig. 26.

Bead—narrow layer or layers of metal, as shown in Fig. 26, deposited on the base metal as the electrode melts.

Ripple—shape of the deposited bead caused by movement of the rod as shown in Fig. 26.

Pass—each layer of beads deposited on the base metal as in Fig. 26.

Crater—depression in the base metal, shown in Fig. 27, made by the arc as the electrode comes in contact with the base metal.

Penetration—depth of fusion with the base metal shown in Fig. 28.

Joints—position of two or more members to be joined as in Fig. 29.

Points to Remember

1. Never look at a welding arc without a shield.

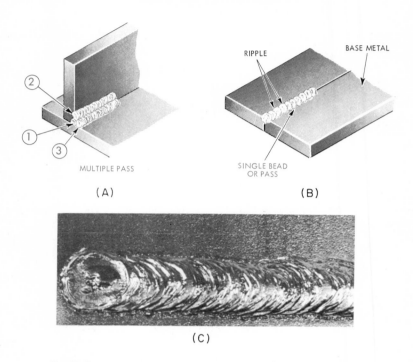

Fig. 26. These views illustrate bead, ripple, pass, and the base metal.

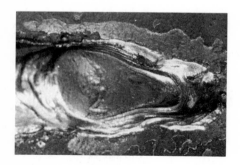

Fig. 27. A crater appears in the base metal. (The Lincoln Electric Co.)

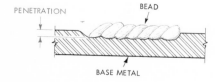

Fig. 28. The depth from the surface of the base metal to the bottom of the bead is called penetration.

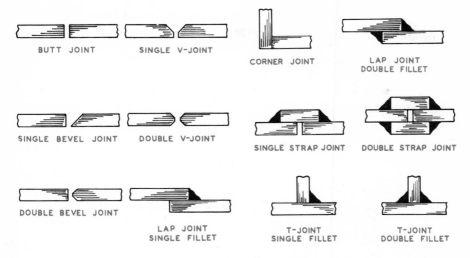

Fig. 29. A variety of joints can be used in welding.

2. Always replace the clear cover glasses when they become spattered.

3. Examine the closed lenses in the helmet. Replace cracked ones at once.

4. Wear goggles when chipping slag off a weld.

5. Always wear gloves and an apron when welding.

6. Use a holder that is completely insulated. If the jaws of your holder are not insulated, never lay it on the bench while the machine is running.

7. Do welding only in areas where there is enough ventilation.

8. If you weld outside of a permanent booth, be sure to have screens so the arc will not harm persons nearby.

9. Prevent welding cables from coming in contact with hot metal, water, oil, or grease. Avoid dragging the cables over or around sharp corners.

10. Make sure that you have a good ground connection.

11. Keep cables in an orderly manner to prevent them from becoming a stumbling hazard. Fasten the cables overhead whenever possible.

12. Do not weld near inflammable materials.

13. Be sure tanks, drums, or pipe lines are completely cleaned of inflammable liquids before welding.

14. Always turn off the machine when leaving the work.

15. Never stand in water or on a wet floor or use wet gloves when welding. Water is an electrical conductor and any wet surface will carry current. Always dry out the work pieces or bench if there is any evidence of moisture.

QUESTIONS FOR STUDY AND DISCUSSION

1. What is a circuit?

2. What is voltage? What instrument is used to measure voltage?

3. What term is used to indicate rate of current flow in a circuit?

4. What is voltage drop? What effect does it have on welding current?

5. What is the difference between AC and DC current?

6. What is the difference between static and dynamic electricity?

7. What is meant by open-circuit voltage and arc voltage?

8. What is polarity?

9. What determines whether the machine is to be set for straight or reversed polarity?

10. How are sizes of welding machines rated?

11. How does a DC motor generator differ from a transformer type unit?

12. What is meant by a constant current, dual control machine?

13. What is meant when a welding machine has a sloping volt-amp curve?

14. What is one main advantage of an AC welder?

15. Why is a rectifier type welding unit often preferred?

16. Why should you never look at an electric arc without eye protection?

17. Why is a helmet more suitable than a hand shield for continuous welding operations?

18. What determines the correct shade of lens to use for welding?

19. Why should shaded lenses be covered with clear glass?

20. Why are goggles important when chipping slag off a weld?

21. Why should welder's gloves be worn when arc welding?

22. What are some of the requirements for a good electrode holder?

CHAPTER 4

Shielded Metal—Arc Welding

Selecting the Electrode

~~~~~~

There are so many different kinds and sizes of electrodes that unless you select the correct one, you will have difficulty in doing a good welding job.

In general, all electrodes are classified into five main groups: *mild steel, high carbon steel, special alloy steel, cast iron,* and *non-ferrous.* The greatest range of arc welding is done with electrodes in the *mild steel* group. Special alloy steel electrodes are made for welding various kinds of steel alloys. Cast iron electrodes are used for welding cast iron, and non-ferrous electrodes for welding such metals as aluminum, copper, and brass. *In this chapter we will discuss mild steel electrodes, and discuss other types of electrodes in subsequent chapters dealing with the welding of special metals.*

What Is an Electrode?

An electrode is a metal rod having approximately the same composition as the metal to be welded, which we will refer to as the base metal. When the current is produced by the generator or transformer and flows to the electrode, an arc is formed between the end of the electrode and the work. The arc melts the electrode and the base metal. The melted metal of the electrode flows into the molten crater and forms a bond between the two pieces of metal being joined.

Electrodes are not only manufactured to weld different metals, but they are also designed for DC or AC welding machines. A few electrodes work equally well on either DC or AC. Then too, electrode usage depends on the welding position. Some electrodes are best suited for flat position welding, others are intended primarily for horizontal and flat welding, and some types are used for welding in any position.

The two kinds of mild steel elec-

49

trodes are known as *bare* and *shielded*. Originally, bare electrodes were uncoated metal rods; today they have a very light coating. Their use for welding is very limited because such electrodes are difficult to weld with and they produce brittle welds with low tensile strength. (Tensile strength is the property of the newly joined metal to resist breaking under a load.) Practically all welding is done with shielded electrodes.

Shielded electrodes have heavy coatings of various substances such as cellulose sodium, cellulose potassium, titania sodium, titania potassium, iron oxide, iron powder as well as several other ingredients. Each of the sub-stances in the coating is intended to serve a particular function in the welding process.

In general, their main purposes are:

1. Act as a cleansing and deoxidizing agent in the molten crater.

2. Releases an inert gas to protect the molten metal from atmospheric oxides and nitrides. See Fig. 1. Since oxygen and nitrogen weakens a weld if allowed to come in contact with the molten metal, the exclusion of these contaminants is important.

3. Form a slag over the deposited metal which further protects the weld until the metal cools sufficiently so it is no longer affected by atmospheric contamination. The slag also slows the

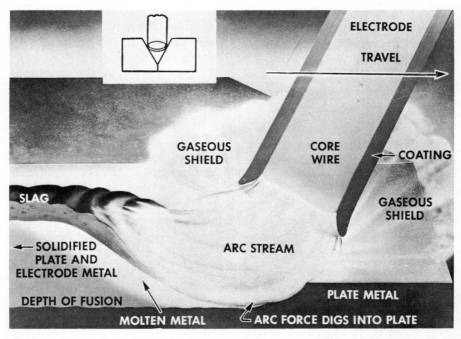

Fig. 1. Cross-section of a coated electrode in the process of welding. (The Lincoln Electric Co.)

cooling rate of the deposited metal thereby permitting a more ductile weld to form.

4. Provide easier arc starting, stabilize the arc better, and reduce splatter.

5. Permit better penetration and improve the x-ray quality of the weld.

The coating of some electrodes contains powdered iron which converts to steel and becomes a part of the weld deposit. The powdered iron also helps to increase the speed of welding and improve the weld appearance.

A group of electrodes known as low hydrogen electrodes have coatings high in limestone and other ingredients with low hydrogen content, such as calcium fluoride, calcium carbonate, magnesium - aluminum - silicate, and ferrous alloys. These electrodes are used to weld high-sulphur and high-carbon steels that have a great affinity for hydrogen which often causes porosity and underbead cracking in a weld.

Identifying Electrodes

You will find that electrodes are referred to by a manufacturer's trade name. To ensure some degree of uniformity in manufacturing electrodes, the American Welding Society and the American Society for Testing of Materials have set up certain requirements for electrodes. Thus different manufacturers' electrodes which are within the classification established by the A.W.S. and A.S.T.M., may be expected to have the same welding characteristics. In this classification,

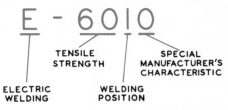

Fig. 2. The letter and each number used to classify electrodes have a specific meaning.

each type of electrode has been assigned specific symbols, such as E-6010, E-7010, E-8010, etc. The *prefix E* identifies the electrode for electric arc welding as illustrated in Fig. 2. The *first two digits* in the symbol designate the minimum allowable tensile strength of the deposited weld metal in thousands of pounds per square inch. For example, the 60 series electrodes have a minimum pull strength of 60,000 pounds per square inch; the 70 series, a strength of 70,000 pounds per square inch.

The *third digit* of the symbol indicates possible welding positions. Three numbers are used for this purpose: 1, 2 and 3. Number 1 is for an electrode which can be used for welding in any position. Number 2 represents an electrode restricted for welding in horizontal and flat positions only. Number 3 represents an electrode to be used in the flat position only. The *fourth digit* of the symbol simply shows some special characteristic of the electrode, such as weld quality, type of arc, and amount of penetration. The fourth digit may be 0, 1, 2, 3, 4, 5, or 6. Their meanings are as follows:

0—Direct current with reverse polarity only except in the case of the

TABLE I

AWS Major Alloying Elements in Electrodes

SUFFIX SYMBOL	MO (MOLYBDENUM)	NI (NICKEL)	CR (CHROMIUM)	MN (MANGANESE)	VA (VANADIUM)
A1	0.5				
B1	0.5		0.5		
B2	0.5		1.25		
B3	1.0		2.25		
B4	0.5		2.0		
C1		2.5			
C2		3.5			
C3		1.0			
D1	0.3			1.5	
D2	0.3			1.75	
G	0.2	0.5		1.0	0.1

xx20 or xx30 classes where either current or polarity may be used. Produces high quality deposits with deep penetration and flat or concave beads.

1 — Alternating current or direct current with reverse polarity. Produces high quality deposits with deep penetration and flat to slightly concave beads.

2—Direct current with straight polarity only or AC current. Medium quality deposits, medium arc, medium penetration and convex heads.

3 — Alternating current or direct current with either polarity. Medium to high quality deposits, soft arc, shallow penetration and slightly convex beads.

4—AC or DC positive, fast deposition rate, deep groove butt, fillet and lap welds, medium penetration, easy slag removal.

5—Direct current with reverse polarity, high quality deposits, soft arc, moderate penetration, flat to slightly convex head, low hydrogen content in weld deposits. Known as lime ferritic.

6—Alternating current with qualities similar to number 5.

Along with the basic digit designation numbers, alloy steel electrodes often carry a symbol suffix such as A1, B2, etc. These AWS suffixes indicate specific additions of alloying elements as shown in Table I.

In addition to the number classification, electrodes are often identified by a *color code* established by the National Electrical Manufacturers Association (N.E.M.A.) See Fig. 3.

Some manufacturers do not use the color code but simply print the AWS classification on each electrode.

The N.E.M.A. color markings of the more commonly used covered electrodes are given in Table II. The location of the colors are shown in the two sketches in Fig. 3.

TABLE II
N.E.M.A. Color Code for Covered Electrodes

CLASS	END COLOR	SPOT COLOR	CLASS	END COLOR	SPOT COLOR
Group Color–Blue			**LOW HYDROGEN LOW ALLOY STEEL** Group Color—Green		
ECu	GREEN	NONE	E-7015	BLUE	RED
ECu-Si	RED	NONE	E-7015-G	NONE	RED
ECu-SnA	YELLOW	NONE	E-7015-A 1	BLUE	WHITE
ECu-Ni	NONE	BLUE	E-7016	BLUE	ORANGE
ECu-SnC	YELLOW	BLUE	E-7016-G	NONE	ORANGE
ECu-A 1-A2	SILVER	BLUE	E-7016-A 1	BLUE	YELLOW
ECu-A 1-B	SILVER	BROWN	E-7018	BLACK	ORANGE
ECu-A 1-C	SILVER	GREEN	E-7018-G	NONE	BLUE
ECu-A 1-D	SILVER	RED	E-7018-A 1	BLACK	YELLOW
ECu-A 1-E	SILVER	YELLOW	E-8015-G	GRAY	RED
			E-8015-B 1	WHITE	BROWN
LOW ALLOY STEEL Group Color—Silver			E-8015-B2	WHITE	GREEN
			E-8015-B4	BROWN	BRONZE
			E-8015-B2L	BLACK	GREEN
E-7020-G	BLUE	GREEN	E-8015-B4L	BLACK	BRONZE
E-7020-A 1	BLUE	YELLOW	E-8015-C1	WHITE	BRONZE
E-8013-G	WHITE	BROWN	E-8015-C2	WHITE	WHITE
E-8013-B 1	WHITE	WHITE	E-8015-C3	WHITE	RED
E-8013-B2	BROWN	WHITE	E-8016-G	WHITE	YELLOW
E-9013-G	BROWN	BROWN	E-8016-B 1	WHITE	BLACK
E-10013-G	GREEN	BROWN	E-8016-B2	WHITE	GRAY
			E-8016-B4	BROWN	VIOLET
SURFACING ELECTRODES Group Color—Red			E-8016-C1	WHITE	BLUE
			E-8016-C2	WHITE	VIOLET
			E-8016-C3	WHITE	ORANGE
EFeMn-A	BLUE	NONE	E-8018-G	BLACK	BLUE
EFeMn-B	BLUE	BLUE	E-8018-B 1	GRAY	BLACK
EFeCr-A 1	WHITE	NONE	E-8018-B2	GRAY	GRAY
EFeCr-A2	WHITE	BLUE	E-8018-B4	BLACK	GRAY
EFe5-A	BROWN	NONE	E-8018-C1	GRAY	BLUE
EFe5-B	BROWN	BLUE	E-8018-C2	GRAY	VIOLET
EFe5-C	BROWN	WHITE	E-8018-C3	BLACK	BLACK
ECoCr-A	GREEN	RED	E-9015-G	BROWN	RED
ECoCr-B	GREEN	GREEN	E-9015-B3	BROWN	GREEN
ECoCr-C	GREEN	BLACK	E-9015-B3L	BLACK	WHITE
ENiCr-A	RED	NONE	E-9015-D1	BROWN	WHITE
ENiCr-B	RED	BLUE	E-9016-G	BROWN	ORANGE
ENiCr-C	RED	WHITE	E-9016-B3	BROWN	BLUE
			E-9016-D1	BROWN	YELLOW
			E-9018-G	VIOLET	BLUE
			E-9018-B3	VIOLET	BLACK
MILD STEEL AND LOW ALLOY STEEL XX10, XX11 and all 60XX Group Color—None			E-9018-D1	VIOLET	VIOLET
			E-10015-G	GREEN	RED
			E-10015-D2	GREEN	YELLOW
			E-10016-G	GREEN	ORANGE
E-6010	NONE	NONE	E-10016-D2	GREEN	GRAY
E-6011	NONE	BLUE	E-10018-G	GREEN	BLUE
E-6012	NONE	WHITE	E-10018-D2	GREEN	VIOLET
E-6013	NONE	BROWN	E-11015-G	RED	RED
E-6014	RED	BROWN	E-11016-G	RED	YELLOW
E-6015	NONE	RED	E-11018-G	RED	BLUE
E-6016	NONE	ORANGE			
E-6018	RED	ORANGE			
E-6020	NONE	GREEN			
E-6024	NONE	YELLOW			
E-6027	NONE	SILVER	**NICKEL, NICKEL-ALLOY AND HIGH TEMPERATURE ELECTRODES** Group Color—White		
E-6028	RED	BLACK			
E-7010-G	BLUE	NONE			
E-7010-A 1	BLUE	WHITE	E3N10	BLUE	WHITE
E-7011-G	BLUE	BLUE	E4N10	BLUE	BROWN
E-7011-A 1	BLUE	YELLOW	E3N14	BLUE	RED
E-7014	BLACK	BROWN	E3N1B	WHITE	GREEN
E-7024	BLACK	YELLOW	E3N1C	WHITE	VIOLET
E-7028	BLACK	BLACK	E4N12	GREEN	BROWN
E-8010-G	WHITE	NONE	E3N11	YELLOW	WHITE
E-8010-B 1	WHITE	BROWN	E4N11	YELLOW	BROWN
E-8010-B2	WHITE	GREEN	E3N12	VIOLET	WHITE
E-8011-G	WHITE	BLUE	E3N19	VIOLET	RED
E-8011-B 1	WHITE	BLACK	ENi	ORANGE	BLUE
E-8011-B2	BROWN	BLACK	ENi-Cu	ORANGE	WHITE
E-8010-G	BROWN	NONE	ENi-Fe	ORANGE	BROWN
E-9011-G	BROWN	BLUE	ENi-CuB	ORANGE	GREEN
E-10010-G	GREEN	NONE	Ni-Cr60-13	GREEN	BLUE
E-10011-G	GREEN	BLUE	Ni-Cr80-15	GREEN	WHITE
E-12015-G	ORANGE	RED	Mil 4N1W	WHITE	YELLOW
E-12016-G	ORANGE	ORANGE	Mil 3N1L	BRONZE	WHITE
E-12018-G	ORANGE	BLUE	Mil 3N1N	BRONZE	ORANGE

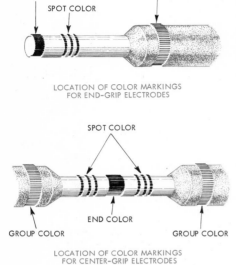

END COLOR SPOT COLOR GROUP COLOR

LOCATION OF COLOR MARKINGS
FOR END-GRIP ELECTRODES

SPOT COLOR

END COLOR

GROUP COLOR   GROUP COLOR

LOCATION OF COLOR MARKINGS
FOR CENTER-GRIP ELECTRODES

Fig. 3. N.E.M.A. Color Code for covered electrodes.

Selecting the Correct Electrode

The ideal electrode is one that will provide good arc stability, smooth weld bead, fast deposition, minimum spatter, maximum weld strength, and easy slag removal. To achieve these characteristics seven factors should be considered in selecting an electrode. These are: (see Fig. 4)

1. *Properties of the base metal.* A top quality weld should be as strong as the parent metal. This means that the electrode to be used must produce a weld metal with approximately the same mechanical properties of the parent metal.

Electrodes are available for welding different classifications of metal. Thus some electrodes are designed to weld carbon steels, others are best suited for low alloy steels and some are intended specifically for high strength alloy steels. Therefore, in undertaking any welding operation, the first requisite is to ascertain the chemical analysis of the metal and then select an electrode that is normally recommended for the metal involved. Most welding supply distributors are usually able to provide this information.

2. *Electrode diameter.* As a rule, never use an electrode having a diameter larger than the thickness of the metal to be welded. Some operators prefer larger electrodes because they permit faster travel along the joint and thus speed up the welding operation; but this requires considerable skill. For example, it takes approximately half the time to deposit a quantity of weld metal from ¼″ coated mild steel electrodes than from ³⁄₁₆″ electrodes of the same type. The larger sizes not only make possible the use of higher current but require fewer stops to change the electrode. Therefore, from the standpoint of economy it is always a good practice to use the largest size electrode that is practical for the work to be done.

When making vertical or overhead welds, ³⁄₁₆″ is the largest diameter electrode that should be used regardless of plate thickness. Larger electrodes make it too difficult to control the deposited metal. Ordinarily, a *fast-freeze* type of electrode is best for vertical and overhead welding. See Table III.

The diameter of the electrode is also influenced by the configuration of the joint design. Thus, in a thick metal section with narrow vee, a small diameter electrode is always used to run the

TABLE III
Electrode Characteristics

TYPE	AWS CLASS	CURRENT TYPE	WELDING POSITION	WELD RESULTS
Mild Steel	E-6010 E-6011	DCR DCR, AC	F, V, OH, H F, V, OH, H	Fast freeze, deep penetrating, flat beads, all-purpose welding
	E-6012 E-6013 E-6014	DCS, AC DCR, DCS, AC DCS, AC	F, V, OH, H F, V, OH, H F, V, OH, H	Fill-freeze, low penetration, for poor fit-up, good bead contour, minimum spatter
	E-6020 E-6024	DCR, DCS, AC DCR, DCS, AC	F, H F, H	Fast-fill, high deposition, deep groove welds, single pass
	E-6027	DCR, DCS, AC	F, H	Iron powder, high deposition, deep penetration
	E-7014	DCR, DCS, AC	F, V, OH, H	Iron powder, low penetration, high speed
	E-7024	DCR, DCS, AC	F, H	Iron powder, high deposition, single and multiple pass
Low Hydrogen	E-6015 E-6016 E-6018 E-7016 E-7018 E-7028	DCR DCR, AC DCR, AC DCR, AC DCR, AC DCR, AC	F, V, OH, H F, V, OH, H F, V, OH, H F, V, OH, H F, V, OH, H F, H	Welding of high-sulphur and high carbon steels that tend to develop porosity and crack under weld bead
Stainless Steel	E-308-15, 16	DC, AC	F, V, OH, H	Welding stainless steel 301, 302, 303, 304, 308
	E-309-15, 16	DC, AC	F, V, OH, H	Welding 309 alloy at elevated temperature application and dissimilar metals
	E-310-15, 16	DC, AC	F, V, OH, H	Welding type 310 and 314 stainless steel where high corrosion and elevated temperatures are required
	E-316-15, 16	DC, AC	F, V, OH, H	Welding type 316 stainless steel and welds of highest quality. Contains less carbon to minimize carbon transfer in the weld. Type 316 reduces pitting corrosion
	E-3437-15, 16	DC, AC	F, V, OH, H	For welding all grades of stainless steels
Low Alloy	E-7011-A1 E-7020-A1	DCR, AC DCR, DCS, AC	F, V, OH, H F	For welding carbon moly steels
	E-8018-C3	DCR, AC	F, V, OH, H	For low alloy, high tensile strength
	E-10013-G	DCS, AC	F, V, OH, H	For low alloy, high tensile steels

DCR — Direct Current Reverse Polarity
DCS — Direct Current Straight Polarity
AC — Alternating Current
F — flat, V — vertical, OH — overhead, H — horizontal

first weld bead or root pass. This is done to ensure thorough penetration at the root of the weld. Successive passes are then made with larger diameter electrodes.

3. *Joint design and fitup.* Joints with insufficient beveled edges require deep penetrating, fast-freeze electrodes. Some electrodes have this particular digging characteristic even

Fig. 4. Be sure to use the right electrode for the job being done. (Hobart Brothers Co.)

though the resulting spatter may require more skillful electrode manipulation by the operator. On the other hand, joints with open gaps need a mild penetrating fill-freeze electrode that rapidly bridges gaps. See Table III.

4. *Welding position.* The position of the weld joint is an important factor in the type of electrode to be used. Some electrodes produce better results when the welding is done in a flat position. Other electrodes are designed for vertical, horizontal, and overhead welding.

5. *Welding Current.* Electrodes are made for use with either AC current or DC current reverse polarity or DC current straight polarity, although some electrodes function as well on both AC or DC current. Since the type of current has a direct influence on the quality of a weld the designated current characteristic of the electrode becomes important.

6. *Production efficiency.* Deposition rate is extremely significant in any production work. The faster a weld can be made the lower the cost. Not all electrodes have a high-speed high current rating and still produce smooth, even bead ripples. Unless electrodes are noted for a fast deposition rate they may prove very difficult to handle when used at high speed travel.

7. *Service Conditions.* The service requirements of the part being welded may necessitate special weld deposits. For example, high corrosion resistance, or ductility, or high strength may

be important factors. In such cases electrodes must be selected that will produce these specific characteristics.

Conserving and Storing Electrodes

Most electrodes are costly; therefore, every bit of the electrode should be consumed. Do not discard stub ends until they are down to only 1½″ to 2″ long. See Fig. 5.

Always store electrodes in a dry place. When exposed to moisture, the coating has a tendency to disintegrate. In storing electrodes, be sure they are

Fig. 5. Do not discard electrodes of this length.

not bumped, bent, or stepped on, since this will remove the coating and make the electrode useless.

Selecting Mild Steel Electrodes

E-6010. This electrode is known as an all-position electrode, meaning that it can be used for welding in any position such as flat, horizontal, vertical, or overhead. It is suitable only on DC machines with reversed polarity, and is designed primarily for welding mild and low alloy steels. The E-6010 electrode is used a great deal for ship construction, buildings, bridges, tanks, and piping. Table IV shows the am-

TABLE IV
Current Settings for E-6010 Electrodes

Dia. of Electrodes	Amperes*	Arc Volt*
1/16	20–40	20–22
5/64	25–60	20–22
3/32	30–80	22–24
1/8	80–120	24–26
5/32	120–160	24–26
3/16	140–220	26–30
7/32	170–250	26–30
1/4	200–300	28–32
5/16	250–450	28–32

*These ranges may vary slightly for electrodes made by different manufacturers.

perage and voltage settings for different sizes of this electrode.

E-6011. The E-6011 electrode is similar to the E-6010 except that it is made especially for AC machines. Although the electrode can be used on DC machines with reversed polarity, it does not work quite as well as the E-6010. The amperage and voltage settings for E-6011 are the same as for E-6010.

E-6012. This electrode may be used on either DC or AC welders. When employed on DC welders the current must be set for straight polarity. The electrode provides medium penetration, a quiet type arc, slight spatter, and dense slag. Although it is considered an all-position electrode, it is used in greater quantities for flat and horizontal position welds. This electrode is especially useful to bridge gaps under conditions of poor *fit-up work;* that is, joints where the edges do not fit too closely together. Higher currents can be used with the E-6012 electrodes than with any other type of all-position electrodes. Current set-

TABLE V
Current Settings for E-6012 Electrodes

Dia. of Electrodes	Amperes*	Arc Volt*
1/16	20–40	17–20
5/64	20–60	17–21
3/32	30–80	17–21
1/8	80–130	18–22
5/32	120–180	18–22
3/16	140–250	20–24
7/32	170–300	20–24
1/4	200–400	20–24
5/16	250–500	22–26

*These ranges may vary slightly for electrodes made by different manufacturers.

tings for this electrode are shown in Table V.

E-6013. Electrodes of this type are very similar to E-6012 with a few slight exceptions. Slag removal is better and the arc can be maintained easier, especially with small diameter electrodes, thus permitting better operation with lower open-circuit voltage. Although the electrode is used particularly for welding sheet metal, it has many other applications. It works well in all positions and it functions very well on AC welders. When used with DC machines the polarity must

TABLE VI
Current Settings for E-6013 Electrodes

Dia. of Electrodes	Amperes*	Arc Volt*
1/16	20–40	17–20
5/16	25–50	17–20
3/32	30–80	17–21
1/8	70–120	18–22
5/32	120–170	18–22
3/16	140–240	20–24
7/32	170–300	21–25
1/4	200–350	22–26
5/16	250–450	23–27

*These ranges may vary slightly for electrodes made by different manufacturers.

be *straight*. Current settings for E-6013 electrodes are shown in Table VI.

E-6015. Electrodes of the E-6015 classification are intended for DC machines with *reversed polarity* only. They are used in welding higher strength, high-carbon, alloy steels without *underbead cracking*. These cracks occur in the center of the weld metal and are caused by the hydrogen present in the conventional electrode coverings. E-6015 electrodes are also used for welding free-machining, high-sulphur steels, and cold-rolled steels. The arc is very quiet and steady, without interference from molten slag. Current settings for E-6015 electrodes are shown in Table VII.

TABLE VII
Current Settings for E-6015 Electrodes

Dia. of Electrodes	Amperes*	Arc Volt*
1/32	70–110	20–22
1/8	100–150	20–22
5/32	135–200	21–23
3/16	160–240	22–24
7/32	260–320	23–25
1/4	300–375	24–27
5/16	350–450	24–28

*These ranges may vary slightly for electrodes made by different manufacturers.

E-6020. The E-6020 electrode is designed to produce flat or slightly concave horizontal welds with either DC or AC current and *straight* or *reversed polarity*. It will take a very high current and produce deep penetration. The electrode is used a great deal to weld pressure vessels, heavy machine bases, and structural sections.

TABLE VIII
Current Settings for E-6020 Electrodes

Dia. of Electrodes	Amperes*	Arc Volt*
1/8	100-140	24-28
5/32	120-180	26-30
3/16	175-250	30-36
7/32	200-325	30-36
1/4	250-400	30-36
5/16	350-450	32-38

*These ranges may vary slightly for electrodes made by different manufacturers.

Current settings are shown in Table VIII.

A development of the E-6020 classification is an electrode containing iron powder in the coating. This electrode is known by special trade names such as "Jetweld" (Lincoln Electric Co.), "Speedex" (Metal & Thermit Corp.), or "Easy Arc" (Airco). The electrode can be used either with AC or DC current and is designed for high speed welding of butt and deep groove joints.

E-6030. This electrode was developed for deep, narrow groove welding of heavy plate. It produces a smaller amount of slag and less fluid slag than the E-6020, thus decreasing the possi-bility of slag interference in deep grooves. However, due to insufficient slag covering, this electrode is not very suitable for horizontal fillet welding. (A fillet weld is a weld applied to a joint where one plate is placed perpen-dicular to another.) Current settings for the E-6030 are approximately the same as those for E-6020. This electrode is no longer used to any great extent since the development of pow-dered metal electrodes such as the E-6024 type.

E-7014. This electrode has a thick coating with approximately 30 per cent of the coating consisting of iron powder. The iron powder permits higher welding currents and therefore means higher deposition rates and welding speed. Although it is consid-ered an all position welding electrode, it is not particularly suited for out-of-position welding on thin-gage mate-rials.

The E-7014 is used for welding mild and low alloy steels when greater tensile strength is required. Current settings for this electrode are shown in Table IX.

E-7016, E-7018. These are low-

TABLE IX
Current Settings for E-7014 Electrodes

DIAMETER OF ELECTRODES	AMPERES*	ARC VOLTS*
3/32	80-125	17-21
1/8	110-160	18-22
5/32	150-210	19-23
3/16	200-275	20-24
7/32	260-340	21-25
1/4	330-415	22-26
5/16	390-500	23-28

*These ranges may vary slightly for electrodes made by different manufacturers.

TABLE X
Current Settings for E-7016 and E-7018 Electrodes

DIAMETER OF ELECTRODE	AMPERAGE	ARC VOLT
3/32	65-110	17-22
1/8	100-165	18-22
5/32	140-220	20-24
3/16	180-275	21-25
7/32	240-340	22-27
1/4	300-400	23-28
5/16	375-475	24-28

hydrogen electrodes designed for welding high sulphur and high-carbon steels. When such steels are welded they tend to develop porosity and cracks under the weld bead because of the hydrogen absorption from arc atmospheres. Low-hydrogen electrodes were developed to prevent the introduction of hydrogen in the weld.

Both the E-7016 and E-7018 are classified as all position electrodes and operate with either AC or DC reverse polarity current. Approximate current settings are shown in Table X.

Special Electrodes

Standard electrodes are used for most general types of welding. With these electrodes fusion is achieved by changing the solid state of metal into a molten mass, which combines with the metal deposit of the electrode, to form a permanent bond. The success of the bond depends on the generation of sufficient heat to produce a completely amalgamated molten puddle. However, metals often undergo unfavorable changes when subjected to high heat, and precautions must be taken to avoid stresses, distortion, warpage, and other metallurgical structural changes.

A wide range of low heat input electrodes are available under the name "Eutectic" for welding where high heat may be a critical factor. These electrodes are designed so a strong joint can be made without heating the parent metal to its full melting point. Such welding is done with considerably lower current values without necessarily sacrificing the strength of the joint. For example, a ⅛″ high nickel content electrode may be used to cold weld castings only five-thirty seconds of an inch thick. An arc of only one-sixteenth of an inch instead of the conventional one-eighth inch arc gap is required.

Low heat input electrodes may be procured to weld all kinds of ferrous and non-ferrous metals. Special information concerning these electrodes can be obtained from the Eutectic Welding Alloys Corporation.

Points to Remember

1. Use the correct type electrode for the welding to be done.

2. Remember, some electrodes can be used only on DC machines and others on AC machines.

3. If welding is to be done on a DC machine, check whether straight or reverse polarity is needed for the particular electrode to be used.

4. Select an electrode with a diameter that is about the same as the thickness of the plate to be welded.

5. Always use up the electrode until the stub is down to $1\frac{1}{2}''$ to $2''$ long.

6. Store electrodes in a dry place where the coating cannot be damaged.

QUESTIONS FOR STUDY AND DISCUSSION

1. What is the difference between a bare and shielded electrode?

2. Why are bare electrodes rarely used today?

3. What are the functions of the heavy coating on shielded electrodes?

4. What has been done to ensure uniformity of electrode specifications?

5. What symbols have been adopted to identify different types of electrodes?

6. In addition to identification symbols, what other means are used to mark electrodes? Where are these markings located?

7. Explain the identifying symbols of the electrode classification E-6010.

8. What is meant by an all-position electrode?

9. How is it possible to determine if an electrode is designed for an AC or DC welder?

10. What factors should be taken into consideration when selecting an electrode for the job to be done?

11. Why are smaller diameter electrodes used for overhead welding?

12. What precautions must be taken in storing electrodes?

13. What is the specific feature of electrodes with coatings containing powdered iron?

14. For what are low hydrogen electrodes used?

CHAPTER 5

Shielded Metal—Arc Welding

Striking an Arc

Learning to arc weld involves mastery of a specific series of operations. Skill in performing these operations requires practice. Once this skill has been acquired, the operations can be applied on any welding job. The first basic operation is learning to strike an arc and run a straight bead.

Checking and Adjusting the Equipment

To start your first welding operation, proceed as follows:

1. Inspect the cable connections to make certain that they are all tight.

2. Make sure the bench top and metal to be welded are dry and free from dirt, rust, and grease.

3. If you are using a DC welder, set the polarity switch for the desired kind of current—straight or reversed.

4. Adjust the control unit for the amperage and voltage needed for the selected electrode. *Remember,* the recommended current setting specified for the electrode is only approximate. Final adjustment of current value is made as you proceed with the welding operation. For example, the amperage range for the electrode may be 90-100. It is best for the beginner to set the control midway between the two limits, which in this case is 95 amperes. If after the welding is started the arc is too hot, turn the control to reduce the amperage. Increase the current setting if the arc is not hot enough for penetration.

No specific rules can be given for the final setting because many factors are involved, such as skill of the operator, welding position, type of metal, and the nature of the welding job. Ability to make the final adjustment comes as you gain experience.

Fig. 1. How to grip the electrode. (Hobart Brothers Co.)

Gripping the Electrode Holder

Place the bare end of the electrode in the holder as shown in Fig. 1. By gripping the electrode near the end, most of the coated portion can be used. *Always keep the jaws of the holder clean* to ensure good electrical contact with the electrode. *Be careful not to touch the welding bench with an uninsulated holder, as this will cause a flash. When not in use, hang the holder in the place provided for it.*

Grip the holder lightly in your hand. If you hold it too tightly, your hand and arm will tire quickly. Whenever possible, drape the cable over the shoulder or knee to lessen its drag on the holder.

Striking the Arc

1. Obtain a piece of ⅛″ or ¼″ steel plate and lay it flat on the bench top. Insert a ⅛″ or ⁵⁄₃₂″ E-6010, E-6011, or E-6012 electrode in the holder and set the machine for the correct current.

2. There are two methods which can be used to start, or strike, the arc—the *tapping* and the *scratching* motion. The tapping method is the one preferred by experienced welders, whereas the scratching motion is found to be easier for the beginner.

In the tapping motion, the electrode is brought straight down and withdrawn instantly, as shown in *A* of Fig. 2. With the scratching method, the electrode is moved at an angle to the plate in a scratching motion much as in striking a match as shown in *B* of Fig. 2. Regardless of which motion you use, upon contact with the plate, promptly raise the electrode a distance equal to the diameter of the electrode. Otherwise, the electrode will stick to the metal. If it is allowed to remain in this position with the current flowing, the, electrode will become red hot.

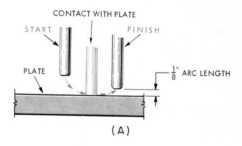

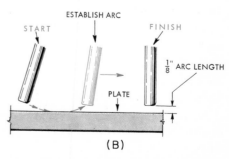

Fig. 2. There are two methods of starting, or striking, the arc.

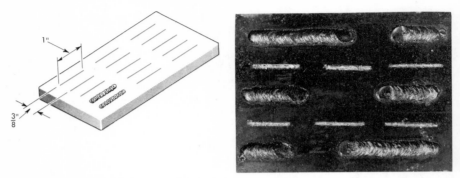

Fig. 3. Lay out guide lines with a soapstone for running short beads.

Should the electrode weld fast to the plate, break it loose by quickly twisting or bending the holder. If it should *fail to dislodge, disengage the electrode by releasing it from the holder.*
    3. Practice starting the arc until this

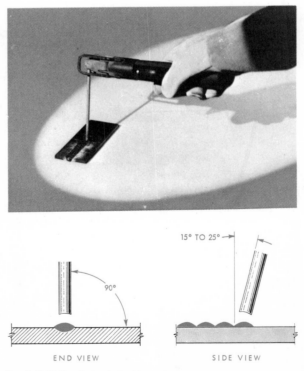

Fig. 4. Hold the electrode in this position for running straight beads.

operation can be performed quickly and easily.

Running Short Beads

With a soapstone, which is a marking chalk used to draw lines on metal, draw a series of lines on a steel plate, each line to be approximately 1″ in length and ⅜″ apart as illustrated in Fig. 3. Run a continuous bead over each line, moving the electrode from left to right. Hold the electrode in a vertical position or slant it slightly away from you as shown in Fig. 4. Move the electrode just rapidly enough so the deposited metal has time to penetrate into the base plate. If the current is set properly and the arc is maintained at the correct length, there will be a continuous crackling or frying noise. Learn to recognize this sound. An arc that is too long will have somewhat of a humming sound. Too short of an arc makes a popping sound. Notice the action of the molten puddle and how the trailing edge of the puddle solidifies as the electrode travels forward.

The appearance of the puddle is often an indication of how good a weld is being made. If the molten metal is clear and bright it means that no molten slag is mixing with the puddle. Slag is brittle and when it flows in the molten metal the weld is weakened. Normally, if the edges of the weld bead have a dull irregular appearance it means that slag is being trapped into the puddle.

Checking the Welding Heat

After you have become accustomed to striking an arc and running short weld beads, vary the welding current to see how it affects the welding heat. First turn the machine down about five amperes and check if there is any difference when you run a bead. Then turn it down another five amperes and again try to run a bead. As you reduce the amperage it soon becomes apparent that there is insufficient heat to melt the base metal. Furthermore, you will find that as the electrode burns off it does not fuse with the base metal but lies as spatter on the surface which easily scrapes off.

Now reverse the process by gradually raising the amperage. Turn the machine up five amperes in several steps and each time run short beads. It will soon become obvious that as the amperage is increased the arc gets hotter and the electrode melts faster.

From this experiment you can appreciate the importance of having the correct welding heat to make a sound weld. However, as you gain experience in welding, proper adjustment of welding current becomes relatively easy.

Points to Remember

1. Inspect the equipment before starting to weld.

2. See that the polarity switch is set in the right position.

3. See that no combustible materials are near where the welding is to be done, as flying sparks from the spatter of the arc may easily ignite the materials.

4. Do not lay the holder on the bench while the current is flowing.

5. Release the electrode if it sticks to the plate.

6. Always shut off the machine when leaving the welding bench.

QUESTIONS FOR STUDY AND DISCUSSION

1. What are some of the items to be checked before proceeding to weld?

2. Why should the electrode be clamped at its extreme end?

3. Why should the holder never be placed on the work bench while the current is on?

4. What two methods may be used in striking an arc?

5. In striking an arc, why should the electrode be withdrawn instantly?

6. What should be done if the electrode welds fast to the plate?

7. The arc should be maintained at approximately what length?

8. If the arc length and current are correct, what is the characteristic noise that is heard?

WELDING ASSIGNMENTS

1. Practice striking an arc on a flat steel plate.

2. Cover both sides of a plate with short beads.

CHAPTER 6

Shielded Metal—Arc Welding

Running Continuous Beads

To produce good welds you must not only know how to manipulate the electrode, but you need to know certain weld characteristics. Especially important is a knowledge of what constitutes a good weld and what causes a poor weld. Some of the more important elements affecting good welds are discussed in this chapter.

Four Essentials of Arc Welding

To secure a weld that has proper penetration, you must keep in mind the following four factors:

1. *Correct electrode* — The choice of an electrode involves such items as position of the weld, properties of the base metal, diameter of the electrode, type of joint, and current value. Since many different kinds of electrodes are manufactured, you must know the results that can be expected from different electrodes. If the characteristics of the electrodes are known, then you

have greater assurance that a correct weld will be made. Without the right kind of electrode it is almost impossible to get the results desired, regardless of the welding technique used.

2. *Correct arc length*—If the arc is too long, the metal melts off the electrode in large globules which wobble from side to side as the arc wavers. This produces a wide, spattered, and irregular bead without sufficient fusion between the original metal and the deposited metal. An arc that is too short fails to generate enough heat to melt the base metal properly. Furthermore, the electrode sticks frequently, producing a high, uneven bead with irregular ripples.

The length of the arc depends on the size of electrode used and the kind of welding done. Thus for small diameter electrodes, a shorter arc is necessary than for larger electrodes. As a rule, the length of the arc should be

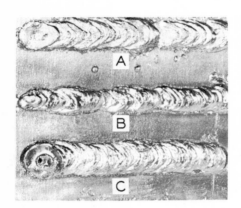

Fig. 1. This is how the beads appear when (A) the arc is too long, (B) the arc is too short, and (C) the arc is the correct length.

too, that a shorter arc is required for vertical and overhead welding than for most flat position welds because it gives better control of the molten puddle.

The use of a short arc is important because it prevents impurities from entering a weld. A long arc allows the atmosphere to flow into the arc stream, thereby permitting impurities of nitrides and oxides to form. Moreover, when the arc is too long, heat from the arc stream is dissipated too rapidly, causing considerable metal spatter. Study Fig. 1 and notice the condition of the three sample welds shown. Sample *A* illustrates a weld formed when the arc is too long. This is indicated by the large amount of spatter and the fact that the beads are too coarse.

approximately equal to the diameter of the electrode. For example, an electrode ⅛" in diameter should have an arc length of about ⅛". You will find,

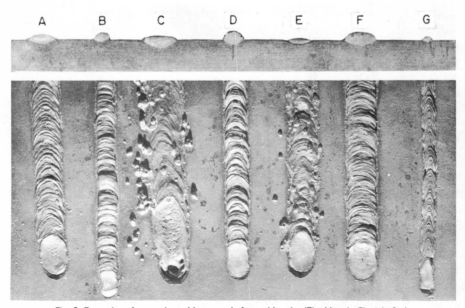

Fig. 2. Examples of properly and improperly formed beads. (The Lincoln Electric Co.)

A. Current, voltage, and speed normal.   E. Voltage too high.
B. Current too low.   F. Speed too slow.
C. Current too high.   G. Speed too fast.
D. Voltage too low.

Sample *B* shows a weld made with an arc that is too short. Notice the excessive height of the beads. Such beads are a sign of improper penetration. Sample *C* is an example of a good weld. In this case the beads have the proper height and width, and the ripples are uniformly spaced.

3. *Correct current*—If the current is too high, the electrode melts too fast and the molten pool is large and irregular. When the current is too low, there is not enough heat to melt the base metal and the molten pool will be too small. The result is not only poor fusion but the beads will pile up and be irregular in shape. See Fig. 2.

4. *Correct travel speed*—Where the speed is too fast, the molten pool does not last long enough and impurities are locked in the weld. The bead is narrow and the ripples pointed. If the rate of travel is too slow, the metal piles up excessively and the bead is high and wide with straight ripples as illustrated in Fig. 2.

Crater Formation

As the arc comes in contact with the base metal, a pool, or pocket, is formed. As previously stated, this pool is known as a *crater*. The size and depth of a crater indicate the amount of penetration. In general, the depth of penetration should be from one-third to one-half the total thickness of the bead, depending upon the size of the electrode, as pictured in Fig. 3.

To secure a sound weld, the metal deposited from the electrode must fuse completely with the base metal. Fusion will result only when the base metal

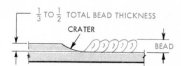

Fig. 3. This crater and bead show proper penetration.

has been heated to a liquid state and the molten metal from the electrode readily flows into it. Thus, if the arc is too short, there will be insufficient *spread* of heat to form the correct size crater of molten metal. When the arc is too long, the heat is not centralized or intense enough to form the desired crater.

Remelting and Controlling a Crater

An improperly filled crater may cause a weld to fail when a load is applied on a welded structure. Therefore, be sure to fill a crater properly. There is always a tendency when starting an electrode for a large globule of metal to fall on the surface of the plate with little or no penetration. This is especially true when beginning a new electrode at the crater left from a previously deposited weld. To fill the crater and secure proper fusion, strike the arc approximately ½ ″ in front of the crater as shown at *A* in Fig. 4.

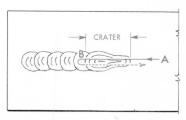

Fig. 4. Fill the crater by moving the electrode from **A** to **B**, and then back again through the crater to **A**.

Then bring it back through the crater to point *B* just beyond the crater, and weld back through the crater.

Occasionally, you will find that the crater is getting too hot and the fluid metal has a tendency to run. When this happens, lift the electrode quickly and shift it to the side or ahead of the crater. Such a movement reduces the heat, allows the crater to solidify momentarily, and stops the deposit of metal from the electrode. Then return the electrode to the crater and shorten the arc.

Another method used by welders to control the temperature of the molten puddle is a *whipping* action of the electrode. This technique is especially helpful when welding pieces that do not have a tight fit and large openings have to be filled. It is also used in overhead welding to better control the weld puddle.

In a whipping action the electrode is struck and held momentarily. Then it is moved forward about ¼ ″ or ⅜ ″ and raised a similar distance at the same time. Raising the electrode temporarily reduces the heat. Then just as the puddle begins to freeze the electrode is moved back into the center of the puddle and the sequences repeated. The movement of the electrode should be done by pivoting the wrist and not moving the arm.

Undercutting and Overlapping

Undercutting is a condition that results when the welding current is too high. The excessive current leaves a groove in the base metal along both sides of the bead which greatly reduces

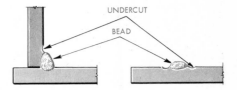

Fig. 5. Undercutting greatly weakens a weld.

the strength of a weld as illustrated in Fig. 5. *Overlapping* occurs when the current is set too low. In this instance, the molten metal falls from the electrode without actually fusing with the base metal as shown in Fig. 6.

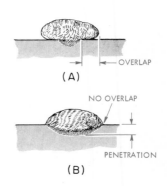

Fig. 6. When not enough heat is used overlapping occurs as shown in (A). A satisfactory weld appears in (B).

Cleaning a Weld

It has already been mentioned that when a weld is made, a layer of slag covers the deposited bead. If additional layers of weld metal are deposited, this slag must be removed; otherwise it will be melted in with the

Fig. 7. Slag is removed from the weld by chipping.

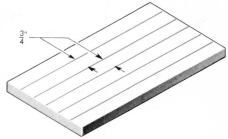

Fig. 9. Using a steel plate with lines ¾″ apart, deposit continuous beads from left to right.

deposited metal and cause a weak weld. To remove the slag, strike the weld with a chipping hammer. Hammer the bead so the chipping is away from the body and thus away from the eyes and face as pictured in Fig. 7. Do not pound the bead too hard; otherwise the structure of the weld may be damaged. After the slag is loosened, drag the pointed end of the hammer along the weld where it joins the plate. This will remove the remaining particles of slag. Follow the chipping with a good, hard brushing, using a stiff wire brush as illustrated in Fig. 8.

Welding Continuous Beads

Plate No. 1. After you have mas-

tered the operation of depositing short beads, secure another steel plate ¼″ x 4″ x 6″. With a soapstone, draw a number of lines approximately ¾″ apart as shown in Fig. 9. Use a ⅛″ diameter E-6010 or E-6011 electrode and run continuous beads on these

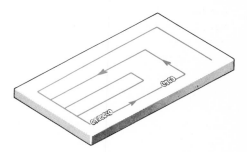

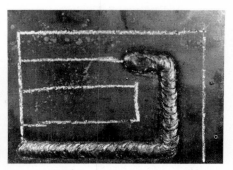

Fig. 8. After chipping, brush the weld with a wire brush. (Hobart Brothers Co.)

Fig. 10. To practice moving the electrode in several directions, deposit beads along the lines as indicated by the arrows (above) and the finished work (below).

lines, starting from the left edge and working to the right. After the plate is filled, remove the slag and examine the beads.

Plate No. 2. This exercise provides practice in moving the electrode in several directions. Draw the lines on the plate as shown in Fig. 10. Then deposit a continuous bead, moving the electrode from left to right, bottom to top, right to left, and top to bottom.

Plate No. 3. The purpose of this plate is to develop skill in re-striking an arc while making a continuous

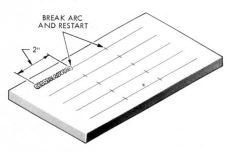

Fig. 11. To develop skill in re-starting an arc, break the arc and re-start every 2 inches.

bead. Draw a series of straight lines on the plate and divide these lines into 2-inch sections as shown in Fig. 11. Run a bead over the first line but break the arc when reaching the end of the 2-inch mark. Re-start the arc and continue the deposit for another two inches; then repeat the practice of breaking the arc and refilling the crater. Follow this procedure until skill is mastered in depositing uniform and continuous beads with properly filled craters.

Weaving the Electrode

Weaving is a technique used to in-

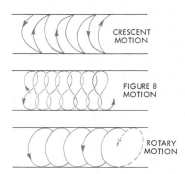

Fig. 12. The Crescent, Figure-8, and Rotary motions are three typical weaving patterns.

crease the width and volume of the bead. Enlarging the size of the bead is often necessary on deep groove or fillet welds where a number of passes must be made. Fig. 12 illustrates several weaving patterns. The pattern used depends to some extent on the position of the weld. In subsequent chapters additional instructions will be given as to the most suitable weaving pattern for specific weld joints.

Plate No. 4. Lay out a series of straight lines on a ¼″ x 4″ x 6″ plate. Run continuous beads over these lines and then clean each bead. Now proceed to practice weaving by depositing a weld back and forth between the first

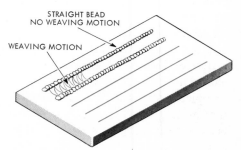

Fig. 13. Practice weaving by depositing a weld from left to right between the straight beads.

pair of continuous beads as illustrated in Fig. 13. Use one type of weaving motion to fill the first space and then try several other weaves on the remaining sections. Make certain that the short beads are fused into the long, straight beads. Continue the weaving practice on several plates until a workmanlike job is accomplished.

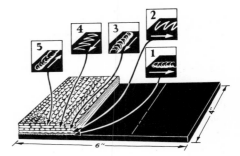

Fig. 15. A weld metal pad is built up by depositing successive layers of beads on top of each other.

Fig. 14. This shaft is being built up by padding. (Hobart Brothers Co.)

Plate No. 5 — depositing a weld metal pad. *Padding* is a process often used in building up worn surfaces of shafts, wheels, and other machine parts. The operation consists of depositing several layers of beads, one on top of the other as pictured in Fig. 14. For this exercise divide the standard 4″ x 6″ plate into three sections as shown in Fig. 15. Fill the first section completely with beads, clean the weld thoroughly, and then deposit a second layer of weaving beads about ½″ wide at right angles to the first layer. After the weld is cleaned, deposit a third

layer at right angles to the second layer. Clean this surface and deposit a fourth and a fifth layer. Follow a similar procedure to build up the two remaining sections on the plate.

Points to Remember

1. Use the correct type of electrode.

2. Use an arc that is about as long as the diameter of the electrode.

3. Maintain the correct welding current.

4. Move the electrode just fast enough to produce evenly spaced ripples.

5. Keep the penetration a depth equal to one-third to one-half the total thickness of the bead.

6. Be sure the molten metal from the electrode fuses completely with the base metal.

7. Always re-start the electrode ½″ in front of the previously made crater.

8. Avoid undercutting and overlapping.

9. Clean the slag from a weld. Remember, chip away from your body to prevent the slag from flying up into your face.

QUESTIONS FOR STUDY AND DISCUSSION

1. What causes a bead to overlap the base metal? Why does this produce a poor weld?

2. What causes undercutting? How can undercutting be avoided?

3. What is meant by a crater?

4. What should be the depth of penetration? How thick should the bead be?

5. How is a crater affected when the arc is too short? What happens when the arc is too long?

6. What are the four essentials for securing a sound weld?

7. What factors must be taken into consideration when selecting an electrode?

8. When an arc is too long what happens to the metal as it melts from the electrode?

9. How is it possible to identify a weld that has been made with an arc that is too long?

10. What is likely to happen to the electrode when the arc is too short?

11. What are some of the characteristics of a weld made with an arc that is too short?

12. What are some of the factors that you must think of in deciding the length of an arc?

13. In what way does the current affect a weld?

14. What determines the speed at which an electrode should be moved?

15. How should an electrode be re-started to fill a crater left from a previously deposited weld?

16. What should be done when the crater gets too hot and the metal has a tendency to run?

17. How should slag from a weld be removed?

18. What is meant by weaving?

19. When is a weaving motion used?

20. What is the purpose of padding?

WELDING ASSIGNMENTS

1. Fill a plate with straight lines of beads.

2. Fill a plate with beads running in different directions.

3. Fill a plate with beads, re-starting the arc every two inches.

4. Fill a plate with beads, using a weaving motion.

5. Build a pad on a flat plate.

CHAPTER 7

Shielded Metal—Arc Welding

The Flat Position

〜〜〜〜〜〜〜〜〜〜〜〜〜〜〜〜〜〜〜〜〜〜〜〜〜〜〜

Although welding can be done in any position, the operation is simplified if the joint is flat. When placed in this way, the welding speed is increased, the molten metal has less tendency to run, better penetration can be secured, and the work is less fatiguing. Some structures may appear at first glance to require horizontal, vertical, or overhead welding, but upon more careful examination you may be able to change them to the easier and more efficient flat position. See Fig. 1.

Making a Single Pass Fillet Lap Weld

The lap joint is one of the most frequently used joints in welding. It is a relatively simple joint, since no beveling or machining is necessary. One

Fig. 1. Welding with the work in a flat position is not only easier, but will also result in better quality and greater economy. (The Lincoln Electric Co.)

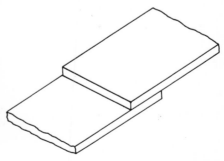

Fig. 2. The lap joint is used frequently in welding to provide greater strength.

standard requisite is to have clean, evenly aligned surfaces. As shown in Fig. 2 the joint consists of lapping one edge over another and joining. The amount the edges should overlap depends upon the thickness of the plates and the strength required of the welded piece. Usually the thicker the plates the greater the amount of overlap. This is done to provide sufficient support to prevent the plates from bending. When the structure is subjected to heavy bending stresses, it is advisable to weld the edges of both sides of the joint as illustrated in Fig. 3.

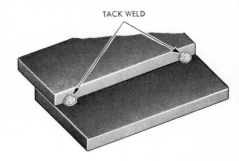

Fig. 4. Tack the plates at each end before starting to weld a flat lap joint.

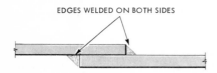

Fig. 3. For a strong joint weld both edges.

The lap joint is adaptable for a variety of new construction work as well as for making numerous types of repairs. For example, such a joint can be employed when joining a series of metal plates together or in reinforcing another structural member. Since a lap weld stiffens the structure where the plates are lapped, this joint is used a great deal in tank and ship building.

To practice welding a single pass lap joint, obtain two pieces of $3/16''$ or $1/4''$ steel plate. A *single pass* simply means depositing one layer of beads. When a weld is built up of more than one layer it is known as a *multiple pass* weld. Use $1/8''$ electrodes and adjust the machine for the correct current. Then tack the plates at each end. A *tack* weld is made by depositing

several short beads on the ends of the base plates to hold them in position as shown in Fig. 4.

With the plates properly tacked, run a $1/4''$ fillet along the edge. Hold the electrode at a 45° angle and point it toward the weld as shown in Fig. 5. Weave the electrode slightly, maintaining the arc for a slightly longer period

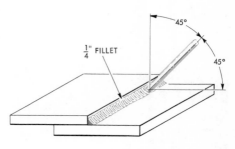

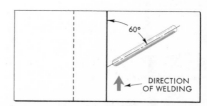

Fig. 5. For a flat lap weld, hold the electrode as shown in the above two views.

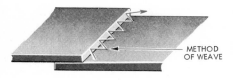

Fig. 6. Use this weave for a flat lap weld.

on the lower plate. See Fig. 6. Be sure to get complete fusion at the *root,* or joining point, of the joint and avoid overlaps on the top surface. Watch the crater carefully to prevent an undercut on the bottom plate. Fig 7A illustrates a *properly made fillet weld* on a lap joint. A weld made as in Fig. 7B usually is too weak because it lacks sufficient reinforcing material, while the weld shown in Fig. 7C has waste metal, which is of no value to the joint.

Making a Multiple Pass Fillet Lap Weld

When an exceptionally strong lap joint is required, especially on heavy plates ⅜" and over in thickness, a multiple pass fillet weld is recommended. This joint has two or more layers of beads along the seam, with each bead lapping over the other.

To make such a weld, deposit the first bead as shown in Fig. 8 by moving the electrode straight down the seam without any weaving motion. Clean the weld carefully and lay the second pass over this *stringer bead,* a term used to describe a narrow single bead over the seam of the base plates. During the second pass, weave the electrode, pausing for an instant at the top of the weave to favor or deposit extra metal on the vertical edge of the upper plate.

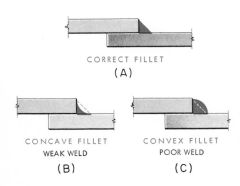

Fig. 7. How a good lap weld and two poor lap welds appear from a side view.

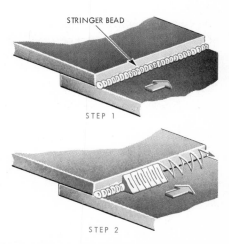

Fig. 8. Making a multiple pass fillet weld on a lap joint.

Fig. 9. Single pass T-fillet joint. (The Lincoln Electric Co.)

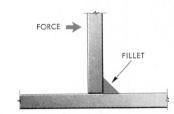

Fig. 11. This joint would be weak if subjected to stresses from the direction indicated by the arrow.

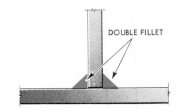

Fig. 12. A double fillet T-joint is stronger.

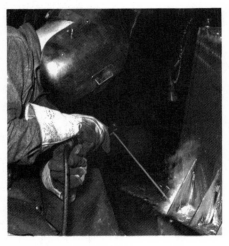

Fig. 10. Example of work where a T-joint is used. (Hobart Brothers Co.)

Making a Single Pass T-Fillet Joint

The T-fillet joint is frequently used in fabricating straight and rolled shapes. Sees Figs. 9 and 10. The strength of this joint depends considerably on having the edges of the joint fit close together. The T-joint should not be used if it is subjected to heavy stresses from the opposite direction of the welded seam. This weakness can be partially overcome by using a double fillet—that is, welding both sides of the joint. See Figs. 11 and 12.

To practice welding a T-fillet joint, obtain two $\frac{3}{16}''$ or $\frac{1}{4}''$ plates. Set the vertical plate on the middle of the horizontal plate and tack weld each end. Deposit a $\frac{1}{4}''$ fillet bead along the edge. Hold the electrode as shown in Fig. 13 and advance it in a straight line without any weaving motion. Point the tip of the electrode toward the completed portion of the weld and travel rapidly enough to stay ahead of the molten pool. Concentrate the arc more on the lower plate to prevent under-

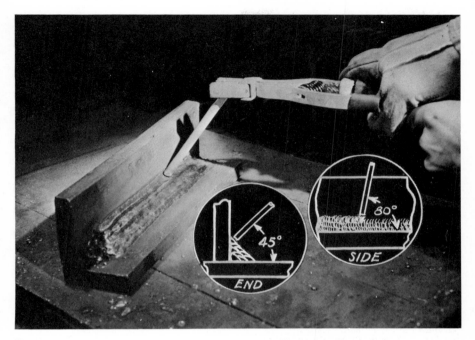

Fig. 13. Position of the electrode for welding a T-fillet joint. (The Lincoln Electric Co.)

cutting the upper plate. Watch the crater closely so it will form a bead with the correct contour.

Fig. 14. A multiple pass T-fillet joint.

Making a Multiple Pass T-Fillet Joint

When a very strong T-joint is required, make a wider fillet along the seam. You can get a wider fillet by running several layers of beads as illustrated in Fig. 14. Deposit the first bead as described in making a single pass T-fillet joint. Remove the slag and lay the second bead over the first,

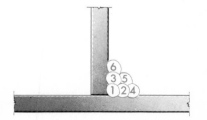

Fig. 15. Sequence of passes for a multiple T-fillet weld.

weaving the electrode sufficiently to secure the desired width fillet. Deposit additional layers if necessary to get the right size fillet, but *be sure to clean off the slag after each pass.* See Fig 15.

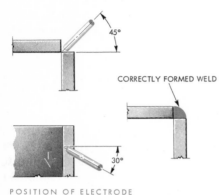

CORRECTLY FORMED WELD

POSITION OF ELECTRODE

Fig. 16. An outside corner weld. The angle of the electrode is viewed from the side (top), and overhead (bottom).

How to Make an Outside Corner Weld

The outside corner weld, as shown in Fig. 16, is often used in constructing rectangular shaped objects such as tanks, metal furniture, and other machine sections where the outside corner must have a smooth radius. See Fig. 17.

To make an outside corner weld, tack the two plates and run a bead along the edge with the electrode held as indicated in Fig. 16. On light stock, one bead is usually enough. Heavy stock will probably require a series of passes to fill in the corner.

How to Weld a Butt Joint

The butt joint is often used when structural pieces have flat surfaces, such as in tanks, boilers, and a variety

Fig. 17. An outside corner weld is used in fabricating this structure. (Hobart Brothers Co.)

Fig. 18. The narrow section in this tank is welded with a butt joint. (Hobart Brothers Co.)

of machine parts. See Fig. 18. The joint may be opened, closed, or the edges beveled, as pictured in Fig. 19. A *closed butt joint* has the edges of the two plates in direct contact with each other. This joint is suitable for welding steel plates *that do not exceed 1/8″ to 3/16″ in thickness.* Heavier metal can be welded but only if the machine has sufficient amperage capacity and if heavier electrodes are used. *Remember that on heavy metal it is difficult to secure ample penetration to produce a strong weld by a single pass bead.*

In the *open butt joint* the edges are placed slightly apart, usually 3/32″ to 1/8″, to allow for expansion. You will find a more detailed discussion of expansion in Chapter 2. As a rule, a backup strip or block of scrap steel, copper, or brick is placed under this joint as shown in Fig. 20. A backup strip prevents the bottom edges from burning through.

BACKUP BLOCK

Fig. 20. A backup strip or block should be used on an open butt joint.

When the thickness of the metal exceeds 1/8″ the edges of a butt joint must be beveled. The beveling can be done by cutting the edges with a flame torch or by grinding them on an emery wheel. The included angle of the vee should not exceed 60 degrees, to limit the amount of contraction that usually

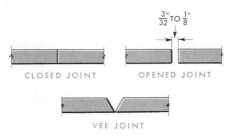

$\frac{3}{32}″$ TO $\frac{1}{8}″$

CLOSED JOINT   OPENED JOINT

VEE JOINT

Fig. 19. There are three types of butt joints.

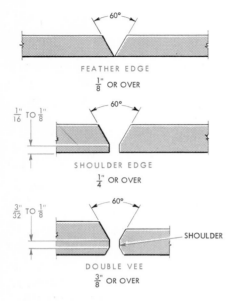

FEATHER EDGE
$\frac{1}{8}''$ OR OVER

SHOULDER EDGE
$\frac{1}{4}''$ OR OVER

DOUBLE VEE
$\frac{3}{8}''$ OR OVER

Fig. 21. There are three methods of preparing a vee joint.

results when the metal cools. The edges may be shaped in several ways

as shown in Fig. 21. Notice that on heavy metal $\frac{3}{8}''$ or more in thickness the edges are beveled on both sides. Beveling in this manner will ensure better penetration.

Fig. 22 illustrates the position of the electrode for welding a butt joint. However, when the joint consists of two pieces of different thicknesses, adjust the position of the electrode so the greatest portion of the heat is concentrated on the thickest plate.

When a multiple pass bead is made in a vee joint, hold the electrode down in the groove so it almost touches both sides of the joint. Move the electrode fast enough to keep the slag flowing back on the finished weld. If the electrode is not moved rapidly enough, the slag may become trapped in the bottom of the weld, thereby preventing proper fusion.

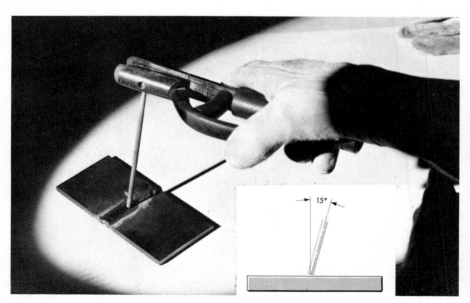

Fig. 22. Position of the electrode for welding a butt joint. (The Lincoln Electric Co.)

Fig. 23. The edges of round stock are beveled on **both sides** and held in place with a piece of angle iron. (The Lincoln Electric Co.)

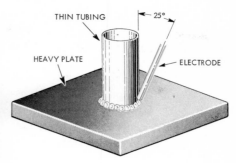

Fig. 24. Position of the electrode when welding pipe to a flat plate.

How to Weld Round Stock

A butt joint is generally used to weld round shafts or rods. First bevel both sides of the stock, leaving a shoulder in the center. Be sure to grind the edges so they have the same angle. Then place the pieces in a vise or section of angle iron, as shown in Fig. 23, to hold them in position. To prevent the shaft from warping, deposit a small bead on one side and then lay a similar bead on the opposite side. Use a slight weaving motion on the final pass.

Sometimes you may have to weld a thin-walled pipe to a heavier flat plate. If you change the position of the electrode from the usual angle to approximately 25°, you can direct more heat on the flat plate and thus prevent the pipe from burning through. See Fig. 24.

Points to Remember

1. When welding a lap or T-joint, weld the edges on both sides if the structure is subjected to heavy stresses.

2. Tack the two pieces before starting to weld. This will keep them in position.

3. Hold the electrode at a 45° angle when welding a lap joint, keeping the arc more on the upper plate.

4. For an exceptionally strong lap or T-joint on heavy metal, use several layers of beads.

5. Place the edges of an open butt joint slightly apart to allow for expansion.

6. When the thickness of the metal exceeds $\frac{1}{8}''$ on a butt joint, always bevel the edges.

7. When a butt joint is used to weld a round shaft, bevel both sides to the same angle.

8. To weld a thin-walled pipe to a heavy flat plate, change the angle of the electrode so the arc is directed more on the plate.

QUESTIONS FOR STUDY AND DISCUSSION

1. What is an advantage of welding in a flat position rather than in an overhead or vertical position?

2. What is meant by a single pass fillet weld?

3. When making a lap weld, how much should the edges overlap?

4. How is it possible to avoid undercutting when welding a lap joint?

5. What is the purpose of using a double fillet on a lap joint?

6. When should a multiple bead be used on a lap joint?

7. What are some of the factors that must be considered when using or making a T-joint?

8. When welding a T-joint, using flat plates, why should the arc favor the bottom plate?

9. How many passes should be made on an outside corner weld?

10. When is a butt joint used in welding?

11. What is the difference between an open and closed butt joint?

12. When should the edges of butt joints be beveled?

13. How should the edges of round stock be prepared for welding?

14. In what position should the electrode be held when welding a thin-walled pipe to a heavier flat plate?

WELDING ASSIGNMENTS

1. Weld a single pass lap joint.

2. Weld a multiple pass lap joint.

3. Weld a single pass T-joint.

4. Weld a multiple pass T-joint.

5. Make an outside corner weld.

6. Make a closed butt weld.

7. Make an open butt weld.

8. Make a vee butt weld.

9. Weld two pieces of round stock.

10. Weld a short section of pipe to a flat plate.

CHAPTER 8

Shielded Metal—Arc Welding

The Horizontal Position

On many jobs it is practically impossible to weld pieces in the flat position. Occasionally, the welding operation must be done while the work is in a horizontal position. A weld is in a horizontal position when the joint is on a vertical plate and the line of weld runs on a line with the horizon as in Fig. 1.

Fig. 1. Welding a horizontal seam.

To perform welds of this kind, you must use a slightly shorter arc than for flat position welding. The shorter arc will minimize the tendency of the molten puddle to sag and cause overlaps. An overlap occurs when the puddle runs down to the lower side of the bead and solidifies on the surface without actually penetrating the metal. See Fig. 2. A sagging puddle usually leaves an undercut on the top side of the seam as well as improperly shaped beads, all of which weaken a weld.

How to Hold the Electrode

For horizontal welding, hold the

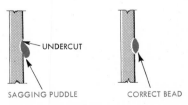

Fig. 2. The sagging puddle at the left can be avoided by shortening the arc.

85

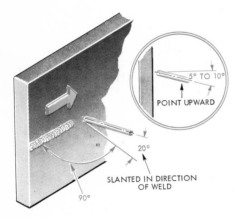

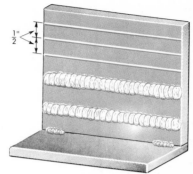

Fig. 5. Tack the plate so it is in a vertical position.

Fig. 3. Position of the electrode for horizontal welding.

electrode so that it points upward 5° to 10°, and slants approximately 20° away from the deposited bead as illustrated in Fig. 3. In laying the bead, use a narrow weaving motion as shown in Fig. 4. By weaving the electrode, the heat will be distributed more evenly, thereby reducing still further any tendency for the puddle to sag.

Depositing Straight Beads in a Horizontal Position

1. Obtain a ¼″ plate and draw a series of lines ½″ apart.

2. Fasten the plate on the bench in a vertical position as pictured in Fig. 5. To keep the piece in place, tack it to a flat piece.

3. Adjust the machine to the correct current and, with a weaving motion, deposit beads between the horizontal lines. Lay one bead by starting from the left side of the plate and working to the right. Then reverse the direction and run the bead from the right side to the left. Continue this operation until uniform beads can be made without overlapping and undercutting.

Making a Single Pass Lap Joint in a Horizontal Position

1. Tack two ¼″ plates to form a

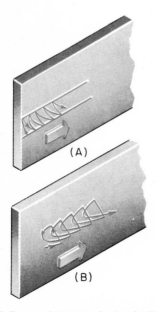

Fig. 4. The weaving pattern in view A will result in a normal width bead, while the pattern in view B will result in a wider bead.

lap joint. Clamp the piece in a vertical position as shown in Fig. 6.

2. Run a single bead along the edge, using a slight weaving motion.

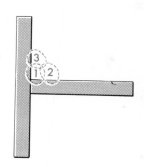

Fig. 7. Depositing a multiple bead on a T-joint.

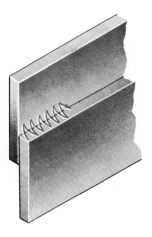

Fig. 6. This is how to make a single pass lap weld.

Watch the surface of the top plate closely to prevent any undercutting. Continue this operation on additional lap joints until a satisfactory weld is made.

Welding a Multiple Pass Fillet T-joint in a Horizontal Position

1. Tack two plates to form a T-joint and fasten the base plate in a vertical position as illustrated in Fig. 7.

2. Run a bead along the root of the joint without any weaving motion. Clean the slag and deposit a second bead, using a slight weaving motion, penetrating the first bead and the plate. See Fig. 7.

3. Clean the slag off the second bead and deposit a third layer. Notice that the third bead penetrates into the first and second layers as well as into the upright plate. This penetration is

important; otherwise a weak weld will result.

Welding a Multiple Pass Butt Joint in a Horizontal Position

1. Obtain two pieces of $\frac{1}{4}''$ steel plate and *bevel the edge of one plate.*

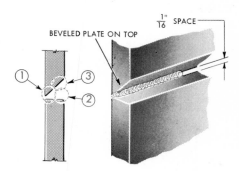

Fig. 8. Position of the butt joint for horizontal welding.

2. Tack the two plates together to form a butt joint, allowing $\frac{1}{16}''$ space at the root opening. Fasten the plates in a vertical position with the beveled plate on top as shown in Fig. 8. The plate that is not beveled should be on the bottom since its flat edge serves as a shelf, thus helping to prevent the molten metal from running out of the joint.

3. Deposit the first bead deep in the

root of the joint. Remove the slag and lay the second bead. Then follow with a third bead.

4. Make a similar weld on heavier stock, using either ⅜″ or ½″ plate. Bevel the edge of one piece to a 20° angle and the edge of the other to a 50° angle. Tack the two sections together, allowing a 1/16″ root opening. Fasten the joint in a vertical position so the plate with the 20° bevel is located below. Proceed to deposit the necessary layers of beads as shown in Fig. 9, making sure to clean off the slag after each pass is completed.

The number of passes on the joint will depend on the thickness of the metal as well as the diameter of the electrode. The important thing is to

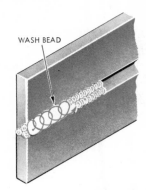

Fig. 10. A wash bead produces a smooth finish.

secure sufficient penetration into each adjacent layer. It is common practice on a wide joint to finish the weld with a *wash bead,* as illustrated in Fig. 10, to produce a smooth finish. A wash bead is made by using a wide weaving motion that covers the entire area of the deposited beads.

Points to Remember

1. Use a lower welding current and shorter arc for horizontal welding.

2. For horizontal welding, tilt the electrode upward 5° to 10° and slant it slightly away from the weld.

3. Use a slight weaving motion.

4. Do not allow the molten pool to sag and cause overlaps.

5. On a multiple pass weld, use a wash bead on the final pass.

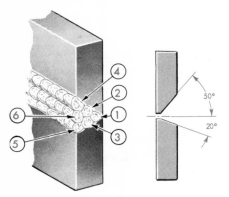

Fig. 9. Position of the various layers in a deep butt joint.

1. Why is it essential to use a lower current and a shorter arc when welding in a horizontal position?

2. What can be done to avoid overlaps on horizontal welds?

3. In what position should the electrode be held for horizontal welding?

4. Why should a weaving motion be used when making horizontal welds?

5. What determines the number of passes that should be made on a weld?

6. What practice should be followed in beveling the edges for a multiple pass weld?

7. Where and why is a wash bead used?

WELDING ASSIGNMENTS

1. Deposit straight beads on a plate in a horizontal position.

2. Weld a single pass lap joint in a horizontal position.

3. Weld a multiple pass lap joint in a horizontal position.

4. Weld a butt joint in a horizontal position.

CHAPTER 9

Shielded Metal—Arc Welding

The Vertical Position

In the fabrication of many structures such as steel buildings, bridges, tanks, pipelines, ships, and machinery, the operator must frequently make vertical welds. A vertical weld is one with a seam or line of weld running up and down as shown in Fig. 1.

Position and Movement of the Electrode

Vertical welding is done by depositing beads either in an upward or downward direction. *Downward welding* is very practical for welding light gage metal because penetration is shal-

Fig. 1. After tacking the metal strips together, this operator will lay vertical welds. (Hobart Brothers Co.)

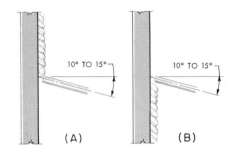

Fig. 2. Position of the electrode for downward and upward vertical welding.

low, thereby forming an adequate weld without burning through the metal. Moreover, downward welding can be performed much more rapidly, which is important in production work.

On heavy plates of ¼" or more in thickness, *upward welding* is more practical, since deeper penetration can be obtained. Welding upward also makes it possible to create a shelf upon which successive layers of beads can be placed.

For downward welding, tip the electrode as in Fig. 2A. Start at the top of the seam and move downward with little or no weaving motion. If a slight weave is necessary, swing the electrode so the crescent is at the top.

For upward welding, start with the electrode at right angles to the plates. Then, lower the rear of the electrode, keeping the tip in place, until the electrode forms an angle of 10°-15° with the horizontal as shown in Fig. 2B.

Laying Straight Beads in a Vertical Position

1. Obtain a ¼" plate and draw a series of straight lines. Then fasten the piece so the lines are in a vertical position.

2. Strike the arc on the bottom of the plate. As the metal is deposited, move the tip of the electrode upward in a rocking motion as shown in Fig. 3. In rocking the electrode, do not break the arc but simply pivot it with a wrist movement so the arc is moved up ahead of the weld long enough for the bead to solidify. Then return it to the crater and repeat the operation, work-

Fig. 3. Use a rocking motion in depositing upward vertical beads.

ing up along the line to the top of the plate. *Remember, do not break the arc while moving the electrode upward.* Withdraw it just long enough to permit the deposited metal to solidify and form a shelf so additional metal can be deposited. Continue to lay beads from bottom to top until each line is smooth and uniform in width.

Laying Vertical Beads with a Weaving Motion

On many vertical seams it is neces-

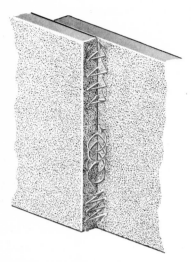

Fig. 4. Weaving patterns can be used to vary bead width.

Fig. 5. Deposit two beads to weld a vertical lap joint.

sary to form beads of various widths. The width of the bead can be controlled by using one of the weaving patterns shown in Fig. 4. Each pattern will produce a bead approximately twice the diameter of the electrode. Notice that each weave is shaped so the electrode can dig into the metal at the bottom of the stroke, and the upward motion momentarily removes the heat until the metal can solidify. When a smooth weld is required on the final pass of a wide joint, the *wash bead* should be used.

Before applying these weaving motions on actual joints, practice running them on a vertical plate. Continue this practice until a smooth bead of uniform width can be deposited.

Welding a Vertical Lap Joint

1. Obtain two ¼″ plates and tack them together to form a lap joint. Sup-

port the joint in a vertical position by tacking it to a flat scrap piece.

2. Deposit a small stringer bead in the root by slightly rocking the electrode as previously described.

3. Lay an additional layer as illustrated in Fig. 5. Use a weaving motion and work from the bottom to the top. Make certain that the second bead is thoroughly fused with the first.

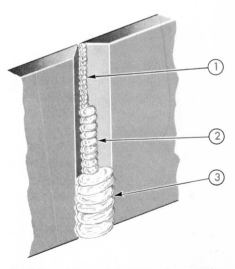

Fig. 6. Several layers of straight beads are used to provide a vertical butt weld.

Welding a Vertical Butt Joint

1. Obtain two ¼″ plates and bevel the edges to form a 60° vee.

2. Tack the plates together with a ¹⁄₁₆″ root opening and fasten them in an upright position to provide a vertical butt joint.

3. Deposit a straight bead in the root opening and follow with additional layers as illustrated in Fig. 6. Be sure to clean off the slag after each bead and test to make certain that there is good fusion between the beads and sides of the vee by bending it in a vise.

4. Try another butt weld, using either ⅜″ or ½″ plate. Bevel the edges to form a 60° vee with a ⅛″ root face. Tack the pieces together leaving a ⅛″ root opening. Support the joint in a vertical position with a backing strip. Deposit the necessary layer of beads and finish with a wash weld.

Welding a Vertical T-Joint

1. Obtain two ¼″ plates and tack them to form a T-joint. Support the joint in a vertical position.

2. Deposit a narrow, straight bead in the root, using a rocking motion.

3. Remove the slag and deposit at least one or two additional layers as shown in Fig. 7.

Points to Remember

1. For welding light gage metal in a vertical position, the downward technique is more practical.

2. For plates ¼″ or more in thickness, better results will be obtained by using the upward method of welding.

3. Rocking the electrode will provide better control of the molten puddle in upward welding.

4. On grooved joints, always lay the first bead deep into the root opening.

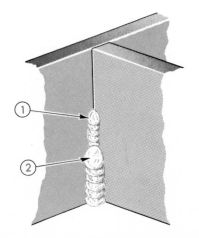
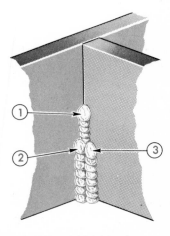

Fig. 7. A strong T-joint is attained by depositing 2 (left) to 3 (right) beads.

QUESTIONS FOR STUDY AND DISCUSSION

1. Why is welding downward on a vertical joint more applicable on light gage metal?

2. How should the electrode be held in making a vertical upward weld?

3. In laying a straight bead on a vertical seam, why should the electrode be rocked?

4. How can the width of a bead be controlled on a vertical weld?

5. When making a three pass vertical lap weld, in what sequence should the beads be placed?

6. Why should a small opening be provided between the plates when making a vertical butt weld?

7. How should the edges be beveled for a vertical butt weld on $\frac{1}{2}''$ plates?

WELDING ASSIGNMENTS

1. Deposit vertical beads on a plate.
2. Weld a vertical lap joint.

3. Weld a vertical butt joint.
4. Weld a vertical T-joint.

CHAPTER 10

Shielded Metal—Arc Welding

The Overhead Position

Welding in an overhead position is probably the most difficult operation to master. It is difficult because you must assume an awkward stance, and at the same time work against gravity, which exerts a downward force. See Fig. 1. In an overhead position, therefore, the puddle has a tendency to drop, making it harder to secure uniform beads and correct penetration. Nevertheless, with a little practice it is possible to secure welds as good as those made in other positions.

Fig. 1. Although it is a difficult position in which to work, overhead welding is often necessary.

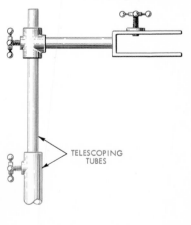

TELESCOPING TUBES

Fig. 2. A jig is necessary to raise the work to the correct height and position.

Position for Overhead Welding

In learning to weld in an overhead position, you will need some kind of a jig. The one shown in Fig. 2 is recommended, since the work can be adjusted to any height or position.

To start welding, place the electrode in the holder as illustrated in Fig. 3. Hold the electrode at right angles to the seam. Then tilt the rear of the electrode away from the crater until the electrode forms an angle of 10°-15° with the horizontal as shown in Fig. 4. The line of weld may be in any direction — forward, backward, left, or right.

Grip the holder so that your knuckles are up and your palm down. This prevents particles of molten metal from being caught in the hollow palm of the glove. To gain as much protection as possible from falling sparks and hot metal drippings, stand to the side rather than directly underneath the arc. The discomfort of the cable can be minimized by dropping it over the shoulder if you are welding in a standing position, or over the knees if in a sitting position. See Figs. 5 and 6.

Fig. 3. Position of the holder and hand for overhead welding. (The Lincoln Electric Co.)

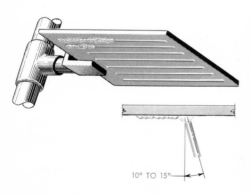

10° TO 15°

Fig. 4. Position of the electrode for overhead welding.

Fig. 5. If you are standing, drape the cable over your shoulder. (Hobart Brothers Co.)

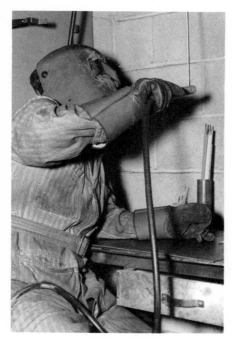

Fig. 6. If you are sitting, drape the cable over your knees.

Running Straight Beads in an Overhead Position

1. Clamp a $\frac{1}{4}''$ plate in the overhead jig.

2. Run a series of straight beads, rocking the electrode in the same manner as in vertical welding. To prevent the puddle from dropping, keep the

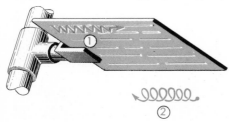

Fig. 7. Two weaving motions are used in overhead welding.

arc as short as possible and rock the electrode a little faster.

3. Continue to deposit straight beads until proper control of the puddle is mastered. Practice running the beads in one direction and then in another.

4. Obtain another $\frac{1}{4}''$ plate and practice weaving the arc as shown in Fig. 7.

Welding a Lap Joint in an Overhead Position

1. Tack two $\frac{1}{4}''$ plates to form a lap joint and clamp them in the overhead jig.

2. Hold the electrode so it bisects the angle between the plates and is inclined slightly away from the crater as illustrated in Fig. 8.

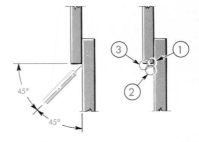

Fig. 8. Position the electrode at a 45° angle (left), and deposit three beads (right) to weld an overhead lap joint.

3. Lay the first bead deep in the root of the joint, using a wrist-pivot motion as described in Chapter 9.

4. Remove the slag and deposit the second bead on the wide side of the plate. Clean off the slag and deposit the third bead. See Fig. 8.

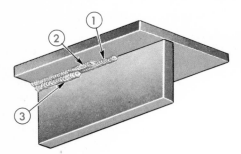

Fig. 9. Welding a T-joint in an overhead position.

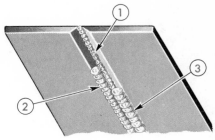

Fig. 10. Welding a butt joint in an overhead position.

Welding a T-Joint in an Overhead Position

1. Tack two ¼″ plates to form a T-joint and clamp them in the overhead jig.

2. Deposit the first bead in the root of the vee. Clean off the slag and deposit two additional beads as shown in Fig. 9.

Welding a Butt Joint in an Overhead Position

1. Bevel the edges of two ¼″ plates and tack them together with a ¹⁄₁₆″ root opening. Clamp the joint in the overhead jig.

2. Deposit three layers of beads as illustrated in Fig. 10. Be sure to clean off the slag after each layer.

Points to Remember

1. In overhead welding, incline the electrode 10° to 15° away from the crater.

2. Grip the electrode so that your knuckles face up and your palm down.

3. Stand to the side of the arc instead of directly underneath.

4. Drape the cable over the shoulder if welding in a standing position, or over your knees if in a sitting position.

QUESTIONS FOR STUDY AND DISCUSSION

1. Why is overhead welding more difficult?

2. How should the electrode be held for overhead welding?

3. Why should the holder be grasped so the palm of your hand is facing down?

4. What position should you assume for overhead welding?

5. What can be done to minimize the discomfort of the cable?

6. What should be done to prevent the puddle from falling?

WELDING ASSIGNMENTS

1. Run straight beads on a plate in an overhead position.
2. Weld an overhead lap joint.
3. Weld an overhead T-joint.
4. Weld an overhead butt joint.

CHAPTER 11

Shielded Metal—Arc Welding

Cast Iron

Most structures made of cast iron can be welded successfully. Because of the peculiar characteristics of cast iron, you will find that welding this metal requires a great deal more care than welding mild steel. However, if certain precautions are observed you should, with a little practice, be able to arc weld almost any cast iron piece. See Fig. 1.

Types of Cast Iron

Cast iron is an iron-base material with a high percentage of carbon. The five types of cast iron are gray, white, malleable, alloy, and nodular.

Gray cast iron results when the silicon content is high and the iron is permitted to cool slowly. The combination of high silicon and slow cooling forces the carbon to separate in the form of graphite flakes, sometimes

Fig. 1. This cast iron frame is being welded by the arc welding process. (Hobart Brothers Co.)

called free carbon. It is this separation of the carbon from the iron that makes gray cast iron so brittle.

Gray cast iron is used a great deal for machine castings. It can readily be identified by the dark gray, porous structure when the piece is fractured. If brought in contact with a revolving emery wheel, the metal gives off short streamers that follow a straight line and are brick red in color, with numerous fine, repeating yellow sparklers as shown in Fig. 2. Gray cast iron can be arc welded with comparative ease.

White cast iron possesses what is known as combined carbon. Combined carbon means that the carbon element has actually united with the iron instead of existing in a free state as in gray cast iron. This condition is brought about through the process of rapidly cooling the metal, leaving it very hard. In fact it is so hard that it is exceedingly difficult to machine, and special cutting tools or grinders must

be used to cut the metal. White cast iron is often used for castings with outer surfaces that must resist a great deal of wear. It is also used to make malleable castings.

The fracture of a piece of white cast iron will disclose a fine, silvery white, silky, crystalline formation. The spark test will show short streamers that are red in color. There are fewer sparklers than in gray cast iron and these are small and repeating as illustrated in Fig. 2.

Although white cast iron can be welded, generally speaking it has poor welding qualities.

Malleable cast iron is actually white cast iron which has been subjected to a long annealing process. The annealing treatment draws out the brittleness from the casting, leaving the metal soft but possessing considerable toughness and strength.

The fracture of a piece of malleable cast iron will indicate a white rim and

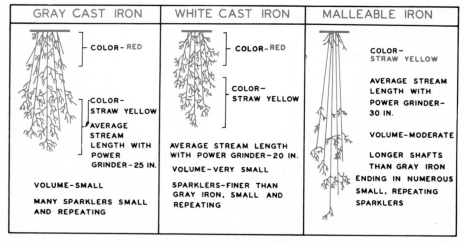

GRAY CAST IRON	WHITE CAST IRON	MALLEABLE IRON
COLOR- RED	COLOR- RED	COLOR- STRAW YELLOW
COLOR- STRAW YELLOW	COLOR- STRAW YELLOW	AVERAGE STREAM LENGTH WITH POWER GRINDER- 30 IN.
AVERAGE STREAM LENGTH WITH POWER GRINDER- 25 IN.	AVERAGE STREAM LENGTH WITH POWER GRINDER- 20 IN.	VOLUME- MODERATE
VOLUME- SMALL	VOLUME- VERY SMALL	LONGER SHAFTS THAN GRAY IRON ENDING IN NUMEROUS
MANY SPARKLERS SMALL AND REPEATING	SPARKLERS- FINER THAN GRAY IRON, SMALL AND REPEATING	SMALL, REPEATING SPARKLERS

Fig. 2. Notice how the spark characteristics vary for different kinds of cast iron.

a dark center. The spark test will show a moderate amount of short, straw-yellow streamers with numerous sparklers that are small and repeating as shown in Fig. 2.

Malleable cast iron can be welded; however, you must be sure that the metal is not heated above a critical temperature (approximately 1382° F). If it is heated beyond this point, the metal reverts back to the original characteristics of white cast iron.

Alloy cast irons are those which contain certain alloying elements such as copper, aluminum, nickel, titanium, vanadium, chromium, molybdenum, and magnesium. By adding one or more of these elements to the iron it is possible to improve its tensile strength, machinability, fatigue resistance, and corrosion resistance. The alloy combinations cause the graphite to separate in a fine and evenly distributed structure, resulting in a cast iron possessing much higher mechanical properties.

Most alloy cast irons can be arc welded but greater precautions must be taken in the preheating and post-heating stages to prevent the destruction of the alloying elements.

Nodular iron sometimes called ductile iron, has the ductility of malleable iron, the corrosion resistance of alloy cast iron and a tensile strength greater than grey cast iron. These special qualities are obtained by the addition of magnesium to the iron at the time of melting and then using special annealing techniques. The addition of magnesium and control of the cooling rate causes the graphite to change from a

stringer structure to rounded masses in the form of spheroids or nodules. It is the formation of these nodular forms that gives the cast iron better mechanical properties.

Nodular iron can be arc welded providing adequate preheat and postheat treatments are used, otherwise some of the original properties are lost.

Preparing Cast Iron for Welding

Follow this procedure to prepare cast iron for welding:

1. Grind a narrow strip along each edge of the joint to remove the surface layer known as *casting skin*. See Fig. 3. Elimination of the surface layer is important because it is full of impurities. These impurities were embedded in the skin when the metal was poured

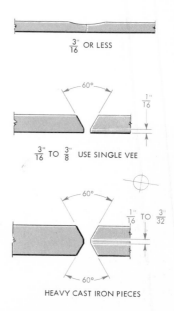

Fig. 3. This is how the edges should be prepared for welding cast iron.

into the sand mold. Unless they are removed, they will interfere with the fusion action of the weld metal.

2. Vee the edges as illustrated in Fig. 3. When the metal does not exceed $\frac{3}{16}$″ in thickness no vee is necessary, but still remove the casting skin. On $\frac{3}{16}$″ to $\frac{3}{8}$″ metal, only a single vee is required. The included angle of the vee should be approximately 60 degrees. Heavy cast iron pieces $\frac{3}{8}$″ or more in thickness should have a double vee with a $\frac{1}{16}$″ to $\frac{3}{32}$″ root face. The included angle should be 60 degrees.

3. If only a crack in a casting is to be welded, vee the crack approximately $\frac{1}{8}$″ to $\frac{3}{16}$″ deep with a diamond point chisel, as shown in Fig. 4, or by grinding. On sections that are less than $\frac{3}{16}$″ in thickness, vee only one-half the thickness.

4. Be sure the casting is entirely free from rust, scale, dirt, oil, and grease, as these substances, if trapped in the weld, will weaken it. Pour kerosene or penetrating oil over the entire area surrounding the crack. After a

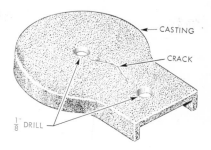

Fig. 5. Drill a $\frac{1}{8}$″ hole beyond each end of the crack.

few minutes, wipe off the kerosene or oil with a clean dry cloth.

Fine, hairline cracks in a casting can be made more visible by rubbing a piece of white chalk over the surface. The chalk leaves a "wet" line exactly where the crack is located.

5. During the welding operation, cracks have a tendency to extend. To prevent this from happening, drill a $\frac{1}{8}$″ hole a short distance beyond each end of the crack as illustrated in Fig. 5.

Keeping Cast Iron Cool

An important point in welding cast iron is to keep the piece as cool as possible. Otherwise, cracks will form. In the case of malleable cast iron, excessive heat will transform it into white cast iron. If possible, preheat the entire section with an oxyacetylene torch. Never heat it beyond a dull red color or a temperature exceeding 1200°F. The critical point where changes occur in cast iron is about 1450°F. Normally a preheat between 500° and 1200°F is recommended.

The preheat should be as uniform as possible over the entire casting and

Fig. 4. Veeing a crack in a casting.

Fig. 6. Peen the bead while it is cooling.

Fig. 7. A crack in a cast iron cylinder head is welded with non-machinable electrodes. (The Lincoln Electric Co.)

kept at this temperature until the welding is completed. Then the piece must be cooled slowly to room temperature. Very slow cooling is extremely essential with malleable and nodular iron.

When it is impossible to preheat the piece, you can keep it cool by running short beads 2″ to 3″ long. After a bead is deposited, allow it to cool until you can touch it with your hand before starting the next bead. *While cooling, peen the bead by striking it lightly with a hammer as shown in Fig. 6.* Peening helps to make the weld tight, and relieves stresses.

Electrodes for Welding Cast Iron

There are two types of electrodes for welding cast iron; machinable and non-machinable. These electrodes are usually known by a manufacturer's trade name, such as *Ferroweld* (non-machinable — Lincoln), *Softweld* (machinable — Lincoln), *Strongcast* (non-machinable—Hobart), *Softcast* (machinable—Hobart). The non-ma-

chinable electrode has a mild steel core covered with a special coating. It leaves a very hard deposit and is used only when the welded section is not to be machined afterwards. This electrode produces a tight and waterproof weld, making it ideal for repairing motor blocks, water jackets, transmission cases, compressor blocks, pulley wheels, pump parts, mower wheels, and other similar structures. See Fig. 7.

Fig. 8. An example of a weld made in a casting with machinable type electrodes. (The Lincoln Electric Co.)

Machinable type electrodes have a copper-nickel or pure nickel core. They are used to repair all kinds of broken castings, correcting for machining errors. filling up defects, or to weld cast iron to steel. The deposited metal is soft enough so it can be readily machined as shown in Fig. 8.

Welding Procedure

1. Set the machine for the correct amperage. Follow the recommendation of the electrode manufacturer. As a rule, the amperage setting for welding cast iron is lower than for welding mild steel.

2. Since it is important to keep the heat to a minimum, always use small diameter electrodes. Operators seldom weld with electrodes greater than $\frac{1}{8}''$ in diameter.

3. Tip the electrode 5 to 10 degrees in the direction of travel. Use a slightly longer arc than in welding mild steel. If more than one layer is to be deposited, use a slight weaving motion after the first bead is made.

4. When welding cracks in castings, start about $\frac{3}{8}''$ before the end of the crack and weld back to the hole, filling the hole. See Fig. 9. Then move slightly beyond the hole. Next move to the other end of the crack and do the same thing. Continue to alternate the weld on each end, limiting the length of each weld $1''$ to $1\frac{1}{2}''$ on thin material and $2''$ to $3''$ on heavier pieces. Always allow each section of weld to cool before starting the next, and peen each short bead.

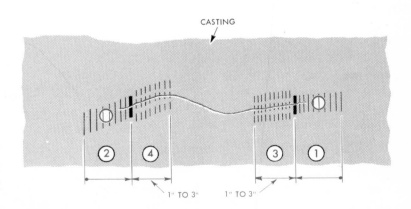

Fig. 9. This is how to weld a crack in a casting. Note the $\frac{1}{8}''$ holes beyond each end of the crack. These holes prevent the crack froom extending. The starting points on each end are shown by the thick black lines.

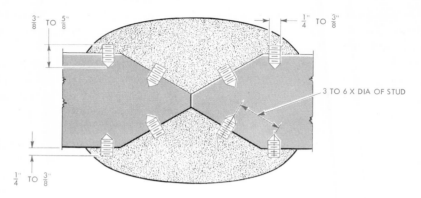

$\frac{3''}{8}$ TO $\frac{5''}{8}$

$\frac{1''}{4}$ TO $\frac{3''}{8}$

3 TO 6 X DIA OF STUD

$\frac{1''}{4}$ TO $\frac{3''}{8}$

Fig. 10. Studs can be used to reinforce the weld in a broken casting.

Welding Sections with Pieces Knocked Out

To weld a section with one or more pieces broken out, fit the parts together. Vee the breaks and tack them before welding.

If the broken part cannot be made to fit in the casting, shape another piece, using mild steel. Place the new section in position and weld.

Studding Broken Castings

When a casting is 1½" or more in thickness and is subjected to heavy stresses, use steel studs to strengthen the joint. Studding is not advisable on castings lighter than 1½" because it tends to weaken rather than strengthen the joint. To apply studs proceed as follows:

1. Vee the crack.
2. Drill and tap ¼" or ⅜" holes in the casting at right angles to the sides of the vee. Space the holes so the center-to-center distance is equal to three to six times the diameter of the stud. See Fig. 10.

3. Screw the studs into the tapped holes. The threaded end of the studs should be about ⅜" to ⅝" in length and should project approximately ¼" to ⅜" above the casting.

4. Deposit beads around the base of the studs, welding them thoroughly to the casting. Remove the slag and deposit additional layers of beads to fill the vee.

Points to Remember

1. Always remove the casting skin before welding cast iron pieces.

2. Vee the edges with a single or double vee, depending upon the thickness of the metal.

3. Clean an old casting very carefully before welding.

4. To weld a crack in a casting, drill a ⅛" hole a short distance beyond each end of the crack to prevent the crack from spreading.

5. Keep the casting as cool as possible.

6. Peen the bead to relieve stresses.

7. Use the correct type of electrode.

8. Use small diameter electrodes and maintain a lower amperage setting than for mild steel.

9. To weld cracks in castings, start the weld about ⅜″ away from the weld and travel to the drilled hole. Alternate the weld on each end of the crack.

10. Run short beads of 1″ to 1½″ on thin metal and 2″ to 3″ on heavy metal.

11. Reinforce heavy castings with studs for added strength

12. Preheat the piece whenever possible, and cool slowly after the weld is completed.

QUESTIONS FOR STUDY AND DISCUSSION

1. What is the difference between gray, white, and malleable cast iron?

2. Why should the outer skin be removed before welding cast iron?

3. How should the joints be prepared for welding cast iron?

4. How should old castings be cleaned before welding?

5. What can be done to make fine cracks in castings more visible?

6. How can cracks in castings be prevented from spreading?

7. Why is it important to keep cast iron cool when welding? How should this be done?

8. If a casting is to be preheated, how can you determine when the correct condition is reached?

9. Why should a bead be peened?

10. What two types of electrodes are used for welding cast iron?

11. Why is a lower amperage setting required for cast iron welding?

12. Why is it a good practice never to use electrodes greater than ⅛″ in diameter for welding cast iron?

13. What is the correct procedure for welding cracks in castings?

14. Why is it advisable to use studs in repairing some broken castings?

15. Why should studs be used only on heavy castings 1½″ or more in thickness?

16. How far apart should studs be fastened?

17. How deep should studs be driven in the castings? How much should they project above the surface?

WELDING ASSIGNMENTS

1. Weld two pieces of cast iron.

2. Weld a broken casting.

CHAPTER 12

Shielded Metal—Arc Welding

Carbon Steels

~~~~~~

Carbon steels can readily be arc welded but some require considerably more control of the welding process. For certain types, special electrodes must be used or some preheating and postheating treatment applied to secure sound welds with the required mechanical properties.

An important point to remember in welding carbon steels is the effects of heat on the welded area. When steel is heated to a high temperature its structure undergoes a change. Depending on the amount of carbon present, the steel changes from a mixture of ferrite (pure iron) and cementite (iron and iron-carbide sometimes called pearlite) to a solid solution known as austenite, where the carbon goes into a solution form and becomes evenly distributed. If an austenic structure is cooled quickly a martensitic condition develops which causes the carbon to precipitate and leave an extremely hard and brittle material. When this happens in a weld area underbead cracking can be expected as well as cracks alongside the weld in the parent metal.

Welding Low-Carbon Steels

As you know carbon steels are those steels whose principal element is carbon. Steels in this group are referred to as low carbon, medium carbon, and high carbon.

Low carbon steels are the easiest to weld. No particular control needs to be taken since the welding heat has no appreciable effect on the parent metal. Any mild steel coated electrodes in the E60 or E70 series will produce good welds. The choice of electrodes in these series is influenced by specific re-

TABLE I

Classification of Mild Steel Electrodes

AWS ASTM	TYPE OF COATING	WELDING POSITIONS	CURRENT
E-6010	High cellulose sodium	F, V, OH, H	DC/RP
E-6011	High cellulose potassium	F, V, OH, H	AC/ or DC/RP
E-6012	High titania sodium	F, V, OH, H	AC/ or DC/SP
E-6013	High titania potassium	F, V, OH, H	AC/ or DC/Both
E-6014	Iron powder, titania	F, V, OH, H	AC/ or DC/SP
E-6015	Low hydrogen sodium	F, V, OH, H	DC/RP
E-6016	Low hydrogen potassium	F, V, OH, H	AC or DC/RP
E-6018	Low hydrogen	F, H-fillets	AC or DC/SP
E-6020	High iron oxide	F, H-fillets	AC or DC/SP
E-6027	Iron powder, iron oxide	F, H-fillets	AC or DC/SP
E-7014	Iron powder, titania	F, V, OH, H	AC or DC/Both
E-7015	Low hydrogen sodium	F, V, OH, H	DC/RP
E-7016	Low hydrogen potassium	F, V, OH, H	AC or DC/RP
E-7018	Iron powder, low hydrogen	F, V, OH, H	AC or DC/RP
E-7024	Iron powder, titania	F, H-fillets	AC or DC/Both
E-7028	Iron powder, low hydrogen	F, H-fillets	AC or DC/RP

quirements such as depth of penetration, type of current, position of the weld, joint design, and deposition rate. See Table I.

Welding Medium-Carbon Steel

A medium carbon steel is one whose carbon content ranges from 0.30 per cent to 0.45 per cent. The main consideration in welding medium-carbon steel is the prevention of underbead cracks along the fusion line. To some extent cracking can be minimized by the use of correct electrodes and proper applications of preheating and postheating.

Electrodes. Recommended electrodes for welding medium-carbon steels are the low hydrogen E-6015, E-6016, and E-6018. Where higher strength and greater weld metal deposits are required, the E-7015, E-7016, and E-7018 are used. Since these electrodes produce less heat, preheating can either be eliminated or reduced considerably.

Preheating

Preheating involves raising the temperature of the base metal before the welding is started. Its main purpose is to reduce cracking by preventing the formation of hard surfaces in the surrounding weld area. Preheating also burns grease, oil, and scale out of the joint and permits faster welding speeds.

A preheating treatment lowers the cooling rate after welding since it reduces the thermal conductivity of the iron. The low thermal conductivity allows a slower withdrawal of heat from the weld zone and therefore lessens the tendency for martensite to form. The preheat also keeps the weld beads more fluid with flatter surfaces thus adding to the strength of the weld joint.

Correct temperature is an important factor in preheating. Preheat temperatures for mild steel should be between 200° to 700°F depending on the carbon content. The greater the carbon content, the higher the preheating temperatures. Preheating temperatures can be measured in various ways. Here are several:

1. Use of surface thermometers or thermocouples.

2. Marking the surface with a carpenters blue chalk. A mark made with this chalk will turn to a whitish gray when the temperature reaches approximately 625°F.

3. Rubbing 50-50 solder on the surface. The solder starts to melt at 360°F.

4. Rubbing a pine stick on the heated surface. The pine stick chars at about 635°F. Preheating can be done by placing the part in a furnace or moving an oxyacetylene torch over the metal.

5. Using "tempilstiks" which are crayons or liquids. When applied, they melt and change color at a specific temperature.

Control Heat Process

For welding most mild steels, the control heat process is often more economical than the use of preheating. The principle of this technique is to induce a large volume of heat into the base metal by welding with high current at low speed or by making multiple-pass welds. The high current and slow welding rate builds up considerable heat in the metal. This naturally slows up the rate of cooling and the subsequent prevention of hard crystaline zones near the weld area.

In the multiple-pass welding the deposit of the first layer preheats the base metal. The heat of the next pass tempers the base metal adjacent to the first weld bead. Each successive pass then leaves just enough heat so there is no rapid cooling and consequently no appreciable hardening.

Postheating

Postheating is intended primarily as a stress-relief treatment. For welding some of the higher range carbon steels, postheating is as important as preheating. Although preheating does control the cooling rate, nevertheless the possibility of stresses becoming locked in the welded area is always a factor. Unless these stresses are removed, cracks may develop when the piece cools completely, otherwise the part may become distorted, especially after a machining operation.

Postheating temperatures for stress relief should be in the range of 900° to 1250°F. Soaking period normally runs about one hour per inch of metal thickness.

Welding High-Carbon Steels

High-Carbon steels are those whose carbon content is 0.45 per cent or higher. These steels are considered more difficult to weld than other carbon steels. However, with proper care, high carbon steels can be arc welded successfully. The following are some of the problems which must be considered when welding high carbon steels:

1. Development of cracks in the weld metal and base metal.

2. Porosity in the weld.

3. Excessive hardening and softening of the parent metal below the weld area.

Formation of Weld Cracks

Cracks in the weld metal may run in a longitudinal or transverse direction and are often invisible to the naked eye. The defects will usually show up under some type of ultrasonic, magnetic, or radiographic inspection.

Basically weld cracks occur when there is a shrinkage of the weld bead. Since high carbon steels do not stretch very much because of their hardness, whenever a weld bead is deposited on the hard, rigid surface the generated contraction forces must be absorbed by the more ductile metal in the deposited weld bead.

Weld cracks can be avoided by keeping the weld penetration as low as possible thus minimizing any excessive stressing of the parent metal. Furthermore, if penetration is kept low there is less of a tendency for the weld bead to pick up an excessive amount of carbon from the base metal, thereby leaving the weld bead considerably more ductile and better able to absorb shrinkage stresses.

The use of low-hydrogen electrodes with iron-powder coatings produce minimum penetration and ductile welds. For welding high carbon steels in the upper carbon range, special stainless steel electrodes of the E-310-15 type (25% chromium and 20% nickel) are frequently recommended because of their ductility.

Crater Cracks. These cracks occur across the weld bead crater and result from shrinkage. See Fig. 1. When a weld bead is deposited, solidification of the molten metal takes place from the sides and moves towards the center. The center of the crater cools rapidly because of the smaller amount of

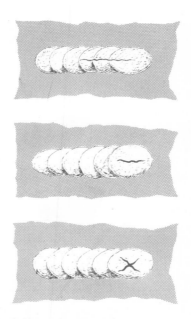

Fig. 1. Types of crater cracks.

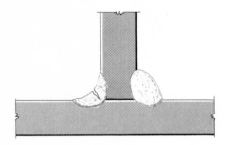

Fig. 2. Crater cracks will often occur on thin concave fillet welds.

metal while the remaining bead cools more slowly, causing a concentration of stresses which eventually result in cracks. Crater cracks are particularly prevalent in thin concave fillet welds. See Fig. 2. Most crater cracks can be prevented by proper electrode manipulation. Care should be taken to completely fill up the craters and the weld bead rounded slightly by using a shorter arc.

Root Cracks. In making a groove or fillet weld, the first pass is in the form of a narrow stringer bead along the weld seam. This is followed by one or more layers of weld beads. It is the first layer, or root bead, that is the most susceptible to cracking. See Fig. 3. The cracking is generally due to the excessive carbon which the bead picks up from the base metal, thereby making the weld metal hard and brittle. As the weld metal cools, it shrinks, and as additional layers of beads are deposited on the root weld, tensile

Fig. 3. The root bead is often more susceptible to cracking.

stresses form which develop into cracks. Root cracks can be prevented by preheating the base metal, using a more ductile weld metal, and providing sufficient space between the plates so they can move as the weld cools.

Porosity. Porosity is a common problem in welding high carbon steel. Molten high-carbon steel readily absorbs gases such as hydrogen and carbon monoxide which are released as the metal begins to cool. If this gas does not reach the surface before the metal begins to solidify it becomes entrapped in the metal, leaving small gas pockets or blowholes. The formation of blowholes is very common in welding steel with a high sulphur content. The presence of sulphur along with phosphorous and silicon when combined with other gases always generate a degree of porosity that seriously affects the strength of the weld.

Skillful welders usually can prevent porosity by proper manipulation of the electrode. The secret of gas-free welds is to keep the surface of the deposited metal pool fluid enough so the gas is rapidly released. Welding with low-hydrogen electrodes as a rule will prevent any extensive formation of porosity.

Excessive Hardening and Softening of Base Metal. As in the case of medium carbon steel, the development of a hard layer in the weld zone is the result of too rapid cooling. The rapid cooling transforms the metal into a martensitic condition which leaves a very brittle area. The best procedure to avoid excessive hardening is to utilize a controlled system of preheating and postheating. Preheat treatment should be between 200° and 400°F for steels with a carbon content of 0.45 to 0.65 per cent and 400°-700°F when the carbon content is over 0.60 per cent. Postheating should be in the 1100° to 1200°F range.

The strength of high carbon steel is dependent upon its hardness which is obtained by a heat treating process. If the part is to be heat treated after welding then excessive hardness or softness is not necessarily important. On the other hand, if the part is not to be heat treated then suitable precautions must be taken to prevent a loss of the hardness properties which are characteristic of high carbon steel after heat treatment.

Welding will often have some softening effect on hardened high-carbon steel especially near the weld. To minimize both excessive hardening and softening, the use of a high chromium, high-nickel stainless steel electrode is recommended. A small diameter electrode and an intermittent welding procedure will also reduce excessive softening and hardening of the base metal.

Points to Remember

1. Use E60 or E70 series electrodes to weld low-carbon steel.

2. Use low hydrogen electrodes when welding medium-carbon steels.

3. Preheat steels having a high carbon content.

4. The control heat welding process will often eliminate the need for preheating carbon steels.

5. For many high carbon steels a postheat treatment is often advisable for stress-relief.

6. Keep the cooling rate of the weld puddle as slow as possible in welding high carbon steel.

7. Low-hydrogen electrodes with iron powder coatings will usually minimize cracking in welding high carbon steel.

8. Use correct electrode manipulation to allow gases to come to the surface in order to avoid gas pockets and blowholes.

QUESTIONS FOR STUDY AND DISCUSSION

1. What happens to high-carbon steel when it develops into a martensitic structure?

2. Why are low-carbon steels relatively easy to weld?

3. What type of electrodes are normally used for welding low-carbon steels?

4. When is a steel classified as a medium-carbon steel?

5. What type of electrodes are required for welding medium-carbon steel?

6. Why is a preheating treatment sometimes necessary in welding medium and high carbon steels?

7. At what temperature should preheating be carried out?

8. What is meant by controlled heat welding?

9. What is the function of post-heating?

10. At what temperature should postheating be done?

11. Why are high-carbon steels more difficult to weld?

12. How can weld cracks be avoided when welding high-carbon steel?

13. What are crater cracks and what causes them?

14. What are root cracks and why do they occur?

15. What causes porosity in a weld?

16. How can porosity in a weld be avoided?

17. Why must the condition of a heat treated part be considered before welding it?

18. How can excessive softening of a heat treatment part be kept to a minimum in a welding operation?

WELDING ASSIGNMENTS

1. Weld fillet, lap, and tee joints using ¼" or ⅜" plate of low, medium, and high carbon steel. Evaluate each weld for strength, cracks, and porosity.

CHAPTER 13

Shielded Metal—Arc Welding

Alloy Steels

〜〜〜〜〜〜〜〜〜〜〜〜〜〜〜〜〜〜〜〜〜〜〜〜〜〜〜〜〜〜〜〜〜〜

An alloy steel is a steel which is mixed with one or more additional elements, other than carbon or iron, in large enough percentages to alter the characteristics and properties of the steel. The addition of such substances as manganese, nickel, chromium, tungsten, molybdenum, or vanadium produces a steel that is greater in strength and toughness. Alloy steels are known by their main alloying elements, such as manganese steel, chromium-nickel steel, molybdenum steel, etc.

Practically all alloy steels can be welded, but as a rule the welding operation is much more difficult to perform than in welding mild steel. This is due to the fact that the characteristics of the basic alloying ingredients are sometimes destroyed as the weld is made. Furthermore, unless precau-

tions are taken, cracks appear near the welded areas, or slag inclusions and gas pockets form in the bead, all of which weaken the weld. Many of the difficulties, however, can be avoided or minimized by using special electrodes designed specifically for welding alloy steels.

Preheating and Postheating

Successful welding of many alloy steels requires a controlled rate of cooling because when heated to a high temperature and cooled rapidly, they readily harden. Welding these steels without proper heat control produces an embrittlement in the heat-affected zone parallel to the weld joint. With proper preheating and postheating, the rate of cooling is delayed and consequently the metal near the weld zone does not harden appreciably.

The application of preheating and postheating is also an important factor in preventing weld cracks caused by shrinkage stresses. By slowing the rate of cooling, the stresses are more readily distributed throughout the weld and released while the metal is still hot.

The preheating and postheating temperatures will depend on the alloying content of the base metal. Some elements produce greater hardenability and therefore the cooling rate must be slower. In any event, the temperature should never exceed the original hardening and tempering temperatures unless the piece is to be heat treated again after the weld is completed.

When a preheat temperature is difficult to ascertain, the *clip test* is often used to make a rapid check. This test is not applicable for thin steels but will produce good results on heavy sections down to ⅜ inches in thickness.

The test involves the welding of a piece of low-carbon steel ½″ in thickness and 2″ or 3″ square to the steel plate which is being checked for a preheat temperature. A convex contour fillet weld is made with similar electrode and welding current to be used for the welding job. The weld is allowed to cool for five minutes and then the clip is hammered until it breaks off. See Fig. 1A. If the lug breaks through the weld after a number of blows, the test indicates that no serious underbead cracking will result when the welding is carried out in the same manner at normal room temperature. If the lug breaks and pulls out some of the parent metal (Fig. 1B) the test shows that this particular steel must be preheated.

Welding Austentic Manganese Steel

Austentic manganese steel is a tough, nonmagnetic alloy noted especially for its high strength, excellent ductility, and outstanding wear resistance. Welding this metal requires considerable attention since it is so sensitive to reheating. Any prolonged period of heating will embrittle the metal and result in loss of tensile strength and ductility. Consequently, low welding current and rapid welding rate without any extensive preheating is necessary.

There are two groups of manganese

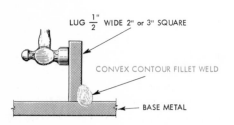

LUG $\frac{1}{2}$″ WIDE 2″ or 3″ SQUARE

CONVEX CONTOUR FILLET WELD

BASE METAL

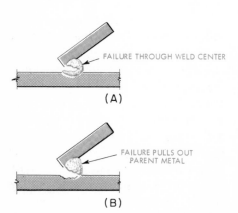

FAILURE THROUGH WELD CENTER

(A)

FAILURE PULLS OUT PARENT METAL

(B)

Fig. 1. Clip test for ascertaining need for preheating.

TABLE I

Filler Metals Recommended for Welding Manganese Steels

FILLER METALS	TYPE OF FABRICATION
Austenitic manganese steel covered electrodes or tubular wire with less than 0.025% phosphorus.*	Recommended for joining austenitic manganese steel where the weldment is subjected to severe wear or structural stress or both. May be used also for multiple pass welding of manganese steel to carbon or low-alloy steel with the latter (the carbon and low-alloy steel only) slightly preheated.
Austenitic manganese steel with phosphorus over 0.025%, electrodes with or without covering.	Recommended for joining and filling only where structural stress and wear are light. For an extra factor of safety in fabrication welds, a root pass of stainless is suggested. Rods and wire in this class are not recommended for joining manganese steels to mild or low-alloy steels unless overlaid with stainless steel.
Nickel-chromium stainless steel electrodes.	Used for joining manganese steels to manganese, or to mild or low-alloy steels where weldments are subjected to little wear and moderate structural stress. NOTE: Welds cannot be oxyacetylene cut.
Austenitic Manganese-Chromium (Stainless) Electrodes (Covered)	Recommended for joining manganese steel or manganese to mild or low-alloy steels where the weldment is subjected to wear and severe structural stress and where considerably higher yield strength is desired. NOTE: Welds cannot be oxyacetylene cut.
Low phosphorus, composite austenitic manganese steel electrodes or tubular wire, or 309 or 310 stainless electrodes.†	Nonmagnetic applications for all types of stresses.

* Usually available only in composite or tubular form.
† 18-8 stainless should be avoided in applications subjected to impact of the weld as some grades become magnetic after severe work hardening.

(AWS)

steel, known as low manganese (2% manganese or less) and high manganese (12—14% manganese minimum).

Low manganese steels are used for fabricating parts or structures where they must withstand impact stresses and resist wear. To weld these metals a 0.5% molybdenum electrode of the E-7010 or E-7020 class is generally used. Since both electrodes are of the deep penetrating type, care must be taken to prevent an excessive amount of the parent metal from mixing into the weld. Slight preheating is advisable since it reduces underbead cracking. When penetrating is impractical, the standard E-6012 electrode can be used. However, if this electrode produces a high number of cracks, the E-6015, E-6016, E-7015, or E-7016 should be substituted. See Table I.

High manganese steel is usually in a cast form because of its tough core and hard abrasion resisting surface. This metal is used widely for stone crushing equipment parts, power shovel buckets, and other structures which are subjected to great wear. See Fig. 2.

Welding high manganese steel involves joining two pieces, repairing cracks, or building up worn surfaces. Building up worn surfaces is commonly referred to as hardfacing. A detailed description of hardfacing is presented in Chapter 18.

Fig. 2. Because of its tough qualities, high manganese steel is often used for power shovel buckets. (Hobart Brothers Co.)

To secure the best possible results in welding pieces of high manganese steel, observe the following:

1. Vee the joint and clean the surfaces carefully.

2. Use the lowest possible current to prevent the formation of a brittle zone next to the weld.

3. The electrode most frequently recommended for high manganese steel is a stainless steel 18-8 type. (E-308-15, E-308-16, E-309-15, E-309-16, E-310-15, E-310-16).

As a rule these electrodes are easier to apply and produce the most satisfactory welds. Other types of electrodes used for welding high manganese steel are molybdenum - copper - manganese

and nickel-manganese. However, more skill is needed to execute good welds with these electrodes.

4. Strike the arc ahead of the crater and continue the weld bead in the direction of travel. Keep the weld beads short (about 2″) and allow them to cool between each run to avoid concentrated and prolonged heat in any localized area of the base metal. Do not continue to weld in an area unless the temperature of the metal is below 750°F. Use tempilstiks to determine temperature by marking the base metal ⅜″ to ½″ from the weld. Actually you should be able to place your hand within 6″ to 8″ of the weld at any time. If you have trouble controlling the heat, place wet rags on areas adjacent to the weld.

5. Use a narrow weave with the electrode held at about a 45 degree angle in the direction of the weld bead travel.

6. Due to the high thermal expansion of manganese steel, many stresses form as the weld cools, causing cracks to develop during contraction. To reduce cracking, peen each run of weld bead when it is completed.

To repair cracks in manganese steel follow this procedure:

1. Cut a hole at the end or ends of the crack to prevent stresses from spreading the crack further.

2. Gouge a U or V groove in the crack and grind away all oxide from the weld area.

3. Deposit a root bead along section 1 as indicated in Fig. 3. Weld additional layers over the root bead until the groove is full. Then follow

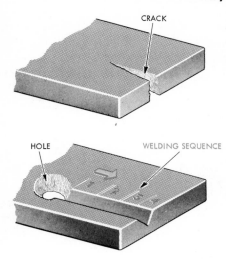

Fig. 3. Welding crack in manganese steel.

the same procedure for sections 2, 3, and 4.

4. When the entire groove is filled, fill the hole or holes at the end of the original crack.

Welding Stainless Steel

The first stainless steel developed was the chromium-iron type, having as the main constituents chromium and iron. Later nickel was introduced into stainless steel, producing a metal that has been popularly referred to as 18-8. (Approximately 18 per cent chromium and 8 per cent nickel.) Further developments have brought into use a whole series of stainless steels designed to meet more rigid fabricating demands.

How Stainless Steel Is Classified

Stainless steel today is classified into two general A.I.S.I. (American Iron and Steel Institute) series—300 and 400. Each series includes several dif-ferent kinds of steel, all of course having some special characteristic. See Table II.

The 400 series. The 400 series is further classified into two groups according to their crystalline structure. One group is known as ferritic and is non-hardenable and magnetic. The other group is referred to as martensitic, which is hardenable by heat treatment and is also magnetic.

The ferritic chromium steels when subjected to the heat of welding will develop some degree of brittleness. This brittleness may be reduced and ductility improved by cold working the weld area by peening and annealing.

The martensitic chromium steels will harden when cooled from welding temperatures. Since these steels are usually subjected to further heat-treating processes, the hardening effects present no problem, especially if the annealing or tempering treatment is begun immediately after the welding operation.

The 300 series. These steels have an austenitic structure which make them extremely tough and ductile in the as-welding condition. Hence, they are the most ideal for welding and require no annealing after welding when used in normal atmospheric conditions or are mildly subjected to corrosive actions. If they are to encounter severe corrosive conditions, it is advisable to anneal the welded structure.

Physical Properties of Stainless Steel

The coefficient of expansion of the 400 chromium types of steel is approximately the same as that of carbon

TABLE II

Types of Stainless Steels

CHROMIUM-NICKEL TYPES

Austenitic Non-Magnetic Non-Hardenable by Heat Treatment

AISI TYPE NUMBER	CARBON %	MAN-GANESE MAX %	PHOS-PHORUS MAX %	SULFUR MAX %	SILICON MAX %	CHROMIUM %	NICKEL %	OTHER ELEMENTS %
301	Over 0.08 to 0.15	2.00	0.04	0.03	1.00	16.0-18.0	6.0- 8.0	
302	Over 0.08 to 0.15	2.00	0.04	0.03	1.00	17.0-19.0	8.0-10.0	
302B	Over 0.08 to 0.15	2.00	0.04	0.03	2.0-3.0	17.0-19.0	8.0-10.0	
303	0.15 max	2.00	X	X	1.00	17.0-19.0	8.0-10.0	
304	0.08 max	2.00	0.04	0.03	1.00	18.0-20.0	8.0-11.0	
304L	0.03 max	2.00	0.04	0.03	1.00	18.0-20.0	8.0-11.0	
305	0.12 max	2.00	0.04	0.03	1.00	17.0-19.0	10.0-13.0	
308	0.08 max	2.00	0.04	0.03	1.00	19.0-21.0	10.0-12.0	
309	0.20 max	2.00	0.04	0.03	1.00	22.0-24.0	12.0-15.0	
309S	0.08 max	2.00	0.04	0.03	1.00	22.0-24.0	12.0-15.0	
310	0.25 max	2.00	0.04	0.03	1.50	24.0-26.0	19.0-22.0	
310S	0.08 max	2.00	0.04	0.03	1.50	24.0-26.0	19.0-22.0	
314	0.25 max	2.00	0.04	0.03	1.5-3.0	23.0-26.0	19.0-22.0	
316	0.10 max	2.00	0.04	0.03	1.00	16.0-18.0	10.0-14.0	Mo-1.75-2.50
316L	0.03 max	2.00	0.04	0.03	1.00	16.0-18.0	10.0-14.0	Mo-1.75-2.50
317	0.10 max	2.00	0.04	0.03	1.00	18.0-20.0	11.0-14.0	Mo-3.00-4.00
317L	0.03 max	2.00	0.04	0.03	1.00	18.0-20.0	11.0-14.0	Mo-3.00-4.00
330	0.25 max	2.00	0.04	0.04	1.00	14.0-16.0	33.0-36.0	
321	0.08 max	2.00	0.04	0.03	1.00	17.0-19.0	8.0-11.0	Ti-5 X C min
347	0.08 max	2.00	0.04	0.03	1.00	17.0-19.0	9.0-12.0	Cb-Ta-10XCmin
347F	0.08 max	2.00	X	X	1.00	17.0-19.0	9.0-12.0	Cb-Ta-10XCmin

CHROMIUM TYPES

Martensitic Magnetic Hardenable by Heat Treatment

AISI TYPE NUMBER	CARBON %	MAN-GANESE MAX %	PHOS-PHORUS MAX %	SULFUR MAX %	SILICON MAX %	CHROMIUM %	NICKEL %	OTHER ELEMENTS %
403	0.15 max	1.00	0.04	0.03	0.50	11.5-13.0		
410	0.15 max	1.00	0.04	0.03	1.00	11.5-13.5		
414	0.15 max	1.00	0.04	0.03	1.00	11.5-13.5	1.25-2.50	
416	0.15 max	1.25	X	X	1.00	12.0-14.0		X
420	Over 0.15	1.00	0.04	0.03	1.00	12.0-14.0		
420F	Over 0.15	1.00	X	X	1.00	12.0-14.0		X
431	0.20 max	1.00	0.04	0.03	1.00	15.0-17.0	1.25-2.50	
440A	0.60-0.75	1.00	0.04	0.03	1.00	16.0-18.0		Mo-0.75max
440B	0.75-0.95	1.00	0.04	0.03	1.00	16.0-18.0		Mo-0.75max
440C	0.95-1.20	1.00	0.04	0.03	1.00	16.0-18.0		Mo-0.75max
440F	0.95-1.20	1.00	X	X	1.00	16.0-18.0		X

CHROMIUM TYPES

Ferritic Magnetic Non-Hardenable by Heat Treatment

AISI TYPE NUMBER	CARBON %	MAN-GANESE MAX %	PHOS-PHORUS MAX %	SULFUR MAX %	SILICON MAX %	CHROMIUM %	NICKEL %	OTHER ELEMENTS %
405	0.08 max	1.00	0.04	0.03	1.00	11.5-13.5		Al-0.10-0.30
430	0.12 max	1.00	0.04	0.03	1.00	14.0-18.0		
430 Ti	0.12 max	1.00	0.04	0.03	1.00	14.0-18.0		Ti-6 X C min
430F	0.12 max	1.25	X	X	1.00	14.0-18.0		X
442	0.20 max	1.00	0.04	0.03	1.00	18.0-23.0		
446	0.35 max	1.50	0.04	0.03	1.00	23.0-27.0		

X Free Machining Stainless Steels—Phosphorus, Sulfur or Selenium—0.07% min , Zr or Mo—0.60% max

steel. Consequently, the allowances for expansion are practically the same as those for carbon steel. The chromium-nickel 300 series have about a 50 to 60 per cent greater coefficient of expansion than carbon steel and therefore require greater consideration in expansion control.

The heat conductivity of the 400 series is approximately 50 to 65 per cent of carbon steel. With the 300 series the heat conductivity is almost 40 to 50 per cent of carbon steel. Consequently in both series the heat is not conducted away as fast as in ordinary steel and as a result, stainless steels take longer to cool. This phenomenon is particularly important to remember in welding thin gages since there is greater danger of burning through the material.

Methods of Reducing Effects of Heat

Unfavorable effects of heat can be reduced substantially by means of chill plates. The use of chill plates such as copper pieces will help conduct the heat away. Rigid jigs and fixtures should be employed wherever possible, especially for the 300 series. When stainless steels are allowed to cool in a jig, warping and distortion is practically eliminated.

If jigs cannot be used, special welding procedures will be necessary to counteract expansion forces. The common practice is to resort to "skip" or "step-back" methods of welding. See Chapter 2.

Weldability of Stainless Steel

It is generally conceded that stainless steels in the 300 series have better welding qualities than those in the 400 series. However, this does not mean that the 400 series stainless steels are not weldable. Greater precautions simply have to be taken, especially in applying proper heat-treating methods after the weld is completed.

All methods of welding may be used in joining stainless steel. Oxy-acetylene

Fig. 4. Large stainless steel vats for chemical processing are arc welded. (Hobart Brothers Co.)

welding is usually recognized as the most effective for welding 20 gage and lighter stainless steel sheets, and the metallic arc for heavier plates. See Fig. 4.

Today the inert-gas-shielded arc is utilized a great deal more for welding stainless steel of all types because of the ease with which welds can be made and since with this process there is less danger of destroying the corrosion-resistant properties in the steel.

Choosing the Correct Joint Design

For thin metal, the flange-type joint is probably the most satisfactory design. Slightly heavier sheets, up to 1/8″ in thickness, may be butted together. For plates heavier than 1/8″, the edges should be beveled to provide a vee so fusion can be obtained entirely to the bottom of the weld.

Since stainless steels have a much higher coefficient of expansion with lower thermal conductivity than mild steels, there are greater possibilities for distortion and warping. Therefore, whenever possible, clamps and jigs should be used to keep the pieces in line until they have cooled.

Electrodes. In arc welding, flux coated electrodes should always be used. The flux shields, or protects, the molten metal from the air, preventing oxidation of the chromium and producing strong, corrosion resistant welds. Also, the flux has a tendency to act as a stabilizing agent helping to maintain a steady arc with an even metal flow into the shielded area.

The slag formed by flux coated electrodes will flow to the surface where it should be brushed off before subsequent beads are laid on the weld. To produce a good strong weld, the electrode should ordinarily be as low in carbon as possible. It is also desirable for the electrode coatings to be free from undesirable elements such as carbon.

The alloy content of electrodes should be higher than that of the base

TABLE III

Electrodes for Welding Stainless Steel

BASE METAL (AISI)	ELECTRODES (AWS)
Austentic	
301, 302, 304	E-308-15, 16
305, 308	E-309-15, 16
309	E-309-15, 16
310	E-310-15, 16
316	E-316-15, 16
317	E-317-15, 16
318	E-318-15, 16
330	E-330-15, 16
347	E-347-15, 16
Ferritic	
405	E-430-15, 16
430	E-430-15, 16, E-308, 309, 310
442	E-308, 309, 310
446	E-308, 309, 310
Martensitic	
403	E-410, 308, 309, 310
410	E-410, 308, 309, 310
416	E-410, 308, 309

metal to compensate for expected alloy loss. Moreover, a columbium bearing electrode must be used for both the columbium (Type 347) and the titanium (Type 321) stabilized grades. Chromium-nickel electrodes are often used in welding chromium grades due to the fact that they provide a ductile weld metal. See Table III.

Stainless steel electrodes are identified in a different way than mild steel. For example, a standard 18-8 electrode for AC-DC current is designated as E-308-16. The prefix "E" indicates a metallic arc electrode. The next three digits are the AISI (American Iron and Steel Institute) symbols for a particular type of metal. Thus "308" represent a metal containing 18 per cent chromium and 8 per cent nickel. The last two dash digits may be either 15 or 16; the "1" indicates an all position welding, and the "5" or "6" specifies the type of covering and applicable welding current. The "5" designates a low hydrogen covering electrode for DC reverse polarity. The "6" is an electrode designed for AC and DC reverse polarity and has a hydrogen type covering.

Welding Current. Both direct and alternating current are used in the arc welding of stainless steel. Reversed polarity will produce deeper weld penetration and more consistent fusion when welding stainless steel sheets and light plates with direct current.

Since stainless steel has a lower melting point than mild steel, at least 20 per cent less current is recommended than would ordinarily be used for mild steel. Also, the low thermal conductivity of stainless localizes the heat from the arc along the weld, again lowering current requirements.

Cleaning. It is necessary to have the material to be welded free from scale, grease, and dirt in order to prevent weld contamination.

Procedure. To produce good welds, all butting edges should be squared. Stainless steel sheets 18 gage and lighter are fitted with no gap. Heavier gage sheets and plates are set up with gaps.

To start arc welding, the arc is struck by touching the metal electrode on the work and quickly withdrawing it a short distance (enough to maintain the proper arc). The tendency for the electrode to stick, or "freeze," to the work may be overcome by using a striking motion similar to that used when striking a match. Any coating on the electrode tip must be removed before an arc can be struck.

To maintain the arc, the electrode should be fed continuously into the arc, to compensate for metal deposited, and also moved rapidly in a continuous movement in the direction of welding.

To finish the weld or break the arc, the electrode should be held close to the work, thus shortening the arc, then moved quickly back over the finished bead.

In order to reduce weld oxidation and porosity, the arc should be as short as possible. Too long an arc is inefficient and increases spattering. Vertical and overhead welding require

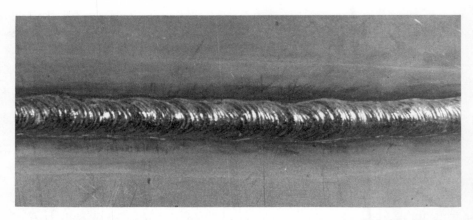

Fig. 5. Appearance of a butt and fillet weld made on stainless steel plate.

a short arc together with smaller diameter electrodes than are used in horizontal welding.

After welding, all slag, scale, and discoloration should be completely removed from the weld bead and adjacent base metal. See Fig. 5. Light weld discoloration may be removed electrolytically. Scale or oxide is best removed by grinding, pickling, or sandblasting. When grinding, re-

finish with progressively finer grits. The smoother and cleaner the surface of any stainless part, the better the corrosion resistance.

Downhand Welding.* In welding butt joints in the flat position, the current selected should be high enough to

---

*Airco

insure ample penetration with good "wash-up" on the sides. When several beads are required it is advisable to use a number of small beads rather than to try and fill up the groove with one or two passes. A fairly short arc should be maintained, and any weaving should be limited to 2½ times the electrode diameter. In general, it is good practice to hold the electrode vertical or very slightly tilted in the direction of travel. The latter case should only be used with small diameter electrodes. For lack of a hard and fast rule it may be said that the correct position is one that gives a clean pool of metal and which solidifies uniformly as the work progresses. The movement of the electrode across the pool controls the flow of the metal and slag. Any weave technique employed should be in the form of a "U" for best results.

Vertical Welding.* The welding of butt joints in the vertical position progressing upward can be accomplished with a reduced current from that used in the flat positions for a given electrode diameter. Oscillation or whipping is not recommended but instead a motion in the form of a "V" may be used for the first pass. The point of the "V" is the root of the joint, hesitating momentarily at this point to assure adequate penetration and to bring the slag to the surface. The arc is then brought out on one side of the point about ⅛" and immediately returned to the root of the joint. After the momentary pause at the root the procedure is repeated on the other side of the weld. Electrodes of $\frac{3}{16}$" in diameter may be used on sections heavy enough to give rapid dissipation of the heat, but $\frac{5}{32}$" diameter electrodes are the generally accepted maximum size for less massive sections. Welding should progress from the bottom upward except for single pass corner welds with $\frac{3}{32}$" and smaller diameter electrodes, which may be used from the top downward. In the usual vertical fillet weld the electrode is inclined slightly below the horizontal position (holder end lower than arc end) and the weave motion should be rapid across the center of the bead.

Overhead Welding.* Stringer beads are recommended when welding in the overhead position, since attempts to carry a large puddle of molten metal will result in an irregular convex bead. To assure best results, a short arc should be maintained and the machine should be set properly thereby providing good penetration of the base metal.

Horizontal Fillet Welding.* Horizontal fillet welds and lap welds require a machine setting high enough to give good penetration into the root of the joint and a well-shaped bead. Too low a current is easily recognized, since difficulty will be experienced in controlling or concentrating the arc in the joint, and a very convex bead with poor fusion will result.

*Airco

When two legs of equal thickness are being welded, the electrode should be held equidistant from each face and tilted slightly forward in the direction of travel. If one leg is lighter than the other, the electrode should be pointed towards the heavier leg. Undercutting on the vertical is caused by dwelling too long on that leg or by too high a current.

Welding Low Alloy Molybdenum Steels

Two of the more common molybdenum alloy steels are known as carbon-moly and chrome-moly. Carbon-moly steels have high strength especially at high temperatures. For this reason they are used extensively in piping systems where high pressures at high temperatures are encountered.

Chrome-moly steels are widely used for highly stressed parts. Many aircraft components are fabricated from this metal, such as landing gear supports, tubular frames and engine mounts. See Fig. 6.

Low-carbon moly steels with carbon content below 0.15 per cent are readily weldable in much the same way as mild steel. Usually E-7010, E-7011, E-7015, E-7016, E-7018, E-7020, E-70270 electrodes will provide approximately the same tensile strength

Fig. 6. "Chrome-moly" steel is used for this engine mount. (The Lincoln Electric Co.)

as the base plate strength. Where the tensile strength of the weld need not be as high as that of the base metal, ordinary E-6010 electrodes can be used.

Some preheating is advisable at temperatures of 400° to 650°F. When the thickness of the metal is over ⅜″, stress relief is often necessary after the welding is completed. Stress relief is accomplished at temperatures of 1200°-1250°F for periods of one hour for each inch of thickness followed by slow cooling in the furnace at a rate of 200°-250°F per hour. When the heat reaches about 150°F the rest of the cooling may be done in still air.

Chrome-moly steels having a low carbon content may be welded with E-6012, E-6013, or E-6024 electrodes. These electrodes will pick up enough alloy from the parent metal to produce the necessary tensile strength in the weld. For higher carbon chrome-moly steels special low hydrogen electrodes of the E-7015, 16 type are used with adequate preheat and postheat treatment to prevent extreme brittleness at the fusion zone.

Welding Low Alloy Nickel Steels

The addition of nickel (3% to 5%) to steel greatly increases the elastic properties as well as the strength, toughness, and corrosion resistance.

To weld low alloy nickel steels where the tensile strength must be equal to the base plate, an E-7010 or E-7020 electrode is used. As a rule, standard E-6012 electrodes are best

for welding thin sheets because they penetrate less than the E-70 series.

If there are persistent signs of cracking during welding, it is best to switch to a low hydrogen electrode of the E-6015, E-6016, E-7015, or E-7016 series. On heavy sections, preheating to a dull red is generally advisable.

Points to Remember

1. Some preheating is required when welding most alloy steels.

2. Use E-7010 or E-7020 to weld low manganese steels.

3. Use the lowest possible current when welding high manganese steel.

4. Best results are obtained with E-308, E-309, or E-310 electrodes for high manganese steel.

5. Peen each bead to minimize cracking when welding manganese steel.

6. Arc welding is more satisfactory when welding stainless steel material over 20 gage in thickness.

7. When welding stainless steel, use a short arc with only a slight weaving motion.

8. Be sure to use the right kind of electrodes for the type of stainless steel to be welded.

9. In flat position welding of stainless steel hold the electrode vertical or tilted only slightly in the direction of travel.

10. When making vertical welds on stainless steel, avoid any whipping action of the electrode, instead use a motion in the form of a "V."

11. Use E-70XX type electrodes to weld low carbon moly steels.

12. Keep preheating temperatures between 400° to 650°F for low carbon moly steels.

13. Chrome moly steels can be welded with E-6012, E-6013, or E-6024 electrodes.

14. Use E-7010 or E-7020 electrodes to weld low alloy nickel steel.

15. If cracks appear in the process of welding low alloy nickel steel, switch to E-7015, E-7016, E-6015, or E-6016 electrodes.

QUESTIONS FOR STUDY AND DISCUSSION

1. Why is some form of preheating recommended when arc welding alloy steels?

2. What is the purpose of a "clip test" and how is it conducted?

3. What are some of the basic characteristics of austentic manganese steel?

4. Why must the lowest possible current be used when welding manganese steel?

5. What type of electrodes produces the most satisfactory results on manganese steel?

6. What should be done to prevent cracks from forming when welding high manganese steel?

7. How are stainless steels classified?

8. What are the particular qualities of stainless steel that makes this metal so valuable?

9. Why are chill plates frequently used when welding stainless steel?

10. How does the symbol classification of stainless steel electrodes differ from mild steel electrodes?

11. Why is less current required in welding stainless steel?

12. Why are martensitic types of stainless steels more difficult to weld?

13. What is the difference between low-carbon moly steel and chrome-moly steel?

14. What kind of electrodes are usually recommended for welding low-carbon moly steel?

15. Why is some form of stress relief often used after welding moly steels?

WELDING ASSIGNMENTS

1. Practice welding the following: Manganese steel, stainless steel, molybdenum alloy steel, and low alloy nickel steel. Use whatever thickness metal that is available and weld: lap joints, tee joints, corner joints, butt joints.

CHAPTER 14

Shielded Metal—Arc Welding

Non-Ferrous Metals

Non-ferrous metals are those which do not contain iron—such as aluminum, copper, brass, bronze, monel, and inconel. Continued experiment and development have now made possible successful welding of these metals. Actually, with a little practice, you can master the art of welding non-ferrous metals as easily as most steels.

Welding Aluminum

Aluminum plays an important role in the manufacture of every conceivable type of equipment ranging from railroad cars, trucks, and buildings, to cooking utensils. See Fig. 1. In most cases, welding is used in fabricating these aluminum products.

Aluminum weighs only about one-third as much as other commonly used metals; it has a high strength-to-weight ratio, is highly resistant to corrosion, possesses great electrical conductivity, and permits unusual ease in fabrication.

Most types of aluminum used in making commercial products are readily weldable either by oxy-acetylene (see Chapter 30) metallic arc, or gas-shielded arc process (Chapters 15 and 16). The welding technique employed depends on such factors as experience of the welder and kind of work to be done. In some instances it is more satisfactory to weld with the oxy-acetylene flame, while for other jobs the task is simplified if the welding is performed with the metallic arc or gas-shielded arc.

Kinds of Aluminum

Aluminum is classified into three main groups: commercially pure aluminum, wrought alloys, and casting

Fig. 1. Welding is used in fabricating many aluminum products. (Aluminum Company of America)

alloys. Commercially pure aluminum has a purity of at least 99 per cent, with the remaining 1 per cent consisting of iron and silicon. Since it lacks alloying ingredients, this aluminum does not possess a very high tensile strength. One of its chief qualities is its ductility, which makes the metal especially adaptable for pressing and forming operations.

Wrought alloys are those which contain one or more alloying elements and possess a much higher tensile strength. The main alloying materials are copper, manganese, magnesium, silicon, chromium, zinc, and nickel. The wrought aluminums are either non-heat-treatable or heat-treatable. The non-heat-treatable types are those which are not hardenable by any forms of heat-treatment; their varying degrees of hardness are controlled only by cold working. The heat-treatable alloys are those in which hardness and strength are further improved by subjecting them to heat-treating processes.

Casting alloys are used to produce aluminum castings, the metal being poured into a sand or permanent metal mold. A great many of the castings are weldable, but extreme care must be exercised when welding the heat-treated types to prevent any loss of the characteristics achieved by the heat-treating process.

Method of Designating Aluminum

The tremendous growth of the aluminum industry in capacity and number of producers has resulted in a multitude of alloys and the use of several commercial designation systems for these alloys. None of these is adequate for use by all. The Aluminum Association recognized this deficiency several years ago and therefore instituted studies directed towards the development of a new and broader system. The system described here is the result, and it is believed it will satisfy the future needs of the industry.

Digit code. Wrought aluminum and wrought aluminum alloys are designated by a four digit index system. The first digit of the designation serves to indicate alloy groups. The last two digits identify the aluminum alloy or indicate the aluminum purity. The second digit indicates modifications of the original alloy or impurity limits.

Pure aluminum and aluminum alloy groups. In the four digit index system the first digit indicates the alloy group as shown in Table I. Thus 1xxx indicates aluminum of at least 99.00% purity, 2xxx indicates an aluminum alloy in which copper is the major alloying element, and 3xxx an aluminum alloy with manganese as the major alloying element, etc. Although most aluminum alloys contain several alloying elements, only one group— 6xxx for alloys with magnesium and silicon as major alloying elements— designates more than one alloying element.

Pure aluminum—In the 1xxx group for aluminum of at least 99.00% purity the last two of the four digits in the designation indicate the minimum aluminum percentage. These digits are the same as the two digits to the right of the decimal point in the minimum aluminum percentage when it is expressed to the nearest 0.01%.

TABLE I

Designations for Aluminum

	AA NUMBER
Aluminum—99.00% minimum and greater	1xxx
MAJOR ALLOYING ELEMENT	

	Major Alloying Element	AA NUMBER
Aluminum Alloys grouped by major Alloying Elements	Copper	2xxx
	Manganese	3xxx
	Silicon	4xxx
	Magnesium	5xxx
	Magnesium and Silicon	6xxx
	Zinc	7xxx
	Other Element	8xxx

TABLE II

Aluminum Alloy Designation Conversions

OLD COMMERCIAL DESIGNATION	NEW AA NUMBER	OLD COMMERCIAL DESIGNATION	NEW AA NUMBER	OLD COMMERCIAL DESIGNATION	NEW AA NUMBER
		17S	2017	56S	5056
99.6, CD1S	1160	A17S	2117	XC56S	X5356
99.75	1175	18S	2018	C57S, K157	5357
99.87, EB1S	1187	B18S	2218	61S	6061
EC	EC	F18S, RR58	2618	62S	6062
AA1S	1095	24S	2024	63S	6063
BA1S	1099	25S	2025	66S	6066
CA1S	1197	B25S	2225	70S	7070
AB1S	1085	32S	4032	72S	7072
EB1S, 99.87	1187	43S, K145	4043	75S	7075
FB1S	1090	C43S, 44S, K143	4343	B77S	7277
AC1S	1070	XE43S	X4543	XA78S	X7178
BC1S	1080	44S, C43S, K143	4343	XB80S	X8280
CC1S, R998, 99.8	1180	45S	4045	K112	8112
JC1S	1075	50S	5050	K143, C43S, 44S	4343
AD1S	1050	A50S, K155, R305	5005	K145, 43S	4043
BD1S	1060	XD50S	X5405	K155, A50S, R305	5005
CD1S, 99.6	1160	A51S	6151	K157, C57S	5357
ED1S	1150	XB51S	X6251	K160, J51S	6951
AE1S	1030	J51S, K160	6951	X162, R306(4)	6003
BE1S	1145	52S	5052	LK183	5083
2S	1100	F52S	5652	K186	5086
3S	3003	53S	6053	R301 Core, 14S	2014
4S	3004	B53S	6253	R305, K155, A50S	5005
XA5S	X3005	XD53S	X6453	R306, K162	6003
11S	2011	E53S	6553	R308	1130
14S, R301 Core	2014	A54S	5154	R399	8099
XB14S	X2214	B54S	5254	R995, 99.35	1235
XC16S	X2316	X55S	X5055	R998, CC1S	1180

The second digit in the designation indicates modifications in impurity limits. If the second digit in the designation is zero, it indicates that there is no special control on individual impurities; while integers 1 through 9, which are assigned consecutively as needed, indicate special control of one or more individual impurities. Thus 1030 indicates 99.30% minimum aluminum without special control on individual impurities and 1130, 1230, 1330, etc. indicate the same purity with special control on one or more impurities. Likewise 1075, 1175, etc. indicate 99.75% minimum aluminum; and 1097, 1197, etc., indicate 99.97%.

Aluminum alloys — In the 2xxx through 8xxx alloy groups the last two of the four digits in the designation have no special significance but serve only to identify the different alloys in the group. Generally these digits are the same as those used to designate the same alloys before the development of this system. Thus 2014 was formerly 14S, 3003 was 3S, and 7075 was 75S. See Table II.

The second digit in the alloy designation indicates alloy modifications. If the second digit in the designation is zero, it indicates the original alloy; while integers 1 through 9, which are assigned consecutively, indicate alloy modifications. In the former system, letters were used to designate alloy modifications. These were assigned consecutively beginning with *A*. Thus 17S is now 2017 and A17S is 2117, 18S is 2018 and B18S is 2218.

Temper designations. The temper designation system in effect since December 31, 1947 is being continued without change. The temper designation follows the alloy designation and is separated from it by a dash. Thus 3S-0 is now 3003-0, Alclad 24S-T8 is Alclad 2024-T8, and 75S-T6 is 7075-T6. The basic designations are:

Non-Heat-Treatable Aluminum

O = Annealed
F = As received condition, no effort made to control the mechanical properties
H = Cold worked

Cold-worked tempers of wrought alloys are designated by the letter *H* followed by a number of two digits. When the temper is produced merely by cold-working the material to the desired extent, the first digit is 1. The second digit depends on the amount of cold-working. When this cold-working has been such as to produce the hardest commercially-practicable temper, the number is 8. Thus, the temper designation for the commercially-hard temper is H18. For material cold-worked to a tensile strength approximately midway between that of the O and the H18 tempers, the designation is H14. Similarly, material with a strength midway between the O and the H14 is designated H12, and that with a strength midway between the H14 and H18 tempers is known as H16.

It also is possible to obtain a given level of strength in the strain-hardened alloys by cold-working to a harder temper and then reducing the strength to the desired level by partially annealing the material. To distinguish material processed to the desired strength in this manner from that cold-worked to the same level of strength, the first digit after the *H* is the number 2. Numbers 2 through 8 are used for the second digit in the same manner as for the H1 series described above.

In the case of certain alloys, the strength developed by cold-work decreases slightly, and the elongation increases when the material is held at room temperature for a long time. These changes can be brought to practical completion by heating the material for a short time at a slightly elevated temperature. Such a stabilizing treatment is indicated by the number 3, plus one or more digits after the *H* designation.

Examples: 1100-O—fully annealed
3003-H18—cold-worked, hardest temper
3003-H24—cold-worked and partially annealed
5052-H32—cold-worked and stabilized

Heat-Treatable Aluminum

T2 = Annealed
T3 = Solution heat-treated and then cold-worked
T4 = Solution heat-treated
T5 = Artificially aged only

TABLE III

Weldability of Aluminum

TYPE	WELDING PROCESS		
	GAS	METAL-ARC	GAS SHIELDED-ARC
1060	A	A	A
1100	A	A	A
3003	A	A	A
3004	A	A	A
5005	A	A	A
5050	A	A	A
5052	A	A	A
2014	X	C	C
2017	X	C	C
2024	X	C	C
6061	A	A	A
6063	A	A	A
6070	C	B	A
6071	A	A	A
7070	X	X	A
7072	X	X	A
7075	X	X	C

A — READILY WELDABLE
B — WELDABLE IN MOST APPLICATIONS—MAY REQUIRE SPECIAL TECHNIQUE
C — LIMITED WELDABILITY
X — NOT RECOMMENDED

T6 = Solution heat - treated and then artificially aged

T7 = Solution heat - treated and then stabilized

T8 = Solution heat-treated, cold-worked, and then artificially aged

T9 = Solution heat-treated, artificially aged, and then cold-worked

T10 = Artificially aged and then cold-worked

Examples: 2017-T4
2024-T2
2014-T6

Welding Characteristics of Aluminum

Nonheat treatable wrought aluminum alloys in the 1000, 3000, and 5000 series are weldable. The heat of the welding may remove some of the material's strength developed by cold working but the strength will never be below that of the material in its fully annealed condition. Nevertheless, the welding procedure should confine the concentration of heat in the narrowest zone possible.

The heat-treatable alloys in the 2000, 6000, and 7000 series can be welded except that the 2000 and 7000 are not generally recommended for oxyacetylene welding. See Table III. Higher welding temperatures and speeds are needed to penetrate these alloys which is impossible with an oxy-acetylene flame. In most instances resistance welding is preferred for high strength alloys.

Welding Procedure

The following paragraphs describe the general procedure for arc welding aluminum alloys.

TABLE IV
Electrode Size, Current, and Number of Passes for Arc Welding Aluminum

Metal Thickness (inch)	Electrode Diameter (inch)	Approximate Current (amperage)	Number of Passes (butt, lap, fillet)
.081	1/8	60	1
.102	1/8	70	1
.125	1/8	80	1
.156	1/8	100	1
.188	5/32	125	1
.250	3/16	160	1
.375	3/16 for laps & fillets 1/4 for butts	200	2
.500	3/16 for laps & fillets 1/4 for butts	300	3
1.000	5/16	450	3

1. Type of electrode — A heavy shielded electrode containing 95 per cent aluminum and 5 per cent silicon is recommended for welding most alloys. See Table IV for correct diameter of electrode.

Fig. 2. Welding brackets to the head of a tank is simplified when performed in a flat position. (Aluminum Company of America)

2. Position of the weld — While welding can be performed in any position, the task is simplified and the quality of the completed joint is more satisfactory if the welding is done in a flat position as shown in Fig. 2. Welding aluminum in an overhead position is particularly difficult and should be avoided whenever possible.

3. Current setting — For the best results, use reversed polarity. See Table IV for the correct setting.

4. Type of joint—Due to the difficulty of controlling the arc at low currents, it is not very practical to arc weld material less than $\frac{1}{16}''$ in thickness. Since it is easy to secure good penetration in aluminum, no edge preparation is necessary on material $\frac{1}{4}''$ or less in thickness. On heavier metal, it is better to bevel the edges as shown in Fig. 3. For some butt welds, beveling can be dispensed with on stock $\frac{3}{16}''$ to $\frac{3}{8}''$ in thickness by run-

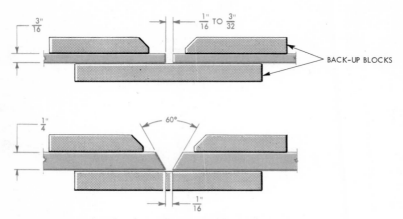

Fig. 3. Bevel the edges for welding heavier aluminum.

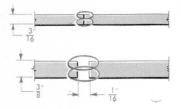

Fig. 4. For some aluminum welds run a bead on both sides.

ning a bead on both sides as in Fig. 4. Copper back-up blocks should be used whenever possible, especially on plates ⅛″ or less in thickness.

5. *Striking the arc*—Brush the end of the electrode across the surface as in striking a match. Starting the arc

in this way is advisable because the electrode melts very fast and the metal solidifies rapidly when the arc is extinguished. If you try to just touch the plate, the electrode will freeze.

6. *Manipulating the rod*—Keep the arc as short as possible, with the electrode coating almost touching the molten pool of metal. Hold the electrode about perpendicular to the work at all times. Direct the arc so both edges of the joint are uniformly heated. Move the electrode either forward or backward along the seam and advance it at such a rate as to produce a uniform bead as illustrated in Fig. 5. Re-

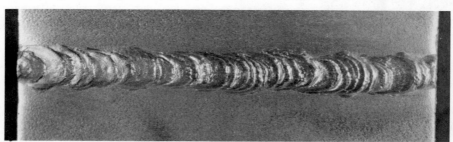

Fig. 5. This is how an aluminum butt weld should appear.

frain from weaving the electrode as in welding mild steel. Just keep it moving in a straight line. Before starting a new electrode, remove the slag from the crater and approximately one inch back of the crater. Then quickly move the electrode back about $\frac{1}{2}''$ over the finished weld and proceed forward as soon as the crater is completely re-melted.

When making a lap weld or fillet weld, hold the electrode so that the angle between the electrode and the plate is approximately 45°. Manipulate the electrode with a small rotary motion, playing the arc first on the vertical member and then on the horizontal plate.

7. *Cleaning the finished weld* — After a weld is completed, it is important that you remove the slag over the bead. This slag is solidified flux from the coating on the electrode. If it is not removed, it will attack the aluminum, especially when moisture is present. To remove the flux, crack it off with a chipping tool and then give it a vigorous brushing with a wire brush. For some welded aluminum products the slag is removed by means of a diluted acid solution followed by a warm water rinse.

Fig. 6. Arc welding an aluminum alloy casting. (Hobart Brothers Co.)

Welding Aluminum Castings

Most aluminum alloy castings can be welded by the metallic arc process as shown in Fig. 6. However, considerable precautions must be taken to prevent the formation of cracks during contraction on cooling and the loss of mechanical properties through excessive heat. To weld a casting successfully proceed as follows:

1. Thoroughly remove oil, grease, and dirt from the weld area with a suitable solvent.

2. Chip out a 45 degree bevel on sections $\frac{3}{16}''$ thick or heavier.

3. Clamp the pieces to be welded to hold them in correct alignment.

4. Preheat the entire casting between 500° and 800° F in a furnace or with a gas torch. Be careful not to overheat the casting.

5. Use an electrode having approximately the same composition as the base metal. Alcoa 43S electrodes usually will produce a good weld.

Welding Copper

Copper is a soft, tough, and ductile

metal. It cannot be heat treated but will harden when cold worked. Commercially available coppers are divided into two groups: oxygen-bearing copper and oxygen-free copper.

Oxygen-bearing Copper. This electrolytic tough pitch copper is practically 99.9 per cent pure and is considered to be the best conductor of heat and electricity. A small amount of oxygen in the form of copper oxide is uniformly distributed throughout the metal but it is insufficient to affect the ductility of the copper. However, if heated above 1680°F for prolonged periods the copper oxide tends to migrate to the grain boundaries, causing a reduction in strength and ductility. Also when exposed to this temperature the copper will absorb carbon monoxide and hydrogen which react with the copper oxide and release carbon dioxide or water vapor. Since these gases are not soluble in copper they exert pressure between the grains and produce internal cracking and embrittlement.

Oxygen-free Copper. This group of copper contains a small percentage of phosphorus or some other deoxidizer, thereby leaving the metal free of oxygen and consequently no copper oxide. The absence of copper oxide gives the metal superior fatigue resistance qualities and better cold working properties over the oxygen-bearing copper.

Weldability. Oxygen-bearing copper is not recommended for gas welding because of the formation of embrittlement. Some welds can be made with the shielded metal-arc process in situations where the tensile strength requirements are extremely low (19,-000 psi or less), providing a high welding current and high travel speeds are used. The high current and speed will not give the embrittlement a chance to develop.

Deoxidized copper is the most widely used type for fabrication by welding. A properly made weld will have a tensile strength of about 30,000 psi. This copper can be welded with all standard welding processes including oxyacetylene, shielded metal-arc, gas tungsten-arc, and gas metal-arc. Since copper has a very high coefficient of expansion and contraction precautions must be taken to provide suitable jigging and clamping to prevent movement while cooling. Contraction forces will often cause cracking during the cooling temperature range.

Due to the rapid heat transfer of copper, the metallic arc is not too practical for welding copper sheets over ¼″ in thickness. Operators prefer the carbon arc (Chapter 15) or some gas shielded arc process.

Special metallic arc electrodes have been developed to weld sheet copper, the most common are phosphor bronze, silicon bronze, and aluminum bronze.

For copper sheets ¼″ or less in thickness, the metallic arc actually is the simplest process to use. With this method it is possible to concentrate the heat and bring about instant fusion of the parent metal and electrode.

The welding procedure for welding copper is much the same as welding other metals with coated electrodes.

Joint design must include relatively large root openings and groove angles. Tight joints should be avoided to prevent buckling, poor penetration, slag inclusions, undercutting, and porosity. Copper backing strips are often advisable.

Welding Brass

Brass is a copper-zinc alloy. Since application of heat tends to vaporize the zinc, arc welding this metal is somewhat difficult. When the zinc volatilizes, the zinc fumes and oxides often obscure vision and make welding hard to perform. Furthermore, the formation of oxides produces a dirty surface which ruins the wetting properties of the molten metal.

To arc weld brass, use heavily coated phosphor-bronze electrodes. Be sure there is an abundance of fresh air circulating around the area to remove the harmful zinc oxide fumes. Best results will be obtained in welding brass if small deposits of metal are made at a time.

Welding Bronze

Bronze is a copper-tin alloy. It possesses higher mechanical properties than either brass or copper. Actually it has about the same mechanical properties as mild steel, but with the corrosion resistance of copper. Hence, bronze is often used in fabricating products requiring superior fatigue-resisting qualities.

Since the thermal conductivity of bronze is near that of steel, this metal can easily be welded. Either the carbon arc or metallic arc may be used. With the metallic arc process, a heavily coated phosphor-bronze electrode is necessary and the current set in reversed polarity. It is very important that the metal be absolutely clean to get sound welds.

Welding Monel and Inconel

Monel metal is an alloy containing approximately 67% nickel, 30% copper, and small quantities of other ingredients such as iron, aluminum, and manganese.

Inconel is an alloy having about 80% nickel, 15% chromium, and 5% iron.

Both Monel and Inconel are not hardened by regular heat treating processes. Their high strength is obtained by cold working such as rolling or drawing. These metals are extensively used as corrosion resisting linings in tanks and liquid carrying vessels.

Monel and Inconel can be welded with good results by the metallic arc process. The operation is performed almost with as much ease as in welding mild steel. Although these metals may be welded in any position, better results are obtained if welded in a flat position. In general, arc welding should not be attempted on sheets lighter than .050″ (18 gage).

The procedure for arc welding Monel or Inconel is as follows:

1. Remove the thin, darkly colored oxide film around the area to be welded. The oxide can be removed by grinding, sandblasting, rubbing with emery cloth, or pickling.

2. No preheating is necessary to arc weld these metals.

3. Use a heavy coated electrode es-

pecially designed for welding Monel and Inconel. Reverse polarity will produce the best results.

4. For welds in a flat position, hold the electrode at an angle of about 20° from the vertical, ahead of the puddle. In this position it is easier to control the molten flux and to eliminate slag trappings. To make welds in other positions, hold the electrode approximately at right angles to the plate.

5. Whenever it is necessary to withdraw the electrode, draw the arc slowly from the crater. Such a procedure permits a blanket of flame to cover the crater, protecting it from oxidation while the metal solidifies.

6. Avoid depositing wide beads. Hold the arc weaving motion to a minimum.

Points to Remember

Welding Aluminum

1. Use a heavy-coated electrode containing about 95 per cent aluminum and 5 per cent silicon.

2. Try to place the weld in a flat position.

3. Use a low current in reverse polarity.

4. Bevel the edges of metal ¼″ or more in thickness.

5. Use a brushing motion to start the electrode.

6. Keep the arc as short as possible and avoid any weaving motion.

7. Clean the bead after the weld is completed.

8. To weld aluminum casting, re-move all oil, grease, and dirt from the weld area.

9. Chip out a groove in the area to be welded.

10. Preheat casting between 500° and 800° F.

Welding Copper

1. Use metallic arc process on sheets ¼″ or less in thickness.

2. Use phosphor-bronze heavily coated electrodes.

3. Whenever possible use the carbon arc to weld heavy copper sections.

4. Carry out metallic arc process on copper the same as in welding mild steel.

Welding Brass

1. Use heavily coated phosphor-bronze electrodes.

2. Make small deposits of beads at a time.

3. Have plenty of fresh air circulating to remove harmful fumes.

Welding Bronze

1. Use heavily coated phosphor-bronze electrodes.

2. Set current in reversed polarity.

3. Clean edges to be welded.

4. Follow same technique as in welding mild steel.

Welding Monel and Inconel

1. Place metal in flat position if at all possible.

2. Do not weld sheets lighter than 18 gage in thickness.

3. Remove oxide film from surface to be welded.

4. Do not preheat.

5. Use heavily coated electrodes especially designed for these metals.

6. Use reverse polarity current.

7. Withdraw the arc slowly from the crater to prevent oxidation.

8. Deposit narrow beads.

QUESTIONS FOR STUDY AND DISCUSSION

1. What is meant by a non-ferrous metal?

2. What are some of the outstanding properties of aluminum?

3. What is the difference between non-heat-treatable and heat-treatable aluminum?

4. In the four digit system used to identify aluminum, what does each digit represent?

5. What temper designations are used for non-heat-treatable aluminum?

6. Why are some heat-treatable aluminum alloys difficult to weld?

7. What kind of an electrode should be used to weld non-heat-treatable aluminum?

8. When should the edges of aluminum be beveled for welding?

9. Why should a brushing motion be used in starting an aluminum electrode?

10. Why should the slag be removed from a weld made on aluminum?

11. What type of copper is the easiest to weld?

12. Why is the metallic arc process better for welding copper sheet less than ¼″ in thickness?

13. Why is it difficult to arc weld brass?

14. Brass is an alloy consisting of what elements?

15. What are the principal alloying ingredients in bronze?

16. What is the advantage of bronze over brass or copper?

17. What are the chief ingredients in Monel and Inconel?

18. What must be done to the surface of Monel and Inconel before welding?

19. When welding Monel or Inconel what type of current should be used?

20. In what position should the electrode be held when welding Monel and Inconel?

WELDING ASSIGNMENTS

Practice welding various types of joints using as many of the following metals as are available:

1. Aluminum
2. Copper
3. Bronze
4. Monel or Inconel

CHAPTER 15

Gas Shielded–Arc Welding
Gas Tungsten Arc–Tig

The primary consideration in any welding operation is to produce a weld that has the same properties as the base metal. Such a weld can only be made if the molten puddle is completely protected from the atmosphere during the welding process. Otherwise atmospheric oxygen and nitrogen will be absorbed in the molten puddle, and the weld will be porous and weak. In gas-shielded arc welding, a gas is used as a covering shield around the arc to prevent the atmosphere from contaminating the weld.

Originally gas-shielded arc welding was developed to weld corrosion resistant and other difficult-to-weld metals. Today the various gas-shielded arc processes are being applied to all types of metals. Gas-shielded arc welding will eventually displace much of the Shielded Metal-Arc and Oxy-

Fig. 1. The gas-shielded arc welding process is used extensively in missile and aerospace fabrication. (U.S. Army)

Acetylene production welding due to the superiority of the weld, greater ease of operation, and increased welding speed. In addition to manual welding, the process can be automated, and in either case can be used for both light and heavy gage ferrous and nonferrous metals. See Fig. 1.

Specific Advantages of Gas-shielded Arc

Since the shielding gas excludes the atmosphere from the molten puddle, welded joints are stronger, more ductile, and more corrosion-resistant than welds made by most other welding processes. The gas-shielded arc particularly simplifies the welding of nonferrous metals, since no flux is required. Whenever a flux is needed, there is always the problem of removing traces of the flux after welding. Furthermore, with the use of flux there is always the possibility that slag inclusions and gas pockets will develop.

Another advantage of the gas-shielded arc is that a neater and sounder weld can be made because there is very little smoke, fumes, or sparks to contend with. Since the shielding gas around the arc is transparent, the welder can clearly observe the weld as it is being made. Even more important, the completed weld is clean and free of the complications often encountered in other forms of metallic-arc welding.

Welding can be done in all positions with a minimum of weld spatter. Inasmuch as the weld surface is smooth, there is a substantial saving in production cost because little or no metal finishing is required. Also, there is less distortion of the metal near the weld.

Types of Gas-Shielded Arc Processes

There are two general types of gas-shielded arc welding. Gas Tungsten-Arc (Tig), and Gas Metal-Arc (Mig). Each has certain distinct advantages, however both produce welds that are deep penetrating and relatively free from atmospheric contamination.

Most industrial metals can be welded easily with either the Tig or Mig process. These include aluminum, magnesium, low-alloy steel, carbon steel, stainless steel, copper, nickel, monel, inconel, titanium, and others.

Both welding processes can be semi-automatic or fully automatic. In semi-automatic the operator controls the speed of travel and direction. With the automatic process the weld size, weld length, rate of travel, start and stop are all controlled by the equipment.

TIG Welding

In the Gas-Tungsten Arc process, a virtually non-consumable tungsten electrode is used to provide the arc for welding. During the welding cycle a shield of inert gas expels the air from the welding area and prevents oxidation of the electrode, weld puddle, and surrounding heat-affected zone. See Fig. 2. In Tig Welding, the electrode is used only to create the arc. It is not consumed in the weld. In this way it differs from the regular Shielded Metal-Arc process, where the stick electrode is consumed in the weld. For joints where addi-

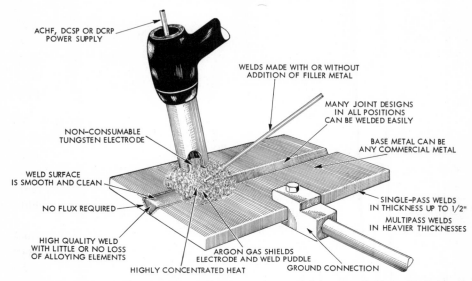

ACHF, DCSP OR DCRP
POWER SUPPLY

WELDS MADE WITH OR WITHOUT
ADDITION OF FILLER METAL

MANY JOINT DESIGNS
IN ALL POSITIONS
CAN BE WELDED EASILY

NON–CONSUMABLE
TUNGSTEN ELECTRODE

BASE METAL CAN BE
ANY COMMERCIAL METAL

WELD SURFACE
IS SMOOTH AND CLEAN

NO FLUX REQUIRED

SINGLE-PASS WELDS
IN THICKNESS UP TO 1/2"

MULTIPASS WELDS
IN HEAVIER THICKNESSES

HIGH QUALITY WELD
WITH LITTLE OR NO LOSS
OF ALLOYING ELEMENTS

ARGON GAS SHIELDS
ELECTRODE AND WELD PUDDLE

HIGHLY CONCENTRATED HEAT   GROUND CONNECTION

Fig. 2. In TIG welding, a non-consumable tungsten electrode is used. It is surrounded by a shield of inert gas. (Linde Co.)

tional weld metal is needed, a filler rod is fed into the puddle in a manner similar to welding with the Oxy-Acetylene flame process. See Fig. 3.

This type of welding is often referred to as "Heliarc" (Linde) or "Heliwelding" (Airco) which are manufacturers' tradenames.

Fig. 3. In TIG welding, when additional weld metal is needed, a filler rod is fed into the weld puddle. (Airco)

Welding Machines

Any standard DC or AC arc welding machine can be used to supply the current for Tig welding. However, it is important that the generator or transformer have good current control in the low range. This is necessary in order to maintain a stable arc. It is especially necessary when welding thin gage materials. If an old DC machine which has poor low range current control is to be used, then it is advisable to install a resistor in the ground line between the generator and the work bench. Such a resistor will enable the electrical system to provide a very low, stable arc.

An AC machine must be equipped with a high frequency generator to supply an even current. Remember that in an AC welder, the current is constantly reversing its direction. Every time the current flow changes direction, there is a very short interval when no current is flowing. This causes the arc to be unstable, and sometimes go out. With a high frequency generator in the system a more even current flow is possible. This stabilizes the arc.

Both the resistor for the DC machine, and the high frequency generator for the AC welder can be obtained from most welding equipment dealers. Automatic or semi-automatic controls are also manufactured. These can be installed on the machines to regulate the flow of gas and the water supply for cooling.

Specially designed machines for tungsten-inert gas welding with all of the necessary controls are available. Many power supply units are made to produce both AC and DC current. See Figs. 4 and 5. See section on Welding Machines—Chapter 3.

The choice of an AC or DC machine depends on weld characteristics that may be required. Some metals

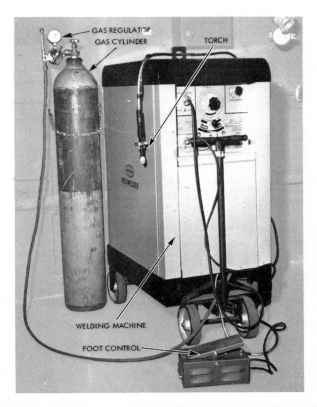

Fig. 4. A complete facility for tungsten inert gas (TIG) welding. (Miller Electric Mfg. Co.)

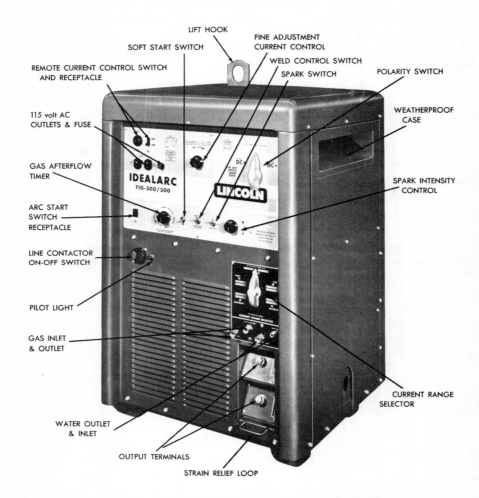

LIFT HOOK

FINE ADJUSTMENT
CURRENT CONTROL

SOFT START SWITCH

WELD CONTROL SWITCH

REMOTE CURRENT CONTROL SWITCH
AND RECEPTACLE

SPARK SWITCH

POLARITY SWITCH

115 volt AC
OUTLETS & FUSE

WEATHERPROOF
CASE

GAS AFTERFLOW
TIMER

SPARK INTENSITY
CONTROL

ARC START
SWITCH
RECEPTACLE

LINE CONTACTOR
ON-OFF SWITCH

PILOT LIGHT

GAS INLET
& OUTLET

CURRENT RANGE
SELECTOR

WATER OUTLET
& INLET

OUTPUT TERMINALS

STRAIN RELIEF LOOP

Fig. 5. Special machines are manufactured to do TIG welding. (The Lincoln Electric Co.)

are joined more easily with AC current while with others better results are obtained when DC current is used. See Table I. To understand the effects of the two different currents an explanation of their behavior in a welding process is necessary.

Direct Current Reverse Polarity (DCRP). With direct current the weld-

ing circuit may be either straight or reverse polarity. When the machine is set for straight polarity the flow of electrons from the electrode to the plate exert considerable heat on the plate. In reverse polarity, the flow of electrons is from the plate to the electrode, thus causing a greater concentration of heat at the electrode. See

TABLE I

Current Selection for TIG Welding

Metal	AC Current with High Frequency Stabilization	DC Current	
		Straight Polarity	Reverse Polarity
Magnesium up to 1/8 in. thick	1	N.R.	2
Magnesium above 3/16 in. thick	1	N.R.	N.R.
Magnesium Castings	1	N.R.	2
Aluminum	1	N.R.	2
Aluminum Castings	1	N.R.	N.R.
Stainless Steel up to 0.050 in.	1	2	N.R.
Stainless Steel 0.050 in. and up	2	1	N.R.
Brass Alloys	2	1	N.R.
Silver	2	1	N.R.
Hastelloy Alloys	2	1	N.R.
Silver Cladding	1	N.R.	N.R.
Hard-Facing	1	2	N.R.
Cast Iron	2	1	N.R.
Low Carbon Steel 0.015 in. to 0.030 in.	2	1	N.R.
Low Carbon Steel 0.030 in. to 0.125 in.	N.R.	1	N.R.
High Carbon Steel 0.015 in. to 0.030 in.	2	1	N.R.
High Carbon Steel 0.030 in. and up	2	1	N.R.
Deoxidized Copper up to 0.090 in.	N.R.	1	N.R.

Key: 1. Excellent Operation — best recommendation.

2. Good Operation — second recommendation.

N.R. Not recommended.

Fig. 6. The intense heat at the electrode tends to melt off the end of the electrode and contaminate the weld. Hence, for any given current DCRP requires a larger diameter electrode than DCSP. For example, a 1/16″ diameter tungsten electrode normally can handle about 125 amperes in a straight-polarity circuit. However, if reverse polarity is used with this amount of current the tip of the electrode would melt off. Consequently a ¼″ diameter electrode would be required to handle 125 amperes of welding current.

Polarity also affects the shape of

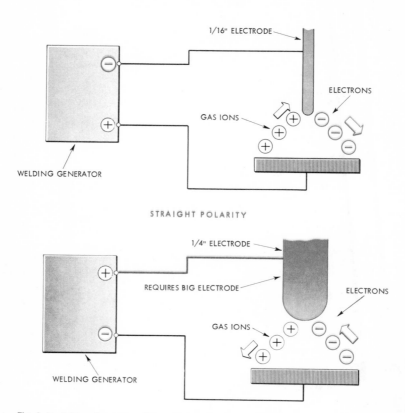

Fig. 6. Straight and reverse polarity in direct current welding.

the weld. DCSP produces a narrow deep weld whereas DCRP with its larger diameter electrode and lower current forms a wide and shallow weld. See Fig. 7. For this reason DCRP is never used in gas tungsten-arc welding except in rare occasions for welding aluminum and magnesium. These metals have a heavy oxide coating which is more readily removed by the greater current cleaning action of DCRP. The same cleaning action is present in the reverse-polarity half of the A-C welding cycle. No other metals require the kind of cleaning action that is normally needed on aluminum and magnesium. The cleaning action develops because of a bombardment of positive charged gas ions that are attracted to the negative charged workpiece. These gas ions when striking the metal have sufficient power to break the oxide and dislodge it from the surface. Generally speak-

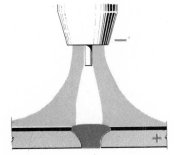

D C STRAIGHT POLARITY

DEEP PENETRATION-NARROW WELD

WELDING WITH DCSP PRODUCES DEEP PENETRATION
BECAUSE IT CONCENTRATES HEAT AT THE JOINT

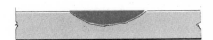

D C REVERSE POLARITY

SHALLOW PENETRATION-WIDE WELD

WELDING WITH DCRP PRODUCES GOOD CLEANING
ACTION BUT WELD PENETRATION IS SHALLOW

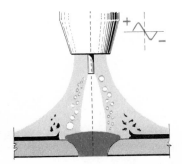

A C H F

DEEP PENETRATION-WIDE WELD

WELDING WITH ACHF COMBINES THE DESIRED CLEANING
ACTION, ON THE POSITIVE HALF OF EACH CYCLE, WITH
THE HEATING REQUIRED FOR GOOD WELD PENETRATION,
ON THE NEGATIVE SWING.

Fig. 7. The different types of operating current directly affect weld penetration, contour, and metal
transfer. (Linde Co.)

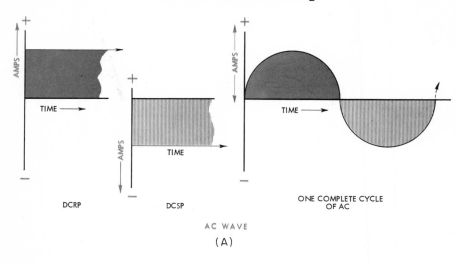

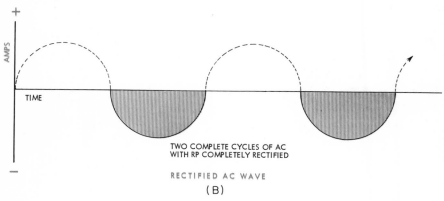

Fig. 8. Characteristic of an AC wave.

ing, better results are obtained in welding aluminum and magnesium with high frequency alternating current.

Direct Current Straight Polarity (DCSP). Direct current straight polarity is used for welding most metals because better welds are achieved. With the heat concentrated at the plate the welding process is more rapid, there is less distortion of the base metal, and the weld puddle is deeper and narrower than with DCRP. Since more heat is liberated at the puddle, smaller diameter electrodes can be used.

Alternating Current (ACHF). AC welding is actually a combination of DCSP and DCRP. Notice in Fig. 8A that half of each complete AC cycle is DCSP and the other half is DCRP. Unfortunately oxides, scale and moisture on the workpiece often tend to prevent the full flow of current in the reverse-polarity direction. If no current whatsoever flowed in the reverse-polarity direction, the current wave would resemble something as shown in Fig. 8B. During a welding operation the partial or complete stoppage of current flow (rectification) would cause the arc to be unstable and sometimes even go out. To prevent such rectification AC welding machines incorporate a high frequency current flow unit. The high-frequency current is able to jump the gap between the electrode and the workpiece piercing

the oxide film and forming a path for the welding current to follow.

Torches. Manually operated welding torches are constructed to conduct both the welding current and the inert gas to the weld zone. These torches are either air- or water-cooled. See Figs. 9 and 10. Air-cooled torches are designed for welding light gage materials where low current values are used. Water-cooled torches are recommended when the welding requires amperages over 200. A circulating stream of water flows around the torch to keep it from overheating. The tungsten electrode which supplies the welding current is held rigidly in the torch by means of a collet that screws into

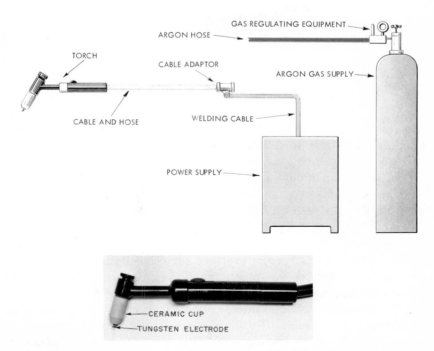

Fig. 9. An air-cooled torch is used for low current setting (below 200 amperes).

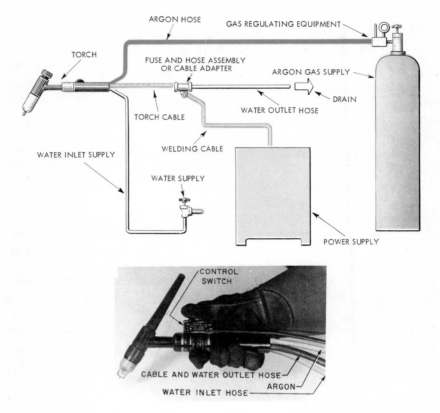

Fig. 10. When high current settings are used, a water-cooled torch is needed (above 200 amperes).

the body of the torch. A variety of collet sizes are available so different diameter electrodes can be used. Gas is fed to the weld zone through a nozzle which consists of a ceramic cup. Gas cups are threaded into the torch head to provide directional and distributional control of the shielding gas. The cups are interchangeable to accommodate a variety of gas flow rates. Some torches are equipped with a "gas lens" to eliminate turbulence of the gas stream which tends to pull in air and cause weld contamination. Gas lenses have a permeable barrier of concentric fine-mesh stainless steel screens that fit into the nozzle. See Fig. 11.

Pressing a control switch on the torch starts the flow of both current and gas. On some equipment the flow of current and gas is energized by a foot control. The advantage of the foot control is that the current flow can be better controlled as the end of the weld is reached. By gradually decreasing the current it is less likely for a cavity to remain in the end of the weld puddle and less danger of cutting short the shielding gas.

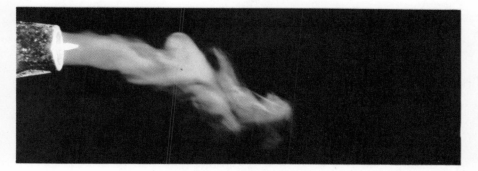

Gas stream of conventional Tig torch.

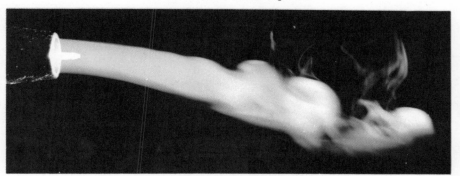

Gas stream of Tig torch with gas lens.

Fig. 11. Gas lens eliminate turbulence of the gas stream.

Gas cups vary in size. The size to be used depends upon the type and size of torch and the diameter of the electrode. See Table II. (It is a good practice to follow the manufacturer's recommendations.)

TABLE II
Approximate Cup Orifice for Tig Welding

TUNGSTEN ELECTRODE DIAMETER	CUP ORIFICE DIAMETER
$\frac{1}{16}$	$\frac{1}{4} - \frac{3}{8}$
$\frac{3}{32}$	$\frac{3}{8} - \frac{7}{16}$
$\frac{1}{8}$	$\frac{7}{16} - \frac{1}{2}$
$\frac{3}{16}$	$\frac{1}{2} - \frac{3}{4}$

TABLE III
Tig Welding—Aluminum

Stock Thickness (inch)	Type of Joint	Amperes, AC Current			Electrode Diameter (inch)	Argon Flow 20 psi		Filler Rod Diameter (inch)
		Flat	Horizontal & Vertical	Overhead		lpm	cfh	
1/16	Butt	60–80	60–80	60–80	1/16	7	15	1/16
	Lap	70–90	55–75	60–80	1/16	7	15	1/16
	Corner	60–80	60–80	60–80	1/16	7	15	1/16
	Fillet	70–90	70–90	70–90	1/16	7	15	1/16
1/8	Butt	125–145	115–135	120–140	3/32	8	17	1/8
	Lap	140–160	125–145	130–160	3/32	8	17	1/8
	Corner	125–145	115–135	130–150	3/32	8	17	1/8
	Fillet	140–160	115–135	140–160	3/32	8	17	1/8
3/16	Butt	190–220	190–220	180–210	1/8	10	21	5/32
	Lap	210–240	190–220	180–210	1/8	10	21	5/32
	Corner	190–220	180–210	180–210	1/8	10	21	5/32
	Fillet	210–240	190–220	180–210	1/8	10	21	5/32
1/4	Butt	260–300	220–260	210–250	3/16	12	25	3/16
	Lap	290–340	220–260	210–250	3/16	12	25	3/16
	Corner	280–320	220–260	210–250	3/16	12	25	3/16
	Fillet	280–320	220–260	210–250	3/16	12	25	3/16

psi — pounds per square inch   (Linde Co.)

lpm — liters per minute

cfh — cubic feet per hour

TABLE IV
Tig Welding—Stainless Steel

Stock Thickness (inch)	Type of Joint	Amperes, DC Current—Straight Polarity			Electrode Diameter (inch)	Argon Flow 20 psi		Filler Rod Diameter (inch)
		Flat	Horizontal & Vertical	Overhead		lpm	cfh	
1/16	Butt	80–100	70–90	70–90	1/16	5	11	1/16
	Lap	100–120	80–100	80–100	1/16	5	11	1/16
	Corner	80–100	70–90	70–90	1/16	5	11	1/16
	Fillet	90–110	80–100	80–100	1/16	5	11	1/16
3/32	Butt	100–120	90–110	90–110	1/16	5	11	1/16
	Lap	110–130	100–120	100–120	1/16	5	11	1/16
	Corner	100–120	90–110	90–110	1/16	5	11	1/16
	Fillet	110–130	100–120	100–120	1/16	5	11	1/16
1/8	Butt	120–140	110–130	105–125	1/16	5	11	3/32
	Lap	130–150	120–140	120–140	1/16	5	11	3/32
	Corner	120–140	110–130	115–135	1/16	5	11	3/32
	Fillet	130–150	115–135	120–140	1/16	5	11	3/32
3/16	Butt	200–250	150–200	150–200	3/32	6	13	1/8
	Lap	225–275	175–225	175–225	3/32	6	13	1/8
	Corner	200–250	150–200	150–200	3/32	6	13	1/8
	Fillet	225–275	175–225	175–225	3/32	6	13	1/8
1/4	Butt	275–350	200–250	200–250	1/8	6	13	3/16
	Lap	300–375	225–275	225–275	1/8	6	13	3/16
	Corner	275–350	200–250	200–250	1/8	6	13	3/16
	Fillet	300–375	225–275	225–275	1/8	6	13	3/16

(Linde Co.)

TABLE V
Tig Welding—Magnesium

Stock Thickness (inch)	Type of Joint	Amperes AC Current	Welding Rod Diameter (inch)	Argon Flow 15 psi		Remarks
		Flat Position		lpm	cfh	
0.040	Butt	45	3/32, 1/8	6	13	Backup
0.040	Butt	25	3/32, 1/8	6	13	No backing
0.040	Fillet	45	3/32, 1/8	6	13	
0.064	Butt	60	3/32, 1/8	6	13	Backup
0.064	Butt and Corner	35	3/32, 1/8	6	13	No backing
0.064	Fillet	60	3/32, 1/8	6	13	
0.081	Butt	80	1/8	6	13	Backup
0.081	Butt, Corner and Edge	50	1/8	6	13	No backing
0.081	Fillet	80	1/8	6	13	
0.102	Butt	100	1/8	9	19	Backup
0.102	Butt, Corner and Edge	70	1/8	9	19	No backing
0.102	Fillet	100	1/8	9	19	
0.128	Butt	115	1/8, 5/32	9	19	Backup
0.128	Butt, Corner and Edge	85	1/8, 5/32	9	19	No backing
0.128	Fillet	115	1/8, 5/32	9	19	
3/16	Butt	120	1/8, 5/32	9	19	1 pass
3/16	Butt	75	1/8, 5/32	9	19	2 passes
1/4	Butt	130	5/32, 3/16	9	19	1 pass
1/4	Butt	85	5/32	9	19	2 passes

(Linde Co.)

TABLE VI
Tig Welding—Silicon Bronze

Stock Thickness (inch)	Type of Joint	Amperes, DC Current—Straight Polarity			Electrode Diameter (inch)	Argon Flow 20 psi		Filler Rod Diameter (inch)
		Flat	Horizontal & Vertical	Overhead		lpm	cfh	
1/16	Butt	100-120	90-110	90-100	1/16	6	13	1/16
	Lap	110-130	100-120	100-120	1/16	6	13	1/16
	Corner	100-130	90-110	90-110	1/16	6	13	1/16
	Fillet	110-130	100-120	100-120	1/16	6	13	1/16
1/8	Butt	130-150	120-140	120-140	1/16	7	15	3/32
	Lap	140-160	130-150	130-150	1/16, 3/32	7	15	3/32
	Corner	130-150	120-140	120-140	1/16	7	15	3/32
	Fillet	140-160	130-150	130-150	1/16, 3/32	7	15	3/32
3/16	Butt	150-200	---	---	3/32	8	17	1/8
	Lap	175-225	---	---	3/32	8	17	1/8
	Corner	150-200	---	---	3/32	8	17	1/8
	Fillet	175-225	---	---	3/32	8	17	1/8
1/4	Butt	150-200	---	---	3/32	9	19	1/8, 3/16
	Lap	250-300	---	---	1/8	9	19	1/8, 3/16
	Corner	175-225	---	---	3/32	9	19	1/8, 3/16
	Fillet	175-225	---	---	3/32	9	19	1/8, 3/16

(Linde Co.)

TABLE VII
Tig Welding—Copper

Stock Thickness (inch)	Type of Joint	Amperes DC Current Straight Polarity	Electrode Diameter (inch)	Argon Flow 20 psi		Filler Rod Diameter (inch)
		Flat Position		lpm	cfh	
1/16	Butt	110–140	1/16	7	15	1/16
	Lap	130–150	1/16	7	15	1/16
	Corner	110–140	1/16	7	15	1/16
	Fillet	130–150	1/16	7	15	1/16
1/8	Butt	175–225	3/32	7	15	3/32
	Lap	200–250	3/32	7	15	3/32
	Corner	175–225	3/32	7	15	3/32
	Fillet	200–250	3/32	7	15	3/32
3/16	Butt	250–300	1/8	7	15	1/8
	Lap	275–325	1/8	7	15	1/8
	Corner	250–300	1/8	7	15	1/8
	Fillet	275–325	1/8	7	15	1/8
1/4	Butt	300–350	1/8	7	15	1/8
	Lap	325–375	1/8	7	15	1/8
	Corner	300–350	1/8	7	15	1/8
	Fillet	325–375	1/8	7	15	1/8

(Linde Co.)

TABLE VIII
Tig Welding—Plain Carbon and Low Alloy Steels

Stock Thickness (inch)	Amperes DC Current Straight Polarity	Filler Rod Diameter (inch)	Argon Flow 20 psi	
			lpm	cfh
0.035	100	1/16	4–5	8–10
0.049	100–125	1/16	4–5	8–10
0.060	125–140	1/16	4–5	8–10
0.089	140–170	1/16	4–5	8–10

(Linde Co.)

Electrodes

Basic diameters of non-consumable electrodes are $\frac{1}{16}''$, $\frac{3}{32}''$, and $\frac{1}{8}''$. They are either pure tungsten, or alloyed tungsten. The alloyed tungsten electrodes usually have one to two per cent thorium or zirconium. The addition of thorium increases the current capacity and electron emission, keeps the tip cooler at a given level of current, minimizes movement of the arc around the electrode tip, permits easier arc starting, and the electrode is not as easily contaminated by accidental contact with the workpiece. The two per cent thoria electrodes normally maintain their formed point for a greater period than the one per cent type. The higher thoria electrodes are used primarily for critical sheet

TABLE IX
Tig Welding—Gray Cast Iron

Stock Thickness (inch)	Type of Joint	Position	Welding Current		Filler Rod Diameter (inch)	Argon Flow 20 psi	
			Type	Amps.		lpm	cfh
1/4	Butt	Flat	*ACHF or **DCSP	160	3/16, 1/4	8	16
1/4	Butt	Vertical	ACHF	150	3/16	8	16
1/4	Butt	Overhead	ACHF	150	3/16	8	16
1	Butt	Flat	DCSP	300–350	3/16 - 1/4 for 1st and 2nd passes. Larger rod for remaining passes.	12	24

*AC High Frequency
**DC Straight Polarity

(Linde Co.)

TABLE X
Tig Welding—Nickel and Monel

Metal	Type of Joint	Stock Thickness (inch)	Argon Flow lpm	Welding Current DCSP
Nickel	Butt	1/8	12	200
Monel	Butt	1/8	12	200

(Linde Co.)

metal weldments in aircraft and missile industries. They have little advantage over the lower thoria electrode for most steel welds. The introduction of the "striped" electrode combines the advantage of the pure, low, and high thoriated tungsten electrodes. This electrode has a solid stripe of two per cent thoria inserted in a wedge the full length of the electrode.

The diameter of the electrode selected for a welding operation is governed by the welding current to be used. Larger diameter tungsten electrodes are required with reversed polarity than with straight polarity. See Tables III thru X for recommended sizes of electrodes, current, and material thickness for Tig welding.

Electrode Shapes

To produce good welds the tungsten electrode must be shaped correctly. The general practice is to use a pointed electrode with DC welding

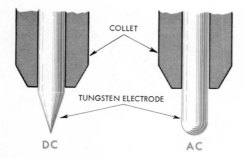

Fig. 12. Be sure the tungsten electrode is shaped properly.

and a spherical end with AC welding. See Fig. 12.

It is also important that the electrode be straight, otherwise the gas flow will be off center from the arc.

Shielding Gas

Shielding gas for gas tungsten-arc welding can be argon, helium, or a mixture of argon and helium. Argon is used more extensively because it is less expensive than helium. Argon is 1.4 times as heavy as air and 10 times as heavy as helium. There is very little difference between the viscosity of these two gases. Since argon is heavier than air it provides a better blanket over the weld. Moreover, there is less clouding during the welding process with argon and consequently it permits better control of the weld puddle and arc.

Argon normally produces a better cleaning action especially in welding aluminum and magnesium with alternating current. With argon there is a smoother and quieter arc action. The lower arc voltage characteristic of argon is particularly advantageous in welding thin material because there is less tendency for burning through the metal. Consequently, argon is used most generally for shielding purposes when welding materials up to 1/8″ in thickness both for manual welding and low-speed machine welding.

The use of argon also permits better control of the arc in vertical and overhead welding. As a rule, the arc is easier to start in argon than in helium and for a given welding speed the weld produced is narrower with a smaller heat-affected zone.

Where welding speed is important especially in machine welding or in welding heavy materials and metals having high heat conductivity helium is sometimes used. Higher welding speeds are possible with helium because higher-arc voltage can be obtained at the same current. Since the arc voltage in helium is higher, a lower current is possible to get the same arc power. Hence, welds can be made at higher speeds inasmuch as the increase in power comes from the increase in voltage rather than in current. A mixture of argon and helium is often used in welding metals that require a higher heat input. See Table XI for the recommended selection of gases.

Argon and helium are supplied in

TABLE XI
Selection of Gases

Al	MANUAL WELDING	ARGON	BETTER ARC STARTING, CLEANING ACTION AND WELD QUALITY; LOWER GAS CONSUMPTION
		HELIUM	HIGH WELDING SPEEDS POSSIBLE
	MACHINE WELDING	ARGON-HELIUM	BETTER WELD QUALITY, LOWER GAS FLOW THAN REQUIRED WITH STRAIGHT HELIUM
Mg	0-1/16"	HELIUM	CONTROLLED PENETRATION
	0-1/16" +	ARGON	EXCELLENT CLEANING, EASE OF PUDDLE MANIPULATION, LOW GAS FLOWS
Mild Steel	0-1/8"	ARGON	EASE OF MANIPULATION, FREEDOM FROM OVERHEATING
	0-1/8" +		(MIG PROCESS PREFERRED)
	SPOT WELDING	ARGON	GENERALLY PREFERRED FOR LONGER ELECTRODE LIFE BETTER WELD NUGGET CONTOUR EASE OF STARTING, LOWER GAS FLOW
		ARGON-HELIUM	HELIUM ADDITION IMPROVES PENETRATION ON HEAVY GAGE METAL
	MANUAL WELDING	ARGON	BETTER PUDDLE CONTROL, ESPECIALLY FOR POSITION WELDING
SS	MACHINE WELDING	ARGON	PERMITS CONTROLLED PENETRATION ON THIN GAGE MATERIAL (UP TO 14 GAGE)
		ARGON-HELIUM	HIGHER HEAT INPUT, HIGHER WELDING SPEEDS POSSIBLE ON HEAVIER GAGES
		ARGON-HYDROGEN (65% - 35%)	PREVENTS UNDERCUTTING, PRODUCES DESIRABLE WELD CONTOUR AT LOW CURRENT LEVELS, REQUIRES LOWER GAS FLOWS
		HELIUM	PROVIDES HIGHEST HEAT INPUT AND DEEPEST PENETRATION
Cu & Ni Cu — Ni Alloys (Monel & Inconel)		ARGON	EASE OF OBTAINING PUDDLE CONTROL, PENETRATION, AND BEAD CONTOUR ON THIN GAGE METAL
		ARGON-HELIUM	HIGHER HEAT INPUT TO OFFSET HIGH HEAT CONDUCTIVITY OF HEAVIER GAGES
		HELIUM	HIGHEST HEAT INPUT FOR HIGH WELDING SPEED ON HEAVY METAL SECTIONS
Ti		ARGON	LOW GAS FLOW RATE MINIMIZE TURBULENCE AND AIR CONTAMINATION OF WELD; IMPROVED METAL TRANSFER; IMPROVED HEAT AFFFCTED ZONE
		HELIUM	BETTER PENETRATION FOR MANUAL WELDING OF THICK SECTIONS (INERT GAS BACKING REQUIRED TC SHIELD BACK OF WELD AGAINST CONTAMINATION)
Si Bronze		ARGON	REDUCES CRACKING OF THIS 'HOT SHORT' METAL
Al Bronze		ARGON	LESS PENETRATION OF BASE METAL

steel cylinders containing approximately 330 cubic feet at a pressure of 2000 pounds per square inch. Either a single or two stage regulator may be used to control the gas flow or a specially designed regulator containing a flowmeter, as shown in Fig. 13, is used. The advantage of the flowmeter

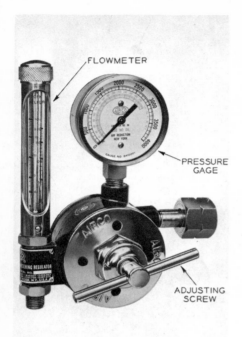

Fig. 13. An argon regulator with flowmeter. (Air Reduction Sales Co.)

the welder from arc radiation. The shade of the lens to be used depends upon the intensity of the arc.

Besides the regulation helmet, protective clothing such as an apron and gloves must be worn whenever welding with the gas tungsten arc.

The Filler Rod

Whenever a joint is to be reinforced, a filler rod is added to the molten puddle. In general, the diameter of the filler rod should be about the same as the thickness of the metal to be welded. For sound welds, it is important that the physical properties of the rod be similar to the base metal.

Joint Preparation

Regardless of the type of joint used, proper cleaning of the metal is essential. All oxidation, scale, oil, grease, dirt, and other foreign matter must be removed.

The following are the most common joints designed for inert-gas-shielded arc welding:

1. Butt Joint—For light materials the *square-edge* butt joint, as shown in Fig. 14, is the easiest to prepare and can be welded with or without filler rod. If the weld is to be made without filler rod, extreme care must be taken to avoid burning through the metal.

The *single-vee butt joint* is prefer-

is that it provides better gas flow control. The flowmeter is either calibrated to show the flow of gas in cubic feet per hour (cfh) or liters per minute (lpm).

The correct flow of argon to the torch is controlled by turning the adjusting screw on the regulator. The rate of flow required depends on the kind and thickness of the metal to be welded. See Tables III thru X.

Protective Equipment

A helmet like the one used in metallic arc welding is required to protect

Fig. 14. Square-edge butt joint.

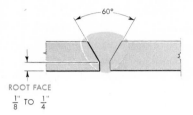

Fig. 15. Single-vee butt joint.

tact along the entire length of the joint as shown in Fig. 17. On metal ¼" or less in thickness, the weld can be made with or without filler rod. As a rule, the lap joint is not recommended for material exceeding ¼" in thickness.

3. Corner Joint—On light material up to ⅛" in thickness, no filler rod is

able on material ranging in thickness from ⅜" to ½" in order to secure complete penetration. The included angle of the vee should be approximately 60° with a root face of about ⅛" to ¼" as illustrated in Fig. 15.

A *double-vee butt joint* is needed when the metal exceeds ½" in thickness and the design is such that the weld can be made on both sides. With a double-vee there is greater assurance

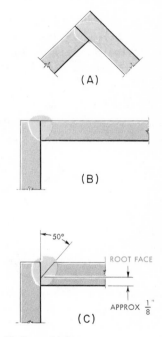

Fig. 18. Corner joints.

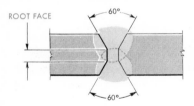

Fig. 16. Double-vee butt joint.

that penetration will be complete. See Fig. 16.

2. Lap Joint — The only special requirement for making a good lap weld is to have the pieces in close con-

required for a corner joint. With heavier metal the use of a filler rod is advisable. If the metal exceeds ¼", one edge of the joint should be beveled. See Fig. 18. The number of passes will depend on the size of the vee and the thickness of the metal.

4. T-Joint—Filler rod is necessary to weld T-joints regardless of the thickness of the metal. As a rule, a weld should be made on both sides of

Fig. 17. Lap joint.

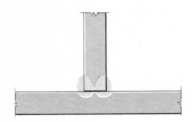

Fig. 19. T-joint.

the joint as illustrated in Fig. 19. The number of passes over the seam will depend on the thickness of the material and the size of the weld to be made.

5. Edge Joint — The edge joint is suitable only on very light material. No filler rod is needed to make this weld. See Fig. 20.

Fig. 20. Edge joint.

Backing the Weld

For many welding jobs, some suitable backing is necessary. On light gage metals, backing is used to protect the underside of the weld from atmospheric contamination and burning through. On heavier stock, backup bars draw some of the heat generated by the intense arc.

The type of material used for backup bars depends on the metal to be welded. Copper bars are suitable for stainless steel. When welding aluminum or magnesium, steel or stainless steel backup bars are needed.

The backup bar should be designed so it does not actually touch the weld zone. See Fig. 21.

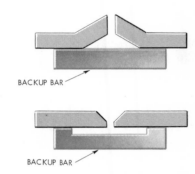

Fig. 21. A backup bar should not touch the weld zone.

Welding Procedure

Preliminary steps. Before starting to weld, follow these steps:

1. Check all electrical circuit connections to make sure they are tight.

2. Check for the proper diameter electrode and cup size. (Follow manufacturer's recommendations.)

3. Adjust the electrode so it extends about ⅛″ to 3⁄16″ beyond the end of the gas cup for butt welding and approximately ¼″ to ⅜″ for fillet welding. See Fig. 22.

4. Check the electrode to be certain that it is firmly held in the collet. Test it by placing the end against a solid surface and pushing the torch down gently but firmly. If the electrode moves into the nozzle, tighten the collet holder or gas cup.

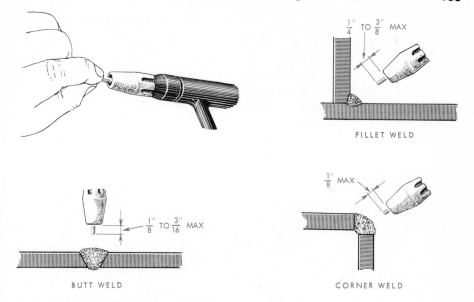

Fig. 22. Adjust the electrode so it extends beyond the edge of the gas cup.

5. Set the machine for the correct welding amperage.

6. If a water-cooled torch is to be used, turn on the water.

7. Turn on the inert gas and set to the correct flow.

Starting the arc. If you are using an AC machine, the electrode does not have to touch the metal to start the arc. To get the arc going, first turn on the welding current and hold the torch in a horizontal position about 2″

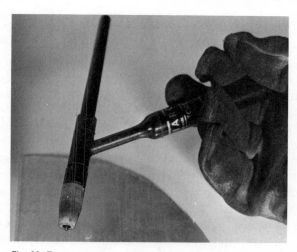

Fig. 23. To start the AC arc, first hold the torch in this manner.

above the work. See Fig. 23. Swing the end of the torch toward the workpiece so the end of the electrode is ⅛″ above the plate. The high-frequency current will jump the gap between the electrode and the plate, establishing the arc. *Be sure the downward motion is made rapidly* to provide the maximum amount of gas protection to the weld zone. See Fig. 24.

crease of current. With such a control it is easier to fill the crater completely and prevent crater cracks.

If you are using a water-cooled cup, do not allow the cup to come in contact with the work when the current is on. The hot gases may cause the arc to jump from the electrode to the cup instead of to the plate, thereby damaging the cup. Be sure, too, that

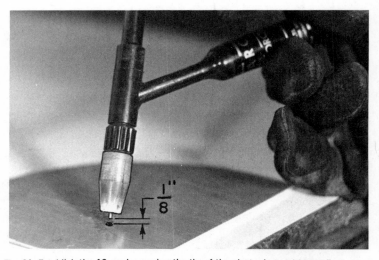

Fig. 24. Establish the AC arc by moving the tip of the electrode to within ⅛″ of the plate.

If a DC machine is used, hold the torch in the same position, but in this case the electrode must touch the plate to start the arc. When the arc is struck, withdraw the electrode so it is about ⅛″ above the workpiece.

To stop the arc on the AC or DC machine, snap the electrode back to the horizontal position. Make this movement rapidly to avoid marring or damaging the weld surface.

Some machines are equipped with a foot pedal to permit a gradual de-

the water flow is set according to the manufacturer's recommendations.

Welding a butt joint. Hold the torch at a 75° angle to the surface of the work as illustrated in Fig. 25. Preheat the starting point of the weld by moving the torch in small circles as shown in Fig. 26. As soon as the puddle becomes bright and fluid, move the torch slowly and steadily along the joint to form a uniform bead. No circular motion of the torch is necessary.

If the filler rod is to be added, hold

the rod about 15° from the work as shown in Figs. 25 and 27. As the puddle becomes fluid, move the arc to the rear of the puddle and add the rod by touching the leading edge of the puddle. Remove the rod and bring the arc back to the leading edge of the puddle. Repeat this sequence for the entire length of the seam.

To weld a butt joint in a vertical position, hold the torch perpendicular to the work. If no filler rod is to be

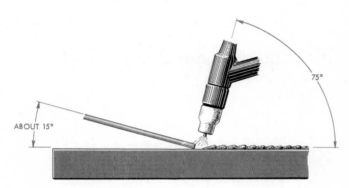

Fig. 25. Hold the torch at a 75° angle.

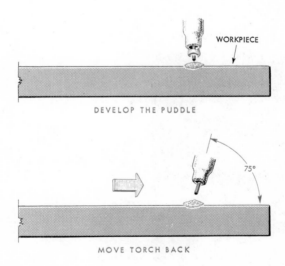

Fig. 26. Start the puddle by a circular movement of the torch. Once the puddle is formed, advance the puddle without circular motion.

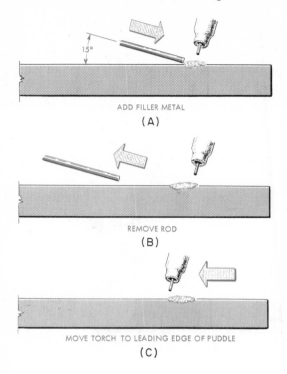

ADD FILLER METAL

(A)

REMOVE ROD

(B)

MOVE TORCH TO LEADING EDGE OF PUDDLE

(C)

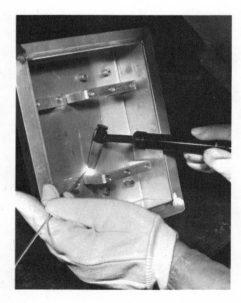

Fig. 27. Follow the steps in the top view in adding filler rod. The bottom view pictures step A during the welding operation.

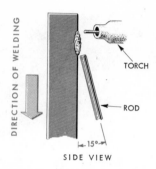

Fig. 28. Positions of the torch and rod for vertical welding.

seam with the end of the electrode just above the edge of the top sheet.

In welding a lap joint, you will find that the puddle forms a vee shape. The center of the vee is called a *notch,* and the speed at which this notch travels determines how fast the torch should be moved. Do not get ahead of it. See Fig. 29. Make certain that this notch is completely filled for the entire length of the seam. Otherwise there will be insufficient fusion and penetration.

used, start the weld at the top and simply progress downward. When filler rod is to be used, add it from the bottom or leading edge of the puddle. See Fig. 28.

Welding a lap and T-joint. To weld a lap or T-joint without filler rod, first form a puddle on the bottom piece. After the puddle is formed, shorten the arc to about $1/16''$. Then rotate the torch directly over the joint until the pieces are joined. After the welding is started, no further torch rotation is necessary. Move the torch along the

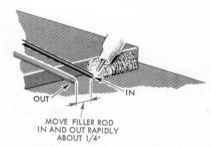

Fig. 30. Welding a lap joint with a filler rod.

If a filler rod is to be used on the lap joint, dip the end of the rod in and out of the puddle about every $1/4''$ travel of the puddle as shown in Fig. 30. Watch carefully to avoid laying bits of filler rod on the cold, unfused base metal. If you add just the right amount of rod at the correct moment, you will get a uniform bead of the proper proportions.

Welding a corner joint. A corner joint does not need any filler rod. Start the puddle at the beginning edge and move the torch straight along the seam. If you find that the molten metal has a tendency to roll off the

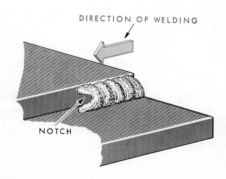

Fig. 29. Advance the torch just fast enough so the notch continues to form and move forward.

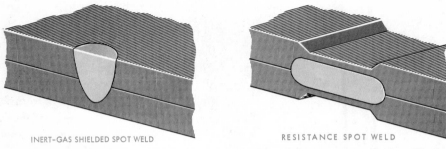

INERT-GAS SHIELDED SPOT WELD   RESISTANCE SPOT WELD

Fig. 31. A comparison of welds made by Tig spot welding and conventional resistance welding. (Airco)

edge, your speed is too slow. On the other hand, if the completed portion of the weld is rough and uneven, then your speed is too fast.

Tig Spot Welding

For many years spot welding was confined to the conventional process commonly referred to as resistance spot welding. With this method, the material to be joined is placed between two copper electrodes which are brought together, and when current is turned on, sufficient heat is generated to fuse the pieces together. The limitation of this process is that pressure must be applied on both sides of the pieces and the work has to be of size to conveniently feed into the spot welding machine.

The development of Tig spot welding now makes it possible to produce localized fusion similar to resistance spot welding without requiring accessibility to both sides of the joint. A special tungsten arc gun is applied to one side of the joint only. Heat is generated from resistance of the work to the flow of electrical current in a circuit of which the work is a part. A comparison of weld cross sections made by resistance spot welding and Tig spot welding is shown in Fig. 31.

The Tig spot welding process has a wide range of applications in fabricating sheet metal products involving joints which are impractical to resistance spot welding because of the location of the weld or the size of the parts or where welding can be made only from one side.

Equipment. Any DC power supply providing up to 250 amperes with a minimum open circuit voltage of 55 can be adapted for spot welding. The gun has a nozzle with a tungsten electrode. See Fig. 32. Various shape nozzles are available to meet particular job requirements. The standard nozzle can also be machined to permit access in tight corners or its diameter reduced to weld on items such as small holding clips. As a matter of fact the nozzle can be shaped for a variety of welding functions as indicated in Fig. 33.

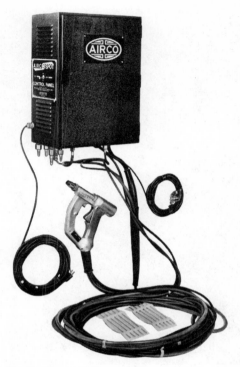

Fig. 32. Tig spot welding gun. (Airco)

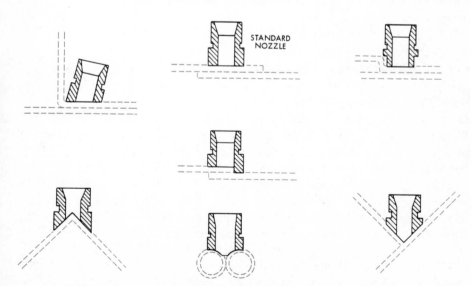

Fig. 33. Tig spot welding gun nozzle can be shaped for a variety of welding jobs. (Airco)

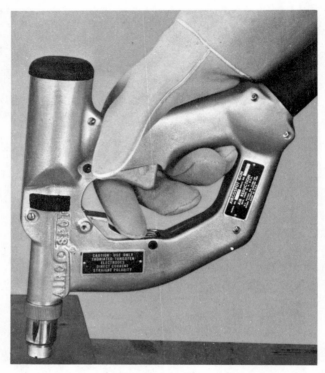

Fig. 34. To make a spot weld, the gun is placed against the work, and the trigger pulled. (Airco)

For most operations a ⅛″ diameter electrode is used. The end of the electrode should normally be flat and of the same diameter as the electrode. However, when working at low amperage settings (100 amperes or less) better results will be obtained if the end of the electrode is tapered slightly to provide a blunt point approximately one half the diameter of the electrode. This will prevent the arc from "wandering."

Whenever the end of the electrode "balls" excessively after only a few welds have been made, it is usually an indication of excessive amperage, dirty material, or insufficient shielding gas.

Making a Weld. To make a spot weld, the end of the gun is placed against the work and the trigger is pulled. See Fig. 34. Squeezing the trigger starts the flow of cooling water and shielding gas and also advances the electrode to touch the work. The electrode automatically retracts establishing an arc which is extinguished at the end of a preset length of time. The electrode is usually set at the factory to provide an arc length of ¹⁄₁₆″ which has been found to be generally satisfactory for practically all welding applications.

Amperage. The amperage required for a weld will naturally be governed by the thickness of the metal to be welded. The major effect of increasing the amperage, when both pieces are approximately the same thickness, is to increase the penetration. However,

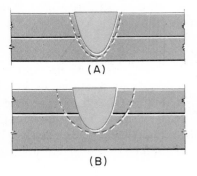

(A)

(B)

Fig. 35. Increasing the amperage will increase the weld diameter. (Airco)

in doing so it also tends to increase the weld diameter somewhat as shown by the dotted line in Fig. 35A. Increasing the amperage when the bottom part is considerably heavier than the top part will result in an increase in weld diameter with little or no increase in penetration as shown in Fig. 35B.

Weld Time. Weld time is set on the dial in the control cabinet. The dial is calibrated in 60ths of a second and is adjustable from 0 to 6 seconds. The effect of increasing the weld time is to increase the weld diameter. But in so doing it also increases the penetration somewhat as shown by the dotted lines in Fig. 35A.

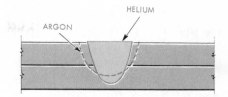

Fig. 36. The effects of shielding gas in making a spot weld. (Airco)

Shielding Gas. Helium will produce greater penetration than argon, although argon will produce a larger weld diameter. See Fig. 36. Gas flow should be set at approximately 6 cfh.

Surface Condition and Surface Contact. Mill scale, oil, grease, dirt, paint, and other foreign materials on or between the contacting surfaces will prevent good contact and reduce the weld strength. The space between

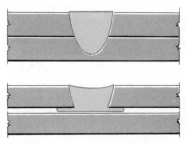

Fig. 37. Good surface contact is important in making a sound spot weld. (Airco)

the two contacting surfaces resulting from these surface conditions or poor fit-up acts as a barrier to heat transfer and prevents the weld from breaking through into the bottom piece. Consequently, good surface contact is important for sound welds. See Fig. 37.

Backing. Although inert-gas-shielded arc welding can be done from one side only, it is obvious that the bottom part must have sufficient rigidity to permit the two parts to be brought into contact with pressure applied by the gun. If the thickness, size or shape of the bottom part is such that it does not provide this rigidity, then some form of backing support or jigging will be required. Backing may be either of steel or copper.

Points to Remember

1. Tig welding can be used for joining practically all metals and alloys in various thicknesses and types of joints.

2. Be sure to use a cup of the correct size. Nozzles having too small an orifice tend to overheat and either crack or deteriorate very rapidly.

3. A water cooled torch is recommended for welding currents over 200 or 250 amperes.

4. Argon is generally the inert gas recommended for Tig welding.

5. The power source can be either a DC or AC machine. With a DC machine better penetration is usually obtained with straight polarity. For some metals better welds are made with an AC machine having a high-frequency voltage.

6. The diameter of the electrode depends on the kind and thickness of the metal to be welded. Make certain the tip is properly shaped for the type of current used.

7. When welding light gage metals, it is often necessary to use backup bars.

8. Before starting to weld, always check to make sure the electrode extends the correct distance.

9. Follow the recommendations for the correct gas flow, otherwise the shielding gas will not be effective.

10. If filler rod is to be used, be sure it is of the right diameter.

11. Always make sure water is flowing before attempting to operate the shielded-gas spot welding gun.

12. Never attempt to adjust the tungsten electrode in the spot welding gun without first shutting down the DC power supply machine.

QUESTIONS FOR STUDY AND DISCUSSION

1. What are some of the advantages of gas-shielded arc welding compared to other welding processes?

2. What is meant by Tig welding?

3. What kind of metal can be welded with the Tig process?

4. When is a filler rod used in Tig welding?

5. In Tig welding, what type of power supply unit may be used?

6. Why should an AC machine be of the high-frequency type?

7. What kind of polarity is used in Tig welding?

8. What determines whether an air-cooled or water-cooled torch is used?

9. Why is it important to use a cup of the correct size?

10. What is meant by an inert gas?

11. Why is argon generally considered a better shielding gas for Tig welding than helium?

12. What is the function of a flowmeter in a gas regulator assembly?

13. In Tig welding, what results can be expected when DCRP or DCSP current is used?

14. What determines the size of the tungsten electrode to be used for welding?

15. What should be the shape of the tungsten electrode for DC and AC welding?

16. How is the arc started and stopped in Tig welding?

17. How far should the electrode extend beyond the end of the gas cup on the torch?

18. What is the proper torch angle for welding a butt joint?

19. What precaution should be observed when using a water-cooled torch?

20. When using a filler rod, how should it be manipulated?

21. What is the advantage of Tig spot welding over the conventional resistance spot welding?

22. What type of equipment is required for Tig spot welding?

23. What diameter tungsten electrode is normally used for Tig spot welding?

24. How is the penetration affected by increasing or decreasing the amperage in Tig spot welding?

25. What is meant by "weld-time" in Tig spot welding?

26. What inert gases are used for spot welding?

27. Why must there be good surface contact for proper Tig spot welding?

28. When is backing or jigging necessary in Tig spot welding?

WELDING ASSIGNMENTS

Practice Tig welding $\frac{1}{16}''$ and $\frac{1}{8}''$ metals of the following types: low carbon steel, stainless steel, aluminum.

1. Run straight beads on flat piece.

2. Weld butt joint.

3. Weld lap joint.

4. Weld T-joint.

5. Weld corner joint.

CHAPTER 16

Gas Shielded-Arc Welding

Gas Metal Arc—Mig

The Gas Metal Arc welding process (Mig) uses a continuous consumable wire electrode. The molten weld puddle is completely covered with a shield of gas. The wire electrode is fed through the torch at pre-set controlled speeds. The shielding gas is also fed through the torch. See Fig. 1.

Fig. 1. High temperature electric arc melts advancing wire electrode into a globule of liquid metal. Wire is fed mechanically through the torch. Arc heat is regulated by conditions pre-set on the power supply. (Linde Co.)

The welding can be completely automatic or semi-automatic. When completely automatic, the wire feed, power setting, gas flow and travel over the workpiece are pre-set and function automatically. When semi-automatic, the wire feed, power setting and gas flow are pre-set, but the torch is manually operated. The welder directs the torch over the weld seam, holding the correct arc-to-work distance and speed. See Figs. 2 and 3.

Mig welding is sometimes referred to by the tradename of the manufacturer such as "Micro-wire Welding" (Hobart), "Aircomatic Welding" (Airco), "Sigma Welding" (Linde), and "Millermatic Welding" (Miller).

Specific Advantages of Mig Welding

The following are considered to be some of the more important advantages of Mig welding:

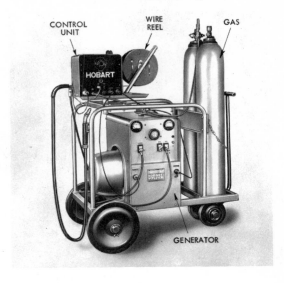

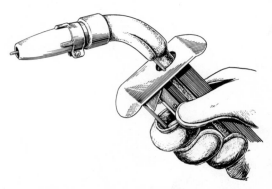

Fig. 2. A semi-automatic welder. (Hobart Brothers Co.)

1. Since there is no flux or slag and very little spatter to remove, there is a considerable saving in total welding cost. Generally speaking, weld cleanup is often more costly than actual welding time.

2. Less time is required to train an operator. As a matter of fact welding operators who are proficient in other welding processes can usually master the technique of Mig welding in a matter of hours. All the operator has to do is pull the gun trigger and weld. His main concern is to watch the angle of the welding gun and speed of travel.

3. The welding process is faster especially when compared with metallic arc stick welding. There is no need to start and stop in order to change electrodes. As a rule weld failures are often due to the starting and stopping of welding, since this condition in-

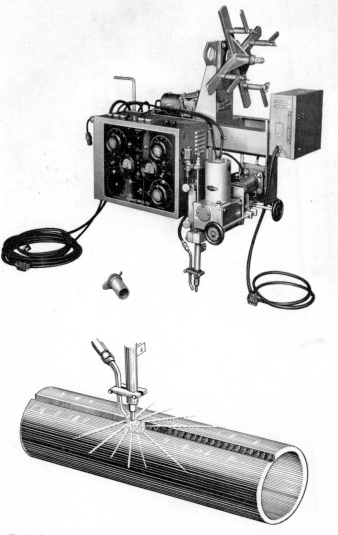

Fig. 3. One of the many types of automatic welders. (Hobart Brothers Co.)

duces slag inclusions, cold lapping and crater cracking.

4. Because of the high speed of the Mig process, better metallurgical benefits are imparted to the weld area. With faster travel there is a narrower heat-affected zone and consequently less molecular disarrangement, less grain growth, less heat transfer in the parent metal, and, even more important, greatly reduced distortion.

5. Although originally Tig welding

was considered more practical for welding thin sheet, because of its lower current, the development of the short circuiting transfer technique now makes it possible to weld thin stock equally as effectively with the Mig process.

6. Since Mig welding has deep penetrating characteristics, narrower beveled joint design can be used. Furthermore, the size of fillet welds is reduced by comparison to other welding methods.

Welding Current

Different welding currents have a profound effect on the results obtained in gas metal-arc welding. Optimum efficiency is achieved with direct current reverse polarity (DCRP). See Fig. 4. The heat in this instance is concentrated at the weld puddle and therefore provides deeper penetration at the weld. Furthermore, with DCRP there is greater surface cleaning action which is important in welding metals having

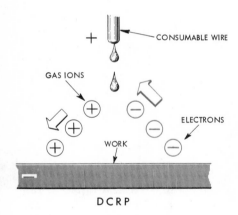

DCRP

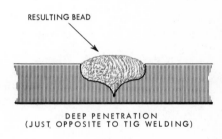

DEEP PENETRATION
(JUST OPPOSITE TO TIG WELDING)

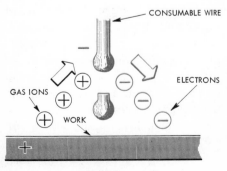

DCSP

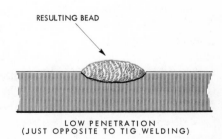

LOW PENETRATION
(JUST OPPOSITE TO TIG WELDING)

Fig. 4. Effects of polarity in Mig welding.

heavy surface oxides such as aluminum and magnesium.

Straight polarity (DCSP) is very impractical with Mig welding because weld penetration is wide and shallow, spatter is excessive, and there is no surface cleaning action. The ineffectiveness of straight polarity largely results from the pattern of metal transfer from the electrode to the weld puddle. Whereas in reverse polarity the transfer is in the form of a fine spray, with straight polarity the transfer is largely of the erratic globular type. The use of AC current is never recommended since the burn-offs are unequal on each half-cycle.

Types of Metal Transfer

When welding with consumable wire electrodes, the transfer of metal is achieved by three methods: spray transfer, globular transfer, and short circuiting transfer. The type of metal transfer that occurs will depend on electrode wire size, shielding gas, arc voltage, and welding current.

Spray transfer. In spray transfer very fine droplets or particles of the electrode wire are rapidly projected through the arc plasma from the end of the electrode to the workpiece in the direction in which the electrode is pointed. The droplets are equal to or smaller than the diameter of the electrode. While in the process of transferring through the welding arc, the metal particles do not interrupt the flow of current and there is virtually a constant spray of metal.

Spray transfer requires a high current density. With the higher current,

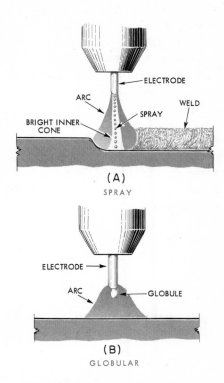

Fig. 5. Types of metal transfer. (Airco)

the arc becomes a steady quiet column having a well defined narrow incandescent cone-shape core within which metal transfer takes place. See Fig. 5A. The use of argon or a mixture of argon and oxygen is also necessary for spray transfer. Argon produces a pinching effect on the molten tip of the electrode, permitting only small droplets to form and transfer during the welding process.

With high heat input, heavy wire electrodes will melt readily and deep weld penetration becomes possible. Since the individual drops are small the arc is stable and can be directed where required. The fact that the metal transfer is produced by an axial force which is stronger than gravity, spray transfer is effective for out-of-position welding. It is particularly adapted for welding heavy gage metal. It is not too practical for welding light gage metal because of the resulting burn through.

Globular transfer. This type of transfer occurs when the welding current is low or below what is known as the transition current. The transition range extends from the minimum value where the heat melts the electrode to the point where the high current value induces spray transfer. Notice in Fig. 6, only a few drops are transferred per second at low current values, while many small drops are transferred at high current values.

In globular transfer the molten ball at the tip of the electrode tends to grow in size until its diameter is two or three times the diameter of the wire before it separates from the electrode and transfers across the arc to the workpiece. See Fig. 5B. As the globule moves across the arc it assumes an irregular shape and rotary motion because of the physical forces of the arc. This frequently causes the globule to

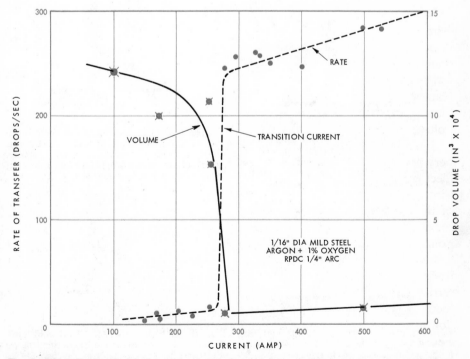

Fig. 6. Effect of current on the size and frequency of drops transferred in an arc shielded by predominantly inert gas. (Airco)

reconnect with the electrode and workpiece, causing the arc to go out and then reignite. The result is poor arc stability, shallow penetration, and excessive spatter.

Short circuiting transfer. The short circuiting transfer permits welding thinner sections with greater ease and is extremely practical for welding in all positions.

With this process a shallow weld penetration is obtained. See illustrations in Fig. 7A-E. It is generally considered to be the most practical at current levels below 200 amperes with fine wire of .045″ or less in diameters. The use of fine wire produces weld pools that remain relatively small and are easily managed, making all-position welding possible.

As the molten wire is transferred to

Fig. 7A. Start of the SHORT ARC cycle-High temperature electric arc melts advancing wire electrode into a drop of liquid metal. Wire is fed mechanically through the welding torch. Arc heat is regulated by the power supply. (Linde Co.)

Fig. 7B. Molten electrode moves toward workpiece. Note cleaning action. Argon gas mixture, developed for SHORT ARC, shields molten wire and seam, insuring regular arc ignition, preventing spatter, and weld contamination. (Linde Co.)

Fig. 7D. Drop of molten wire breaks contact with electrode, causing arc to reignite. Electrode is broken by pinch force, a squeezing power common to all current carriers. Amount and suddenness of pinch is controlled by power supply. (Linde Co.)

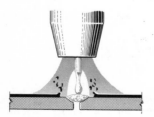

Fig. 7C. Electrode makes contact with workpiece, creating short circuit. Arc is extinguished, allowing to cool. Frequency of arc extinction in SHORT ARC varies from 20 to 200 times per second, according to job requirements. (Linde Co.)

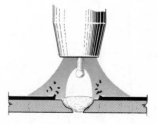

Fig. 7E. With arc renewed, SHORT ARC cycle begins again. Because of precision control of arc characteristics and cool, uniform operation, SHORT ARC produces perfect welds on metals as thin as .030-in. carbon or stainless steel. (Linde Co.)

the weld, each drop touches the weld puddle before it has broken away from the advancing electrode wire. The circuit is "shorted," and the arc is extinguished.

Electromagnetic "pinch force" squeezes the drop from the wire. The short circuit is broken and the arc re-ignites. "Shorting" occurs from 20 to 200 times a second according to preset controls. "Shorting" of the arc pinpoints the effective heat. The result is a small, relatively cool weld puddle which reduces burn-through. Intricate welds are possible in most all of the positions.

In *short-arc welding,* the shielding gas mixture consists of 25 per cent carbon dioxide, which provides increased heat for higher speeds, and 75 per cent argon which controls spatter. However, considerable usage is now

being made of straight CO_2 where bead contour is not particularly important but good penetration is very essential.

Mig Welding Equipment

The Gas-Metal Arc welding equipment consists of four major units: power supply, wire feeding mechanism, welding gun, and gas supply. See Fig. 8.

Power supply. The recommended machine for Mig welding is a rectifier or motor generator supplying direct current with normal limits of 200-250 amperes for all position welding. Direct current reverse polarity (DCRP) is used for optimum efficiency. DCRP contributes to better melting, deeper penetration, and excellent cleaning action.

Constant current versus constant

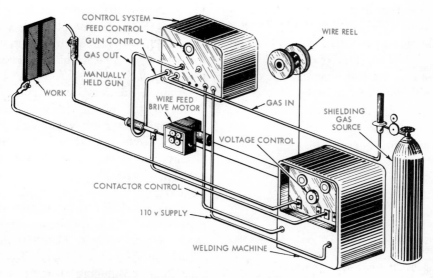

Fig. 8. Mig welding unit. (Hobart Brothers Co.)

potential power supply. In Mig welding, heat is generated by the flow of current through the gap between the end of the wire electrode and the workpiece. A voltage forms across this gap which varies with the length of the arc. To produce a uniform weld, the welding voltage and arc length must be maintained at a constant value. This can be accomplished by (1) feeding the wire into the weld zone at the same rate at which it melts, or (2) melting the wire at the same rate it is fed into the weld zone.

With the conventional constant current welding machine used for many years in shielded metal-arc (stick) welding, the power source produces a constant current over a range of welding voltages. The current has a steep drooping volt-ampere characteristic. See Fig. 9. Remember, the volt-amp characteristic actually shows what occurs at the terminal of the welder (electrode) as the load on the power source varies. It indicates how voltage changes in its relationship to amperage between the "open circuit" stage (static electrical potential but no current flowing) and the "short cir-

cuit" condition (electrode touching the work). When an arc is struck with a power source having a drooping arc voltage the electrode is shorted to the workpiece. The highest voltage potential is present when the circuit is open and no current is flowing. This provides the maximum initial voltage to start the arc. As soon as the arc is struck, the amperage shoots up to maximum and the voltage drops to minimum. Then as the electrode is moved, the voltage rises to maintain the arc and the amperage drops to its normal working level. During welding, the voltage automatically varies directly and amperage inversely with the length of the welding arc. Consequently, the operator can keep reasonable control over the heat input to the work.

When a conventional power source is used for Mig welding, the wire feed speed must be adjusted to narrow limits to prevent the wire from burning back to the nozzle or plunging into the weld plate. Although the operator can, by means of electronic speed controls, adjust the wire speed for a predetermined arc length, nevertheless, whenever the nozzle to work distance changes, the arc length (voltage) changes. Thus, if the nozzle to work distance increases, the arc length increases. The result is a nonuniform weld.

With the need for better arc control, the *constant voltage (potential) power supply* was developed. Constant potential welding power supply has a nearly flat volt-ampere characteristic. See Fig. 10. This means that the preset

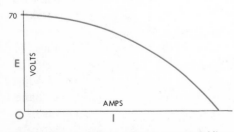

Fig. 9. The conventional constant current welding machine has a drooping volt-ampere characteristic. (Miller Electric Manufacturing Co.)

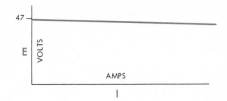

Fig. 10. The constant potential power supply has a nearly flat volt-ampere characteristic. (Miller Electric Manufacturing Co.)

voltage level can be held throughout its range. Although its static voltage potential at open circuit is lower than a machine with drooping characteristic, it maintains approximately the same voltage regardless of the amount of current drawn. Accordingly there is unlimited amperage to melt the consumable wire electrode. The power supply becomes self-correcting with respect to arc length. The operator can change the wire feed speed over a considerable range without affecting the stubbing or burning back the wire. In other words, the arc length can be set on the power supply and any variations in nozzle to work distance will not produce changes in the arc length. For example, if the arc length becomes shorter than the pre-selected value, there is an automatic increase of current and the wire speed automatically adjusts itself to maintain a constant arc length. Similarly, if the arc becomes too long, the current decreases and the wire begins to feed faster.

Stated in another way, when the wire is fed into the arc at a specific rate, a proportionate amount of current is automatically drawn. The constant potential welder therefore provides the necessary current required by the load imposed on it. When the electrode wire is fed faster, the current increases; if it is fed slower the current decreases.

Because of this self-correcting feature, less operator skill is necessary to achieve good welds. There are only two basic controls: a rheostat on the welding machine to regulate the voltage and a rheostat on the wire feed mechanism to control the speed of the wire feed motor.

Slope control. Some power supply units designed for Mig welding have provisions for controlling the slope. The incorporation of slope control gives the machine greater versatility. Thus by altering the flat shape of the slope it is possible to control the pinch force on the consumable wire which is particularly important in the short circuiting transfer method of welding. With better control of the short circuit, the weld puddle can be kept more fluid with better resulting welds. Slope control also helps to decrease the sudden current surge when the electrode makes its initial contact with the workpiece. By slowing down the rate of current rise, the amount of spatter can be reduced.

Wire feeding mechanism. The wire feeding mechanism automatically drives the electrode wire from the wire spool to the gun and arc. See Figs. 11 and 12. Control on the panel can be adjusted to vary the wire feeding speed. In addition, the control panel usually includes a welding power contactor and a solenoid to energize the gas flow. On units designed for welding with a water-cooled gun, a control

Fig. 11. Typical wire feeding unit for Mig welding. (Miller Electric Manufacturing Co.)

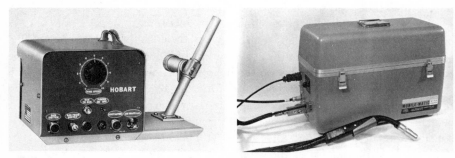

Fig. 12. Types of control panels on wire feed mechanisms.

is also available to turn on and shut off the water flow.

The wire feeder can be mounted on the power supply machine or it can be separate from the welding machine and mounted elsewhere to facilitate welding over a large area.

Welding gun. The function of the welding gun is to deliver the wire, shielding gas, and welding current to the arc area. The manually operated gun is either water- or air-cooled. An air-cooled gun is especially designed to weld light gage metals that require less than 200 amperes with argon as a shielding gas. However, such a torch can usually function at higher amperage (300) with CO_2 because of the cooling effects of this gas. A water-cooled gun generally is best when welding with currents that are higher than 200 amperes.

Guns are either of the push or pull type. The pull gun uses drive rolls in the gun that pulls the welding wire from the wire feeder, and the push gun has the wire pushed to it by drive rolls in the wire feeder itself. The pull gun handles small diameter wires; the push gun moves heavier diameter wires. The pull type is also used to weld with soft wires such as aluminum and magnesium while the push gun is considered more suitable for welding with hard wires such as carbon and stainless steels and where currents are often in excess of 250 amperes. Both guns have a trigger switch that controls the wire feed and arc as well as the shielding gas and water flow. When the trigger is released the wire feed, arc, shielding gas, and water, if a water-cooled torch is used, stop immediately. With some equipment a timer is in-

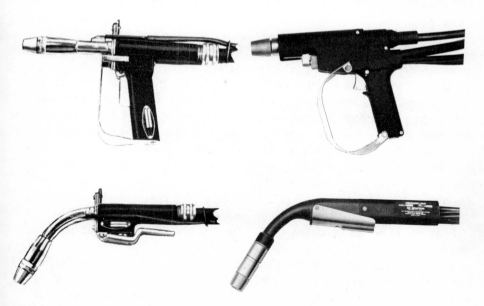

Fig. 13. Types of guns used for Mig welding.

cluded to permit the shielding gas to flow for a predetermined time to protect the weld until it solidifies.

Guns are available with a straight or curved nozzle. See Fig. 13. The curved nozzle provides easy access to intricate joints and difficult to weld patterns.

Shielding Gas*

In any gas shielded arc welding process, the shielding gas can have an appreciable effect upon the properties of a weld deposit. Therefore, welding is done in a controlled atmosphere. In shielded metal-arc welding, this is accomplished by placing a coating on the electrode which produces a non-harmful atmosphere when it disintegrates in the welding arc. In the case of Mig welding, the same effect is accomplished by surrounding the arc area with gases supplied from an external source. See Table I.

The air in the arc area is displaced by the shielding gas. The arc is then struck under the blanket of shielding gas and the welding is accomplished. Since the molten weld metal is exposed only to the shielding gas it is not contaminated and strong dense weld deposits are obtained. The reason for shielding the arc area is to prohibit air from coming in contact with the molten steel.

By volume, air is made up of 21 per cent oxygen, 78 per cent nitrogen, 0.94 per cent argon, and 0.04 per cent other gases (primarily carbon dioxide). The atmosphere will also contain a certain amount of water depending upon its humidity. Of all of the elements that

are in the air, the three which cause the most difficulty as far as welding is concerned are oxygen, nitrogen, and hydrogen.

Oxygen is a highly reactive element and combines readily with other elements in the metal or alloy to form undesirable oxides and gases. The oxide-forming aspect of the oxygen can be overcome with the use of deoxidizers in the steel weld metal. The deoxidizers, such as manganese and silicon, combine with the oxygen and form a light slag which floats to the top of the weld pool. If the deoxidizers are not provided, the oxygen will combine with the iron and form compounds which can lead to inclusions in the weld material which can lower its mechanical properties. On cooling, the free oxygen in the arc area combines with the carbon of the alloy material and forms carbon monoxide. If this gas is trapped in the weld metal as it cools, it collects in pockets which cause pores or hollow spaces in the weld deposit.

Of all of the elements in the air, nitrogen causes the most serious problems in welding steel materials. When iron is molten, it is able to take a relatively large amount of nitrogen into solution. At room temperature, however, the solubility of nitrogen in iron is very low. Therefore, in cooling, the nitrogen precipitates or comes out of the iron as nitrites. These nitrites cause high yield strength, tensile strength, hardness, and a pronounced decrease in the ductility and impact resistance of the steel materials. The loss of duc-

*Courtesy Hobart Brothers Co.

TABLE I

Shielding Gases for Mig Welding

MATERIAL	PREFERRED GAS	REMARKS
Aluminum Alloys	1. Argon	With DC Reverse Polarity removes oxide surface on work piece.
Magnesium Aluminum Alloys	1. 75% He. 25% A.	Greater heat input reduces porosity tendencies. Also cleans oxide surface.
Stainless Steels	1. Argon + 1% O_2	Oxygen eliminates under-cutting when DC Reverse Polarity is used.
	2. Argon + 5% O_2	When DC straight polarity is used 5% O_2 improves arc stability.
Magnesium	1. Argon	With DC straight polarity removes oxide surface on work piece.
Copper (Deoxidized)	1. 75% He. 25% A. 2. Argon	Good wetting and increased heat input to counteract high thermal conductivity. Light gages.
Low Carbon Steel	1. Argon + 2% O_2	Oxygen eliminates under-cutting tendencies also removes oxidation.
Low Carbon Steel	1. Carbon Dioxide (spray Transfer)	High quality low current out of position welding low spatter.
	2. Carbon Dioxide (Buried Arc)	High speed low cost welding accompanied by spatter loss.
Nickel	1. Argon	Good wetting decreases fluidity of weld metal.
Monel	1. Argon	Good wetting decreases fluidity of weld metal.
Inconel	1. Argon	Good wetting decreases fluidity of weld metal.
Titanium	1. Argon	Reduces heat-affected zone, improves metal transfer.
Silicon Bronze	1. Argon	Reduces crack sensitivity of this hot short material.
Aluminum Bronze	1. Argon	Less penetration of base metal. Commonly used as a surfacing material.

NOTE: 1. — First Choice
2. — Second Choice

(Airco)

tility due to the presence of iron nitrites often leads to cracking in and adjacent to the weld metal. As stated above, air contains approximately 78 per cent nitrogen by volume and therefore, if the weld metal is not protected from the air during welding, very pronounced decreases in weld quality will occur. In excessive amounts, nitrogen can also lead to gross porosity in the weld deposit.

Hydrogen is also harmful to welding. Very small amounts of hydrogen in the atmosphere produce an erratic arc. Of more importance is the effect that hydrogen has on the properties of the weld deposit. As in the case of nitrogen, iron can hold a relatively large amount of hydrogen when it is molten but upon cooling it has a low solubility for hydrogen. As the metal starts to solidify, it rejects the hydrogen. Hydrogen that becomes entrapped in the solidifying metal collects at certain points and causes large pressures or stresses to occur. These pressures lead to minute cracks in the weld metal which can later develop into large cracks. Hydrogen also causes defects known as "fish eyes" and under-bead cracking.

The effects of oxygen, nitrogen, and hydrogen make it essential that they are excluded from the weld area during welding. This is done by using inert gases for shielding. The inert gases consist of atoms which are very stable and do not react readily with other atoms. In nature there are only six elements possessing this stability and each of these elements exists as a gas. The six inert gases are helium, neon, argon, krypton, xenon and radon. Since the inert gases do not readily form compounds with other elements, they are very useful as shielding atmospheres for arc welding. Of the six inert gases only helium and argon are important to the welding industry. This is because they are the only two which can be obtained in quantities at an economical price.

Carbon dioxide gas can also be used for shielding the weld area. Although it is not an inert gas, compensations can be made for its oxidizing tendencies and it can readily be employed for shielding the weld. Characteristics of this gas will be explained in detail later.

Argon. Argon gas has been used for many years as a shielding medium for fusion welding. Argon is obtained by the liquification and distillation of air. Air contains approximately 0.94 per cent argon by volume or 1.3 per cent by weight. This seems like a small quantity, but calculations show that the amount of air covering one square mile of the earth's surface contains approximately 800,000 pounds of argon.

In manufacturing argon, air is put under great pressure and refrigerated to very low temperatures. Then, the various elements in air are boiled off by raising the temperature of the liquid. Argon boils off from the liquid at a temperature of $-302.4°F$. For welding the purity of the argon is approximately 99.995 per cent. When greater purity is required, the gas can be chemically cleaned to the purity of 99.999 per cent.

Argon has a relatively low ionization potential. This means that the welding arc tends to be more stable when argon is used in the shielding gas. For this reason argon is often used in conjunction with other gases for arc shielding. The argon gives a quiet arc and thereby reduces spatter. Since argon has a low ionization potential, the arc voltage is reduced when argon is added to the shielding gas. This results in lower power in the arc and therefore lower penetration. The combination of lower penetration and reduced spatter makes the use of argon desirable when welding sheet metal.

Straight argon is seldom used for arc shielding except in welding such metals as aluminum, copper, nickel, and titanium. When welding steel the use of straight argon gas leads to under-cutting and poor bead contour. Also, the penetration pattern obtained with pure argon is shallow at the bead edges and has a deep portion at the center of the weld. This can lead to lack of fusion at the root of the weld if the arm is not directed exactly over the center of the weld.

Argon plus oxygen. In order to re-duce the poor bead contour and pene-tration pattern obtained with argon gas when welding on mild steel, it has been found that the addition of oxygen to the shielding gas is desirable. Small amounts of oxygen added to the argon produce significant changes. Normally, the oxygen is added in amounts of 1, 2, or 5 per cent. Using gas metal-arc welding wires, the amount of oxygen which can be employed is limited to 5 per cent. Additional oxygen might lead to the formation of porosity in the weld deposit.

Oxygen improves the penetration pattern by broadening the deep pene-tration finger at the center of the weld bead. It also improves bead contour and eliminates the undercut at the edge of the weld that is obtained with pure argon when welding steel. Argon-oxy-gen mixtures are very common for welding low alloy steels, carbon steels, and stainless steel.

Carbon dioxide. Unlike argon or helium gases which are made up of single atoms, the carbon dioxide gas is made up of molecules. Each mole-cule contains one carbon atom and two oxygen atoms. The chemical formula for the carbon dioxide molecule is CO_2. Often, carbon dioxide is referred to simply as CO_2 gas.

At normal temperatures, carbon dioxide is essentially an inert gas. However, when subjected to high tem-peratures, carbon dioxide will dis-associate into carbon monoxide and oxygen. In the high temperature of the welding arc this disassociation takes place to the extent that 20 to 30 per cent of the gases in the arc area are oxygen (O_2). Because of this oxidizing characteristic of the CO_2 gas, the wires used with this gas must contain de-oxidizing elements. The deoxidizing elements have a great affinity for the oxygen and readily combine with it. This prevents the oxygen atoms from combining with the carbon or iron in the weld metal and producing low quality welds. The most common de-oxidizers used in wire electrodes are manganese, silicon, aluminum, titan-ium, and vanadium.

Carbon dioxide is manufactured in most plants from flue gases which are given off by the burning of natural gas, fuel oil, or coke. It is aso obtained as a by-product of calcining operations of lime kilns, from the manufacturing of ammonia, and from the fermentation of alcohol. The carbon dioxide given off by the manufacturing of ammonia and the fermentation of alcohol is al-most 100 per cent pure.

The purity of carbon dioxide gas can vary considerably depending upon the process used to manufacture it. However, standards have been set up for the purity that must be obtained in carbon dioxide gas that is to be used for arc welding. The purity specified for welding grade CO_2 is a minimum dew point of minus 40°F. This means that gas of this purity will contain approximately 0.0066 per cent moisture by weight.

Carbon dioxide gas eliminates many of the undesirable characteristics that are obtained when using argon for arc shielding. With the carbon dioxide a broad, deep penetration pattern is obtained. This makes it easier for the operator to eliminate weld defects such as lack of penetration and lack of fusion. Bead contour is good and there is no tendency towards undercutting. Another advantage of CO_2 shielding is its relatively low cost when compared to other shielding gases.

The chief drawback of the CO_2 gas is the tendency for the arc to be somewhat violent. This can lead to spatter problems when welding on thin materials where appearance is of particular importance. However, for most applications this is not a major problem and the advantages of CO_2 shielding far outweigh its disadvantages.

CO_2 is used primarily for mild steel welding, although it has some application in the formulation of other shielding gas mixtures.

Helium*. Helium is an inert gas and may be compared to argon in that respect. There the similarity ends. Helium has an ionization potential of 24.5 volts. It is lighter than air and has high thermal conductivity. The helium arc plasma will expand under heat (thermal ionization) reducing the arc density. With helium there is a simultaneous change in arc voltage where the voltage gradient of the arc length is increased by the discharge of heat from the arc stream or core. This means that more arc energy is lost in the arc itself and is not transmitted to the work. The result is that, with helium, there will be a broader weld bead with relatively shallower penetration than with argon. (For Tig welding, the opposite is true.) This also accounts for the higher arc voltage, for the same arc length, that is obtained with helium as opposed to argon.

Helium is derived from natural gas. The process by which it is obtained is similar to that of argon. First the natural gas is compressed and cooled. The hydrocarbons are drawn off, then nitrogen, and finally the helium. This is a process of liquifying the various gases until at −452°F., the helium is produced.

Helium has sometimes been in short supply due to governmental restrictions and, therefore, has not been used as much as it might have been for welding purposes. It is difficult to initiate an arc in a helium atmosphere with the tungsten arc process. The problem is less acute with the gas metal arc process.

Helium is used primarily for the non-ferrous metals such as aluminum, magnesium and copper. It is also used in combination with other shielding gases.

Argon-CO_2*. For some applications of mild steel welding, welding grade

---

CO_2 does not provide the arc characteristics needed for the job. This will usually manifest itself, where surface appearance is a factor, in the form of intolerable spatter in the weld area. In such cases a mixture of argon-CO_2 has usually eliminated the problem. Some welding authorities believe that the mixture should not exceed 25 per cent CO_2. Others feel that mixtures with up to 80 per cent CO_2 are practical.

The reason for wanting to use as much CO_2 as possible in the mixtures is primarily cost. By using a cylinder of each type of gas, argon and CO_2, the mixture percentages may be varied by the use of flowmeters. This method precludes the possibility of gas separation such as may occur in pre-mixed cylinders. When it is considered that pre-mixed argon-CO_2 gas is sold at the price of pure argon then it makes good sense to mix your own. The price of CO_2 is approximately 15 per cent that of argon in most areas of the country.

Argon-CO_2 shielding gas mixtures are employed for welding mild steel,

---

*Courtesy Miller Electric Mfg. Co.

low alloy steel and, in some cases, for stainless steels.

Argon-Helium-CO_2*. This mixture of shielding gases is used primarily for welding austenitic stainless steels. The combination of gases provides a unique characteristic to the weld. It is possible to make a weld with very little buildup of the top bead profile. The result is excellent for those applications where a high crowned weld is detrimental rather than a help. This gas mixture has found considerable use in the welding of stainless steel pipe.

Gas Flow and Regulation

For most welding conditions, the gas flow rate will approximate 35 cubic feet per hour. This flow rate may be increased or decreased depending upon the particular welding application. See Tables II - VI.

The data presented in these tables are not intended as absolute settings but only as a point in making the starting settings. Final adjustments must often be made on a trial and error basis. Actually the correct settings will

---

TABLE II
Mig Welding-Aluminum (Spray-arc)

PLATE THICKNESS (INCHES)	TYPE OF JOINT	WIRE DIAM. (INCHES)	ARGON FLOW (CFH)	AMPERES (DCRP)	VOLTAGE (VOLTS)	APPROXIMATE WIRE FEED SPEED (IPM)
0.040	FILLET OR TIGHT BUTT	0.030	30	40	15	240
0.050	FILLET OR TIGHT BUTT	0.030	15	50	15	290
0.063	FILLET OR TIGHT BUTT	0.030	15	60	15	340
0.093	FILLET OR TIGHT BUTT	0.030	15	90	15	410

(Linde Co.)

TABLE III

Mig Welding—Aluminum (Spray-Arc)

PLATE THICKNESS	PREPARATION	WIRE DIAMETER (IN.)	ARGON FLOW (CFH)	AMPERES (DCRP)	VOLTAGE
.250	SINGLE VEE BUTT (60° INCLUDED ANGLE) SHARP NOSE BACKUP STRIP USED	3/64	35	180	24
	SQUARE BUTT WITH BACKUP STRIP	3/64	40	250	26
	SQUARE BUTT WITH NO BACKUP STRIP	3/64	35	220	24
.375	SINGLE VEE BUTT (60° INCLUDED ANGLE) SHOP NOSE, BACKUP STRIP USED	1/16	40	280	27
	DOUBLE VEE BUTT (75° INCLUDED ANGLE, 1/16-IN. NOSE). NO BACKUP. BACK CHIP AFTER ROOT PASS	1/16	40	260	26
	SQUARE BUTT WITH NO BACKUP STRIP	1/16	50	270	26
.500	SINGLE VEE BUTT (60° INCLUDED ANGLE) SHARP NOSE. BACKUP STRIP USED	1/16	50	310	27
	DOUBLE VEE BUTT (75° INCLUDED ANGLE 1/16-IN. NOSE). NO BACKUP. BACK CHIP AFTER ROOT PASS	1/16	50	300	27

(Linde Co.)

be governed by the type and thickness of metal to be welded, position of the weld, kind of shielding gas used, diameter of electrode and type of joint.

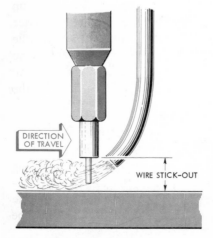

Fig. 14. Gas drift with inadequate gas coverage. (Hobart Brothers Co.)

The proper amount of gas shielding usually results in a rapidly crackling or sizzling arc sound. Inadequate gas shielding will produce a popping arc sound with resultant weld discoloration, porosity, and spatter.

"Gas drift" may result from high weld travel speeds or from unusually drafty or windy conditions in the weld area.

Since one or more of these factors may cause the gas to "drift" away from the arc, the result is inadequate gas coverage. See Fig. 14. The gas nozzle should be adjusted for proper coverage and outside influences should be eliminated by proper windbreakers or shields. See Fig. 15.

Correct positioning of the nozzle with respect to the work will be determined by the nature of the weld. The

TABLE IV
Mig Welding—Carbon Steel

PLATE THICKNESS (IN.)	JOINT AND EDGE PREPARATION	WIRE DIAMETER (IN.)	GAS FLOW (CFH)	DCRP (AMPS)	VOLTAGE	WIRE FEED SPEED (IPM)
.035				55	16*	117
.047				65	17*	140
.063	NON–POSITIONED FILLET OR LAP	.030	10–15	85	17*	170
.078				105	18*	225
.100				110	18*	225
1/8				130	19*	300
1/8	BUTT (SQUARE EDGE)	1/16		280	--	165
3/16	BUTT (SQUARE EDGE)	1/16	MIXTURE (75%A + 25% CO₂)	375	--	260
3/16	FILLET OR LAP	1/16		350	--	230
1/4	DOUBLE VEE BUTT (60° INCLUDED ANGLE, NO NOSE)			375 (1ST PASS) 430 (2ND PASS)	27	83 (1ST) 95 (2ND)
5/16	DOUBLE VEE BUTT (60° INCLUDED ANGLE, NO NOSE)		40–50	400 (1ST PASS) 420 (2ND PASS)	28	87 (1ST) 92 (2ND)
5/16	NON–POSITIONED FILLET			400		8/
1/2	DOUBLE VEE BUTT (60° INCLUDED ANGLE, NO NOSE	3/32	MIXTURE (95% ARGON + 5% O₂)	400 (1ST PASS 450 (2ND PASS)		87 (1ST) 100 (2ND)
1/2	NON–POSITIONED FILLET			450	28	100
3/4	DOUBLE VEE BUTT (90° INCLUDED ANGLE, NO NOSE)			450 (ALL 4 PASSES)	29	100
3/4	POSITIONED FILLET			475	30	110
1	FILLET			450 (ALL 4 PASSES)	28	100

*SHORT ARC

(Linde Co.)

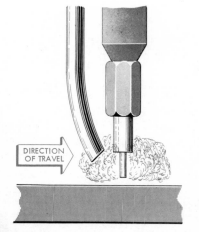

DIRECTION OF TRAVEL

Fig. 15. Adequate gas coverage. (Hobart Brothers Co.)

gas nozzle may usually be placed up to 2″ from the work. Too much space between nozzle and work reduces the effectiveness of a gas shield while too little space may result in excessive weld spatter which collects on the nozzle and shortens its life.

Wire Size

Best results are obtained by using the proper diameter wire for the thickness of the metal to be welded and the position in which the welding is to be done. See Tables II-VI.

Electrode wires should be of the

TABLE V
Mig Welding—Stainless Steel

SHEET OR PLATE THICKNESS (IN.)*	FILLER WIRE DIAM. (IN.)	CURRENT AMPS.	WIRE FEED (IN./MIN.)	GAS AND FLOW CFH	WELDING POSITION**
1/16***	0.035	110/140	230/260	He 20/30	F, H, VD
1/8-3/16	0.035	110/140	230/260	He 20/30	F, H, OH, VD
1/4-1	0.035	110/140	230/260	A+ 1% O_2 20/30	V, OH
1/4-1	0.035	170/190	330/360	A+ 1% O_2 20/30	F, H, OH‡, VD
1/2-1	0.045	140/180	160/200	A+ 1% O_2 20/30	V, OH
3/16-3/8	0.045	190/310	210/340	A+ 1% O_2 30/40	F, H
7/16 & UP	0.045	190/310	210/340	A+ 1% O_2 20/40	OH‡
1/4 & UP	1/16"	280/350	240/330	A+ 1% O_2 30/40	F, H

*ALL JOINT TYPES—BUT, LAP & FILLET   (Linde Co.)
**F—FLAT; H—HORIZONTAL; OH—OVERHEAD; VD—VERTICAL DOWN; V—VERTICAL UP
***GOOD FIT-UP-REQUIRED
‡ WEAVE BEAD
‡ STRINGER BEAD

TABLE VI
Micro-wire Welding
Manual travel, single pass flat fillet welds

MATERIAL THICKNESS T INCH	ELECTRODE SIZE INCH	WELDING CONDITIONS D.C.R.P.		GAS FLOW C.F.H.	TRAVEL SPEED I.P.M.
		ARC VOLTS	AMPERES		
.025	.030	15 – 17	30 – 50	15 – 20	15 – 20
.031	.030	15 – 17	40 – 60	15 – 20	18 – 22
.037	.035	15 – 17	65 – 85	15 – 20	35 – 40
.050	.035	17 – 19	80 – 100	15 – 20	35 – 40
.062	.035	17 – 19	90 – 110	20 – 25	30 – 35
.078	.035	18 – 20	110 – 130	20 – 25	25 – 30
.125	.035	19 – 21	140 – 160	20 – 25	20 – 25
.125	.045	20 – 23	180 – 200	20 – 25	27 – 32
.187	.035	19 – 21	140 – 160	20 – 25	14 – 19
.187	.045	20 – 23	180 – 200	20 – 25	18 – 22
.250	.035	19 – 21	140 – 160	20 – 25	10 – 15
.250	.045	20 – 23	180 – 200	20 – 25	12 – 18

SHIELDING GAS: CO_2 WELDING GRADE   (Hobart Brothers Co.)
TIP-TO-WORK DISTANCE (STICK-OUT) - 1/4 TO 3/8 INCH

same composition as that of the material being welded. Basic wire diameters are .020", .030", .035", .045", 1/16" and 1/8". Generally wires of .020", .030" or .035" are best for welding thin metals. Medium thickness metals normally require .045" or 1/16" diameter electrodes. For thick metals,

$\frac{1}{8}''$ electrodes are usually recommended. However, the position of welding is a factor which must be considered in electrode selection. Thus for vertical or overhead welding, smaller diameter electrodes will be more satisfactory than larger diameter wires.

Welding Current

A wide range of current values can be used with each wire diameter. This permits welding various thicknesses of metal without having to change wire diameter. The correct current to use for a particular joint must often be determined by trial. The current selected should be high enough to secure the desired penetration without cold lapping (cold shuts) but low enough to avoid undercutting and burn through. See Tabes II-VI.

The term current is often related to current density. Current density is the amperage per square inch of cross sectional area of the electrode. Thus at a given amperage the current density of .030″ diameter electrode is higher than with .045″ diameter electrode. Current density is calculated by dividing the welding current by the electrode area.

Each type and size of electrode wire has a minimum and maximum current density. For example, if the welding current falls below the minimum, a satisfactory weld cannot be made.

The success of Mig welding is due to the concentration of a high current density at the electrode tip. Whereas the arc stream of Mig is sharp and deeply penetrating, metallic arc (stick electrode) is soft and widespread. Consequently, the width-to-depth ratio of

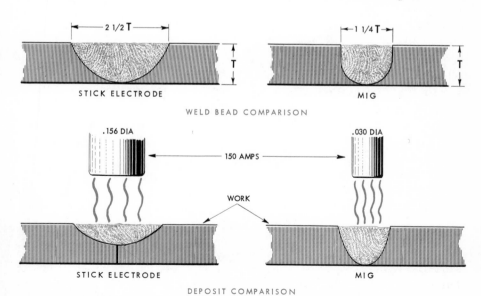

Fig. 16. The high current density of Mig welding produces deeper penetration and narrower beads. (Miller Electric Manufacturing Co.)

gas metal arc will be less than with stick electrode. See Fig. 16.

Wire Feed

The amperage of the welding current used limits the speed of the wire feed to a definite range. However, it is possible to make adjustments of the wire feed within the range. For a specific amperage setting, a high speed of wire feed will result in a short arc. A low speed contributes to a long arc. Also a higher speed must be used for overhead welding than speeds for flat position welding.

Wire Stickout

Wire stickout refers to the distance the wire projects from the nozzle of the gun. See Fig. 17. Stickout influences the welding current since it changes the preheating in the wire. When the stickout increases the preheating increases, which means that the power source does not have to furnish as much welding current to melt the wire at a given feed rate. Since the power source is self-regulating, the current output is automatically decreased. Conversely, if the stickout decreases the power source is forced to furnish more current to burn off the wire at the required rate.

For most Mig welding applications, the wire stickout should measure up to 1". An excessive amount of wire stickout results in increased wire preheating; this tends to increase the deposit rate. Too much wire stickout may result in a "ropy" appearance in the weld bead. Too little stickout results in the wire fusing to the nozzle tip which decreases the life of the tip. As the amount of wire stickout increases, it may become increasingly difficult to follow the weld seam, particularly with a small diameter wire.

The wire, in a near plastic-state between the tip and arc, tends to move (whip) around, describing a somewhat circular pattern. Decreasing the amount of wire stickout and straightening the welding wire tend to decrease the amount of wire whip.

Joint Edge Preparation and Weld Backing

Preparation of the edge of each member to be joined is recommended to aid in the penetration and control of weld reinforcement. For Mig welding, beveling the edges is usually desirable for butt joints thicker than 1/4" if complete root penetration is desired. For thinner sections, a square butt joint is best.

In the Mig process, weld backing is helpful in obtaining a sound weld at the roots. Backing prevents molten metal from running through the joint

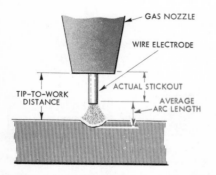

Fig. 17. Correct wire stickout is important to achieve sound welds. (Hobart Brothers Co.)

being welded, especially when complete weld penetration is desired.

There are several types of material used for backing: steel and copper blocks, strips, and bars; carbon blocks, fire bricks, plastics, asbestos, and fire clay. Some of these serve to conduct heat away from the joint and also to form a mold or dam for the metal. The most commonly used backing for Mig welding is copper or steel.

Positioning Work and Welding Wire

The proper position of the welding torch and weldment is important. In Mig welding, the flat position is preferred for most joints because this position improves the molten metal flow, bead contour, and gives better gas protection. However, on gage material, it is sometimes necessary or advantageous to weld with the work inclined 10 to 20 degrees. The welding is done in the downhill position. This has a tendency to flatten the bead and increase the travel speed.

The alignment of the welding wire in relation to the joint is very important. The welding wire should be on the center line of the joint for most butt joints, if the pieces to be joined are of equal thickness. If the pieces are unequal in thickness, the wire may be moved toward the thicker piece. The recommended position of

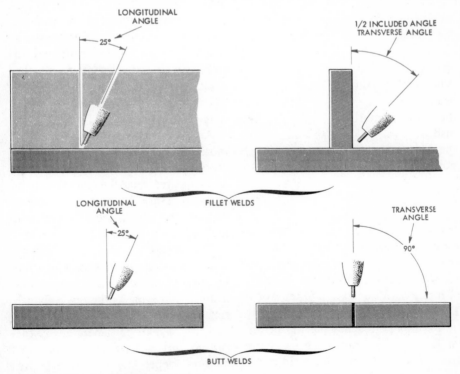

Fig. 18. Correct nozzle angle for Mig welding.

the welding gun for fillet and butt welds is shown in Fig. 18.

Either a pulling or pushing technique may be used with little or no weaving motion. See Fig. 19. Some weaving is desirable for poorly fitted edge joints. The pulling or drag technique is usually best for light gage metals and the pushing technique for heavy materials.

The push technique is recommended for all aluminum because of the gas protection that is needed.

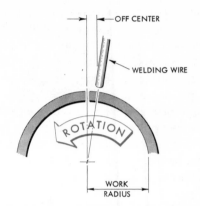

Fig. 20. Position of electrode wire in making a circular weld. (Hobart Brothers Co.)

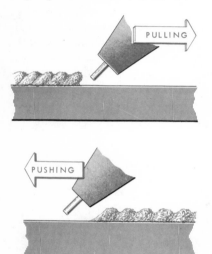

Fig. 19. Use either a pushing or pulling technique in Mig welding.

For welding circular seams, as shown in Fig. 20, the wire should be shifted off-center approximately ⅓ the work radius opposite the direction of rotation, at 90 degrees to the work. This will allow the metal to solidify by the time it reaches the top of the circle. A shift of more than ⅓ of the work radius will cause the weld metal deposit to run ahead of the weld bead.

Arc Starting

Starting an electrical arc for a welding process involves three major factors: electrical contact, arc voltage, and time. To assure good arc starts, it is necessary for the electrode wire to make good electrical contact with the work. The electrode must exert sufficient force on the workpiece to penetrate impurities.

Arc initiation becomes increasingly more difficult as wire stickout increases. A reasonable balance of volts and amperes must be maintained in order to assure the proper arc and to deposit the metal at the best electrode melting rate.

The response time of a power source and circuit is generally fixed by equipment design. Most power sources have an optimum response time for wires.

The arc may be generated by the *run-in start method* or *scratch start method,* depending on the type of equipment used. Some welding units provide circuiting for both by incorporating separate toggle switches on the feeder panel.

In the run-in method the gun is aimed at the workpiece without touching the workpiece. The gun trigger is depressed and this immediately energizes the wire and starts the arc.

With the scratch method, the end of the welding wire must be scratched against the workpiece to start the arc.

Once the arc is started, the gun is simply held at the correct angle and moved at a uniform speed. When reaching the end of a weld, the trigger is released which stops the wire feed and interrupts the welding current. However, the gun should be kept over the weld until the gas stops flowing in order to protect the puddle until it solidifies.

Buried Arc CO$_2$ Welding Process

Buried arc CO$_2$ welding is a high-energy, fast-weld method in which the end of the wire electrode is held either level or below the surface of the work with practically a zero arc length. See Fig. 21. This process is designed for high speed welding of mild steel. Although it can be employed for manual welding its greatest application is in

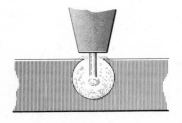

Fig. 21. Buried arc CO$_2$.

mechanized welding. The process is widely used in many industries where the fabrication of parts requires deep penetration and fast deposition of weld metal without critical control of bead contour. In most instances welding wire diameters range from 0.045" to ⅛".

Regular Mig welding equipment is utilized for the buried arc process. The shielding gas is pure carbon dioxide which provides additional economy over the more expensive argon. The metal transfer is globular, but since the wire is buried and a high density current is used, a deep cavity is formed. This deep cavity traps the molten globules that normally would be ejected sideways through the arc. Thus, splatter which otherwise would be severe is minimized and does not affect the welding process.

Pulsed-Spray Arc Welding

The pulsed-spray process is an extension of spray-transfer welding to a current level much below that required for continuous spray transfer. The pulsing current used may be considered as having its peak current in the spray-transfer current range and its minimum value in the globular transfer current range.

The need for current values less than the transition level becomes apparent when attempting to weld under heat transfer conditions which are inadequate relative to the minimum heat input rate with spray transfer. For example, when welding out-of-position, the high current will result in a molten pool which cannot be retained

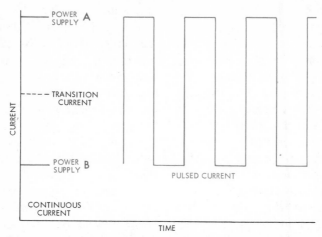

Fig. 22. Illustration of how a switching system can convert two steady-state DC output currents in a simple pulsing-current output waveform. (Airco)

in position unless the material being welded has an adequate thermal-conductivity (coupled with the joint type and plate thickness).

The same factors explain the burn-through obtained when a weld on thin material is attempted with too high a welding current. While smaller diameter electrodes have lower transition currents, the basic limitation cannot be avoided. The net result is that the spray transfer process is very applicable to flat position use but is rather limited in its use for out-of-position and thin material welding.

Pulsed-spray transfer is achieved by pulsing the current back and forth between the spray transfer and globular transfer current ranges. Fig. 22 illustrates, on the left, the current-time relationships for two power sources, A and B, with A putting out a current in the globular transfer range and B putting out a current in the spray-transfer range. Fig. 22 also shows, on the right,

the two outputs combined to produce a simple pulsed output by electrically switching back and forth between them.

Transfer is restricted to the spray mode. Globular transfer is suppressed by not allowing sufficient time for transfer by this mode to occur. Conversely, at the high current level, spray transfer is ensured by allowing more than sufficient time for transfer to occur.

For the given electrode deposited by the pulsed-spray method, all the advantages of the spray-transfer process are available at average current levels from the minimum possible with continuous spray transfer down to values low in the globular transfer range.

The Power Source

To suppress globular transfer, the time period between consecutive pulses must be less than sufficient for

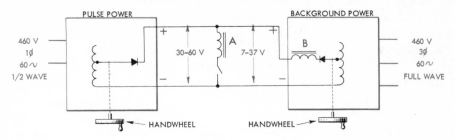

Fig. 23. Block diagram of the essential features of the pulsed-current power supply. (Airco)

a transfer by the globular mode to occur. The time period between pulses produced by the use of the positive half-cycles from a 60 cps power line is short enough to suppress transfer at all current levels in the globular transfer current range. Conversely, the pulse duration is long enough to ensure that transfer by the spray mode will occur at an appropriate current in the spray transfer range.

As Fig. 23 illustrates, the power source combines a standard, three phase, full wave, unit with a single phase, half wave unit, both of the constant-potential type. The three phase unit is termed the "background" unit and the single phase unit is termed

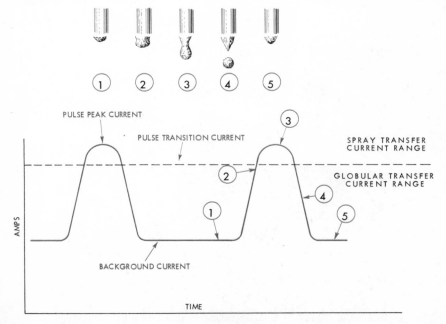

Fig. 24. Illustration of the output current waveform of the pulsed-current power supply; also showing the metal transfer sequence. (Airco)

the "pulsing" unit. These units are connected in parallel but commute in operation. The pulsing current output is schematically illustrated in Fig. 24.

The units are made to switch back and forth in operation by means of the varying output voltage of the pulsing unit. The diode rectifiers in each unit alternately permit or block the passage of current depending upon whether there is a positive or negative voltage difference across their terminals. When the pulse is off or its voltage is less than the background voltage, the diode rectifiers of the background unit pass the full value of the instantaneous current. Conversely, when the pulse voltage exceeds the background voltage, blocking the background diode rectifiers, the pulse

diode rectifiers pass the full value of the instantaneous current.

Two chokes are used. Fig. 23. The choke labeled "A" performs a commutation function. When the pulse voltage drops below the background voltage, it sustains the welding current momentarily, giving the background unit time to respond to the demand for current. Choke B, in series with the output of the background unit, filters the background current and prevents undesirable arc outages at low background current levels. The pulsed-current power source is shown in Fig. 25.

Operation of the pulsed-current power source is similar to that of conventional constant potential sources. With the arc off, the value of the pulse peak voltage, which depends upon the

Fig. 25. Pulsed-current power supply designed for pulsed-spray arc welding. (Airco)

TABLE VII
Typical Pulsed-current Power Supply Settings

ELECTRODE TYPE	ELECTRODE DIAMETER, IN.	PULSE PEAK RANGE, V	AVERAGE CURRENT RANGE, AMP	AVERAGE VOLTAGE
MILD AND LOW ALLOY STEEL	0.035 0.045 1/16	34–36 37–39 42–44	55–130 90–180 110–250	18–20 19–23 20–25
STAINLESS STEEL	0.035 0.045 1/16	33–35 36–38 41–43	55–130 90–180 110–250	18–20 19–23 20–25
ALUMINUM	1/16	34–36	80–250	20–30

TABLE VIII
Average Current vs. Electrode Feed Speed for Typical Diameters of Steel and Aluminum Electrodes when Using Pulsed-current Unit.

ELECTRODE FEED SPEED (IPM)	CORRESPONDING AVERAGE CURRENT, AMP. MILD STEEL AND STAINLESS STEEL (a)			ALUMINUM (b) 1/16 IN. (DIAM.)
	0.035 IN (DIAM.)	0.045 IN. (DIAM.)	1/16 IN. (DIAM.)	
70	. . . .	70	115	70
90	. . . .	90	175	90
105	50	105	215	105
125	60	125	. . . .	125
135	70	135	. . . .	135
155	80	155	. . . .	155
185	90	185	. . . .	185
220	110	220	. . . .	220
235	120			
255	130			
275	140			
300	150			
325	160			
345	170			
365	180			
380	190			
425	210			
500	. . . .			

(a) ARGON + 290 O_2
(b) ARGON

electrode type and diameter (Table VII) is selected and remains constant. This setting is made by rotating the pulse peak voltage handwheel while pressing a button which converts the average voltage meter to a peak voltage meter. The electrode feeder is set at the value which will produce the required current and is determined from Table VIII for the type and di-ameter of electrode to be used. The arc is then initiated and the background voltage handwheel rotated to produce the proper arc length. So long as the type and diameter of electrode remain the same, all further power source adjustments are made by means of the background voltage handwheel. The meters on the power supply read the average voltage and the average current which are the values familiar to every welding operator.

Features of Pulsed-spray Welding

Pulsed-spray welding method provides many features not previously available.

1. The heat input range bridges the gap between, and laps over into, the heat input ranges available from the spray and short-circuiting arc processes. Into its lower heat input range the pulsed-spray process brings the advantages of the continuous spray-transfer process. Also, due to lower heat input, the use of spray transfer is extended greatly into poor heat transfer areas, mainly related to welding out-of-position and on thinner materials.

2. The area of overlap with the spray-transfer process occurs because, having a higher transition current, a larger diameter electrode leaves the continuous spray and enters the pulsed-spray range at a higher current than a smaller electrode. Further, the use of a larger diameter electrode can continue down to a current considerably below the transition current of the smaller diameter eelctrode.

Large diameter electrodes are lower in cost. They have a lower surface-to-volume ratio which is important considering the correlation between material found on the electrode surface and weld porosity and, in certain cases, weld cracking. Also, electrode feeding problems are more often experienced with the smaller diameters of electrodes.

3. The pulsed-spray and the short-circuiting arc processes are different. In general, where applicable, the minimum heat inputs obtainable are approximately equal but, conversely, the maximum heat input of the globular transfer range is achieved by the pulsed-spray but not by the short-circuiting arc process. The pulsed-spray method produces the higher ratio of heat input to metal deposition, permits the use of a completely inert gas shield where necessary, and is essentially free from spatter.

The pulsed-spray process will not displace the short-circuiting arc process in those areas where the short-circuiting arc process is properly applicable and more economical.

4. The pulsed-spray process is characterized by a uniformity of root penetration which approaches that possible with the gas tungsten-arc process; because of this feature, the process may permit deletion of weld backing in some cases.

Tubular Wire Welding

Tubular Wire welding is a gas-metal arc welding process in which a continuous fluxed core wire instead of a solid wire serves as the electrode. The wire can be used on any automatic or semi-automatic Mig welding equipment and is used principally in combination with CO_2 as a shielding gas. See Fig. 26. The wire is frequently referred to by the manufacturer's trade name such as "Fluxcor" (Airco) and "FabCo" (Hobart).

The flux ingredients in the wire include ionizers to stabilize the arc, de-

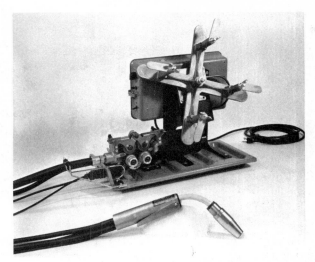

Fig. 26. Tubular wire has a flux core and is designed for heavy duty and continuous operation. (Airco)

oxidizers to purge the deposit of gas and slag and elements to produce high strength, ductility and toughness in weld deposits. The flux generates a gas shield, which is also augmented by the regular CO_2 shield, and a slag blanket that retards the cooling rate and protects the weld deposit as it solidifies.

Tubular wire is designed for high current densities and deposition rates which when combined with high duty cycles result in sharply increased production speeds. It is especially intended for application in large fillet single and multi-pass welds in either a horizontal or flat position using DCRP current. Because of its deep penetrating qualities into the weld root, tubular wire fillet welds of smaller leg size will have the same strength as stick fillet welds of larger size. Double welded butt joints up to ¾ " thick can be welded without edge penetration.

The actual operation of tubular wire welding is similar to other Mig welding processes.

Vapor-Shielded Arc Welding[1]

Vapor-shielded arc welding, known as *Innershield,* is a welding process introduced by Lincoln Electric Company. This process uses a vapor instead of a gas to shield the arc and molten metal. (A *vapor* in its natural state is a liquid or a solid, as distinct from a *gas,* which is in its natural state.) The vapor is generated by a continuous tubular electrode, containing vapor-producing materials. The electrode also serves as a filler rod.

Equipment. Equipment for the vapor-shielded arc consists of a DC power source, a control station for adjusting amperage and voltage, and a continuous wire feed mechanism.

[1]Courtesy The Lincoln Electric Co.

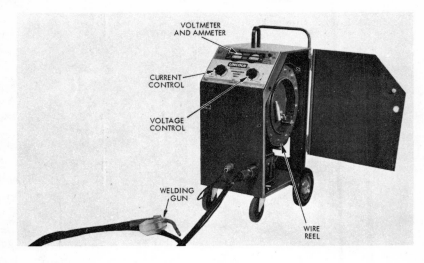

Fig. 27. A semi-automatic welder. (The Lincoln Electric Co.)

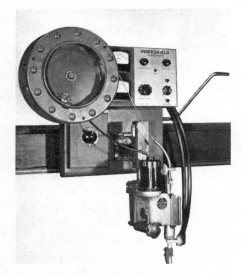

Fig. 28. A fully automatic Innershield welder. (The Lincoln Electric Co.)

The equipment can be fully automatic or semi-automatic. See Figs. 27 and 28.

With semi-automatic equipment, the operator moves a gun-type nozzle along the weld seam. See Fig. 29. To

weld, he simply pulls the trigger which starts the welding current and wire feed. When he wants to stop welding, he merely releases the trigger.

How does vapor shielding work? The tubular mild steel wire which serves as a filler rod, contains all of the necessary ingredients for shield-

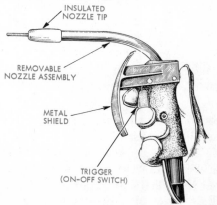

Fig. 29. The gun used in welding with a semi-automatic Innershield welder. (The Lincoln Electric Co.)

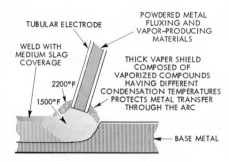

TUBULAR ELECTRODE

WELD WITH
MEDIUM SLAG
COVERAGE

2200°F

1500°F

POWDERED METAL
FLUXING AND
VAPOR–PRODUCING
MATERIALS

THICK VAPER SHIELD
COMPOSED OF
VAPORIZED COMPOUNDS
HAVING DIFFERENT
CONDENSATION TEMPERATURES
PROTECTS METAL TRANSFER
THROUGH THE ARC

BASE METAL

Fig. 30. Action of the tubular electrode in Inner-shield welding. (The Lincoln Electric Co.)

ing, deoxidizing, and fluxing. Some of the ingredients are metallic salts and oxides, which melt before the electrode melts, thereby vaporizing at a temperature lower than the melted electrode metal. These metallic salts vaporize and expand when they meet the intense heat of the arc. The vaporized salts expand until they reach a distance surrounding the arc where the temperature corresponds to their condensing temperature. Then the vaporized salts recondense, forming a thick vapor shield around the arc and molten metal. This shield prevents contamination by the surrounding atmosphere. Other materials in the electrode have oxidizing and alloying functions in creating high grade weld metal. See Fig. 30.

Submerged Arc Welding

Submerged arc welding is a process wherein an electric arc is submerged or hidden beneath a granular material. The electric arc provides the necessary heat to melt and fuse the metal. The granular material, called flux, completely surrounds the electric arc, thus shielding the arc and the metal from the atmosphere. A metallic wire is fed into the welding zone underneath the flux.

The welding process can be either semi-automatic or fully automatic. In the semi-automatic, a special hand welding gun is used. See Fig. 31. Any regular Mig welding DC power source can be adapted for submerged arc welding. The difference between submerged arc welding and other forms of gas-metal arc welding is that no inert shielding gas is required. The gun hopper is simply filled with flux, pointed over the weld area and the gun trigger depressed. As soon as the trigger is pulled, the wire is energized and the arc is started. At the same time the flux begins to flow. The actual welding operation is now carried out in the same way as in Mig welding.

As the metallic wire is fed into the weld zone the feeding hopper deposits the granulated flux over the weld puddle and completely shields the welding action. The arc is not visible since it is buried in the flux, thus there is no

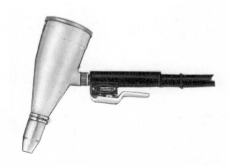

Fig. 31. Hand gun used for submerged arc welding. (Hobart Brothers Co.)

Fig. 32. An automatic submerged arc welder is being used here to weld the cylindrical housing of a missile.

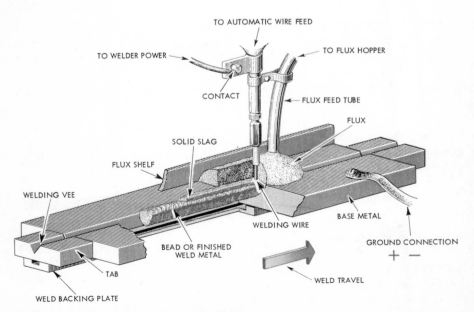

Fig. 33. Cutaway view of submerged arc welding (Linde Co.)

flash or spatter. That portion of the granular flux immediately around the arc fuses and covers the molten metal but after it has solidified it can be tapped off easily.

With the fully automatic process, the welding unit is arranged to move over the weld area at a controlled speed. On some arrangements, the welding head moves and the work remains stationary. In others the head is stationary and the work moves. See Figs. 32 and 33.

Submerged arc welding is usually best adapted where relatively thick sections are to be joined and deep penetration is required. For example, it is possible to weld three-inch plate in a single pass. Little, if any, edge preparation is necessary—as a rule none on material under one-half inch in thickness. Generally back-up support is essential. Welding is done on a horizontal or nearly horizontal plane.

Preliminary Welding Checks for Mig Welding

Before starting to weld, it is always a good practice to check the following:

1. All electric power controls are in the off position.

2. All hose and cable connections from the gun to the feeder are in good condition, properly insulated, and connections correctly secured.

3. Correct nozzle for the diameter wire.

4. Wire is properly threaded through gun.

5. Apertures of contact tube and nozzle are clean.

6. Wire speed and feed have been predetermined and adjusted on the feeder control.

7. Shielding gas and water coolant sources are on and adjusted for desired output.

8. Wire stickout is correct.

Possible Weld Defects

Mig welding like any other form of welding must be controlled properly to produce consistently high quality welds. The beginner, in practicing Mig welding, should analyze each completed weld to avoid repeated weld defects. The following are a few of the more common defects which may be encountered during the early stages of the learning process.

1. Cold lap. Cold laps usually occur when the arc does not melt the base metal sufficiently, causing the slightly molten puddle to flow into the unwelded base metal. See Fig. 34. Very often if the puddle is allowed to become too large, this too will result in cold laps. For proper fusion, the arc should be kept at the leading edge of the puddle. When directed in such

Fig. 34. Example of cold lap. (Hobart Brothers Co.)

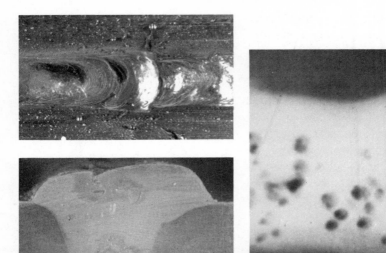

Fig. 35. Examples of surface and subsurface porosity. (Hobart Brothers Co.)

a manner, the molten puddle is prevented from flowing ahead of the welding arc. Also remember that the size of the puddle can be reduced by increasing the travel speed or reducing the wire speed feed.

2. *Surface porosity.* Generally, surface porosity is the direct result of atmospheric contamination. See Fig. 35. It is caused by having the shielding gas set too low or too excessive. If it is too low the air in the arc area is not fully displaced; if the gas flow is too much an air turbulence is generated which prevents complete shielding. On occasions porosity will occur if the welding is being done in a windy area. Without some protective wind shield the gas envelop may be blown away exposing the molten puddle to the air.

Fig. 36. Examples of crater porosity and cracks. (Hobart Brothers Co.)

3. Crater porosity or cracks. The chief cause of crater defects is removing the gun and shielding gas before the puddle has solidified. See Fig. 36. Other possible causes of crater porosity or cracks are moisture in the gas, dirt, oil, rust or paint on the base metal, or excessive tip-to-work distance.

4. Insufficient penetration. Lack of penetration is due to a low heat input in the weld area or failing to keep the arc properly located on the

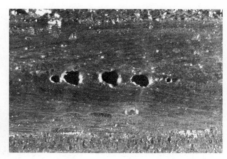

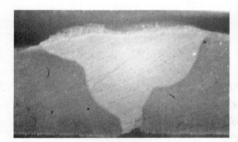

Fig. 37. Example of insufficient penetration. (Hobart Brothers Co.)

Fig. 38. Examples of burn through and excessive penetration. (Hobart Brothers Co.)

leading edge of the puddle. See Fig. 37. If the heat input is too slow, increase the wire feed speed to get a higher amperage.

5. Excessive penetration. Too much penetration or burn-through is caused by having excessive heat in the weld zone. See Fig. 38. By reducing the wire speed feed, the amperage is lowered and there will be less heat. Excessive penetration can also be avoided by increasing the travel speed. If the root opening in the joint is too wide too much burn through may result. Usually improper joint design

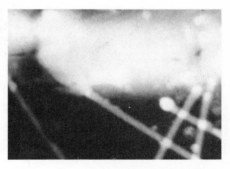

Fig. 39. Examples of whiskers through a weld joint. (Hobart Brothers Co.)

can be remedied by increasing the stickout and by weaving the gun.

6. *Whiskers.* Whiskers are short lengths of electrode wire sticking through the weld joint. See Fig. 39. They are caused by pushing the wire past the leading edge of the puddle. The small section of wire then protrudes inside the joint and becomes welded to the deposited metal. The best way to remedy this is to reduce travel speed, increase slightly the tip-to-work distance, or reduce the wire feed speed.

Points to Remember

1. Mig welding is often referred to by the manufacturer's trade name as Micro-wire Welding, Aircomatic Welding, Sigma Welding, and Miller-matic Welding.

2. Mig welding is faster than stick electrode welding and is much easier to learn.

3. Spray transfer type of welding is particularly adapted for welding heavy gage metals.

4. Short circuiting transfer welding is best for welding light gage metals.

5. For optimum efficiency, DCRP current is required for Mig welding.

6. For Mig welding, a constant potential power supply with a nearly flat volt-ampere characteristic produces the best results.

7. As a general rule, an air cooled gun is satisfactory when welding with amperage around 200 and a water cooled gun for welding heavy metals requiring higher amperages.

8. The use of CO_2 as a shielding gas is most effective and less expensive when welding steel.

9. Argon or a mixture of argon and oxygen will produce the most effective results in welding aluminum and stainless steel.

10. The rate of gas flow for welding most metals is approximately 35 cubic feet per hour. However, this rate may have to be varied somewhat, depending on the type, electrode size, and thickness of metal.

11. The effectiveness of the shielding gas is often governed by the distance of the gun from the workpiece. Generally the gas nozzle should not be more than 2″ from the workpiece.

12. The use of correct diameter wire electrode is necessary for good welds. Check recommendations for correct electrode diameters.

13. The correct current for welding must often be determined by trial. Check recommendations for starting current.

14. Be sure the wire feed is set for the amperage which is to be used for welding.

15. For most Mig welding applications, the wire stick-out should be about 1″.

16. Keep the gun properly positioned to ensure uniform weld with proper penetration.

17. Cold laps will occur if the arc does not melt the base metal sufficiently.

18. Check the weld for surface porosity. Surface porosity is usually caused by improper gas shielding.

19. Do not remove the gun from the

weld area until the puddle has solidified, otherwise cracks may develop.

20. Remember, insufficient or excessive penetration is the result of improper heat input control.

QUESTIONS FOR STUDY AND DISCUSSION

1. How does Mig welding differ from Tig welding?

2. What are some of the specific advantages of Mig welding?

3. What is the difference between spray and globular metal transfer?

4. Why is globular transfer ineffective for welding heavy gage metals?

5. What is meant by short-circuiting transfer? For what type of welding is this most effective?

6. Why is DCRP current best for Mig welding?

7. What results can be expected if DCSP current is used?

8. How does a constant potential power supply unit differ from the conventional constant current welding machine?

9. What is the advantage of using a constant potential power supply unit for Mig welding?

10. What is meant by slope control?

11. How is the electrode wire fed to the welding gun?

12. When should a water-cooled or air-cooled gun be used?

13. What are the elements that make up air?

14. Why is oxygen a harmful element in welding?

15. Why does nitrogen cause the most serious problems in welding?

16. When is argon or a mixture of argon and oxygen considered the ideal gas for shielding purposes?

17. When is CO_2 better for shielding purposes?

18. How is it possible to determine if the gas flow is proper for shielding?

19. What is likely to happen if the gas flow is allowed to drift from the weld area?

20. What factors must be taken into consideration in selecting the correct diameter electrode?

21. What is meant by current density?

22. Why is it impossible to make a proper weld if the current density falls below the required minimum?

23. What determines the rate at which the wire feed should be set?

24. Why is correct wire stickout important?

25. What position should the gun be held for horizontal fillet welding?

26. What position should the gun be held for flat fillet welding?

27. What determines whether a pulling or pushing technique of the gun should be used?

28. How does the buried arc CO_2 process differ from regular Mig welding?

29. How does the pulsed-spray arc welding technique differ from regular Mig welding?

30. How does the run-in start differ

from the scratch start method in starting a weld?

31. How does vapor-shielded arc welding differ from other gas shielded-arc welding processes?

32. In vapor shielded arc welding, how is the vapor generated for the cover shield?

33. What is submerged arc welding?

34. What is the probable cause for the formation of cold laps in a weld?

35. What should be done to avoid surface porosity in a weld?

36. How can crater porosity or cracks be avoided?

37. If weld penetration is insufficient, what should be done?

38. What causes whiskers in a weld?

WELDING ASSIGNMENTS

Practice Mig welding on 1/16" and 1/8" pieces of mild steel, aluminum and stainless steel. Perform the following welds:

1. Run straight beads.
2. Flat fillet weld—lap and Tee joints.
3. Flat butt joints.
4. Corner joints.
5. Horizontal fillet joints.

If equipment is available, practice welding mild steel plate with

1. Tubular wire.
2. Submerged arc.

CHAPTER 17

Gas Shielded—Arc Welding

The Carbon Arc

~~~~~~

Although metallic arc welding is the most commonly used process, carbon arc welding is better for certain jobs. The techniques for performing some of the common carbon arc operations are described in this chapter.

What is Carbon Arc Welding?

Carbon arc welding is a process in which fusion is achieved by heat produced from an electric arc between a carbon electrode and the work. The carbon arc serves only as a source of heat and does not function as a medium for transferring metal as in the metallic arc process. When extra weld metal is necessary for the joint a welding rod is introduced into the heat of the arc and melted as required.

Carbon Arc Welding-DC Machine

Any standard DC arc welding machine will supply the current for carbon arc welding. Better results will be obtained if a high voltage welding generator is used because a greater arc length is needed for the carbon electrodes.

The holder. The holder shown in Fig. 1 is designed for carbon arc welding. The regular metallic arc holder is not suitable since the carbon electrode becomes white hot and the intense heat soon ruins the ordinary holder.

Different sizes of clamps are available to accommodate electrodes of various diameters. A shield is often located near the handle to protect the operator's hand from the intense heat of the carbon electrode. The handle of the holder is made so air circulating around it keeps it cool. When the car-

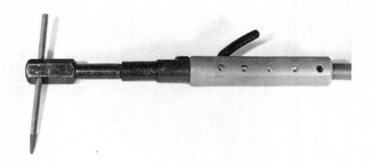

Fig. 1. A common type of carbon arc holder for DC machines.

bon arc is employed for continuous operations, especially on heavy work, the holder is often water-cooled.

Carbon electrodes. There are two kinds of electrodes for carbon arc welding, the *pure graphite* and the *baked carbon*. The pure graphite type

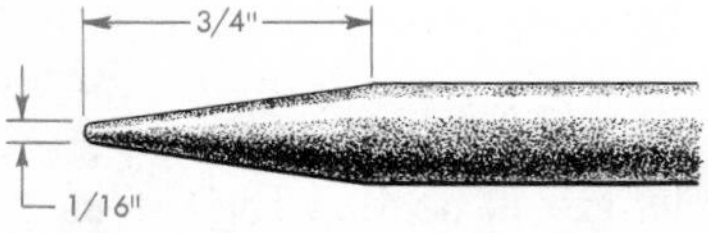

Fig. 2. Use a carbon electrode with a long, tapering point.

lasts longer under high currents but is more expensive. For most welding, baked carbon is satisfactory.

The electrode should have a long, tapering point as shown in Fig. 2, and should be about the same diameter as the thickness of the plates to be welded. The tip needs to be at least $\frac{1}{16}''$ in diameter with the taper extending back about $\frac{3}{4}''$. A carbon electrode with a blunt point burns off too quickly, leaving a broad face that makes the arc too difficult to control. The electrode

Fig. 3. Shape the carbon electrode on an emery wheel.

is shaped by grinding it on an emery wheel as illustrated in Fig. 3.

Current values. The diameter of the electrode depends upon the current values you intend to work with. In turn, the current values will be governed by the thickness of the metal to be welded. Thus, as in the metallic arc process, the thicker the metal, the greater the heat required and the higher the current setting. As a matter of fact, when it comes to selecting the proper current and electrode sizes, you may have to make a few tests. You will find that if the amperage is set too high, the carbon burns rapidly and overheats the metal. A good rule to remember is: *If the carbon burns cherry red more than 1¼" from the tip, the amperage is too high.* Keep in mind, too, that if the amperage setting and the carbon size are correct, the flame will be mild and the arc quiet.

Table I gives the approximate current values for carbon electrodes to be used on DC machines.

TABLE I

Approximate Current Values for Carbon Electrodes on DC Machines

Dia. of Electrodes	Common Carbon Electrodes (amperes)	Special Graphite Electrodes (amperes)
1/8	15–30	15–35
3/16	25–55	25–60
1/4	50–85	50–90
5/16	75–115	80–125
3/8	100–150	110–165

Polarity. To carry out carbon arc welding operations with a DC welder, the machine must be set for straight polarity. If the welder does not have a polarity switch, be sure that the holder is connected to the negative terminal and the work to the positive terminal. Reversed polarity not only produces an unstable arc but, even worse, it causes greater quantities of vaporized carbon to enter the molten metal, producing brittleness in the weld area.

Filler rod. When the joint requires additional metal, a filler rod is necessary. The filler rod should be of the same composition as the base metal. For most copper and brass welding, a phosphor bronze rod is desirable. The diameter of the filler rod should be about the same size as the thickness of the base plates.

DC Carbon Arc Welding Procedure for Non-Ferrous Metals

1. Prepare the joint—On light material of ⅛" in thickness or less, the edges need not be beveled. Plates over ⅛" should be beveled and if the thick-

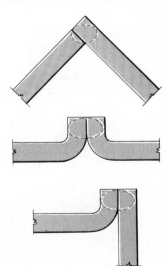

Fig. 4. These joints can be welded without using a filler rod.

ness is ¼″ or more, a double vee is necessary so both sides can be welded. Thin plates of 14 to 18 gage can often be joined without filler rod if the edges are shaped as shown in Fig. 4. The edges of these joints can be welded simply by fusing the two pieces together.

The use of steel or heavy copper backing bars is often advisable, particularly in welding non-ferrous metals. The position of the backing bars

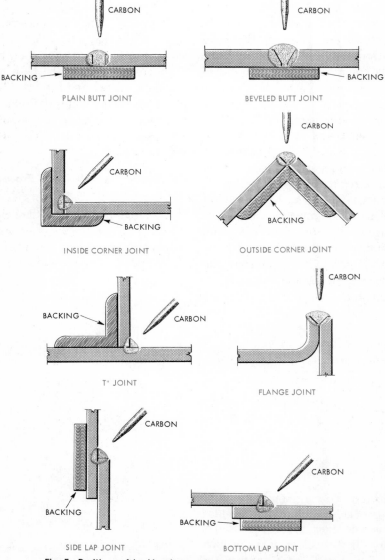

Fig. 5. Positions of backing bars and electrodes for different joints.

for various joints is illustrated in Fig. 5.

For butt joints on light material, no spacing between the edges is necessary. Usually metal $\frac{3}{16}''$ or over in thickness should be spaced about $\frac{1}{8}''$ apart at the root.

The surfaces of the metal must be free from grease, oil, scale, or other foreign matter. If possible, clamp the pieces in position. If clamping is impractical, tack weld them at intervals of 8'' to 10''.

2. Position the joint — Place the piece to be welded in a flat position. Since carbon arc welding is essentially a puddling process, it is almost impossible to carry out the welding operation with the joint in a horizontal, vertical, or overhead position.

3. Adjust length of the electrode— Arrange the carbon so not more than 3'' of the end extends beyond the grip of the holder as shown in Fig. 6. Be sure the carbon is shaped correctly. During the welding process, you may have to push the carbon through occasionally to compensate for burning off.

4. Adjust the machine—Make certain that the current is set for straight polarity and the amperage is correct for the electrode. If necessary, run a trial weld on a scrap piece before proceeding with the regular weld.

5. Strike the arc—To strike the arc, bring the carbon electrode in contact with the work and withdraw it to the proper arc length. A considerably longer arc is necessary than that used for metallic arc welding. As a rule, the arc length should be 3 to 4 times the thickness of the metal. This is necessary to prevent excessive transfer of carbon to the weld pool. For some metals, such as copper, an arc length up to 1'' will often produce better results.

If the arc is broken and needs to be re-started, do not strike the carbon directly over the hot metal weld. Bringing the tip of the carbon electrode directly in contact with the hot metal

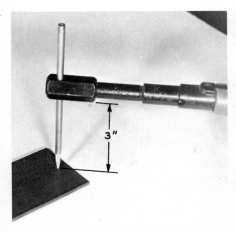

Fig. 6. The carbon electrode should not extend more than 3'' beyond the holder.

Fig. 7. Hold the filler rod in this manner.

will cause a hard spot in the weld, since some of the carbon will be absorbed by the metal. To re-start the arc, strike it on the adjacent cold metal and then bring it over the weld area.

6. *Add filler rod*—Hold the filler rod almost parallel with the seam, with the end resting lightly on the work metal as shown in Fig. 7. Keep the electrode at right angles to the joint but inclined slightly away from the melting end of the filler rod. Play the

arc on the filler rod and move the molten pool along the line of weld.

Carbon Arc Welding with an AC Machine

The holder illustrated in Fig. 8 is especially designed for AC machines. This holder requires two carbon electrodes. In the single carbon electrode used on DC machines, the flame is maintained between the carbon electrode and the work, and as soon as

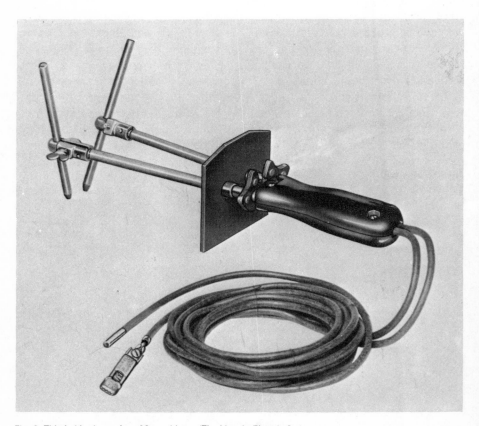

Fig. 8. This holder is used on AC machines. (The Lincoln Electric Co.)

the electrode is removed from the metal the flame goes out. With the AC holder, the flame is formed between the two electrodes and is kept intact even though the electrodes are withdrawn from the work.

The electrodes are inserted into the head of the holder and fastened by turning the thumb screws as shown in Fig. 9. Although the selection of carbons varies with each job, the following serves as a guide:

$\frac{1}{4}''$ dia. carbon—20 to 50 amperes.

$\frac{5}{16}''$ dia. carbon—30 to 70 amperes.

$\frac{3}{8}''$ dia. carbon—40 to 90 amperes.

The actual welding procedure is similar to that described for DC welding. The torch handle is gripped firmly with the thumb resting on the push-button. To establish the arc, push the button forward until the electrodes touch. Then release the pressure on the button just enough to permit the points of the electrodes to part and establish the arc. The control of the arc is maintained by pressure on this thumb button. When the correct distance between the two carbon elec-

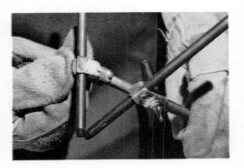

Fig. 9. The carbon electrodes in this holder are adjusted by turning thumb screws. (The Lincoln Electric Co.)

trodes is obtained, there will be a quiet, soft flame. As the carbon burns away, more pressure will have to be exerted on the button.

The size of the arc can be varied by raising or lowering the amperage within the recommended limits and by using large or small electrodes to fit the particular job. When the electrodes are burned away so the arc cannot be established, reset them in the head to the correct distance.

Points to Remember

1. Do not use the regular metallic arc holder for carbon arc welding.

2. For most welding, use the baked carbon type electrodes.

3. Shape the electrode so it has a long, tapering point.

4. In general, use a carbon electrode with a diameter equal to about the thickness of the metal to be welded.

5. When using a DC machine for carbon arc welding, set the current for straight polarity.

6. Use a filler rod having the same composition as the base metal.

7. Whenever possible, use backing blocks when welding non-ferrous metals.

8. Either clamp or tack the pieces before welding.

9. Perform carbon arc welding with the pieces in a flat position.

10. Clamp the carbon electrode so not more than 3″ extends beyond the grip of the holder.

11. Maintain an arc length equal

to 3 to 4 times the thickness of the plates.

12. Do not re-start the arc directly over the hot metal weld.

QUESTIONS FOR STUDY AND DISCUSSION

1. How does the carbon arc process differ from the metallic arc process?

2. For what kind of welding is the carbon arc process particularly useful?

3. Why must a special holder be used for carbon arc welding?

4. How does the holder used on a DC machine differ from the one commonly employed on an AC machine?

5. How should the carbon electrode be shaped?

6. What is the objection to using an electrode with a blunt point?

7. What determines the diameter of the electrode?

8. How can you determine if the amperage is correct for the carbon electrode being used?

9. Why must the current be set for straight polarity for carbon arc welding?

10. What size and kind of filler rod should be used for carbon arc welding?

11. What consideration should be given to the preparation of the joint on pieces to be welded with the carbon arc?

12. How far should the carbon electrode project from the grip of the holder on DC machines?

13. How long should the carbon arc be maintained on a DC machine?

14. With a DC machine, what is the procedure for re-starting a carbon arc?

15. Why shouldn't a carbon arc be re-started over the hot metal?

16. How should the filler rod be held during the carbon arc welding process?

17. How is the arc established with a dual carbon holder on an AC machine?

WELDING ASSIGNMENT

Obtain several pieces of copper and brass, and weld a butt, a lap, a tee, and an outside corner joint.

CHAPTER 18

Special Arc Processes

Hardfacing

The application of welding for hardfacing operations has contributed greatly to conserving and extending the life of machines, tools, and building equipment. Hardfacing is considered the most effective and economical way to repair parts which have been subjected to severe wear.

Hardfacing, or hard surfacing as it is sometimes called, is a process of applying a hard wear-resistant layer of metal to surfaces or edges of parts.

Fig. 1. The edges of these plowshares are repaired with abrasive-resistant hardfacing material. (The Lincoln Electric Co.)

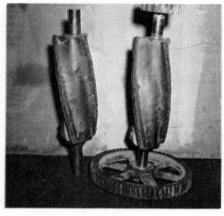

Fig. 2. Here are other examples of parts which have been repaired with hardfacing material. (The Lincoln Electric Co.)

This is done to build up worn areas so as to make them as good as new, or to put hard, wear-resistant cutting edges on soft, ductile materials. See Figs. 1 and 2.

This chapter describes how various hardfacing operations are performed.

Types of Wear

Parts in service are subjected to different kinds and degrees of wear. Thus surfaces may have to withstand great resistance to abrasion or excessive resistance to chipping or cracking under heavy loads. Since hardfacing involves the building-up of surfaces which have become worn, you need to know the exact nature of the wear in order to determine the kind of wear-resistant material to use in the hardfacing operation.

There are two main types of wear: impact and abrasion. *Impact wears* are those in which the metal is lost or deformed by chipping, upsetting, cracking, or crushing. With *abrasion wears,* surfaces are worn away because the parts are subjected to continuous grinding or rubbing action.

Properties of Parts to be Hardfaced

An additional requirement of any hardfacing operation is a knowledge of the composition of the component to be serviced. By and large, metals of these parts can be grouped into two categories. In one group are the metals whose physical properties are not changed significantly or are subject to cracking when heated and cooled in a hardfacing operation. These metals include the low range carbon and medium carbon steels, the low alloy steels, and the stainless steels. The second group includes metal parts made of steels whose physical characteristics are changed with the application of hardfacing materials. These metals usually have been hardened by some heat treating process and any subsequent exposure to heat may jeopardize this hardness or produce cracks. Metals in such a group include the higher range medium-carbon steels, high-carbon steels, cast irons, and other alloy steels.

Metals in the first group can be hardfaced without any particular precautions since no harmful cracking on adjacent weld hardness will result. With metals in the second group special care must be taken to minimize the sudden shock of localized heat. This is done by reducing the hardness by annealing or through gradual and uniform preheating and post cooling. Preheating from 300° to 500°F will usually prevent weld hardening in medium and high-carbon steels. High-carbon alloy steels and wear-resistance alloy steels require preheating to the same temperature. After the surfacing operation is completed, reheating to a temperature of 800° to 1300°F and slow cooling should follow.

Electrodes for Hardfacing

The operation of hardfacing would be simplified if one electrode could be used for all jobs. Unfortunately, this is not possible because no one electrode will build-up a worn surface that can withstand both impact and abrasion wear.

Hardfacing electrodes are classified into three groups. Most of them are referred to by a manufacturer's trade name.

1. Severe abrasion-resistant—Electrodes in this group are of the tungsten carbide and chromium carbide types. These electrodes deposit a very hard abrasive-resistant material. They are not suitable for impact wear, since the material they deposit chips and cracks when subjected to shock.

Chromium and tungsten electrodes come either in coated tubular form or as regular coated cast alloy. The tube rods contain a mixture of powder metal, powder ferroalloys, and fluxing ingredients. The tubes are coated for arc stabilization and arc shielding. Both types of electrodes are used with the metallic arc. The same material is available in powder form. The powder alloy is used when hard surfacing is performed with the carbon arc.

Tungsten electrodes have tiny crystals of tungsten carbide embedded in the steel alloy. When applied on a surface, the steel wears away, leaving toothlike particles of tungsten carbide exposed. Since tungsten carbide is very hard, the exposed particles make the edge of the part self-sharpening. This property is particularly desirable for earth digging equipment, scraping tools, plowshares, rotary digger blades, cultivator sweeps, and other similar machinery as shown in Fig. 3.

Still another type of tungsten carbide electrode deposits fine particles of tungsten carbide that are so close that they form a smooth cutting edge. These electrodes are useful in repairing steel cutting edges such as lathe tool bits.

Chromium carbide electrodes are slightly less hard and less abrasion-resistant than the tungsten carbide type but are tougher. Most of them are not affected by heat treatment and are too hard to be machined. In addition to being hard, chromium carbide electrodes produce surfaces that provide better protection against corrosion.

2. Moderate abrasion and impact resistant — Electrodes in this group are of the high carbon type and leave a very hard and tough deposit. They are excellent for repairing surfaces

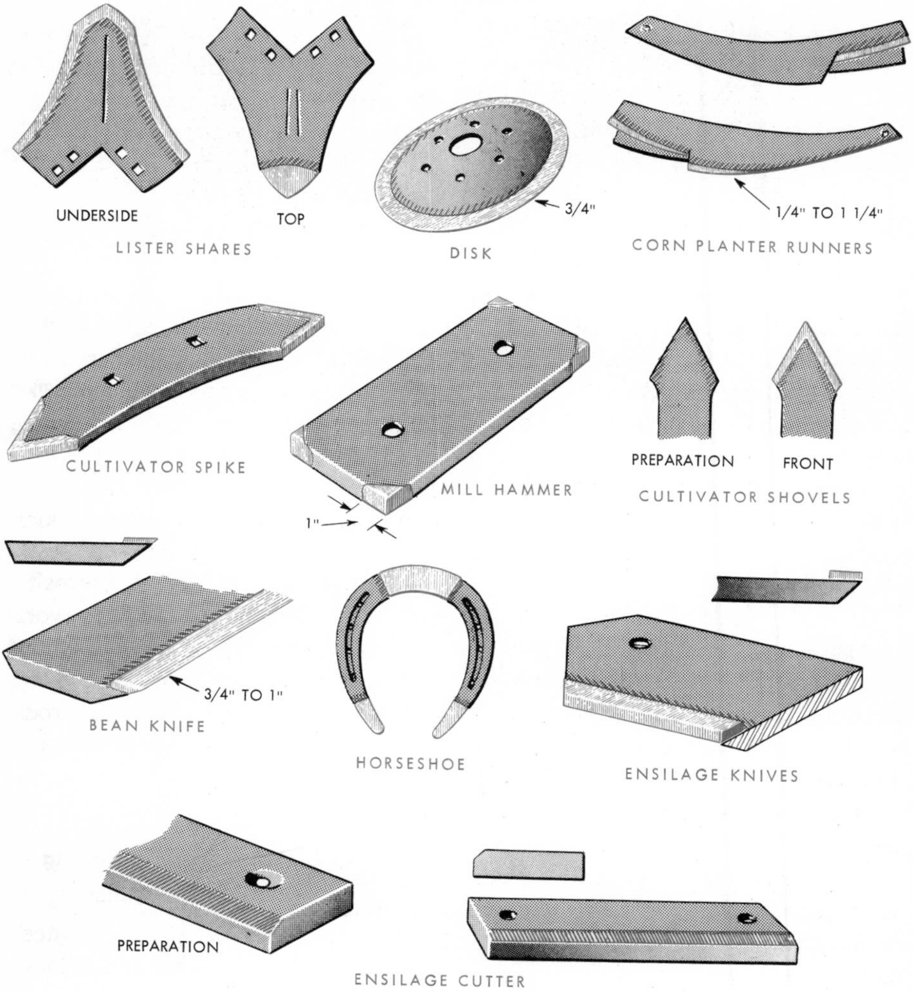

Fig. 3. Examples of farm tools that can be hardfaced with tungsten carbide electrodes to increase their useful life. (The Lincoln Electric Co.)

which must withstand both abrasion and impact forces, such as chisels, hammers, sprockets, gears, tractor lugs, bucket teeth on loaders, scraper blades, etc., as illustrated in Fig. 4. These electrodes are good for general purpose surfacing and cost consider-

ably less than the tungsten carbide electrode.

Deposits from high carbon electrodes can be heat treated to produce even harder surfaces, or they can be annealed to soften them for machining. The hardness of the deposit de-

Fig. 4. Examples of tools surfaced with high carbon electrodes. These tools must withstand both impact and abrasion forces.

pends on the rate of cooling. The faster the part is cooled, the harder will be the deposit.

In this group are also the electrodes having a high percentage of manganese as an alloying element. Manganese electrodes are tougher but not so abrasion-resistant as the high carbon types.

3. Severe impact and moderately severe abrasion-resistant — Deposits of these electrodes are not hard but are very tough. As such, they are highly resistant to impact and produce good resistance to abrasion. They are often referred to as self-hardening because the deposited surface hardens as it is pounded. While the outside surface is hard, the material underneath remains soft. This prevents cracking, even though there may be some deformation. These electrodes are especially adaptable for hard surfacing rock crusher parts, chain hooks, scraper blades, pins, and links.

Stainless steel electrodes are often used for hardfacing parts that must resist impact forces without cracking. These electrodes offer the least resistance to abrasion in the "as deposited condition"; however, they will work-harden (cold working). In addition to their toughness they are very corrosion-resistant. Stainless steel electrodes are often used as base layers for other hardfacing electrodes.

Methods of Applying Hardfacing

There are many metals that can be hardfaced, including all of the steels, cast iron, nickel alloys, copper, brass, and bronze. Either the shielded metal arc or carbon arc method can be used for hardfacing. The method will, to a considerable extent, depend on the job to be done. As a rule, the carbon arc is more satisfactory for hardfacing thin-edged parts requiring low heat. With the carbon arc the heat can be controlled more easily and therefore there is less danger of burning through the metal. For this process, the hardfacing material is in powder form and

Fig. 5. Spread hardfacing paste evenly over the entire area.

is applied as a paste as shown in Fig. 5.

When burn-through is not a problem, the metallic arc with electrodes is much more effective. However, it is important that the correct type of electrodes be used. It is always wise to follow the manufacturer's directions in selecting the correct electrode.

Hardfacing with the Shielded Metal-Arc

1. Clean the surface thoroughly of

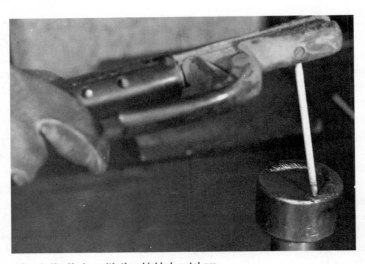

Fig. 6. Hardfacing with the shielded metal arc.

rust, scale, and all other foreign matter.

2. Use only enough amperage to provide sufficient heat to maintain the arc. This is very important to prevent dilution of the deposit by the base metal.

3. Arrange the work so it is in a flat position. Most hardfacing electrodes are designed to be run in a flat position only, as illustrated in Fig. 6.

4. Maintain a medium long arc and do not allow the coating of the electrode to touch the base metal. In making the deposit, use either a straight or weaving bead. A weaving bead is preferred when only a thin deposit is required. Do not extend the width of the weave over ¾″.

5. Remove all the slag from the surface before depositing additional layers.

6. Manipulate the electrode carefully to secure adequate penetration into the adjoining beads. This can be done by holding the electrode a moment over the deposited bead to allow the heat to build up in the adjoining beads. Such a procedure will also minimize undercutting.

A whipping action is often used when surfacing an area along a thin edge. The arc is held over the heavy portion and then whipped out to the thin edge. In this manner a shallow deposit is made before the heat builds up enough in the base metal to burn through.

Hardfacing with the Carbon Arc

1. Clean the surface and place the work in a flat position.

2. Spread hardfacing paste over the area to be faced. If the powder has not been mixed commercially to a paste, add water, alcohol, or other liquid as recommended by the manufacturer. Spread the paste evenly to a depth two

Fig. 7. Move the carbon in a circular motion, keeping the tip of the flame in contact with the surface.

to three times the desired thickness of the final deposit. Then allow the paste to dry momentarily.

3. Set the arc so just enough heat is provided to obtain a free-flowing puddle. If the amperage is too high, there will be an excessive dilution of the base metal and the hardness of the finished surface will be lowered.

4. Move the carbon electrode in a circular motion with the tip of the flame in contact with the surface. When the metal becomes red hot, the paste melts and fuses to the base metal as shown in Fig. 7.

5. If the hard-surfacing material is being applied to a section which tapers to a sharp edge or point, apply most of the heat to the heavier area and rotate the flame to the thin edge just long enough to carry the puddle to the edge or point. Usually it is best to start the puddle at the point and work toward the heavier section.

6. Avoid heavy deposits. If after the first pass the surface is not sufficiently built up, add paste, repeat.

Points to Remember

1. Determine if the part must withstand impact or abrasion or both.

2. Use a tungsten carbide or chromium carbide surfacing electrode for parts that must withstand abrasion.

3. Use high carbon or manganese electrodes for parts subjected to moderate abrasion and impact.

4. Use special electrodes for hardfacing parts which must withstand severe impact loads.

5. Clean the surface thoroughly before depositing hardfacing.

6. Always place the work flat.

7. Use the carbon arc when facing thin-edge materials.

8. Use a minimum amount of heat with both carbon arc and metallic arc.

9. Do not allow the coating of the electrode to contact the base metal.

10. With the metallic arc, be sure to remove all slag before depositing all additional layers.

11. If the shielded metal-arc is employed to hardface thin-edge material, use a weaving or whipping action.

12. When using the carbon arc, spread the paste evenly two to three times the thickness of the final deposit.

13. Move the carbon electrode in a circular motion and concentrate the heat on the thicker section.

QUESTIONS FOR STUDY AND DISCUSSION

1. What is hardfacing?

2. Of what value is hardfacing?

3. What types of wear do parts encounter in service?

4. Why must the correct type of electrode be used for hardfacing?

5. Why are tungsten carbide or chromium carbide electrodes used for

hardfacing parts which must withstand heavy abrasion forces?

6. What are the advantages of chromium carbide electrodes over tungsten carbide?

7. For what type of surfacing are high carbon electrodes used?

8. When are stainless steel electrodes used for hardfacing?

9. What are some factors in choosing the method of hardfacing?

10. Why should excessive heat be avoided in hardfacing?

11. Why should all hardfacing be done in a flat position?

12. How should the shielded metal-arc be manipulated in hardfacing?

13. When is a whipping action used in hardfacing with a shielded metal-arc?

14. How is hardfacing powder applied when using a carbon arc?

15. How thick should the hardfacing material be spread?

16. How should the carbon arc be manipulated?

WELDING ASSIGNMENTS

1. Hardface some worn surface by using the shielded metal-arc process.

2. Hardface a section by the carbon arc method.

CHAPTER 19

Special Arc Processes

Pipe Welding

Pipe of all types and sizes is used a great deal today in transporting oil, gas, and water. It is also used extensively for piping systems in buildings, refineries, and industrial plants. Furthermore, pipe has gained acceptance in construction, and often takes the place of beams, channels, angles, and other standard shapes.

Welding is the easiest and simplest

Fig. 1. Welding is used extensively in joining pipe. (Hobart Brothers Co.)

method of joining sections of pipe together as illustrated in Fig. 1. Welding eliminates complicated threaded joint designs, permits free flow of liquids, and reduces installation costs. Although pipe is often welded by the oxy-acetylene process (see Chapter 31), a faster, less expensive process is the shielded metal-arc, especially for large diameter pipe. A considerable amount is also welded with gas-shielded arc.

Pipe Joints for Welding

The type of joint selected depends considerably on such factors as what is to be conveyed, size of the pipe, pressure of the liquid, pipe material, and code requirements under which the work must be done. In general,

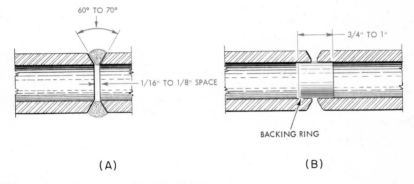

Fig. 2. Two types of joints are commonly used for welding pipe.

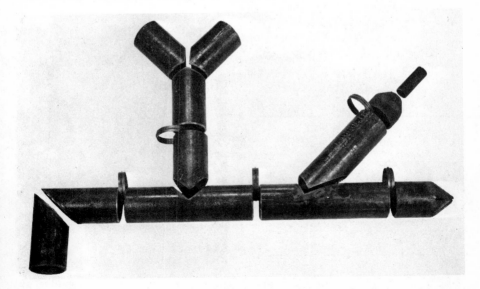

Fig. 3. Backing rings are fitted into the pipe before welding. (Hobart Brothers Co.)

the two types of joints which are the most practical and are used more extensively today are those shown in Fig. 2. The joint at *A* is a plain butt joint and is standard for many gas, oil, and water lines. The joint at *B* is a butt joint with a metal liner. The liner, which is often referred to as a backing ring, is fitted into the pipe before welding. Its function is to assist the welder to secure complete penetration without burning through as well as to prevent spatter and slag from entering the pipe at the joint. Such a ring also assists in securing proper alignment and prevents the formation of masses of metal, sometimes called icicles, on the inside of the joint. See Fig. 3.

Backing rings are either split or continuous. Split rings have the advantage that they can be contracted or expanded slightly to fit the inside diameter snugly. With continuous rings, the pipe must be of the correct diameter so the rings will fit properly.

The outer surface of backing rings —that is, the side which bears against the inside wall of the pipe—is either flat, ridged, or grooved as illustrated in Fig. 4.

Roll and Position Welding

Pipe welding in the field is done in several ways. In one method two or more sections are lined up and tack welded. Special pipe clamps, as shown in Fig. 5, are used to hold the pipe in alignment until they are tacked. The weld is then completed in the flat

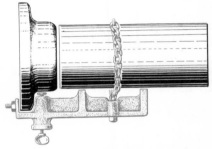

Fig. 5. Fast-action clamps hold the pipe in alignment while tack welds are made.

Fig. 6. Performing a pipe weld in a vertical position. (Hobart Brothers Co.)

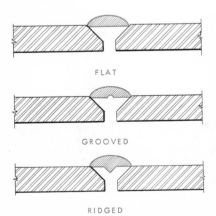

FLAT

GROOVED

RIDGED

Fig. 4. Typical backing rings.

position while helpers rotate the pipe. After the short sections are joined, the long pipe is placed in line with the connecting pipe and the weld made with the entire length in a stationary position. This operation is called *roll welding*.

The *stove pipe* or position method consists of lining up each section, length by length, and welding each joint while the pipe remains stationary. Since the pipe is not revolved, the welding has to be done in various positions — flat, horizontal, vertical, and overhead. See Fig. 6.

Pipe Welding Procedure

1. Tack the pipe joint in three or four places as shown in Fig. 7A.

2. The weld can then be executed in one of three ways:

a. Start the bead at the top and carry it down to the bottom center. Then weld the other side, starting again at the top center and welding downward to the bottom as shown in Fig. 7B. This procedure is often used for welding light walled pipe.

b. For heavy walled pipe, start the weld at the bottom and work upward first on one side and then on the opposite side. Welding upward ensures better penetration. See Fig. 7C.

c. On some welding jobs, the weld is started on the top and carried completely around the pipe as illustrated in Fig. 7D.

Use E-6010 or E-6011 electrodes for pipe welding. With light walled pipe no beveling is needed. Pipe that

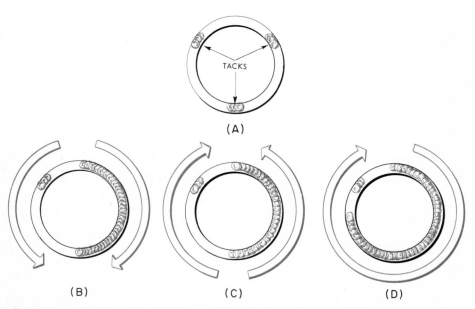

Fig. 7. After tack welding the pipe joint (A), weld the pipe by one of the three methods shown in (B), (C), or (D).

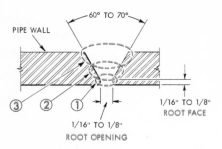

Fig. 8. This is the order in which beads are deposited when welding beveled pipe joints.

shown in Fig. 9A. Weave the electrode slightly to ensure complete penetration on both sides of the vee. On the remaining beads, hold the electrode at an angle of about 30° from the perpendicular and use a wider weaving motion. See Fig. 9B.

Pipe Templates

is ¼″ or more in thickness should be beveled to have an included angle of 60° to 70°.

On beveled pipe, run the first bead with ⅛″ electrodes. Make the second and if necessary the third bead with ⁵⁄₃₂″ or ³⁄₁₆″ electrodes. See Fig. 8.

For the first bead, hold the electrode tip in place and angle the electrode 60° from the perpendicular as

When other than straight end-to-end butt welding is required for pipe, templates of some kind are needed to shape the connecting sections. The pipe may have to be shaped for a 90° turn or a branch line in the form of a tee.

Various procedures are used to fit connecting pieces for angles and tee connections. A simple method is to make a layout of the connection on heavy paper. The paper template is wrapped around the pipe and a line

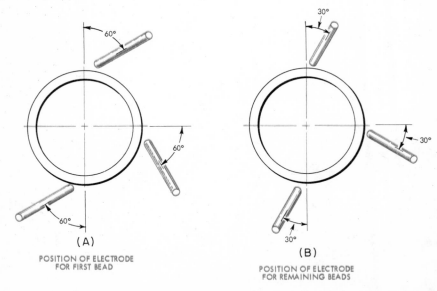

Fig. 9. The positions of the electrode for welding the first bead (A) differ from the positions for laying the remaining beads (B).

TABLE I

Pipe Layout Spacing

Nominal Pipe Size (inches)	Thickness of Metal Std. Wt. Pipe (inches)	Circumference of Pipe (inches)	Spacing of 16 Ordinates (inches)
2	5/32	7 15/32	15/32
2 1/2	13/64	9 1/32	9/16
3	7/32	11	11/16
3 1/2	1/4	12 9/16	25/32
4	1/4	14 1/8	7/8
4 1/2	1/4	15 23/32	31/32
5	17/64	17 15/32	1 3/32
6	9/32	20 13/16	1 5/16
7	5/16	23 31/32	1 1/2
8	11/32	27 3/32	1 11/16
9	11/32	30 1/4	1 7/8
10	3/8	33 25/32	2 1/8
12	3/8	40 1/16	2 1/2
14	3/8	43 31/32	2 3/4
15	3/8	47 1/8	2 15/16
16	3/8	50 1/4	3 5/32
18	3/8	56 9/16	3 17/32
20	3/8	62 27/32	3 15/16

traced with a piece of soapstone. The pipe is then cut with a cutting torch. Several examples are illustrated here on how to lay out pipe templates.

Pipe Template Layout Procedure

1. Assume that a template for a 45° cut on a 6″ pipe is required. Obtain a strip of stout paper, perhaps 12″ wide and long enough to wrap around the pipe.

2. Determine the circumference of the pipe. See Table I under the column headed *Circumference of Pipe*. Note that for a 6″ pipe the circumference is 20 $^{13}/_{16}$″.

3. Find the spacing of the ordinates by dividing the circumference by 16. This spacing may be found in Table I.

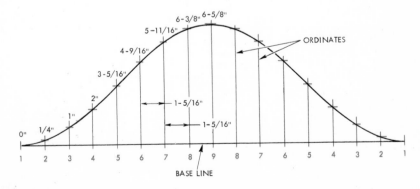

Fig. 10. Laying out the template for a 45° cut.

4. Draw a base line and on this base line space off the ordinates and erect perpendicular lines of indefinite lengths as shown in Fig. 10. Multiply the circumference of the pipe, in this case 20 $^{13}\!/_{16}''$, by the factors in Table II and lay off these values on the ordinates.

5. When all the ordinates have been measured, draw a smooth curve through the points.

6. Table II gives the multiplication factors for 90° turns only. When making turns of other angles, see Table III.

Additional Examples of Pipe Template Layout

Following are additional examples for laying out pipe templates:

90° intersection of cylinders with like diameters. Draw a side view of two cylinders, as shown in Fig. 11, one at right angles to the other. Lines *AB* and *CD* represent the diameters of the desired cylinders *H* and *K*.

On one end of each cylinder draw a semi-circle and divide it into any number of equal parts, numbering the

TABLE II
90° Bends Only

For Ordinate No.	Multiply Circumference of Pipe by Ordinate Factor	For Ordinate No.	Multiply Circumference of Pipe by Ordinate Factor
1	0.0	6	0.22
2	0.012	7	0.272
3	0.047	8	0.306
4	0.098	9	0.318
5	0.159		

TABLE III
Factors for Other Angles

For Angle of Turn Equal to	Multiply Circumference of Pipe by	Remarks
80 deg.	0.839	
70 deg.	0.700	
60 deg.	0.577	
50 deg.	0.466	
45 deg.	0.414	Two welds per 90 deg. turn.
40 deg.	0.364	
30 deg.	0.268	Three welds per 90 deg. turn.
22 1/2 deg.	0.198	Four welds per 90 deg. turn.
20 deg.	0.176	
10 deg.	0.087	

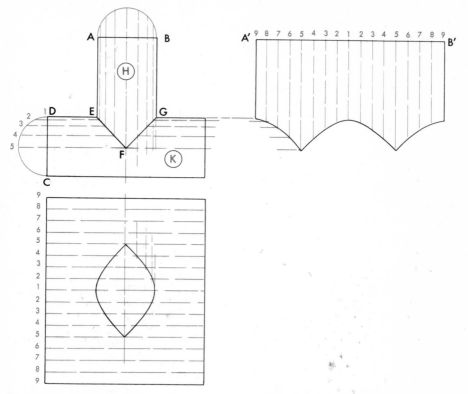

Fig. 11. This is the method of laying out a pattern for a 90° intersection of cylinders with like diameters.

division points 1, 2, 3, 4, etc. Draw the lines *EF* and *FG* at a 45° angle, the intersection *F* lying on the center line of cylinder *K*. Project lines through the numbered division points on both cylinders.

Draw line *A′B′* for the stretchout, and on it lay off the divisions spaced on the semi-circle of cylinder *H*. Draw vertical lines through these points.

From the points where the vertical lines of cylinder *H* intersect the horizontal lines of cylinder *K*, project horizontal lines to intersect the vertical stretchout lines. Finally connect the

intersections on the stretchout with an irregular curve.

Draw the outline of the stretchout for cylinder *K* by laying out the true length of the circumference of that cylinder and locate the divisions as above. Then draw horizontal lines through these division points. Project vertical lines from the semi-circle of cylinder *H* until they intersect the corresponding horizontal stretchout lines of cylinder *K*. Connect the intersection points with an irregular curve.

90° bend. Draw a side view of the cylinder as shown in Fig. 12. The line

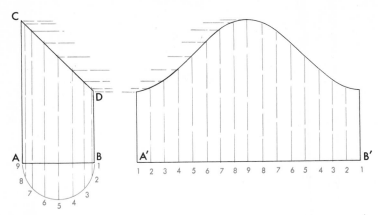

Fig. 12. This is how to lay out a pattern for a 90° bend.

AB represents the diameter of the cylinder, and the mitered line *CD* has the desired angle for the plane of intersection. Using *AB* as a diameter, draw a semi-circle at the base of the cylinder. Divide this semi-circle into any number of equal parts, and number the division points 1, 2, 3, 4, etc. From these points project vertical lines to the slanting line *CD*.

Draw line *A′B′* for the stretchout, and on it space out the numbered divisions of the semi-circle. From these points draw vertical lines of unlimited lengths. Project the points from the slanting line *CD* to intersect the corresponding vertical lines on the stretchout. The horizontal line for point 1 on the mitered line should meet the vertical line for point 1 on the stretchout; the two lines for point 2 should meet; and so on. Connect these intersecting points with an irregular curve.

90° intersection of cylinders with unlike diameters. Draw a side view of two cylinders of the desired diameters. On lines *AB* and *CD*, as shown

in Fig. 13, scribe semi-circles and divide each into any number of equal parts. Number the division points on the semi-circle for cylinder *H*, starting at the end and running to the center. Repeat the same numbers for the opposite half. Since the cylinders have unlike diameters, also draw an end view of the intersecting cylinders. Turn this view of the cylinders around to bring the point numbered 1 on the semi-circle to show in the center position.

Draw line *A′B′* for the stretchout and lay out the divisions, numbering them as shown in Fig. 13. The true outline of the intersection is then found by projecting lines from the end view of the cylinder *H* to the corresponding vertical lines on the stretchout.

Determine the shape for the opening of the cylinder *K* by laying out the true length of the circumference of that cylinder. Draw a vertical line *MN* through the center of this layout. Starting from the point where this line crosses the middle point of pattern

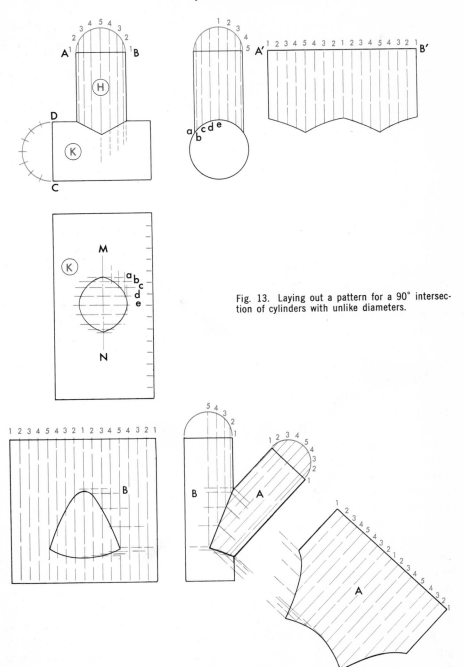

Fig. 13. Laying out a pattern for a 90° intersection of cylinders with unlike diameters.

Fig. 14. This is the procedure for laying out a pattern for angle intersection of cylinders of like diameters.

K, mark off the distances from *e* to *d*, *d* to *c*, *c* to *b*, and *b* to *a*, these distances to be taken along the arc of the end view of cylinder *K*. Draw horizontal lines through these points. From the divisional points of the side view of cylinder *H*, project vertical lines until they intersect the corresponding horizontal lines in the stretchout. Connect the intersection points with an irregular curve.

Angle intersection of cylinders of

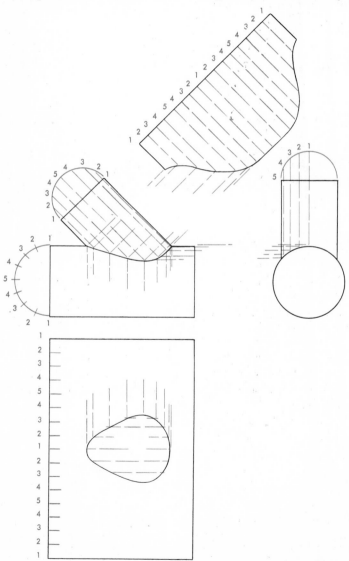

Fig. 15. Laying out a pattern for angle intersection of cylinders of unlike diameters.

like diameters. The method for laying out an angle intersection of two cylinders is similar to that for laying out an intersection of cylinders of unlike diameters. Any desired angle may be used. Details for making the stretchouts for the two cylinders are shown in Fig. 14. Be sure that the center line of cylinder *A* intersects the center line of cylinder *B*.

Angle intersection of cylinders of unlike diameters. The procedure for this problem is practically the same as that used for laying out the 90° intersection of cylinders of unlike diameters. To find the true shape of the angular intersection, end views of both cylinders must be drawn as shown in Fig. 15.

Cutting Branches Without Templates

It frequently happens in the installation of a pipeline that unexpected changes in the layout make it necessary to construct turns or branches for which templates have not been provided. If there is no time to procure a template for such a connection, Fig. 16

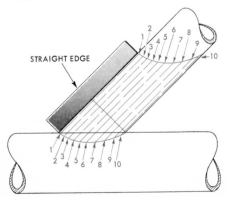

Fig. 16. Method of planning cut for branch without templates.

shows a method of cutting pipe which will give a satisfactory fit for most purposes. Proceed as follows:

1. Set up the two pieces of pipe at the required angle of intersection.

2. Lay a straightedge parallel to the branch and just resting on the main pipe.

3. Punch marks at points 1 and 1.

4. Move the straightedge around the pipe in such a manner that it is always kept parallel to the branch and the lower end just touching the main pipe. At regular intervals mark the end points, such as 2, 3, 4, 5, etc., on both the main and the branch pipe.

5. After the straightedge has been carried completely around the branch, draw a smooth curve with a soapstone through the punch marks.

Points to Remember

1. Bevel the edges of the pipe if the wall thickness is $\frac{1}{4}''$ or more.

2. Tack the pipe in as many places as necessary to keep it in alignment.

3. Use E-6010 or E-6011 electrodes for welding pipe.

4. On light wall pipe start the weld on top and carry it downward. On thick wall pipe start the weld from the bottom and carry it upward.

5. On beveled pipe, run the first bead with $\frac{1}{8}''$ electrodes and the remaining beads with $\frac{5}{32}''$ or $\frac{3}{16}''$.

6. When making the first bead, hold the electrode approximately 60° from the perpendicular. On the remaining passes, hold the electrode about 30° from the perpendicular.

7. Remove all slag before depositing additional beads.

QUESTIONS FOR STUDY AND DISCUSSION

1. Why is the metallic arc used more extensively for welding pipe?

2. What two types of joints are commonly used in welding pipe?

3. What is the function of a backing ring?

4. What types of backing rings are used in welding pipe? How are the outer surfaces of these rings shaped?

5. What is the difference between roll welding and stove pipe welding?

6. In what ways can a pipe be welded?

7. What kind of electrodes are used for pipe welding?

8. How should pipe be beveled?

9. How should the electrode be held for welding pipe?

10. What is meant by a template?

WELDING ASSIGNMENTS

1. Deposit layers of beads around a scrap piece of pipe.

2. Obtain two pieces of ¼″ wall pipe and use a top to bottom weld.

3. Obtain two pieces of ¼″ wall pipe and use a bottom to top weld.

4. Practice making a continuous weld around the pipe.

5. Weld a joint with a 90° bend.

6. Make a tee pipe joint.

CHAPTER 20

Special Arc Processes

Cutting Operations

~~~~~~

Both the metallic arc and carbon arc can be used to cut metal. Cutting with the arc does not produce a smooth, precision cut as with the gas cutting torch (see Chapter 32) but it is quick and reasonably economical. The arc is particularly effective for cutting cast iron and steel for salvage purposes, small pieces, and areas which are hard to reach.

It is easy to understand why cutting with the arc is possible. Heat of the arc ranges from about 6500° to 10,000° F whereas steel, for example, melts at about 2400° F. Since cutting actually is a melting process, the excessive heat of the arc readily melts the metal.

Cutting with the Shielded Metal-Arc

Coated mild steel electrodes are used for cutting purposes with either AC or DC machines. Follow this procedure to carry out a cutting operation:

1. Set the machine for the same polarity as in welding for the electrode selected.

2. Use a mild steel coated electrode such as E-6010 or E-6011. The diameter of the electrode will depend on the thickness of the metal to be cut and the amperage capacity of the machine. For most general purpose cutting use $3/32''$ electrodes for metals up

TABLE I
Suggested Ampere Setting for Cutting

Metal Thickness (inch)	Electrode Diameter (inch)	Ampere Range
up to 1/8	3/32	75–100
up to 1/8	1/8	125–140
over 1/4	5/32	140–180

to ⅛″ in thickness and ⁵⁄₃₂″ electrodes for materials which exceed ¼″ in thickness. Table I gives the approximate ampere setting for cutting.

Keep in mind that the amperage settings listed in Table I apply only to machines limited to 180 amperes. If you are using machines with higher ampere capacity, you can employ larger diameter electrodes with higher ampere settings.

3. Place the metal in a flat position. Start the cut at the bottom edge of the plate; that is, the edge in the lowest position. When the diameter of the electrode is larger than the thickness of the plate being cut, simply move

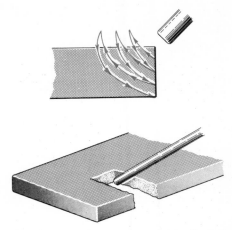

Fig. 2. Use a quick upward motion and then push the molten metal out with a downward motion.

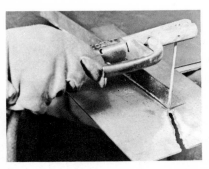

Fig. 1. To cut thin stock, move the electrode in a straight line. Use a guide to ensure a straight cut.

the electrode in a straight line. Check Fig. 1 and note the position of the electrode.

4. When the metal is heavier than the electrode, use a weaving motion to make the cut. Move the electrode with a quick upward motion and then push the electrode downward as shown in Fig. 2. The downward movement helps

to force the molten metal out of the slot.

5. Flat stock over ⅛″ in thickness is often easier to cut if placed in a vertical position. The cut is made from top to bottom as illustrated in Fig. 3.

Fig. 3. For flat stock over ⅛″, make the cut from top to bottom. (The Lincoln Electric Co.)

6. To cut round stock, start the cutting at the outside edge so the metal can flow from the round bar. Carry

Fig. 4. Cut round stock from each side. (The Lincoln Electric Co.)

Fig. 6. To pierce holes in metal over ¼", place the metal on edge. (The Lincoln Electric Co.)

the cut to the center of the piece and then start a new cut on the opposite side as shown in Fig. 4.

Piercing holes. To burn a small hole through thin stock, strike the arc and keep a long arc over the spot to be pierced until the plate begins to sweat.

Next, bring the arc down into the molten pool of metal, moving the electrode in a circular motion as illustrated in Fig. 5. Continue the circular motion until the hole is pierced. It is a good idea to have a punch or bolt on hand so it can be driven into the hole while the metal is still hot. This will help true-up the hole.

To pierce holes in metal over ¼″ in

thickness, place the metal so the hole is made in a vertical position. This permits the molten metal to run out of the hole as shown in Fig. 6. The metal that adheres to the outside surface is easily removed with a chisel or by the heat of the arc.

Cutting large holes. For cutting large holes, follow this procedure:

1. With a soapstone or center punch lay out the hole to be cut.

2. Pierce a small hole in the center of the area to be cut out as shown in Fig. 7.

3. Move the electrode from the center around the edge of the marked circle.

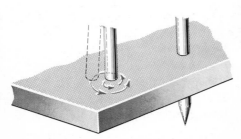

Fig. 5. To pierce a hole, bring the arc into the molten pool and move the electrode in a circular motion.

Fig. 7. For large holes, start the cut in the center and move the electrode around the marked edge.

Cutting with the Carbon Arc

The carbon arc can also be used effectively for cutting. Just as with the metallic arc, the cutting is a melting process and as such does not produce smooth, even edges. Although the carbon arc will cut as well as the metallic arc, it is not generally as satisfactory for burning holes.

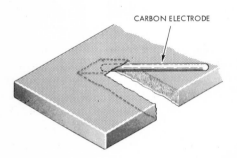

CARBON ELECTRODE

Fig. 8. Keep the lower side of the cut ahead of the upper edge.

The actual cutting process is similar to that of the metallic arc. The current, as in the case of the metallic arc, must be set to a higher value than ordinarily used in welding material of comparable thickness.

Manipulate the carbon electrode so

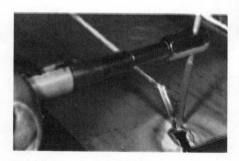

Fig. 9. Cutting with the carbon arc.

as to keep the lower side of the slot ahead of the upper edges as shown in Fig. 8. Move the arc from top to bottom of the cut to force the molten metal down. See Fig. 9.

Plasma Arc Cutting[1]

Plasma arc cutting, better known as Plasmarc cutting was developed by the Linde Company. It is regarded as one of the best processes for high-speed cutting of non-ferrous metals and stainless steels. It cuts carbon steel up to ten times faster than oxy-fuel, with equal quality more economically. See Fig. 10.

Fig. 10. Plasma arc cutting. (Linde Co.)

Plasma is often considered the fourth state of matter. The other three are gas, liquid, and solid. Plasma results when a gas is heated to a high temperature, and changes into posi-

[1] Linde Company

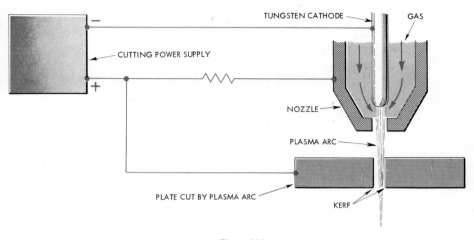

Figure 11A.

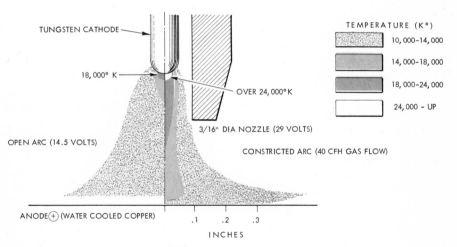

Fig. 11A-B. In Plasmarc cutting the gas flowing through the torch produces a supersonic jet which is hotter than any flame. (Linde Co. Division of Union Carbide Corporation.)

tive ions, neutral atoms and negative electrons. When matter passes from one state to another latent heat is generated. Latent heat is required to change water into steam, and simi-

larly, the plasma torch supplies energy to a gas to change it into plasma. When the plasma changes back to a gas, the heat is released.

In a Plasmarc torch, the tip of the

electrode is located within the nozzle. The nozzle has a relatively small opening (orifice) which constricts the arc. The high-pressure gas must flow through the arc where it is heated to the plasma temperature range. Since the gas cannot expand due to the constriction of the nozzle, it is forced through the opening, and emerges in the form of a supersonic jet, hotter than any flame. This heat melts any known metal and its velocity blasts the molten metal through the kerf. See Figs. 11A and 11B.

Because maximum transfer of heat to work is essential in cutting, Plasmarc torches use a transferred arc (the workpiece itself becomes an electrode in the electrical circuit). The work is thus subjected to both plasma heat and arc heat. Direct current, straight polarity is used. Precise control of the plasma jet is feasible by controlling the variables — current, voltage, type of gas, gas velocity, and gas flow (cfh).

The power supply for cutting is a special rectifier type with an open-circuit rating of 400 volts. A control unit automatically controls the sequence of operations—pilot arc, gas flow, and carriage travel.

A water pressure input of 60 to 80 psi for gas cutting, and 100 psi for air cutting is necessary to keep the torch cool.

When cutting aluminum and stainless steel best results are obtained with an argon-hydrogen, or nitrogen-hydrogen gas mixture. Carbon steels require an oxidizing gas. Air has proven to be the most efficient gas, however oxygen can also be used.

The first steps in making a Plasmarc cut are—adjust the power supply and the gas flow to the appropriate

TABLE II
Typical Plasmarc Cutting Conditions

	THICKNESS (IN.)	SPEED (IPM)	ORIFICE INSERT TYPE	DIA. IN	POWER (KW)	GAS FLOW (CFH)
STAINLESS STEEL	1/2	25	4 x 8	1/8	45	130 N_2
	1/2	70	4 x 8	1/8	60	130 N_2
	1 1/2	25	5 x 10	5/32	85	130 N_2 10 H_2
	2 1/2	18	8 x 16	1/4	150	175 N_2 15 H_2
	4	8	8 x 16	1/4	160	175 N_2 15 H_2
ALUMINUM	1/2	25	4 x 8	1/8	50	100 ①
	1/2	200	4 x 8	1/8	55	100 ①
	1 1/2	30	5 x 10	3/32	75	100 ①
	2 1/2	20	5 x 10	5/32	80	150 ①
	4	12	6 x 12	3/16	90	200 ①
CARBON STEEL	1/4	200	4 x 12M ②	1/8	55	250
	1	50	5 x 14M ②	5/32	70	300
	1 1/2	35	6 x 16M ②	3/16	100	350
	2	25	6 x 16M ②	3/16	100	350

① 65% Argon, 35% Hydrogen Mixture ② Multiport Orifice

Fig. 12. A mechanical plasmarc cutting unit. (Linde Co.)

settings. See Table II. Then, when the operator pushes the start button on the remote-control panel, the control unit performs all on-off and sequencing functions. The cooling water must also be turned on, or the water-flow interlock will block the starting circuit.

To make a mechanized cut, the operator locates the center of the torch about ¼ in. above the surface of the plate to be cut and pushes the start button. Current flows from the high-frequency generator to establish the pilot arc between the electrode (work-piece) and the cathode in the nozzle. Gas starts to flow, and welding current flows from the power supply.

The pilot arc sets up an ionized path for the cutting arc. As soon as the cutting arc is established, the high-

frequency current is shut off, and the carriage starts to move. See Fig. 12.

When the cutting operation is completed, the arc goes out because it has no ground, and the control stops the carriage, opens the main contactor, and shuts off the gas flow.

Arc-Air Cutting

A regular A.C. or D.C. welding machine and compressed air are used in the arc-air cutting process. A carbon-graphite electrode held in a special holder (Fig. 13) provides the electric arc to melt the metal. As the metal melts, a jet of compressed air is directed at the point of arcing to blow the molten metal away. The compressed air line is fastened directly to the torch. The jet air stream is controlled by simply depressing a

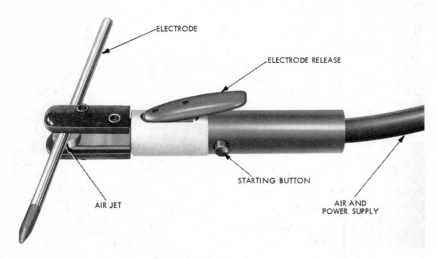

ELECTRODE

ELECTRODE RELEASE

AIR JET

STARTING BUTTON

AIR AND
POWER SUPPLY

Fig. 13. Arc-Air cutting electrode holder. (Arcair Co.)

push-button valve on the holder. See Fig. 13.

Air is supplied by an ordinary compressor. In general pressure will range from 80 to 100 psi. For light work, however, a pressure as low as 60 psi is sufficient. Either plain or copperclad carbon-graphite electrodes can be used. Plain electrodes are less expensive, however copperclad electrodes last longer, carry higher currents and produce more uniform cuts.

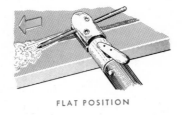

FLAT POSITION

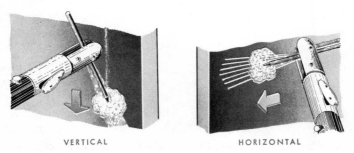

VERTICAL

HORIZONTAL

Fig. 14. Electrode position for gouging. (Arcair Co.)

Gouging Procedure. Hold the torch so the electrode slopes back from the direction of travel. The air blast should be behind the electrode. See Fig. 14. Maintain a short arc and progress fast enough to keep up with metal removal. The depth and contour of the groove is controlled by the electrode angle and travel speed. For a narrow deep groove, a steep electrode angle and slow speed is used. A flat electrode angle and fast speed produces a wide shallow groove. The width of the groove is governed by the diameter of the electrode.

Cutting Procedure. The technique for cutting is the same as gouging, except that the electrode is held at a steeper angle.

Beveling Procedure. Hold the holder parallel to the edge to be beveled, with the electrode at 90° to the holder. The air jet should be on the plate side of the electrode in order to blow the molten metal away from the plate and the beveled edge. See Fig. 15.

Safety Precautions

In any cutting operation, a large

Fig. 15. Electrode position for beveling. (Arcair Co.)

amount of metal always falls on the floor. *Therefore be sure there are no combustible materials nearby.* Turn the cuffs of your trousers down over your shoes to prevent the possibility of molten metal getting inside the cuffs or shoes.

When an excessive amount of cutting is to be done, it is a good idea to sprinkle sand over the concrete floor. This prevents the molten metal from heating the concrete so that it cracks and causes particles to fly upward. Another method is to cut over a work bench drawer partially filled with sand. If the bench lacks a drawer, a sand filled pan can be placed on the floor.

QUESTIONS FOR STUDY AND DISCUSSION

1. Why is it possible to cut metal with an arc?

2. What kind of coated electrodes can be used to cut metal?

3. What determines the diameter of electrodes to be used for cutting?

4. How does the amperage setting for cutting compare with the amperage for welding?

5. Why should the electrode be moved in a weaving motion when the electrode is smaller in diameter than the thickness of the metal?

6. How are holes pierced in metal with electrodes?

7. To pierce holes in metal over ¼" thick, why is it better to do the cutting with the metal in a vertical plane?

8. What is meant by plasmarc cutting?

9. How does arc-air cutting differ from metallic-arc cutting?

10. What are the precautions that should be observed in any cutting operation?

CHAPTER 21

Special Arc Processes

Production Welding

Production welding refers to welding techniques used in the fabrication of goods on a mass production basis. Industries involved in manufacturing such products must rely on welding processes where hand manipulation is kept to a minimum and the joining of metal is performed rapidly and automatically. See Fig. 1.

Since production techniques depend on the nature of the goods made, the kind of welding equipment used will vary from one industry to another. Very often special welding machines are designed for a particular industry. Thus an aircraft company may need a spot welding machine designed to join certain types of aluminum structures. An automotive manufacturer may require a resistance type of seam welder especially made to handle a body structure. Another concern may have

Fig. 1. An automatic welder is used in the fabrication of a missile. (Sciaky Bros. Inc.)

to use a stud welding gun to fasten studs on some metal component. It is the purpose of this chapter to describe briefly some of the more common production welding techniques used in industry.

Resistance Welding

Of the many welding techniques applicable to production processes, resistance welding dominates the field. The fundamental principle upon which all resistance welding is based is this: (1) heat is generated by the resistance of the parts to be joined to the passage of a heavy electrical current, (2) this heat at the juncture of the two parts changes the metal to a plastic state, and (3) when combined with the correct amount of pressure, fusion takes place.

There is a close similarity in the construction of all resistance welding machines whether they are of simple design or are very complex and costly. The main difference is in the type of jaws or electrodes which hold the object to be welded. A standard resistance welder has four principal elements:

1. The frame is the main body of the machine which differs in size and shape for both stationary and portable types.

2. The electrical circuit consists of a step down transformer which reduces the voltage and proportionally increases the amperage to provide the necessary heat at the point of weld.

3. The electrodes include the mechanism for making and holding contact at the weld area.

4. The timing controls represent the switches which regulate the volume of current, length of current time, and the contact period.

The principal forms of resistance welding are classified as spot welding, seam welding, projection welding, flash welding, and butt welding.

Spot welding. This type of welding is probably the most commonly used type of resistance welding. The material to be joined is placed between two electrodes, pressure is applied, and a quick shot of electricity is sent from one electrode through the material to the other electrode.

There are three stages in making a spot weld. First the electrodes are brought together against the metal and pressure applied before the current is turned on. Next the current is turned on momentarily. This is followed by the third, or hold time, in which the current is turned off but the pressure continued. The hold time forges the metal while it is cooling.

Regular spot welding usually leaves slight depressions on the metal which are often undesirable on the "show side" of the finished product. These depressions are minimized by the use of larger-sized electrode tips on the show side.

Spot welders are made for both direct and alternating current. The amount of current used is very important. Too little current produces a light tack giving insufficient strength, too much causes burned welds.

To dissipate the heat and cool the weld as quickly as possible, the electrodes are water-cooled.

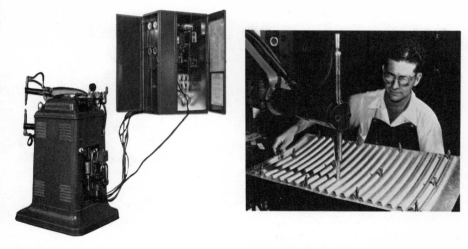

Fig. 2. Single-spot type of spot welding machine. (American Electric Fusion Corp.)

The two basic types of spot welding machines are single spot and multiple spot. The single spot, Fig. 2, has two long horizontal horns, each holding a single electrode, with the upper arm providing the moving action.

Multiple-spot welders have a series of hydraulically or air operated welding guns mounted in a framework or header but using a common mandrel or bar for the lower electrode. The guns are connected by flexible bands to individual transformers or to a common buss bar attached to the

Fig. 3. A Multiple-spot welding machine. (The Taylor-Winfield Corp.)

transformer. See Fig. 3. With some machines two or four guns are often attached to a transformer.

Spot welders are utilized extensively for welding steel, and when equipped with an electronic timer, can be used for other commercial metals such as aluminum, copper, and stainless steel. They are also very effective for welding galvanized metal.

Fig. 5. A self-contained portable spot welder. (Miller Electric Mfg. Co.)

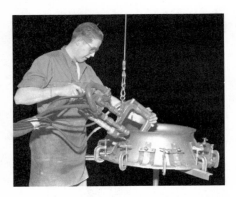

Fig. 4. A spot welding gun is used to weld the intake housing of a commercial fan. (Clarage Fan Co.)

Although many spot welders are of the stationary design, there is an increased demand for the more maneuverable, portable type. The portable, or spot welding gun, as it is often called, consists of a welding head connected by flexible cables which run to the transformer. The jaws are operated either manually, pneumatically, or hydraulically. With this apparatus many spot welds may be made on irregular shaped objects as shown in Fig. 4.

A comparatively recent innovation in the spot welding field is the self-contained portable spot welder as shown in Fig. 5. The welding head contains a built-in timer, electrode contactors, and transformer which requires only a 115 volt power connection. It is especially suitable for sheet metal and auto body welding.

On spot welders, the electrodes which conduct the current and apply the pressure are made of low resistance copper alloy and are usually hollow to facilitate water cooling. These electrodes must be kept clean and shaped correctly to produce good results. Thus if a $\frac{1}{4}''$ diameter electrode face is allowed to increase to $\frac{3}{8}''$ by wear or mushrooming, the contact area is doubled with a corresponding decrease in current density. Unless this is compensated for by an increase in current setting, the result will be weak welds. Additional factors which cause poor welds are: misalignment of electrodes, improper electrode pressure, and convex or concave electrode surfaces.

Pulsation Welding

This is actually a form of spot welding. In regular spot welding the interruption of the flow of welding current

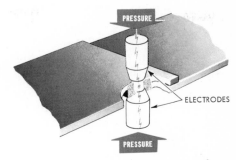

Fig. 6. In pulsation spot welding the current flow is interrupted by precise electronic control. (Republic Steel Corp.)

is controlled manually; with pulsation welding the current is regulated to go on and off a given number of times during the process of making one weld. This method permits spot welding thicker material as well as to increase the life of the electrode. The interrupted current helps to keep the electrodes cooler, thereby minimizing electrode distortion and reducing the tendency of the weld to spark. See Fig. 6.

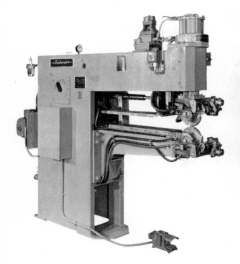

(Aluminum Company of America)

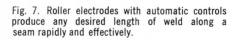

(The Federal Machine & Welder Co.)

Fig. 7. Roller electrodes with automatic controls produce any desired length of weld along a seam rapidly and effectively.

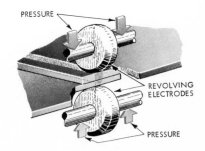

Seam welding. Seam welding is like spot welding except that the spots overlap each other, making a continuous weld seam. In this process the metal pieces pass between roller type electrodes as shown in Fig. 7. As the electrodes revolve, the current is automatically turned on and off at intervals corresponding to the speed at which the parts are set to move. With proper control, it is possible to obtain airtight seams suitable for containers such as

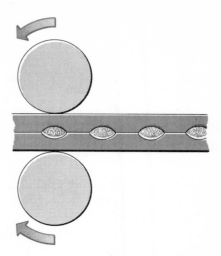

Fig. 9. With proper control setting, intermittent welds of a certain length are produced.

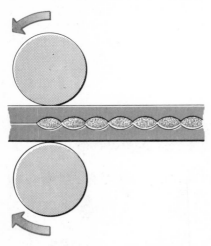

Fig. 8. If welds are spaced close enough, an air-tight seam can be made.

barrels, water heaters, and fuel tanks as shown in Fig. 8. When spots are not overlapped long enough to produce a continuous weld, as illustrated in Fig. 9, the process is sometimes referred to as *roller spot welding*.

Because of the short current cycle, seam welding has several advantages. The rollers may be cooled to prevent overheating with consequent wheel dressing and replacement problems reduced to a minimum. Cooling is ac-

Fig. 10. A portable seam welder is ideal where the structure to be welded is large and cannot conveniently be carried to the welding machine. (The Federal Machine & Welder Co.)

complished either by internally circulating water or by an external spray of water over the electrode rollers. Since the heat input is low, very little of the welded area is hardened and, therefore, the yield point is not materially affected. The fact that very little grain growth takes place in the seam welding process is also important from the standpoint of corrosion-resistant alloys such as stainless steel.

An unusual seam welder is one having a combination of portable welding features with special longitudinal seam welding electrodes. This adaptation permits seam welding on large assemblies where the welder must be brought to the work as shown in Fig. 10.

Projection welding. Projection welding involves the joining of parts by a resistance welding process which closely resembles spot welding. This type of welding is widely used in attaching fasteners to structural members.

The point where the welding is to be done has one or more projections which have been formed by embossing, stamping, casting, or machining. The projections serve to concentrate the welding heat at these areas and facilitate fusion without the necessity of employing a large current. The welding process consists of placing the projections in contact with the mating fixtures and aligning them between the electrodes as illustrated in Fig. 11. Either single or a multitude of projections can be welded simultaneously.

There are many variables involved in projection welding, such as stock thickness, kind of material, and num-

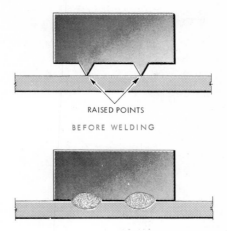

Fig. 11. In projection welding, the weld area has been preformed with raised points.

ber of projections, that make it impossible to predetermine the correct current setting and pressure required. Only by trial runs followed by careful inspection can proper control settings be established.

Not all metals can be projection welded. Brass and copper do not lend themselves to this method because the projections usually collapse under pressure. Aluminum projection welding is limited to extruded parts (shapes formed by forcing metal through a die). Galvanized iron and tin plate, as well as most other thin gage steels, can be successfully projection welded.

Flash welding. In the flash welding process the two pieces of metal to be joined are clamped in dies which conduct the electric current to the work. The ends of the two metal pieces are moved together until an arc is established. The flashing action across

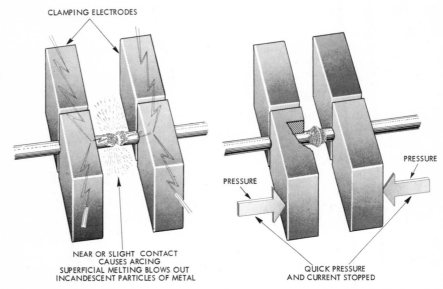

CLAMPING ELECTRODES

NEAR OR SLIGHT CONTACT
CAUSES ARCING
SUPERFICIAL MELTING BLOWS OUT
INCANDESCENT PARTICLES OF METAL

PRESSURE

PRESSURE

QUICK PRESSURE
AND CURRENT STOPPED

Fig. 12. In flash welding the two edges are brought into proximity, causing intense arcing which results in melting the metal. (Republic Steel Corp.)

the gap melts the metal and as the two molten ends are forced together, fusion takes place as shown in Fig. 12. The current is cut off as soon as the forging action is completed. See Fig. 13.

Flash welding is used to butt or mitre weld sheet, bar, rod, tubing, and extruded sections. It has unlimited application for both ferrous and non-ferrous metals. It is not generally rec-

Fig. 13. A steel ring is shown here being flash welded. (The Federal Machine & Welder Co.)

ommended for welding cast iron, lead, or zinc alloys.

Parts to be welded are clamped by copper alloy dies shaped to fit each piece. For some operations the dies are water cooled to dissipate the heat from the welded area. The most important factor to be considered in flash welding is the precision alignment of the parts. Misalignment not only results in a poor joint but also produces uneven heat and telescoping of one piece over another.

The only serious problem encountered in flash welding is the resultant bulge or increased size left at the point of weld. If the finish area of the weld is important, then it becomes necessary to grind or machine the joint to the proper size.

Butt welding. In butt welding the metals to be welded are brought into contact under pressure, an electric current is passed through them, and the edges are softened and fused together as illustrated in Fig. 14. This process differs from flash welding in that constant pressure is applied during the heating process which eliminates flashing. The heat generated at the point of contact results entirely from resistance. Although the operation and control of the butt welding process is almost identical to flash welding, the

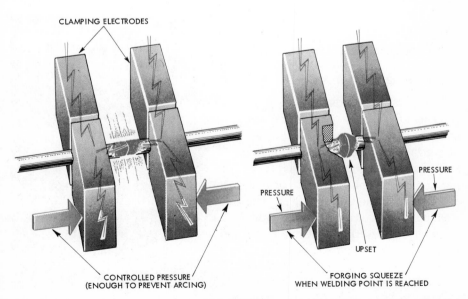

Fig. 14. In butt welding the two ends are butted together and a high current passed through which melts the metal. Continuous pressure fuses the ends. (Republic Steel Corp.)

Fig. 15. An automatic butt welding machine. (The Federal Machine & Welder Co.)

basic difference is in the use of less current and allowing more time for the weld to be completed. See Fig. 15.

Automatic Gas-Metal Arc Welding

Gas-metal arc welding has been acclaimed as the most economical and effective method of joining light gages of hard-to-weld metals such as nickel, stainless steel, aluminum, brass, copper, titanium, columbium, molybdenum, inconel, monel, and silver. This welding process is performed either manually, as described in Chapter 16, or by means of automatic machines.

There are two types of automatic machines: the portable and the stationary. With the portable, the operator holds the unit as in Fig. 16. When

Fig. 16. A portable inert-gas-shielded arc gun being used to join a metal structure. (Airco)

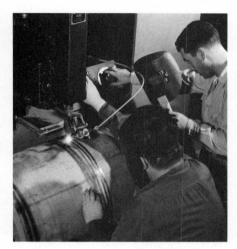

Fig. 17. The automatic inert - gas - shielded arc process produces dependable welds rapidly. (Bell Aircraft Corp.)

the trigger is pressed, the gas, current, and wire automatically begin to flow. The operator simply has to concentrate on performing the weld in the designated area.

The stationary gas-metal arc unit differs from the gun type mainly in the welding head. The welding head

is stationary instead of being portable. The head is either mounted on a carriage which travels over the work or it is in a fixed position and the structure to be welded is moved under the unit as shown in Fig. 17.

Stud Welding[1]

Stud welding is a form of electric arc welding. It was used to some extent in the early thirties or before, but did not reach its present form of complete utility until the late forties. At present there have been two methods developed, each with a different principle of operation. One of these is recognized by the use of a flux and a ceramic ferrule. Equipment consists of a gun, a timing device which controls the DC welding current, the specially designed studs and ceramic ferrules. Studs are available in a wide variety of shapes, sizes and types to meet a variety of purposes. These studs

---

[1]**Republic Steel Corp.**

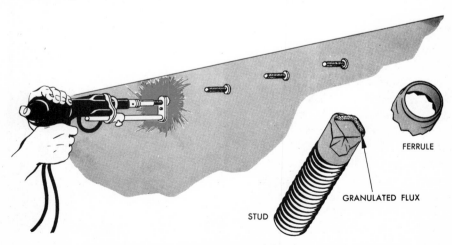

FERRULE

GRANULATED FLUX

STUD

Fig. 18. Stud welding—Nelson Method. (Republic Steel Corp.)

have a recess in the welding end which contains the flux. This flux acts as an arc stabilizer and a deoxidizing agent. An individual porcelain ferrule is used with each stud when welding. It is a most vital part of the operation in that it concentrates the heat, acts (with the flux) to restrict the air from the molten weld, confines the molten metal to the weld area, shields the glare of the arc, and prevents charring of the material (if any) through which the stud is being welded.

In operation, a stud is loaded into the chuck of the gun and a ferrule positioned over the stud. When the trigger is depressed the current energizes a solenoid coil which lifts the stud away from the plate, causing an arc which melts the end of the stud and the area on the plate. A timing device shuts off the current at the proper time. The solenoid releases the stud and a spring action plunges the stud into the molten pool and the weld is made.

Another method is characterized by a small cylindrical tip on the joining face of the stud. The diameter and length of this tip vary with the diameter of the stud and the material being welded. This method operates on alternating current, and a source of about 85 pounds air pressure is also required. The gun is air-operated with a collet (to hold the stud) attached to the end of a piston rod. Constant air pressure holds the stud away from the metal until ready to make the weld, then air pressure drives the stud against the work. When the small tip touches the workpiece, a high amperage, low voltage discharge results, creating an arc which melts the entire area of the stud and the corresponding area of the work. Arcing time is about one mil second (0.001), thus a weld is completed with little heat penetration, no distortion and practically no fillet. The stud is driven at a velocity of about 31 inches per second and the

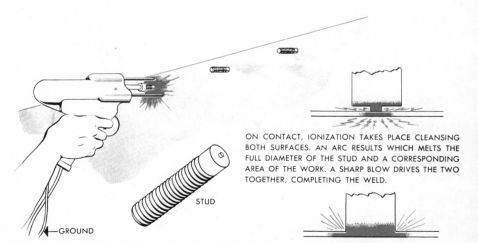

ON CONTACT, IONIZATION TAKES PLACE CLEANSING BOTH SURFACES. AN ARC RESULTS WHICH MELTS THE FULL DIAMETER OF THE STUD AND A CORRESPONDING AREA OF THE WORK. A SHARP BLOW DRIVES THE TWO TOGETHER, COMPLETING THE WELD.

STUD

GROUND

Fig. 19.   Stud welding—Graham Method. (Republic Steel Corp.)

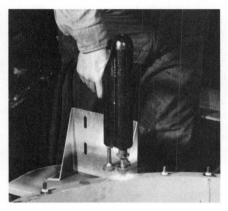

Fig. 20. Stud welding eliminates the necessity of drilling and tapping in the coverplate assembly on this tank. (Nelson Stud Welding Co.)

explosive action as it meets the workpiece cleanses the area to be welded. A minimum thickness of the workpiece of 0.02 inches is desired, particularly if no marking on the reverse side is required.

Both methods of stud welding are adaptable to welding of most ferrous and non-ferrous metals, their alloys, and any combination thereof. See Figs. 18, 19, and 20.

Thermit Welding

Thermit welding is probably one of the oldest methods of welding and is almost extinct today. Its use is restricted to joining large or heavy cross-sectional pieces such as railroad rails and large castings.

This form of welding is actually a foundry casting process. A mold is built around the ends to be welded. A thermit charge consisting of a mixture of iron oxide and granulated aluminum

with small quantities of alloying element is placed in a crucible. When the mixture is ignited, the liberated heat combines the aluminum with the oxygen in the iron oxide and produces free molten steel. The molten steel is then allowed to flow into the mold and its great superheat fuses together the ends of the piece to be joined.

Electron Beam Welding

Electron beam welding is essentially a fusion welding process. Fusion is achieved by focusing a high power density beam of electrons on the area to be joined. Upon striking the metal, the kinetic energy of the high velocity electrons changes to thermal energy, causing the metal to melt and fuse.

The electrons are emitted from a tungsten filament heated to approximately 2000° C. Since the filament would quickly oxidize at this temperature, if it were exposed to normal atmosphere, the welding must be done in a vacuum chamber. Therefore a vacuum chamber is necessary to prevent the electrons from colliding with molecules of air which would make the electrons scatter and lose their kinetic energy.

Electron beam welding can be used to join materials ranging from thin foil to 2 inches in thickness. It is particularly adaptable to the welding of refractory metals such as tungsten, molybdenum, columbium, tantalum, and metals which readily oxidize, such as titanium, beryllium, and zirconium. It also has wide application in joining dissimilar metals, aluminum, standard steels, and ceramics.

Advantages: Electron beam welding has several distinct advantages according to John Meir, Chief Engineer Electron Beam System of Hamilton Standard Division of United Aircraft Corporation. "It facilitates welding with a low total energy input. Workpiece distortion and effects on the material properties of the workpiece are reduced to a minimum. The weld size and location can be controlled relative to the energy input. The process is extremely chemically clean and facilitates welding without contamination of the workpiece."

Electron beam welding is often associated with the joining of difficult to weld metals. It is used in Aerospace fabrication where new metals require more exacting joining characteristics, however, adaptation of the process to commercial products is in-

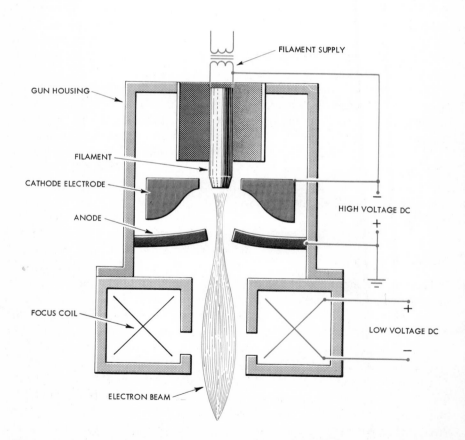

FILAMENT SUPPLY

GUN HOUSING

FILAMENT

CATHODE ELECTRODE

ANODE

HIGH VOLTAGE DC

+

FOCUS COIL

LOW VOLTAGE DC

+

−

ELECTRON BEAM

Fig. 21, Typical elements of an electron beam gun. (Sciaky Bros., Inc.)

creasing. There is every indication that this growth in commercial application will continue.

Limitations

One of the major limitations of electron beam welding is that the work must be done in a vacuum chamber. Consequently, the piece must be small enough to fit into the chamber. This limitation is being reduced to some extent because larger chambers are now manufactured to accommodate a vast variety of products. Another limitation is that when the workpiece is in the chamber in a vacuum it becomes inaccessible. It must be manipulated by some special device. However, engineers believe that in a few years electron beam welding, with all of its advantages, can be done without a vacuum chamber and applied to any normal atmospheric requirement.

Major Units of the System

Electron beam welding equipment usually includes the following basic modules:

1. Electron Gun consisting of a filament, cathode, anode, and focusing coil. See Fig. 21. The electrons emit-

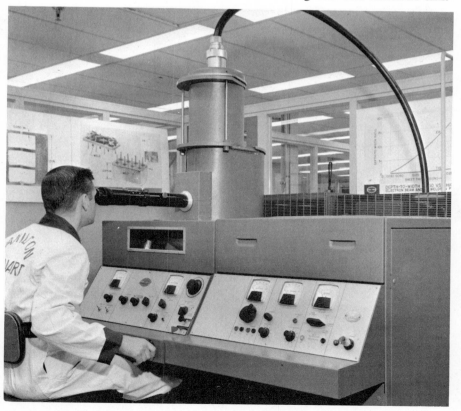

Fig. 22. Electron beam welding machine. (Hamilton Standard-United Aircraft Corp.)

ted from the heated filament carry a negative charge and are repelled by the cathode and attracted by the anode. The electrons pass through an aperture in the anode and then through a magnetic field generated by the electromagnetic focusing coil. An optical viewing system provides a line of sight down the path of the electron beam centerline to the weld area when the beam is off. See Figs. 22 and 23. By varying the current to the focusing coil, the operator can focus the beam for gun-to-work distances ranging from

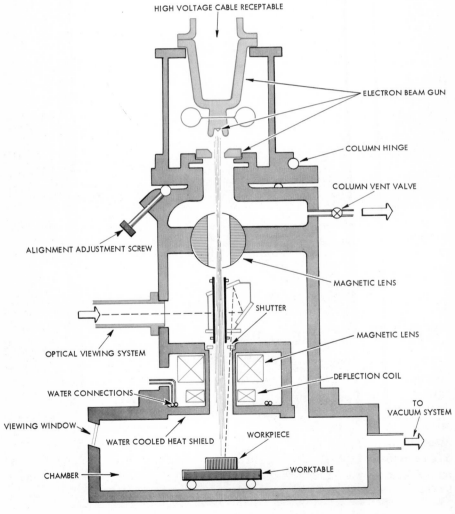

HIGH VOLTAGE CABLE RECEPTABLE

ELECTRON BEAM GUN

COLUMN HINGE

COLUMN VENT VALVE

ALIGNMENT ADJUSTMENT SCREW

MAGNETIC LENS

SHUTTER

MAGNETIC LENS

OPTICAL VIEWING SYSTEM

DEFLECTION COIL

WATER CONNECTIONS

TO VACUUM SYSTEM

VIEWING WINDOW

WATER COOLED HEAT SHIELD

WORKPIECE

CHAMBER

WORKTABLE

Fig. 23. Schematic of electron beam gun column. (Hamilton Standard-United Aircraft Corp.)

Fig. 24. Vacuum chamber where the workpiece to be welded is positioned. (Hamilton Standard-United Aircraft Corp.)

½ inch to 25 inches. The electron beam can be controlled with a focusing coil to produce a spot diameter of less than .005 of an inch.

2. Vacuum Chamber usually rectangular in shape has heavy glass windows or ports to permit viewing the work. A work table in the chamber is arranged so it can be operated either manually or electrically in the X and Y directions. "T" slots are provided on the table to attach fixtures or workpieces for welding as shown in Fig. 24.

3. Vacuum Pumping System de-

signed to provide a clean, dry vacuum chamber in a relatively short time. The capacity of the pump required is governed by the volume and area of the chamber and the time required to evacuate the chamber. The pumping equipment is usually completely automatic.

4. Electrical Controls include set-up controls and operating controls. The set-up controls include instruments required for the initial setup of the welding operation, such as meters for beam voltage, beam current, focusing current, and filament current.

The operating controls consist of stop-and-start sequence, high voltage adjustment, focusing adjustment, filament activation, and work table motion. These controls are mounted so they are easily accessible to the operator while he is observing the welding action through the viewing window.

5. Power Unit furnishes the main high voltage supply up to 150 kv and a low filament power up to 6 volts.

Operating the Equipment

Set Up Procedure. The workpiece is positioned on the work carriage in the chamber. The set up steps are begun. The beam gun, and work-to-gun distance are aligned manually, and visually by use of the optical system. Work travel or gun travel (depending on the type of welding facility used) are checked and adjusted for alignment.

The vacuum chamber is then closed. Vacuum-controls are initiated and the chamber is pumped down to the required vacuum (usually prescribed in a weld schedule).

Beam voltage, beam current, filament current and focusing current controls are then set from the weld schedule. This schedule is usually made by a welding engineer. When these control settings have been checked, the beam current may be switched on and off instantaneously for a weld spot alignment check. By viewing the weld spot through the optical system, determination is made with regard to operation for the actual welding.

The weld or weld area is viewed by opening the shutter only when the beam current is turned off. If the shutter is opened when beam current is on, the result will be severe damage to the optical system.

Weld Procedure. After all the aforegoing have been checked and all switching made operative, the welding is begun by switching the sequence start switch to the 'on' position. The weld is made automatically.

It has been mentioned that the growth of applications for electron beam welding no longer limit it exclusively to exotic metal welding. It may also be assumed that electron beam welding will never entirely replace other welding processes.

All welding processes in their proper application should continue to serve a useful purpose in the wide spectrum of welding functions.

Inertia Welding

Inertia or friction welding is a process where stored kinetic energy is used to generate the required heat for fusion. The two workpieces to be joined are axially aligned. One is held stationary by means of a chuck or fixture, and the other is securely clamped in a rotating spindle.

The rotating member is brought up to a certain speed so as to develop sufficient energy. Then the drive source is disconnected and the pieces brought into contact under a pre-computed thrust load. At this point the kinetic energy contained in the rotating mass converts to frictional heat. The metal

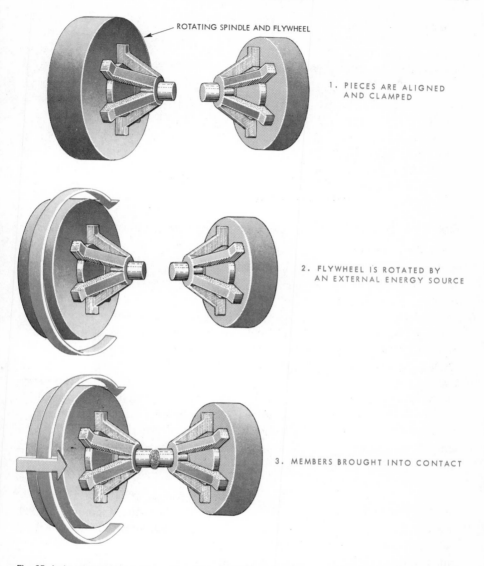

ROTATING SPINDLE AND FLYWHEEL

1. PIECES ARE ALIGNED AND CLAMPED

2. FLYWHEEL IS ROTATED BY AN EXTERNAL ENERGY SOURCE

3. MEMBERS BROUGHT INTO CONTACT

Fig. 25. In inertia welding, heat resulting from stored kinetic energy is used to forge the pieces together. (Caterpillar Tractor Co.)

at and immediately behind the interface is softened, permitting the workpieces to be forged together. See Figs. 25 and 26.

Inertia welding has several advantages over conventional flash or butt welding. It produces improved welds at higher speed and lower cost, less electrical current is required, and costly copper fixtures for hold parts

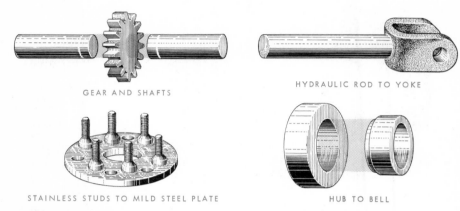

GEAR AND SHAFTS

HYDRAULIC ROD TO YOKE

STAINLESS STUDS TO MILD STEEL PLATE

HUB TO BELL

Fig. 26. Typical examples of parts welded by inertia welding. (Caterpillar Tractor Co.)

are eliminated. With inertia welding there is less shortening of the components, which often results in flash or butt welding. Also the heat-affected zone adjacent to the weld is confined to a narrow band and therefore does not draw the temper of the surrounding area.

The inertia welding process is applicable for welding many dissimilar or exotic metals as well as similar metals. Weld strength is normally equal to that of the original metals.

Laser Welding

Laser welding is like welding with a white-hot needle. Fusion is achieved by directing a highly concentrated beam to a spot about the diameter of a human hair. The highly concentrated beam generates a power intensity of one billion or more watts per square centimeter at its point of focus. Because of its excellent control of heat input, the laser can fuse metal next to glass or even weld near varnished

coated wires without damaging the insulating properties of the varnish.

Since the heat input to the workpiece is extremely small in comparison to other welding processes, the size of the heat affected zone and the thermal damage to the adjacent parts of the weld are minimized. Thus it is possible to weld heat-treated alloys without affecting their heat-treated condition. As a matter of fact the weldment can be held in the hand immediately after the weld is completed.

The laser can be used to join dissimilar metals and other difficult to weld metals such as copper, nickel, tungsten, aluminum, stainless steel, titanium and columbium. Furthermore, the laser beam can pass through transparent substances without affecting them, thereby making it possible to weld metals that are sealed in glass or plastic. The fact that the heat source is a light beam, the effects of atmospheric contamination on the weld joint is not a problem.

The current application of laser

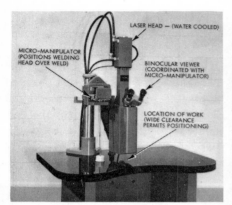

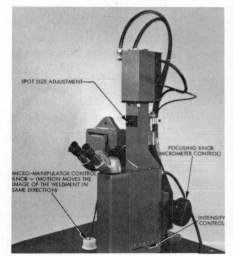

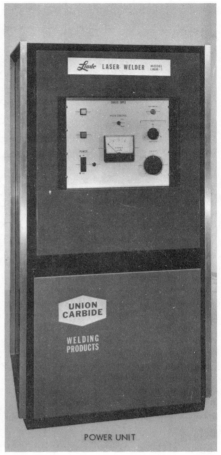

Fig. 27. Laser welding unit. (Linde Co.)

welding is largely in aerospace and electronic industries where extreme control in weldments is required. Its major limitation is the shallow penetration. Present day equipment restricts it to metals not over 0.020 inches in thickness.

The duration of the beam is usually about 0.002 seconds with a pulse rate of one to ten times per second. As each point of the beam hits the metal, a spot is melted but solidifies in microseconds. The line of weld thus consists of a series of round solidified puddles each overlapping the other. The workpiece is either moved beneath the beam or the energy source is moved across the line of weld.

Focusing the beam onto the workpiece is accomplished with an optical system and the actual control of the welding energy by means of a switch. See Fig. 27.

Theory of the Laser Beam[1]. Atoms have been made to generate energy by exciting them in such common devices as fluorescent lights and television tubes. Fluorescence refers to the ability of certain atoms to emit light when they are exposed to external radiation of shorter wave lengths.

In the Laser Welder, the atoms that are excited to produce the laser light beam are locked in a man-made ruby rod 3⁄8-in. in diameter. See Fig. 28. The ruby is identical to a natural ruby but has a more perfect crystal structure. About .05 per cent of its weight consists of chromium oxide.

The chromium atoms give the ruby its red color because they adsorb green light from external light sources. When the atoms adsorb this light energy, some of their electrons are excited. Thus, green light is said to pump the chromium atoms to a higher energy state.

The atoms eventually return to their original state. In doing so, they give up a portion of the extra energy they previously adsorbed (as green light) in the form of red fluorescent light.

When the red light emitted by one excited atom hits another excited atom, the second atom gives off red light which is in phase with the colliding red light wave. In other words, the red light from the first atom is amplified because more red light exactly like it is produced.

By using a very intense green light to excite the chromium atoms in the ruby rod, a larger number of atoms can be excited and the chances of collisions are increased.

To further enhance this effect, the parallel ends of the rod are mirrored to bounce the red light back and forth within the rod. When a certain critical intensity of pumping is reached (the so-called threshold energy), the chain reaction collisions become numerous enough to cause a burst of red light. The mirror at the front end of the rod is only a partial reflector, allowing the burst of light to escape through it.

---

[1]Courtesy Union Carbide Corp.—Linde Division.

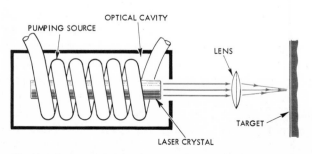

Fig. 28. Schematic diagram of laser welder. (Linde Co.)

Plasma Welding

Plasma welding is a process which utilizes a central core of extreme temperature surrounded by a sheath of cool gas. The required heat for fusion is generated by an electric arc which has been highly intensified by the injection of a gas into the arc stream. The super-heated columnar arc is concentrated into a narrow stream and when directed on metal makes possible butt welds up to one-half inch in thickness or more in a single pass without filler rods or edge preparation. See Fig. 29.

In some respects plasma welding may be considered as an extension of the conventional gas tungsten arc welding. The main difference is that in plasma welding the arc column is constricted and it is this constriction that produces the much higher heat transfer rate.

The arc plasma actually becomes a

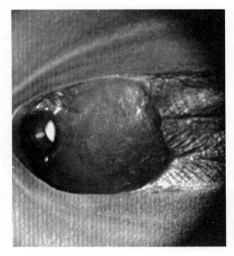

Fig. 30. Top view of "keyhole" with bead in ½ inch thick plate of titanium. (Thermal Dynamics Corp.)

jet of high current density. The arc gas upon striking the metal cuts or "keyholes" entirely through the piece producing a small hole which is carried along the weld seam. See Fig. 30. During this cutting action, the melted metal in front of the arc flows around the arc column, then is drawn together immediately behind the hole by surface tension forces and reforms in a weld bead.

The specially designed torch (Fig. 31) for plasma welding can be hand held or mounted for stationary or mechanized applications. See Fig. 32. The process can be used to weld stainless steels, carbon steels, Monel, Inconel, titanium, aluminum, copper and brass alloys. See Fig. 33. Although for many fusion welds no filler rod is needed, a continuous filler wire can be added for various fillet types of weld joints.

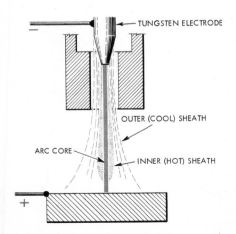

TUNGSTEN ELECTRODE

OUTER (COOL) SHEATH

ARC CORE

INNER (HOT) SHEATH

Fig. 29. Plasma welding uses a central core of extreme temperature surrounded by a sheath of cool gas. (Thermal Dynamics Corp.)

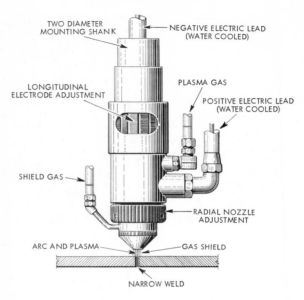

TWO DIAMETER MOUNTING SHANK

NEGATIVE ELECTRIC LEAD (WATER COOLED)

LONGITUDINAL ELECTRODE ADJUSTMENT

PLASMA GAS

POSITIVE ELECTRIC LEAD (WATER COOLED)

SHIELD GAS

RADIAL NOZZLE ADJUSTMENT

ARC AND PLASMA

GAS SHIELD

NARROW WELD

Fig. 31. Torch for plasma welding. (Thermal Dynamics Corp.)

Fig. 32. Plasma welding torch can be mounted for stationary or mechanized applications. (Thermal Dynamics Corp.)

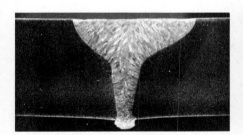

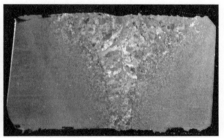

Single-pass butt weld in ½ in. thick Type 304 stainless steel. Welds produced by "keyholing" have this typical "wine glass" shape. No edge preparation or filler metal.

Single-pass butt weld in ½ in. thick titanium. "Wine glass" configuration bounds coarse grain structure. No edge preparation or filler metal.

Single-pass butt weld in ¼ in. thick mild steel using "keyhole" technique. No edge preparation or filler metal.

Fig. 33. Types of weld penetration on different types of metal produced with plasma welding. (Thermal Dynamics Corp.)

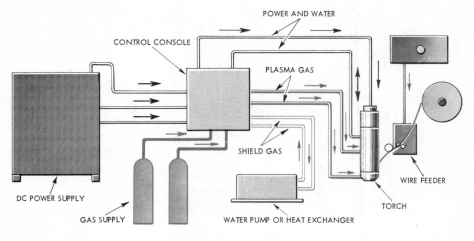

Fig. 34. Typical plasma welding installation and control console. (Thermal Dynamics Corp.)

Equipment. A regular heavy duty DC rectifier is used as the source of power for plasma welding. A special control console is required to provide the necessary operating controls. A water cooling pump is usually needed to assure a controlled flow of cooling water to the torch at a regulated pressure. Proper cooling prolongs the life of the electrode and nozzle. See Fig. 34.

Gas supply is either argon or helium. In some application, argon is used as the plasma gas and helium as the shielding gas. However in many operations argon is used for shielding and generating the plasma arc.

Ultrasonic Welding

If two metal pieces with perfectly smooth surfaces were brought into intimate contact, the metal atoms of one piece conceivably could unite with

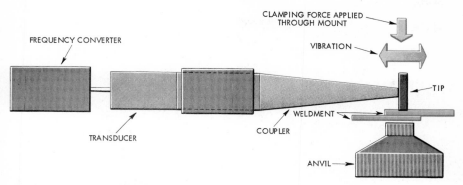

Fig. 35. Schematic of a typical ultrasonic welder. (Sonobond Corp.)

the atoms of the other piece to form a permanent bond. However, regardless of how smooth such surfaces could be produced, a sound metallurgical bond normally would not occur because it is virtually impossible to prepare surfaces that are absolutely smooth. No matter what means were used to smooth surfaces, they would still possess peaks and valleys as measured on an atomic scale. As a result only the peaks of both workpieces which came into intimate contact would unite, leaving the countless atoms of valleys without the power of forming a bond. Furthermore, smooth surfaces are never actually clean. Oxygen molecules from the atmosphere react with the metal to form oxides. These oxides attract water vapor, forming a film of moisture on the oxidized metal surface. Both the moisture and oxide film also act as barriers to prevent intimate contact.

In the ultrasonic welding process, these three existing barriers are broken down by plastically deforming the interface between the workpieces. This is done by means of vibratory energy which disperses the moisture, oxide, and irregular surface to bring the areas of both pieces into close contact and form a solid bond. Vibratory energy is generated by a transducer. A schematic of a typical ultrasonic welding unit is shown in Fig. 35.

The welding equipment consists of two units: a power source or frequency converter which converts 60 cycle line power into high-frequency electrical power and a transducer which changes the high-frequency electrical power into vibratory energy. The components to be joined are simply clamped between a welding tip and supporting anvil with just enough pressure to hold them in close contact. The high frequency vibratory energy is then transmitted to the joint for the required period of time. The bonding is accomplished without applying external heat, filler rod or melting metal. Either spot-type welds or continuous-seam welds can be made on a variety of metals ranging in thickness from .00017″ (aluminum foil) to

Fig. 36. Ultrasonic continuous-seam welder.(Sono-bond Corp.)

0.10″. Thicker sheet and plate can be welded if the machine is specifically designed for them. High strength bonds are possible both in similar and dissimilar metal combinations.

Ultrasonic welding is particularly adaptable for joining electrical and electronic components, hermetic sealing of materials and devices, splicing metallic foil, welding aluminum wire and sheet, and fabricating nuclear fuel elements. See Fig. 36.

Welding variables such as power, clamping force, weld time for spot welds or welding rate for continuous-seam welds can be preset and the welding cycle completed automatically. A foot switch or some other trig-gering mechanism lowers the welding head, applies the necessary clamping force and starts the flow of ultrasonic energy. Successful ultrasonic welding depends on the proper relationship between these welding variables which is usually determined experimentally for a specific application. Thus clamping force may vary from a few grams for very light materials to several thousand pounds for heavy pieces. Weld time may range from 0.005 to 1.0 seconds for spot welding and a few feet per minute to 400 fpm for continuous-seam welding. The high-frequency electrical input to the transducer may be anywhere from a fraction of a watt to several kilowatts.

QUESTIONS FOR STUDY AND DISCUSSION

1. What are some of the production welding processes?
2. What is the basic principle of resistance welding?

3. How does a portable spot welder differ from an ordinary stationary spot welder?
4. What is a seam welder?

5. What is roller spot welding?

6. What is projection welding?

7. How does flash welding differ from butt welding?

8. What is meant by pulsation welding?

9. How does the stud welding gun operate?

10. How is thermit welding accomplished?

11. How is fusion obtained in electron beam welding?

12. What are some advantages, and what are some limitations of electron beam welding?

13. How does plasma welding differ from regular Tig welding?

14. What is the function of the transducer in ultrasonic welding?

15. How is fusion of metal accomplished in ultrasonic welding?

16. In laser beam welding how is the high intensity laser light beam generated?

17. What is the basic principle of inertia welding?

CHAPTER 22

Oxy-Acetylene Welding

Machines and Accessories

〜〜〜〜〜〜〜〜〜〜〜〜〜〜〜〜〜〜〜〜〜〜

The process of oxy-acetylene welding is possible because of the principle that, when acetylene is mixed with oxygen in correct proportions and ignited, the resulting flame is one of the hottest known. This flame, which reaches a temperature of 6300° F, melts all commercial metals so completely that metals to be joined actually flow together to form a complete bond without application of any mechanical pressure or hammering. In most instances, some extra metal in the form of a wire rod is added to the molten metal in order to build up the seam slightly for greater strength. On very thin material the edges are usually flanged and just melted together. In either case, if the weld is performed correctly, the section where the bond is made will be as strong as the base metal itself.

With the oxy-acetylene flame, such

Fig. 1. Flame hardening with an oxy-acetylene flame permits hardening just those surfaces of the gear teeth that are subjected to wear in service. (Linde Co.)

metals as iron, steel, cast iron, copper, brass, aluminum, bronze, and other alloys may be welded. In many instances dissimilar metals can be joined, such as steel and cast iron, brass and steel, copper and iron, brass and cast iron.

The oxy-acetylene flame is also employed for a variety of other purposes, notably for cutting metal, case hardening, and annealing. It is used for several types of metallic spray guns which spray fine particles of molten metal on worn surfaces that need refacing or building up. As a matter of fact it can be used in practically any situation which involves joining metal parts. See Fig. 1.

Separating Oxygen for Use in Welding

The atmosphere, which we commonly refer to as air, is composed of approximately 20 per cent oxygen, the rest being nitrogen and a small percentage of rare gases such as helium, neon, and argon. To obtain the oxygen in a state that makes it usable for welding, it is necessary to separate it from the other gases.

The two general methods that may be used to produce oxygen are the electrolytic and the liquid-air methods. In the electrolytic method, the fact is utilized that water is a chemical compound consisting of oxygen and hydrogen. By sending a current through a solution of water containing caustic soda, oxygen is isolated at one terminal plate and hydrogen at the other, thereby making possible the separation of the two gases. Because of the greater cost in manufacturing oxygen in this manner, the liquid-air method is more commonly used to produce commercial oxygen.

In a plant where oxygen is made by the liquid-air method, the air is drawn from the outside into huge containers known as washing towers, where the air is washed and purified of carbon dioxide. A solution of caustic soda is used to wash the air, this solution being run from a nearby tank and circulated through the towers by means of centrifugal pumps. As the air leaves the washing towers, it is compressed and passed through *oil-purging cylinders* in which oil particles and water vapor are removed. From this point the air goes into drying cylinders. These cylinders contain dry, caustic potash which dries the air and removes any remaining carbon dioxide and water vapor. On the top of each cylinder, special cotton filters are provided to prevent any particles of foreign matter from being carried into the high-pressure lines. The dry, clean, compressed air then goes into rectifying or liquification columns where the air is cooled and then expanded to approximately atmospheric pressure. The process of changing the extremely cold air under high pressure to the lower atmospheric pressure causes the air to liquify.

The separation of the nitrogen from the oxygen becomes possible at this stage because of the difference in the boiling point between the nitrogen (—320° F) and the oxygen (—296° F). The nitrogen, having the lower boiling point, evaporates first, leaving the liquid oxygen in the bottom of the condenser. The liquid oxygen next passes through a heated coil which changes the liquid into a gaseous form. From here the gas goes into a storage tank, flowing through a gas meter which registers the amount of gas entering the storage tank. The gas is then drawn from this tank and compressed into receiving cylinders.

The oxygen cylinder. Oxygen cylinders are made from seamless, drawn steel and tested with a water pressure of 3360 pounds per square inch. The cylinders are equipped with a high-pressure valve which can be opened by turning the hand wheel on top of the cylinder. See Fig. 2. *This valve should always be opened by hand and not with a wrench. The hand wheel must be turned slowly to permit a*

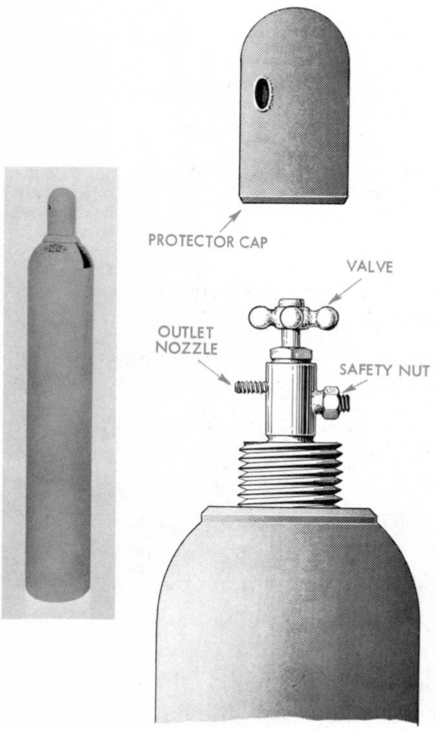

Fig. 2. Oxygen cylinders are available in three sizes, one of which is shown above (left). The view at the right shows the top of the cylinder with the cap removed.

gradual pressure load on the regulator, and then opened as far as the valve will turn, to full gas pressure. Unless the valve is wide open the high oxygen pressure may cause the oxygen to leak around the valve, resulting in considerable waste.

There are three common sizes of oxygen cylinders. The large size, which is the one popularly used by industrial plants and shops consuming large quantities of gas, is filled with 244 cubic feet of oxygen. The medium cylinder contains 122 cubic feet, and the small cylinder 80 cubic feet.

Cylinders are charged with oxygen at a pressure of 2200 lbs per sq in. at a temperature of 70° F. Gases expand when heated and contract when cooled, so the oxygen pressure will increase or decrease as the temperature changes. For example, if a full cylinder of oxygen is allowed to stand outdoors in near freezing temperature, the pressure of the oxygen will register less than 2200 lbs per sq in. However, this does not mean that any of the oxygen has been lost; cooling has only reduced the pressure of the oxygen.

Since the pressure of gas will vary with the temperature, all oxygen cylinders are equipped with a safety nut that permits the oxygen to drain slowly in the event the temperature increases the pressure beyond the safety load of the cylinder. Thus if a cylinder were exposed to a hot flame, the safety nut would relieve the pressure before the cylinder would reach the point where it would explode.

A *protector cap* which screws onto the neck ring of the cylinder is furnished to protect the valve from any damage. This cap must always be in place when the cylinder is not in use.

Separating Acetylene for Use in Welding

Acetylene is a gas formed by the mixture of calcium carbide and water. The commercial generator in which the gas is made consists of a huge tank containing water. A specified quantity of carbide is dumped into a hopper and raised to the top of the generator. The carbide is then allowed to fall into the water, and upon coming in contact with the water, bubbles of gas are given off. This gas is collected, purified, cooled, and slowly compressed into cylinders.

Acetylene is a colorless gas, with a very distinctive nauseating odor. It is highly combustible when mixed with oxygen or air. Although it is stable under low pressures, it becomes very unstable if compressed to more than 15 pounds per square inch. Therefore, *acetylene becomes dangerous if used beyond a 15 pound pressure.*

The acetylene cylinder. To ensure safety in storing acetylene, the cylinder is packed with a porous material. This material is saturated with acetone, which is a chemical liquid that dissolves or absorbs large quantities of acetylene under pressure without changing the nature of the gas itself. See Fig. 3A.

The acetylene cylinder is equipped with a fusible plug to relieve any excess pressure if the cylinder should be subjected to undue heat, or any other mechanical pressure.

The cylinder valve is operated by

Fig. 3A. Acetylene cylinders come in three common sizes—60, 100, and 300 cubic feet. A typical cylinder is shown above as it normally appears (left) and in a cutaway view (right). (Linde Co.)

Fig. 3B. The acetylene cylinder valve is operated by a T-wrench.

means of a T-wrench. *This valve should never be opened more than one and one-half turns.* A slight opening is advisable since it permits closing the valve in a hurry in case of an emergency. See Fig. 3B.

Handling Cylinders

To move a cylinder rotate it on its bottom edge. Place the palm of one hand over the protector cap and tilt the cylinder toward you. Start the tank rolling by pushing it with the other hand as shown in Fig. 4.

Here are a few precautions that must be observed when handling oxygen and acetylene cylinders:

1. Never use the valve-protector caps for lifting cylinders.

2. Do not allow cylinders to lie in a horizontal position.

Fig. 4. Correct way to move a cylinder. The rolling motion not only is less dangerous but an easy way to handle a heavy cylinder.

3. Never permit grease or oil to come in contact with cylinder valves. Although oxygen is in itself noninflammable, if it is allowed to come in contact with any inflammable material it will quickly aid combustion.

4. Avoid exposing cylinders to furnace heat, radiators, open fire, or sparks from the torch.

5. Never transport a cylinder by dragging, sliding, or rolling it on its side. Avoid striking it against any object that might create a spark. There may be just enough gas escaping to cause an explosion.

6. If cylinders have to be moved, be sure that the cylinder valves are shut off.

7. Never tamper with or attempt to repair the cylinder valves. If the valves do not function properly or if they leak, notify the supplier immediately.

The Welding Outfit

A single welding apparatus consists of a torch with an assortment of different-sized tips; two lengths of hose, one red for the acetylene and the other green or black for the oxygen; two pressure regulators; two cylinders, one containing acetylene and the other oxygen; a pair of dark-colored goggles; and a sparklighter. See Fig. 5. When considerable work is to be done, an acetylene generator is used to produce acetylene at a reduced cost.

As a rule, the cylinders are chained to a two-wheel truck to permit moving the equipment to any desired place. If the cylinders are positioned near the work bench, they should be chained to some fixed object. Securing cylin-

Fig. 5. A welding outfit on a truck permits transporting the unit to wherever a welding job is to be done. (Linde Co.)

Fig. 6. Always chain cylinders to prevent them from tipping over. (Linde Co.)

ders is important; otherwise they may tip over and cause an explosion or ruin the regulators. See Fig. 6.

Using an Acetylene Generator

When considerable welding is done, such as in industry or in a school welding shop, the oxygen cylinders are frequently connected to a manifold with pipe lines carrying the gas to the welding stations as shown in Fig. 7. Although it is also possible to manifold acetylene cylinders, the acetylene generator, as illustrated in Fig. 8, is often more economical to operate than resorting to a manifold system.

Two kinds of acetylene generators are made—the low-pressure and the high-pressure type. The low-pressure generator furnishes acetylene under pressures of less than 1 lb per sq in. With this kind of generator only the injector type of blowpipes can be used. (See the following section entitled *The Welding Torch.*) Today the low-pressure generator is rarely installed.

The high-pressure generator supplies acetylene up to pressures of 15 lbs per sq in. This generator is the one that is more commonly used.

The operation of a generator is relatively simple. The unit feeds controlled amounts of calcium carbide into the water. When these ingredients are mixed, acetylene gas is produced. Various devices are incorporated in the generator to ensure safe operation. However, there are definite official codes which must be followed as to where a generator is to be located and how it is to be used.

Fig. 7. The oxygen and acetylene manifold makes a convenient and efficient system when a great deal of welding is done. (Airco)

Fig. 8. Many welding shops manufacture their own acetylene in a generator such as this. (Airco)

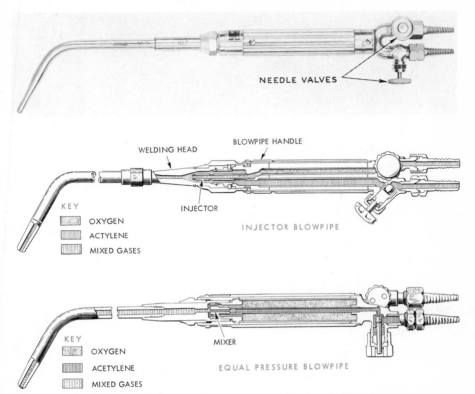

NEEDLE VALVES

WELDING HEAD BLOWPIPE HANDLE

KEY
OXYGEN
ACTYLENE
MIXED GASES

INJECTOR

INJECTOR BLOWPIPE

KEY
OXYGEN
ACETYLENE
MIXED GASES

MIXER

EQUAL PRESSURE BLOWPIPE

Fig. 9. The injector (above) and equal pressure (below) gas welding torches are the two main types in use today. (Linde Co.)

The Welding Torch

The torch, or blowpipe, as it is sometimes called, is a tool which mixes acetylene and oxygen in the correct proportions and permits the mixture to flow to the end of a tip where it is burned. Although blowpipes vary to some extent in design, basically they are all made to provide complete control of the flame during the welding operation.

The two main types of blowpipes ·are the *injector* and the *medium*

(equal) pressure. The injector torch is designed to use acetylene at very low pressures, from 1 lb or less per sq in. The equal pressure type requires acetylene pressures of 1 to 15 lbs per sq in. Both will operate when acetylene is supplied from cylinders or medium-pressure generators. Whereas the injector blowpipe will function with a low-pressure generator, the equal-pressure torch cannot be used on this type of generator.

With the injector blowpipe, the oxygen, as it passes through a small open-

ing in the injector nozzle, draws acetylene into the oxygen stream. See Fig. 9.
One advantage of this blowpipe is that
small fluctuations in the oxygen supplied to it will produce a corresponding change in the amount of acetylene
drawn, thereby making the proportions of the two gases constant while
the torch is in operation. In the equal-
pressure type the acetylene and oxygen are fed independently to a mixing
chamber, after which they flow out
through the tip. See Fig. 9. The equal
pressure type of blowpipe is the one
most generally used.

Both kinds of torches are equipped
with two needle valves, one regulates
the flow of oxygen and the other the
acetylene. On the rear end of the torch
there are two fittings for connecting
the two hoses. In order to eliminate
any danger of interchanging the hoses,
the oxygen fitting is made with a right-
hand thread and the acetylene with a
left-hand thread.

Care of the torch. When the welding is completed, always suspend the
torch securely so it will not fall. The
needle valves are especially delicate,

and care must be taken never to drop
the torch so they will strike some hard
object. Occasionally the needle valves
will turn too freely, making it difficult
to secure and keep the adjustment for
the proper mixture. When this occurs,
give the safety-lock nuts on the stem
of the needle valves a slight turn with
a correct fitting wrench as shown in
Fig. 10.

Welding Tips

To make possible the welding of
different thicknesses of metal, blowpipes are equipped with an assortment
of different size heads, or tips, as
shown in Fig. 11. The size of the tip
is governed by the diameter of its
opening which is marked on the tip.
The system of digits used depends
largely on the manufacturer of the
welding equipment. The most common system consists of numbers which
range from 0 to 15. With this system,

Fig. 10. Tighten the needle valve lock nuts with
a correct fitting wrench.

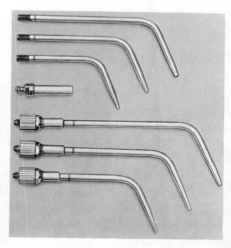

Fig. 11. The size of a welding tip is governed by
the diameter of the opening. (Air Reduction Sales
Co.)

the larger the number the greater the tip diameter.

Care of welding tips. At some time or other you will have to remove a tip. Always change a tip with a wrench especially made for this purpose as illustrated in Fig. 12. *Under no condition should pliers be used to remove a welding tip.* Pliers quickly ruin the nut on the tip, rendering it practically useless.

Never insert a tip while the torch is hot. Heat expands the threads, causing the tip to "freeze" onto the torch after it has cooled. Attempting to force a tip loose from the torch later may result in breaking off the threaded section, thereby ruining the tip. Moreover you also have the problem of removing the broken section from the opening of the torch.

Keep the tip clean at all times to produce satisfactory welds. Frequent use of the torch will cause a formation of carbon in the passage of the tip. Remove this carbon by inserting a

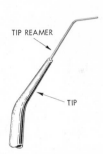

Fig. 13. Clean the opening of the tip with a tip reamer.

tip reamer. See Fig. 13. Brushing the end of the tip with a fine grade of sandpaper is also advisable at times. Brushing the end of the tip with a fine grade of sandpaper is also advisable at times.

Regulators

The oxygen and acetylene pressure regulators perform two functions. They reduce the cylinder pressure to the required working pressure and produce a steady flow of gas under varying cylinder pressures. To illustrate this more clearly, let us assume that the oxygen in the cylinder is under a pressure of 1800 lbs per sq in., and a pressure of 6 pounds is needed at the torch. The regulator must maintain a constant pressure of 6 pounds even if the cylinder pressure drops down to 500 pounds.

There are two types of regulators, the *two-stage* and the *single-stage*. With the two-stage regulator, the reduction of the cylinder pressure to that required at the torch is accomplished in two stages. In the first stage, the gas

Fig. 12. Change the tip with the proper tip wrench.

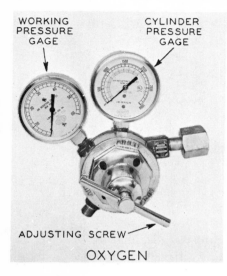

WORKING   CYLINDER
PRESSURE   PRESSURE
GAGE   GAGE

ADJUSTING SCREW

OXYGEN

ACETYLENE

Fig. 14. The oxygen and acetylene regulators control the flow of gas to be used for welding.

flows from the cylinder into a high pressure chamber. A spring and diaphragm keeps a predetermined gas pressure in this chamber. For oxygen such a pressure is usually set at 200 lbs per sq in. and for acetylene 50 lbs per sq in. From the high pressure chamber the gas then passes into a second reducing chamber. Control of the pressure in the reducing chamber is governed by an *adjusting screw*. The principal advantage of the two-stage regulator is that it provides a more uniform flow of gas.

The single-stage regulator is not as expensive as the two-stage type. With this regulator, there is no intermediate chamber through which the gas passes before it enters the low pressure chamber. The gas from the cylinder flows into the regulator and is controlled entirely by the adjusting screw. The disadvantage of this regulator is that as the cylinder pressure drops, the regulator pressure also falls, thereby necessitating occasional readjustment of the pressure. With the two-stage regulator the pressure remains constant until the gas in the cylinder is exhausted.

Both types of regulators have two gages. One gage indicates the actual pressure in the cylinder and the other shows the working or line pressure used at the torch. The oxygen high pressure gage is usually graduated to 3000 pounds. As a rule this gage also has a second scale which is calibrated to register the content of the cylinder in cubic feet. The acetylene high pressure gage is graduated to 350-400 pounds as shown in Fig. 14.

The oxygen working pressure gage is graduated to 50-60 pounds and the working pressure gage on the acetylene regulator to 15-30 pounds.

The most important thing to remember when using a regulator is to make absolutely certain that *the ad-*

justing screw is released (turned out) before the cylinder valve is opened. If the adjusting screw is not released and the cylinder valve opened, the tremendous pressure of the gas in the cylinder is forced on to the working pressure gage, resulting in possible damage to the regulator.

Care of regulators. Regulators are sensitive instruments and must at all times be regarded as such. It takes only a slight jar to put a regulator out of commission. Be extremely careful in handling the regulator while removing it from the cylinder. *Never allow a regulator to remain on a bench top or floor for any length of time,* as someone may come along and carelessly move it, which may result in breaking the glass on the gages or damaging the regulator itself. Here are a few more rules that should be followed:

1. Always check the adjusting screw before the cylinder valve is turned on, and release this screw when the welding has been completed.

2. *Never use oil on a regulator.* Use only soap or glycerine to lubricate the adjusting screw.

3. *Do not try to interchange the oxygen and acetylene regulators.*

4. If a regulator does not function properly, shut off the supply of gas and have a qualified repairman check it.

5. If a regulator creeps (does not remain at set pressure), have it repaired immediately. Creeping will be noticed on the working pressure gage after the needle-valves on the torch are closed. A creeping regulator usually requires a change of valve seat or stem.

6. If the gage pointer fails to go back to the pin when the pressure is released, this condition should be repaired. The trouble is probably due to a sprung mechanism brought about by allowing the pressure to enter a gage suddenly.

7. Always keep a tight connection between the regulator and the cylinder. If the connection leaks after a reasonable force has been used to tighten the nut, close the cylinder valve and remove the regulator. Clean both the inside of the cylinder valve seat and the regulator inlet-nipple seat. If the leak still persists, the seat and threads are probably marred, in which case the regulator will have to be returned to the manufacturer for repair.

Oxygen and Acetylene Hose

A special non-porous hose is used for welding. To prevent mistakes in connecting them, *the oxygen hose is either green or black* and *the acetylene hose red.* If oxygen were to pass through an old acetylene hose, a dangerous combustible mixture might result.

A standard connection is used to attach the hose to the regulator and torch. This connection consists of a nipple which is forced into the hose and a nut that connects the nipple to the regulator and torch. The acetylene nut may be distinguished from the oxygen by the groove that runs around the center, indicating a left-hand thread as illustrated in Fig. 15. A clamp of some type is used to squeeze

ACETYLENE   OXYGEN

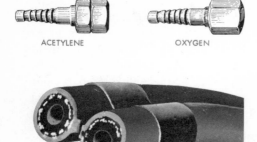

Fig. 15. Hose connections (above) and welding hose (below).

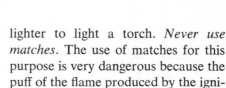

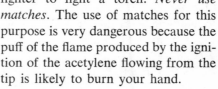

Fig. 16. Always use a sparklighter to light a torch.

the hose around the nipple to prevent it from working loose.

Care of welding hose. The acetylene and oxygen hose is an important part of the welding equipment. First of all, as previously mentioned, all the connections on the hose must be perfectly tight. These connections should be tightened with close-fitting wrenches to prevent damaging the nuts.

Avoid dragging the hose around on a greasy floor, since grease or oil eventually will soak into it. Be careful in pulling the hose around sharp objects and especially over hot metal. Prevent anyone from stepping or dropping anything on the hose. When the welding has been completed, roll up the hose and suspend it in such a manner that it will not drop to the floor.

The Sparklighter

The sparklighter, as illustrated in Fig. 16, is the implement used for igniting the torch. While welding, form the habit of always employing a spark-

lighter to light a torch. *Never use matches.* The use of matches for this purpose is very dangerous because the puff of the flame produced by the ignition of the acetylene flowing from the tip is likely to burn your hand.

Goggles

An oxyacetylene flame produces light rays of great intensity and also heat rays which, if meeting the naked eye, may eventually prove destructive to the eye tissues. Consequently, always wear goggles having suitable, approved, colored glass. The density of the colored lenses should be such that no more of the light rays are shut off than are necessary to the welder. One test which may be performed to check the suitability of the colored lenses is to use one pair of goggles for a few

Fig. 17. Always wear proper goggles when welding.

minutes while welding and then re-move them, noting whether or not white spots dance before your eyes. If these white spots are noticeable the lenses do not provide sufficient protec-tion, and a darker shade should be used.

Goggles, as shown in Fig. 17, also protect the eyes from flying sparks and pieces of molten metal that may splat-ter around.

Protective Clothing

It is a good idea to wear an apron, shop coat, or coveralls while welding with oxyacetylene equipment. Sparks will invariably shoot away from the molten metal, and, without some suit-able covering, numerous holes will be burned in your clothes. *Under no cir-cumstances should a sweater be worn.* A small spark falling on this garment may burst into a rapid-spreading flame that may have dire consequences.Some type of skull cap is also desirable to prevent any hot metal particles from falling on the hair.

The beginner should wear a pair of lightweight gloves to avoid possible burns. Occasionally the hot end of a rod or a piece of metal, which has been momentarily laid aside to cool, is picked up by mistake, and without gloves serious burns are apt to result. It is true, however, that experienced oxyacetylene welders frequently do not wear gloves.

Points to Remember

1. Handle oxygen and acetylene cylinders with care. Never expose them to excessive heat and prevent oil and grease from coming in contact with them.

2. Be sure the adjusting screw on a regulator is fully released before opening a cylinder valve.

3. Always hang up a torch when not in use to prevent it from dropping to the floor and being damaged.

4. Never remove tips with pliers. If a tip has to be cleaned, insert a piece of soft wire or tip drill in the opening.

5. Do not lubricate the adjusting screw on a regulator with oil. Use soap or glycerine.

6. Never interchange the hoses. Avoid dragging them over greasy floors.

7. Always wear proper goggles when welding, as well as suitable pro-tective clothing.

8. Never light a torch with a match.

9. Never use oxygen or acetylene from the tank to blow dirt and dust from clothing.

QUESTIONS FOR STUDY AND DISCUSSION

1. What safety devices are used to prevent cylinders from exploding when subjected to intense pressure?

2. What is the purpose of the pro-tector cap on a cylinder?

3. How much should the cylinder

valve be opened on an acetylene cylinder? On the oxygen cylinder?

4. Why is it dangerous to allow grease or oil to come in contact with the oxygen cylinder valve?

5. What is the function of the needle valves on a welding torch?

6. Why are the oxygen and acetylene hose fittings made with different screw threads?

7. How are sizes of welding tips indicated?

8. Why should a close-fitting wrench be used in removing welding tips?

9. What is the objection to using pliers for removing welding tips?

10. What is a tip drill, and when and why should it be used?

11. What is meant by a two-stage regulator?

12. Why should the adjusting screw on a regulator be fully released before opening a cylinder valve?

13. What precautions should be observed in handling a pressure regulator?

14. Why is it a poor practice to light a torch with a match?

CHAPTER 23

Oxy-Acetylene Welding

Setting-Up and Operating

One of the first things you should learn in starting your oxy-acetylene welding operations is to assemble a welding outfit. A certain sequence must be followed if the equipment is to be properly and safely connected. Once you have learned to do this then you need to know how to light the torch and adjust the flame. This chapter explains how these operations are performed.

Assembling the Welding Outfit

To assemble a welding outfit follow these steps:

1. Chain cylinders—Fasten the cylinders securely to a truck or to some other fixed object where they are to be located. Remove the protector cap from each cylinder and examine the outlet nozzles closely. Make sure the connection seat or screw threads

are not damaged. A damaged screw thread is apt to ruin the regulator nut, while a poor connection seat will cause the gas to leak.

2. Crack cylinder valves—Particles

Fig. 1. Crack cylinder valves to blow out dirt which may be lodged in the outlet nozzles.

of dirt frequently collect in the outlet nozzle of the cylinder valve. This dirt, if not cleaned out, will work into the regulator when the pressure is turned on. To avoid any possibility of dirt clogging up any passage, open the valves of each cylinder for just an instant. Then with a clean cloth, wipe out the connection seat. See Fig. 1.

Fig. 3. Connect the hoses to the regulator.

Fig. 2. Fasten the regulators to the cylinders with a proper fitting wrench.

3. Attach regulators—Connect the oxygen pressure regulator to the oxygen cylinder and the acetylene regulator to the acetylene cylinder as shown in Fig. 2. Use a close-fitting wrench to tighten the nuts, and avoid stripping the threads. Always use a proper wrench to tighten the nuts, as a loose-fitting wrench will eventually ruin the corners of the regulator nuts.

4. Connect hoses to cylinders — Connect the green or black hose to the oxygen regulator and the red hose to the acetylene regulator as illustrated in Fig. 3. Check the adjusting screw on each regulator to make certain that it is released, and open the

cylinder valves. Then blow out any dirt that may be lodged in the hoses by opening the regulator adjusting screws and promptly closing them again when the hoses have been cleaned out. See Fig. 4.

Fig. 4. Blow out each hose.

5. Connect hoses to the torch — Connect the hoses to the respective fittings on the torch, the red hose to the needle valve fitting, marked *AC,* and the green or black hose to the oxygen needle valve, marked *OX,* as

Fig. 5. Connect the hoses to the torch.

shown in Fig. 5. *Remember, acetylene hose connections always have left-hand threads and oxygen hose connections have right-hand threads.*

6. *Test for leaks*—All new welding apparatus needs to be tested for leaks before being operated. Thereafter it

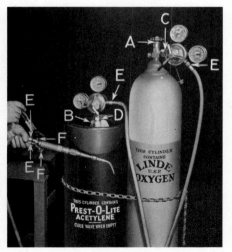

Fig. 6. Test these points with soapy water for leakage. (Linde Co.)

is advisable to periodically apply this same test in order to ensure that no leakage has developed. A leaky apparatus is very dangerous, since a fire may develop. Furthermore, leaks mean wasted gas.

To test for leaks, open the oxygen and acetylene cylinder valves and with the needle valves on the torch closed, adjust the regulators to give about normal working pressure. Test the following points as shown in Fig. 6:

A—Oxygen cylinder valve
B—Acetylene cylinder valve
C—Oxygen regulator inlet connection
D—Acetylene regulator inlet connection
E—Hose connections at the regulators and torch
F—Oxygen and acetylene needle valves

Apply soapy water with a brush to test for leaks. Under no circumstances should any other means be used for this operation. If bubbles form, a leak is present.

To remedy any leakage, tighten up the connections a little with a wrench. If this does not stop the leak, shut off the gas pressure, open the connections, and examine the screw threads. Also, old hose should be tested very closely, since it has a tendency to become porous.

Selecting the Proper Welding Tip

The size of the tip will depend upon the thickness of the metal to be welded. If very light sheet iron is to be welded, a tip with a small opening is used, while

TABLE I
Tip Sizes vs. Metal Thickness

Tip Number	Thickness of Metal (inches)	Oxygen Pressure (pounds)	Acetylene Pressure (pounds)
00	1/64	1	1
0	1/32	1	1
1	1/16	1	1
2	3/32	2	2
3	1/8	3	3
4	3/16	4	4
5	1/4	5	5
6	5/16	6	6
7	3/8	7	7
8	1/2	7	7
9	5/8	7 1/2	7 1/2
10	3/4 & up	9	9

(Airco)

a large-sized tip is needed for thick metal. Table I lists the sizes of tips for various thicknesses of metals and the approximate working pressures required.

It is very important to use the correct tip, with the proper working pressure. If too small a tip is employed, the heat will not be sufficient to fuse the metal to the proper depth. When the tip is too large, the heat is too great, thereby burning holes in the metal. A good weld must have the right penetration and smooth, even, overlapping ripples. Unless the conditions are just right, it is impossible for the torch to function the way it should and, consequently, the weld will be poor.

Fig. 7. Standing in this position is **dangerous** when opening a cylinder valve.

Lighting the Torch

1. Select a tip for welding ⅛″ or ¹⁄₁₆″ metal and screw it into the torch.

2. Open the oxygen and acetylene cylinder valves and set the working pressure to correspond to the size of tip that is to be used. *Do not stand too close to the regulator when opening the cylinder valve.* A defect in the

regulator may cause the gas to blow through, shattering the glass and blowing it into your face. See Fig. 7. *Make it a practice to stand to one side of the regulator, as in Fig. 8, and turn the cylinder valve slowly.* Remember, oxygen and acetylene are charged in the tanks under a high pressure and if the gas is permitted to come against the regulator suddenly, it is apt to cause

Fig. 8. Stand to one side of the regulator when opening a cylinder valve.

some damage to the equipment. Open the acetylene cylinder valve approximately one complete turn and the oxygen all the way. Next turn the oxygen and acetylene regulator adjusting valves to the required working pressures.

Then turn the acetylene needle valve on the torch approximately three quarters of a turn. With the sparklighter held about one inch away from the end of the tip, ignite the acetylene as

Fig. 9. Some people prefer to hold the torch in the right hand and the sparklighter in the left hand. Others find it more convenient to hold the torch in the left hand and the sparklighter in the right.

it leaves the tip as shown in Fig. 9. Do this as rapidly as possible to avoid unnecessary wasting of gas. If not enough acetylene is turned on, the flame will produce considerable smoke; therefore, quickly turn on more acetylene until the flame has a slight tendency to jump away from the tip.

Never use a match to light a torch. This procedure brings your fingers too close to the tip and the sudden ignition of the acetylene is very apt to burn them.

When igniting a torch, keep the tip facing downward and preferably against the bench top. Lighting the torch while it is facing outward or upward may result in burning someone nearby as the ignited flame spurts out. If other people are welding around the same area, *never reach over to the other fellow for a light.* He may be welding, and bringing your torch near his will not only disturb his work but might burn his face or hands.

Make no attempt to relight a torch from the hot metal when welding in an enclosed box, tank, drum, or other small cavity. There may be just enough unburned gas in this confined space to cause an explosion as the acetylene from the tip comes in contact with the hot metal. Instead, *move the torch into the open,* relight it in the usual manner, and make the necessary adjustments before resuming the weld.

Adjusting the Flame

With the acetylene burning, gradually open the oxygen needle valve until a well-defined white cone appears near

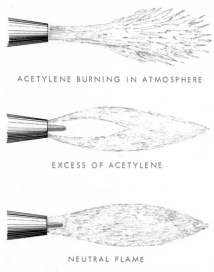

ACETYLENE BURNING IN ATMOSPHERE

EXCESS OF ACETYLENE

NEUTRAL FLAME

Fig. 10. Steps in adjusting for a neutral flame.

If the mixture consists of a slight excess of acetylene, the flame is *carbonizing,* or *reducing.* This flame can easily be identified by the existence of three flame zones instead of the usual two found in the neutral flame. The end of the brilliant white cone is no longer as well defined, and it is also surrounded by an intermediate white cone, which has a feathery edge in addition to the usual bluish outer envelope. See Fig. 11.

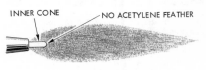

INNER CONE — NO ACETYLENE FEATHER

NEUTRAL FLAME

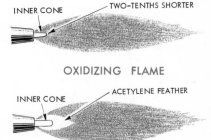

INNER CONE — TWO-TENTHS SHORTER

OXIDIZING FLAME

INNER CONE — ACETYLENE FEATHER

REDUCING OR CARBONIZING FLAME

Fig. 11. Three types of oxy-acetylene welding flames. (Linde Co.)

the tip, surrounded by a second, bluish cone that is faintly luminous. This is known as a *neutral flame* and is so called because there is an approximate one-to-one mixture of acetylene and oxygen resulting in a flame which is chemically neutral. The brilliant white cone should be from $\frac{1}{16}''$ to $\frac{3}{4}''$ long, depending on the tip size. See Fig. 10. The neutral flame is the one used for most welding operations.

Any variation from the one-to-one mixture will alter the characteristics of the flame. When an excess amount of oxygen is forced into the mixture, the resulting flame is said to be *oxidizing.* This flame resembles the neutral flame slightly, but has a shorter and more pointed inner cone with an almost purple color rather than brilliant white. It is sometimes used for brazing. See Fig. 11.

Testing the Flames

You will probably have a little difficulty at first in making the correct flame adjustment, but if the characteristics of the carbonizing and oxidizing flames are understood, the adjustment for a neutral flame will be relatively easy. As an aid in becoming familiar with the effects of these various flames, try the following experiments:

Carbonizing flame. Obtain a piece of scrap metal. Light the acetylene and turn on the oxygen until a white cone appears on the end of the tip enveloped by another fan-shaped cone which has a feathered edge.

Put on a pair of goggles and apply this flame to the metal, holding the point of the white cone close to the metal. You will notice that as the metal melts it has a tendency to boil. This is an indication that carbon is entering the molten metal. You will also discover, after the metal has cooled, that the surface is pitted and very brittle.

Oxidizing flame. Now, open the oxygen needle valve. The white cone becomes short and the color changes to a purplish hue. The flame burns with a decided roar.

Apply this flame to a piece of metal, allowing the cone to come in contact with the surface. You will find that as the metal melts there are numerous sparks given off and a white foam or scum forms on the surface. After this piece cools, the metal will be shiny.

Neutral flame. Now, adjust the needle valve until the flame is balanced. Apply this neutral flame to a piece of metal. The molten metal flows smoothly like syrup, with very few sparks, clean and clear.

Flame Characteristics

A flame may be harsh or quiet. The harsh type is induced by forcing too much pressure of both gases to the tip. This flame is undesirable, since it has a tendency to depress the molten surface and cause the metal to splatter around the edges of the puddle. Such a flame is noisy, and its use makes it extremely difficult to bring about perfect fusion, with smooth, uniform ripples.

The quiet flame is just the opposite of the harsh flame and is achieved by the correct pressure of gases flowing to the tip. The flame is not a forcing, noisy flame but one that permits a continuous flow of the molten puddle without any undue amount of splatter.

To secure a soft neutral flame, see that (1) the tip is absolutely clean, and (2) the mixture is correct. Even if the proportion of acetylene and oxygen is right, a good weld is difficult to achieve unless the opening in the tip permits a free flow of gases. Any foreign matter in the tip will simply restrict the source of heat necessary to melt the metal.

Flame Control

Once the flame has been properly set, it does not mean that further adjustments are unnecessary. From time to time, as the welding progresses, it is necessary to observe the flame cone to be certain that the mixture has not altered. Changes in the flame will occur as a result of some slight fluctuation in the flow of the gases from the regulators. A slight turn of one needle valve or the other will quickly readjust the flame.

In the course of welding, a torch may occasionally start "popping." This noise is an indication that there is an insufficient amount of gases flowing to the tip. Such popping can be stopped by opening both the oxygen and acetylene needle valves on the torch to a greater extent. Another reason for popping is the overheating of the molten pool by lingering or keeping the flame too long in one position and not melting enough rod into the pool.

Backfire and Flashback

When the flame goes out with a loud "pop," it is called a *backfire*. A backfire may be caused (1) by operating the torch at lower pressures than required for the tip used, (2) by touching the tip against the work, (3) by overheating the tip, or (4) by an obstruction in the tip. If a backfire should occur, shut the needle valves and after remedying the cause, relight the torch.

A *flashback* is a condition that results when the flame flashes back into the torch and burns inside with a shrill hissing or squealing noise. If this should happen, close the needle valves immediately. A flashback generally is an indication that something is wrong. Perhaps it is a clogged tip, or the improper functioning of the needle valves, or even an incorrect acetylene or oxygen pressure. In any case, investigate the cause before relighting the torch.

Shutting Off the Torch

Following is the correct sequence of steps for shutting off a torch:

1. Close the acetylene needle valve first.

The acetylene needle valve is closed first, since shutting off the flow of this gas will immediately extinguish the flame, whereas if the oxygen is shut off first, the acetylene will continue to burn, throwing off a great deal of smoke and soot.

2. Close the oxygen needle valve.

3. If the entire welding unit is to be shut down, shut off both the acetylene and the oxygen cylinder valves.

4. Remove the pressure on the working gages by opening the needle valves until the lines are drained. Then promptly close the needle valves.

5. Release the adjusting screws on the pressure regulators.

Points to Remember

1. Be sure to fasten the cylinders securely so they will not fall over.

2. Crack the cylinder valves before attaching regulators.

3. Periodically test the welding outfit for leaks. Use soapy water only.

4. Use the correct size tip for the thickness of metal to be welded.

5. Always stand to one side of the regulator when opening cylinder valves and be sure the regulator adjusting valves are fully released.

6. Never use a match to light a torch; use a regulation sparklighter.

7. Adjust the torch to a soft, neutral flame for welding unless the nature of the metal calls for a different type of flame.

8. Keep the passage in the welding tip clean.

9. Avoid conditions that may cause a backfire or flashback.

QUESTIONS FOR STUDY AND DISCUSSION

1. Why should the cylinders be securely fastened before being used?

2. Why should the outlet nozzles be examined closely?

3. What is meant by the term "cracking the valve?" Why is this done?

4. List the proper order for setting up the welding apparatus.

5. Why should a close-fitting wrench be used in fastening all connections?

6. Why should a flame never be used in testing for leaks?

7. What is the proper method of testing for leaks?

8. What governs the size of the tip which should be used?

9. Why must the working pressure be correct for the size of tip used?

10. How can you determine the amount of acetylene to turn on at the needle valve control when lighting the torch?

11. What is meant by an oxidizing flame?

12. What is a carbonizing flame?

13. How can you distinguish these flames from the neutral flame?

14. How can you determine when you have a neutral flame?

15. Why should the acetylene needle valve be closed first in shutting off the torch?

16. What is the difference between a harsh and soft flame?

17. What are some of the conditions that may cause a backfire?

18. What is meant by a flashback?

WELDING ASSIGNMENTS

1. Light, adjust, and shut off a welding torch.

2. Test the effects of a carbonizing, oxidizing, and neutral flame.

CHAPTER 24

Oxy-Acetylene Welding

The Flat Position

To master the skill of welding with an oxy-acetylene torch, you will have to practice a series of operations in a definite order. These operations involve carrying a puddle without a rod, laying beads with a filler rod, and welding various types of joints. All of this welding should be done with the metal lying in a flat position.

Carrying a Puddle Without a Filler Rod

Obtain a piece of metal $\frac{1}{16}''$ or $\frac{1}{8}''$ in thickness and approximately 5" in length. Be sure the surface is free of oil, dirt, and scale. Light the torch and adjust it for a neutral flame. Then proceed as follows:

1. Holding the torch—A torch may be held in either one of two ways, depending on which is the more comfortable for you. When welding light-

Fig. 1. This is one way to hold the torch.

gage metal, most operators prefer to grasp the handle of the blowpipe, with the hose over the outside of the wrist, in the same manner a pencil ordinarily is held. See Fig. 1. In the other grip, the torch is held like a hammer, with the fingers lightly curled underneath as shown in Fig. 2. In either case the

Fig. 2. Here is another way to hold the torch.

torch should balance easily in the hand to avoid fatigue.

2. Position and motion of the torch —Hold the torch so the flame points in the direction you are going to weld and at an angle of about 45° with the completed part of the weld. See Fig. 3. If you are right handed, start the weld at the right edge of the metal and bring the inner cone of the neutral flame to within ⅛" of the surface of the plate. The left-handed person reverses this direction. Hold the torch still until a pool of molten metal forms. Then move the puddle across the plate. As the puddle travels forward, rotate the torch to form a series of overlapping ovals as shown in Fig. 3.

Do not move the torch ahead of the puddle, but slowly work forward, giving the heat a chance to melt the metal. If the flame is moved forward too rapidly, the heat fails to penetrate far enough and the metal does not melt properly. If the torch is kept in one

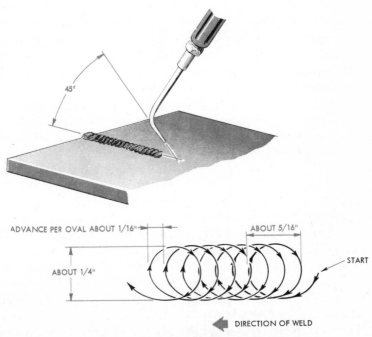

Fig. 3. Hold and rotate the torch in this manner while moving the puddle forward.

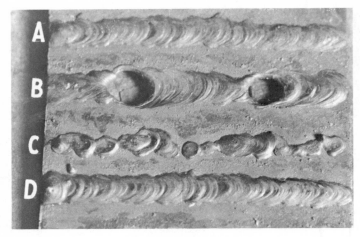

Fig. 4. Strip A and D show correct procedure for carrying the puddle without a filler rod. Strip B shows excess heat. Strip C shows insufficient heat. (Linde Co.)

position too long, the flame will burn a hole through the metal. See Fig. 4.

Laying Beads with a Filler Rod

On some types of joints it is possible to weld the two pieces of metal without adding a filler rod. In most instances the use of a filler rod is advisable because it builds up the weld, thereby adding strength to the joint. The strength of a weld depends largely on the skill with which the rod is blended, or interfused, with the edges of the base metal.

The use of a filler rod requires coordination of the two hands. One hand must manipulate the torch to carry a puddle across the plate, while the other hand must add the correct amount of filler rod. To gain experience in coordinating these movements, practice laying a bead across a flat plate. To do this, obtain a flat plate $\frac{1}{16}''$ or $\frac{1}{8}''$ in thickness and then proceed as follows:

1. Selecting the filler rod — A welded joint should always possess as much strength as the base metal itself. If this is to be accomplished it is necessary to employ a welding rod that has the same properties as the base metal. It is a mistake to attempt to use just any kind of wire, because an inferior rod contains so many impurities that it is extremely difficult to use and makes a weld that is weak and brittle. A good welding rod will flow smoothly and readily unite with the base metal without any excessive amount of sparking. A rod of poor weldability will spark profusely, flow irregularly, and leave a rough surface filled with punctures like pinholes.

Filler rods come in a variety of sizes ranging from $\frac{1}{16}''$ to $\frac{3}{8}''$ in diameter. The size of rod to use will depend largely upon the thickness of the metal. *The general rule is to use a rod with a diameter equal to the thickness of the base metal.* In other words, if a $\frac{1}{16}''$ metal is to be welded, a $\frac{1}{16}''$ diameter rod should be used.

A great many different kinds of rods are available for welding a variety of metals. For example, a mild-steel rod is used for welding mild steel, a cast-iron rod for cast iron, a nickel rod for nickel steel, a bronze rod for bronzing malleable cast iron and other dissimilar metals, an aluminum rod for aluminum welding, a copper rod for copper products, etc.

2. Manipulating the filler rod — Hold the rod at approximately the same angle as the torch but slant it away from the torch. It is advisable to bend the end of the rod at right angles, since this permits holding the rod so that it is not in a direct line with the heat of the flame. See Fig. 5.

Melt a small pool of the base metal and then insert the tip of the rod in this pool. Remember, to secure perfect fusion, the correct diameter rod is important. If the rod is too large the heat of the pool will be insufficient to melt the rod, and if the rod is too small the heat cannot be absorbed by the rod,

with the result that a hole is burned in the plate.

As the rod melts in the pool, advance the torch forward. Concentrate the flame on the base metal and not on the rod. Do not hold the rod above the pool. If you do this the molten metal will fall through the air to the puddle. When this happens it combines with the oxygen of the air and part of it burns up, causing a weak, porous weld. Always dip the rod in the center of the pool.

3. Laying beads—Rotate the torch to form overlapping ovals and keep raising and lowering the rod as the molten puddle is moved forward. *An alternate torch movement* is the semicircular motion as shown in Fig. 6. When the rod is not in the puddle, keep the tip just inside the outer envelope of the flame.

At the start of this exercise, you will find that the end of the rod may stick occasionally. This is because a beginner often experiences difficulty in holding the welding rod steady and, instead of inserting the rod in the middle of the puddle where the heat is sufficient to melt it readily, he may insert it near the edge of the pool where the temperature is lower. The heat at the edge is not enough to melt the rod. When this

Fig. 5. Position for holding a rod. (Linde Co.)

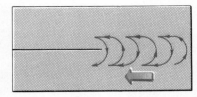

Fig. 6. Instead of the circular torch motion shown in Fig. 3, you can use this semicircular movement.

Fig. 7. Examples of straight beads laid with a filler rod.

happens, do not try to jerk it loose, since such an action will simply interrupt the welding. To loosen the rod, play the flame directly on the tip of the rod and the rod will be freed immediately. In all probability, while the rod is being freed, the puddle will have solidified; therefore be sure to reform the puddle before moving forward.

4. Travel speed—To secure beads of uniform width and height you must keep the forward movement of the torch just right. If the puddle is carried forward too slowly, it becomes too large and you may even burn through the metal. If it is moved too rapidly, the rod is not actually fused with the base metal but merely stuck on the

surface. Furthermore, it will be impossible to form even ripples.

When it appears that the puddle is getting too large, withdraw the flame slightly so only the outer envelope of the flame is touching the molten puddle. *Do not flip the flame off to one side, since such a movement allows the air to strike the hot metal and oxidize it.*

Continue to practice melting filler rod on scraps of metal until you are able to lay straight ripple beads 4″ to 5″ in length as shown in Fig. 7.

Welding Butt Joints

After you have mastered the knack of carrying a puddle across the surface of a plate while adding filler rod, your next task is to fuse two pieces together. Follow these steps when practicing this exercise:

1. Space plates—Obtain two pieces of 1/16″ or 1/8″ metal 4″ to 5″ in length and set them on two firebricks. Allow a gap of about 1/16″ at the starting end of the joint and approximately 1/8″ at the other. This is known as progressive spacing. The purpose of the space is to

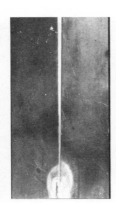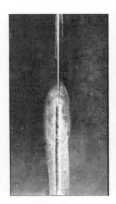

Fig. 8. This illustrates the manner in which the spacing closes up during welding. (Linde Co.)

allow for expansion of the metal; otherwise the edges will overlap before the weld is completed as illustrated in Fig. 8. Furthermore, this space permits the flame to melt the edges all the way to the bottom of the plates.

2. Tack plates—If progressive spacing between the edges of a seam is not used, then the plates must be tacked at various intervals to restrict expansion forces. See Fig. 9.

To make a tack weld, simply apply the flame to the metal until it melts and then add a little filler rod.

Fig. 10. A good ripple weld on a butt joint will look like this. (Linde Co.)

the metal is flowing freely before you dip in the rod. Watch closely the course of the flame to make certain that its travel along both edges of the plates is the same, maintaining a molten puddle approximately $\frac{1}{4}''$ to $\frac{3}{8}''$ in width. Advance this puddle about $\frac{1}{16}''$ with each complete motion of the torch. Unless the molten puddle is kept active and flowing forward, correct fusion will not be achieved.

Keep the motion of the torch as uniform as possible. This will produce smooth, even ripples as shown in Fig. 10. At first such a task may appear very difficult but after a little practice a uniform motion of the torch will be mastered.

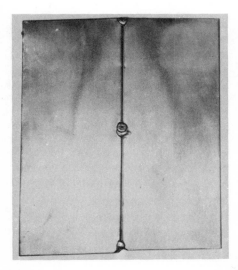

Fig. 9. Tack the plates before welding.

3. Weld plates—Begin welding at the right end (or the left end if you are left-handed), using the same torch and rod movement as previously described. Work the torch slowly to give the heat a chance to penetrate the joint, and add sufficient filler rod to build up the weld about $\frac{1}{16}''$ above the surface. Be sure the puddle is large enough and

Fig. 11. Test the weld by striking it with a hammer, bending the metal against the weld.

4. Test the weld—The welded piece should next be tested. Pick the metal up with a pair of pliers and clamp it in a vise with the weld parallel to the top of the jaws and the welded joint just above the top of the vise. Strike the metal with a hammer, bending it against the weld as illustrated in Fig. 11. The test should be made so that the underside or bottom of the weld is put in tension and the top in compression.

Hammer the metal until the joint has been bent to an angle of 90° to 180°. If the fusion has been correct no cracks will show in the weld joint.

5. Check for defects—It is only natural to assume that your first few welds will break easily. Continue trying until you can make a straight, smooth weld that will not open when bent.

The following are some of the common defects that you may expect to find in your first few welds:

1. Uneven weld bead, caused by moving the torch too slowly or too rapidly.

2. Holes in the joint, caused by holding the flame too long in one spot.

3. A brittle weld, due to improper flame adjustment.

Fig. 12. The underside of this plate shows uneven penetration.

4. Excessive metal hanging underneath the weld, showing too much penetration. See Fig. 12.

5. Insufficient penetration, caused by moving the torch forward too rapidly. When the penetration is correct, the underside of the seam should show that fusion has taken place clear to the bottom edges as shown in Fig. 13.

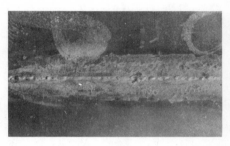

Fig. 13. If penetration is correct, the underside of the plate will look like this.

6. Hole in the end of the joint, caused by not lifting the torch when the end of the weld was reached.

7. Very often a joint appears to have correct penetration and still cracks open when tested. This may be caused by a number of reasons, such as:

   a. Improper space allowances between the edges of the plates.

   b. Filling the space between the metal plates with molten rod without sufficiently melting the edges of the plates to ensure a good bond between the parent metal and rod.

   c. Holding the torch too flat, causing the molten puddle to lap over an area that has not been properly melted.

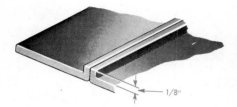

Fig. 14. A flange joint.

Welding a Flange Joint

A flange joint is used a great deal in sheetmetal work, particularly on material that is 20 gage or less. The flange should extend above the surface of the sheet a distance equal to about the thickness of the sheet. See Fig. 14.

To weld a flange joint, no filler rod is needed. The position of the torch should be the same as for welding a butt joint. Place the two pieces with the flange edges touching and tack weld them. Hold the torch flame on the right end (left end for a left-handed person) until a puddle forms and then move the puddle forward.

Welding a Corner Joint

The corner joint is used extensively in fabricating numerous products as well as in repair work. To weld such a joint, set up the plates as illustrated in Fig. 15 and tack them in position. The edges are then fused as in welding a flange joint; that is, without a filler rod. If you must build the edge up slightly, add a little filler rod from time to time as the puddle is moved forward. Test the completed weld by bending the piece out flat and then fold it a little farther over to put stress on the bottom of the weld.

Fig. 15. A corner weld.

Welding a Lap Joint

Obtain two pieces of $\frac{1}{16}''$ or $\frac{1}{8}''$ metal 4″ to 5″ in length. Lay the plates on the workbench with one piece of metal overlapping as in Fig. 16.

Weld the two plates, using a semicircular movement of the torch and

Fig. 16. A lap joint.

Fig. 17. Use a chisel and hammer to open up the back side of a lap joint. (Linde Co.)

working from right to left, or the reverse for a left-handed person. Since it requires less heat to melt the edge of the upper plate than the flat surface of the lower one, direct more heat onto the lower plate. This may be accomplished by prolonging the travel of the flame on the lower surface and cutting short the flame on the edge of the upper metal. Weld one side of the plate, test it as shown in Fig. 17, and then practice on the reverse side. Repeat the exercise until a satisfactory weld is made.

Welding a T-Joint

This joint is made by standing one piece of metal at right angles to a second plate. Proceed as follows to weld a T-joint:

1. Tack plates in position—Obtain two pieces of $\frac{1}{16}''$ or $\frac{1}{8}''$ metal 4″ to 5″ in length and tack them in position to form a T-joint.

2. Weld the joint—Start the welding at the right end if you are right-handed (the reverse applies if you are left-handed) and proceed to the left, using a semicircular torch movement.

Hold the torch so the tip forms an angle of about 45° to the flat plate and the same angle to the line of the weld. Point the rod toward the welding tip at an angle of approximately 30° to the line of weld and 15° to 20° to the horizontal plate. See Fig. 18.

Direct the flame evenly over both plates, keeping the inner cone of the flame about $\frac{1}{8}''$ away from the surface. In a weld of this type the tendency is to heat the vertical plate too much, causing an undercutting above

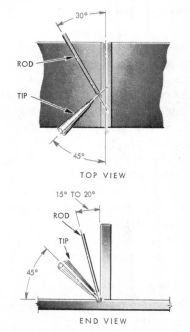

Fig. 18. Position of the torch and rod for welding a T-joint. (Linde Co.)

the weld. To prevent undercutting, keep the molten puddle moving, adding the rod nearer the vertical plate.

3. Test the weld — Pick up the welded piece with a pliers and fasten it in a vise as shown in Fig. 19. Hammer the flat plate downward, bending it against the weld.

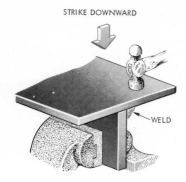

STRIKE DOWNWARD

WELD

Fig. 19. Testing a T-weld.

Points to Remember

1. Move the torch just fast enough to keep the puddle active and flowing forward.

2. When reaching the end of a joint, raise the flame away momentarily to give the puddle a chance to solidify partly.

3. Use a filler rod that has the same composition as the base metal.

4. Use a rod with a diameter equal to the thickness of the base metal.

5. Do not hold the rod too high above the pool so the molten metal falls drop by drop onto the puddle.

6. When welding with a filler rod, move the torch in a semicircular or circular motion.

7. Allow a space between plates to compensate for expansion forces.

QUESTIONS FOR STUDY AND DISCUSSION

1. What governs the rate at which the flame should be moved forward?

2. What happens if the torch is moved forward too slowly?

3. Why should the torch be raised when it nears the end of the weld?

4. What are some of the common defects of a beginner's weld?

5. How should the top and bottom surfaces appear when proper fusion has taken place?

6. If the metal does not melt readily, what is the probable cause for it?

7. Why is a filler rod used in welding?

8. How can you determine whether or not a rod is good or poor?

9. What determines the size of the rod that should be used?

10. What happens if the rod is too large for the size of metal that is being welded? If too small?

11. How should the torch be manipulated when using a filler rod on a butt weld?

12. Why is the length of the arc prolonged on the bottom plate of a lap joint?

13. What precautions should be observed in welding a T-joint?

14. If the metal does not melt freely, what should be done?

15. What should be the position of the torch for welding the T-joint?

WELDING ASSIGNMENTS

1. Carry a puddle across a plate without a filler rod.

2. Deposit straight beads on a flat plate with a filler rod.

3. Weld a butt joint using $\frac{1}{16}''$ or $\frac{1}{8}''$ metal.

4. Weld a flange joint using $\frac{1}{16}''$ or $\frac{1}{8}''$ metal.

5. Weld a corner joint using $\frac{1}{16}''$ or $\frac{1}{8}''$ metal.

6. Weld a lap joint using $\frac{1}{16}''$ or $\frac{1}{8}''$ metal.

7. Weld a T-joint using $\frac{1}{16}''$ or $\frac{1}{8}''$ metal.

CHAPTER 25

Oxy-Acetylene Welding

Other Welding Positions

Welding with an oxy-acetylene torch cannot always be done with the work in a flat position. On some occasions the location of the piece will be such as to require horizontal, vertical, or overhead welding. Undoubtedly welding in a flat position is easier and somewhat faster; nevertheless after a little practice, welds in other positions can be performed without too much difficulty.

Vertical Welding

1. Obtain two pieces of $\frac{1}{16}''$ or $\frac{1}{8}''$ metal and tack them to form a butt joint. Then mount the plates in a jig (see Fig. 2, Chapter 9).

2. Hold the torch and rod at about the same angle as in flat welding as shown in Fig. 1. As the welding progresses you may have to vary the angle slightly to control the puddle.

3. Start the weld at the bottom and work upward, using a semicircular torch motion. Do not allow the puddle to become too large. If the puddle gets too big or too fluid, it will get out of control and run down the face of the weld. When you find that the weld is getting too hot, pull the flame away

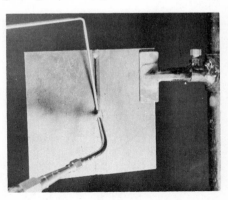

Fig. 1. Hold the torch and rod in this position for vertical welding. (Linde Co.)

319

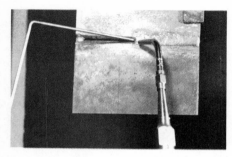

Fig. 2. Hold the torch and rod in this manner for horizontal welding. (Linde Co.)

slightly so that it does not play directly on the puddle.

4. To prevent the puddle from getting too fluid, direct more of the flame on the filler rod. Continue to practice this weld until you can obtain beads that appear good and have correct penetration. Test each weld by bending it in a vise as previously described.

Horizontal Welding

1. Tack two pieces of $\frac{1}{16}''$ or $\frac{1}{8}''$ plates to form a butt joint. Allow a space between the edges for expansion.

2. Clamp the joint in a jig so the surfaces are in a vertical position with the line of weld running horizontally. See Fig. 2.

3. Start welding from the right edge (or left, if you are left-handed) using a semicircular torch motion. As the welding progresses, you will find that the metal has a tendency to build up much more on the edge of the lower plate. To overcome this direct the flame longer on the lower edge of the plate without allowing the molten puddle to drop. Keep the tip of the filler rod nearer the upper plate. After each weld, be sure to test the joint by bending it in the vice.

Overhead Welding

The overhead weld is a little more difficult to perform because of the unusual position in which you are required to work and the skill needed to keep the molten puddle from dropping off the plates.

Overhead welding is possible because of the fact that molten metal has cohesive qualities as long as the puddle is not permitted to get too large. In other words, molten metal will not fall if the puddle is not allowed to form in complete drops. The amount of heat directed on the seam must be very carefully regulated, since excessively intense heat will increase the flow of the molten metal. With the correct flame, proper torch manipulation, and practice, the overhead weld can be mastered quickly.

Practicing overhead welds. Tack two $\frac{1}{16}''$ or $\frac{1}{8}''$ plates together and set the work up on a suitable jig that will permit sufficient freedom for manipulating the torch. See Fig. 3. Use the same semicircular motion of the torch as previously described. To help keep the puddle shallow, move the filler rod slowly in a circular or swing-

Fig. 3. Notice the positions of the torch and rod for overhead welding. (Linde Co.)

ing motion. The movement of the rod will distribute the molten puddle and prevent it from forming into large drops and falling off. Watch the flame very closely and, if the puddle has a tendency to run, pull the torch away slightly. After the weld is completed, subject it to the bending test. Continue practicing overhead welds until you can make joints that will not break.

Points to Remember

1. Use a semicircular torch move-ment for vertical, horizontal, and overhead welding.

2. Do not allow the puddle to become too large.

3. If the puddle has a tendency to become too fluid, raise the flame slightly.

4. In horizontal welding direct the flame more on the edge of the lower plate.

5. On overhead welds move the filler rod slowly in a circular or swinging motion.

QUESTIONS FOR STUDY AND DISCUSSION

1. What can be done to prevent the puddle from sagging in vertical welding?

2. At what angle should the torch be held for vertical welding?

3. How should the torch be manipulated for vertical, horizontal, and overhead welding?

4. In horizontal welding, why should the flame be directed more on the edge of the lower plate?

5. What should be done to prevent the puddle from becoming too fluid?

6. Why is overhead welding somewhat more difficult to perform?

7. How can the puddle be prevented from dropping off in overhead welding?

8. How should the filler rod be manipulated in overhead welding?

WELDING ASSIGNMENTS

1. Weld a butt joint in a vertical position.

2. Weld a butt joint in a horizontal position.

3. Weld a butt joint in an overhead position.

CHAPTER 26

Oxy-Acetylene Welding

Heavy Steel Plate

Rolled steel stock is commonly labeled as sheet, or plate, depending upon the thickness. Generally speaking, if the metal is ⅛″ or less in thickness, it is referred to as sheet. If the thickness is over ⅛″ it is designated as plate.

Although the technique for welding heavy plate is about the same as in welding light material, the problems associated with heavy plate welding are somewhat more complicated. For this kind of welding more attention has to be given to the manner in which the joints are prepared and to the amount of heat required for sufficient penetration.

Welding a Single-Vee Butt Joint

To have the greatest maximum strength, a weld must possess complete penetration. Full penetration in stock ⅛″ or less in thickness is reasonably easy to achieve. When the thickness exceeds ⅛″, penetration cannot be obtained if the edges are left square. Therefore, on such metal the edges must be beveled. The easiest method of beveling plates is by means of the cutting torch. See Chapter 31. Another way to prepare the edges is by grinding them on an emery wheel.

For plates up to ½″ in thickness, the single-vee, as shown in Fig. 1, is ample. In the single-vee, the included angle should be between 60° and 90°. The bottom of the vee can have a ¹⁄₁₆″ or ⅛″ square root face (unbeveled) or the edges feathered to a sharp point.

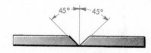

Fig. 1. For a single-vee butt joint, bevel the edges like this.

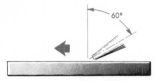

Fig. 2. For heavy plate welding hold the torch at a 60° angle.

To practice welding a single-vee butt joint, proceed as follows:

1. Obtain two pieces of ¼″ plate and bevel the edges.

2. Separate the plates about ¹⁄₁₆″ and tack weld them together. Use a filler rod that is approximately ³⁄₁₆″ in diameter.

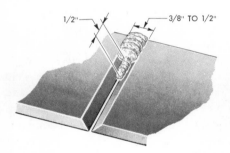

Fig. 3. Fill in the bottom of the vee and then carry the puddle to the top.

3. Hold the torch so the flame will be at an angle of 60° from the vertical rather than the 45° angle used on light stock as previously described. See Fig. 2. Be sure you have the correct size tip for this weld. See Chapter 22.

4. Direct the flame on the vee and, as the edges begin to melt, dip the tip of the rod in the puddle. Before adding filler rod make certain that the sides of the vee are in a molten state all the way to the bottom of the vee. Fill in the bottom of the vee for a length of about ½″ with the puddle extending upward to one-half the depth of the vee. Then, while the puddle is still in a plastic state, swing the torch in a semicircular motion and fill the vee as shown in Fig. 3. The completed bead should be between ³⁄₈″ to ½″ in width and project slightly above the surface of the plate. Return the flame to the bottom of the vee, advance another ½″, and again raise this section of the bead to the top of the vee. Continue to do this until the weld is finished. See Fig. 4.

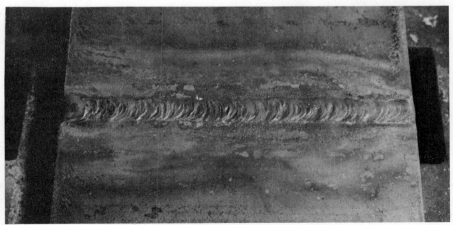

Fig. 4. A good ripple weld in heavy plate should look like this. (Linde Co.)

Fig. 5. Cut off a specimen and grind off the weld surplus.

5. To test the weld, cut off several 1″ strips as shown in Fig. 5. Grind off the surplus weld metal so that the top of the weld (face) is flush with the top of the plate. Place the specimen in a vise with the face of the weld towards you and bend the piece so the weld is under tension. A good weld should bend at least 90° with no indication of cracking or fracturing. See Fig. 6.

Backhand Welding

All of the welding that has been described so far is known as forehand welding. As you know, in this method the welding progresses from right to left for the right-handed person with the flame between the welding rod and the completed portion of the weld.

In the *backhand* technique, the weld is carried from left to right (right to left for a left-handed person). The welding flame is directed backward at the completed portion of the weld and the rod is between the flame and the completed weld section. See Fig. 7. Since the flame is constantly directed on the edges of the vee ahead of the puddle, no sidewise motion of the torch is necessary. As a result, a narrower vee can be utilized than in forehand welding.

Fig. 6. A good weld specimen should withstand bending without cracking.

Fig. 7. In the backhand technique, the welding progresses from left to right for right-handed persons. (Linde Co.)

In backhand welding the puddle is less fluid. This results in a slightly different appearance of the weld surface. The ripples are heavier and spaced further apart.

To practice a backhand weld, proceed as follows:

1. Place two ¼" thick plates on the bench with the beveled edges separated about ⅟₁₆" and tack them together.

2. Start the weld at the left (right, if left-handed) and bring the edges of the vee to a molten puddle. While doing so, hold the end of the rod in the outer envelope of the flame so it will be ready to melt as soon as the puddle starts to form.

3. At the start, concentrate the flame a little more on the bottom of the vee. As soon as the puddle is fluid enough, dip the rod into it. Once the puddle begins to move, direct the flame more on the filler rod and build up the puddle to the top of the vee. As the molten metal begins to fill up the vee, move the filler rod slightly from side to side to make sure that the weld metal fuses evenly with the edges of the base metal.

4. Test the joint in the same manner as described in making a single-vee butt weld with the forehand method.

Welding a Double-Vee Butt Joint

When a plate is ½" or more in thickness, it is much better to run a weld on both sides. For this purpose a double-vee is required. See Fig. 8. Notice that in a double-vee a ⅟₁₆" or ⅛" root face is provided in the cen-

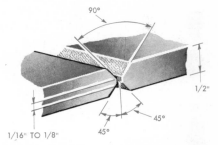

Fig. 8. For extremely heavy plates a double-vee should be used.

ter. Either the forehand or backhand method can be used to execute the weld.

In making a double-vee weld it will be necessary to build up the weld in layers, because it is too difficult to control the molten puddle and secure good penetration in attempting to fill the vee in one lap. The usual practice is to first run one layer near the bottom of the vee on both sides of the plate. Then successive layers are added to fill the vee. Extreme care must be taken when applying the successive layers to fuse each layer with the one already deposited and with the sides of the vee.

Welding High Carbon Steel

Any metal having a carbon content of 0.80 per cent carbon or more is considered to be a high carbon steel. This includes all carbon machine steels, spring steel, and common tool steels.

Whether a steel is weldable or not depends upon the effects the heating and cooling cycle has on the physical properties of the weld area and the base metal itself. If the metal can be taken through the heating and cooling cycle without cracks developing in the weld zone or without seriously affecting the characteristics of the original metal, a steel is assumed to be weldable. See Chapter 2 for a more complete discussion of the effects of heat on steel.

To weld a high carbon steel, it must be preheated first. This can be done by playing the oxyacetylene flame uniformly over the metal until it reaches a faint, red color. The welding should be done with an excess acetylene flame with just enough heat to secure fusion between the weld metal and the base metal. For thin parts where there is likely to be considerable intermingling of base metal and weld metal, a low-carbon filler rod should be used. On heavier sections and especially when the parts are to be heat-treated again, a high carbon rod is advisable.

Points to Remember

1. Plate thicker than ⅛″ should be beveled before welding.

2. Plate ½″ or more in thickness should have a double-vee.

3. When beveling plate, the included angle should be between 60° and 90°.

4. Hold the torch at a 60° angle when welding heavy plate.

5. Be sure the bottom surfaces of the vee have reached the proper temperature before adding filler rod.

6. The backhand welding technique is particularly adaptable for welding heavy plate.

7. In backhand welding do not swing the torch; move the filler rod instead.

8. On plates ½″ or more in thickness do not try to fill the vee in a single pass. Use several passes.

9. Remember that a high carbon steel will lose its hardness if welded. To restore its hardness it must be put through a heat-treating process after welding.

10. Use a slightly excess acetylene flame for welding high carbon steel.

11. Use a high carbon filler rod on steels that are to be heat-treated after welding.

QUESTIONS FOR STUDY AND DISCUSSION

1. Why is some metal called sheet and other plate?

2. Why should the edges be beveled when the plate is ¼″ or more thick?

3. At what angle should the torch be held when welding heavy plate?

4. Why should the edges of heavy plate be spaced for welding?

5. How should test specimens of

heavy plate be prepared for checking the strength of the weld?

6. How does the backhand welding technique differ from the forehand?

7. How should the torch and rod be handled in backhand welding?

8. At what angle should heavy plates be beveled?

9. Why is a double-vee used on some plates?

10. In welding plates over ½″ thick, why use more than one pass?

11. Why must extreme care be taken when welding high carbon steel that has been heat-treated?

12. What kind of flame should be used in welding high carbon steel?

13. What kind of a filler rod is needed to weld high carbon steel?

WELDING ASSIGNMENTS

1. Weld a single-vee butt joint using the forehand technique.

2. Weld a single-vee butt joint using the backhand technique.

3. Weld a plate using a double vee.

CHAPTER 27

Oxy-Acetylene Welding

Stainless Steel

~~~~~~

Stainless steels, particularly the 300 series (See Chapter 13), can readily be welded with the oxy-acetylene flame. However, better results are obtained with the gas shielded-arc processes.

Choosing the Correct Joint Design

For thin metal, the flange-type joint is probably the most satisfactory design. Slightly heavier sheets, up to ⅛" in thickness, may be butted together. For plates heavier than ⅛", the edges should be beveled to provide a vee so fusion can be obtained entirely to the bottom of the weld.

Since stainless steels have a much higher coefficient of expansion with lower thermal conductivity than mild steels, there are greater possibilities for distortion and warping. Therefore whenever possible clamps and jigs should be used to keep the pieces in line until they have cooled.

Selecting the Proper Tip Size

In welding stainless steel with oxy-acetylene, it is necessary to use a tip that is one or two sizes smaller than the one ordinarily employed for welding mild steel. Since heat has a tendency to remain longer in the weld zone of stainless steel, a smaller flame reduces the possibility of destroying the properties of the metal.

Adjusting the Flame

A neutral flame is very essential for welding stainless steel. Even a slightly oxidizing flame oxidizes the chromium in the steel, thereby materially reducing its corrosion-resistant qualities. An excessive carbonizing flame is also undesirable because it increases the carbon content in the weld area, making the weld weak and brittle. Since it is often difficult to maintain an exact neutral flame, it is often better to use a slight excess of acetylene.

Selecting the Filler Rod

Special treated columbium 18-8 filler rods are essential for achieving satisfactory welding of stainless steel. As a matter of fact, it is often desirable to have a rod that contains 1 to $1\frac{1}{2}$ per cent more chromium than the base metal. Such a rod allows for the slight oxidation losses that may occur during the welding operation. If special rods are not available, the next best thing is to cut strips from the base metal and use these as filler rods.

Using Flux

Not only does the chromium in stainless steel oxidize easily, but the oxide formed during welding acts as an insulating barrier between the flame and the work. Hence a flux is needed to ensure better control of the molten metal and to make possible a sound, clean, good-appearing weld.

Most fluxes are prepared by mixing the powder with water to a consistency of thin paste. You then apply the flux by brushing it on the seam, on the filler rod, or on both. It is also a good policy to coat the underside of the seam with flux, since this prevents oxidation and allows a more perfect union to be made along the bottom of the seam.

Welding Procedure

1. Use the forehand technique on light sheets and either the backhand or forehand method on heavy plate.

2. Keep the tip of the inner cone of the flame to within $\frac{1}{16}''$ of the

Fig. 1. For welding stainless steel, incline the pieces downward from the point where you start.

molten puddle. This will help prevent oxidation. Hold the torch at an angle of about 45° to the work. It is usually helpful to elevate the starting end of the joint so the line of the weld inclines slightly downward in the direction of the finishing end. In this way the flux, which fuses at lower temperatures than the steel, can flow forward and provide protection for the metal as it fuses. See Fig. 1.

3. When adding filler rod, hold it close to the cone of the flame. Upon withdrawing it from the puddle, remove it entirely from the flame until you are ready to dip it back into the puddle. A columbium-treated rod flows freely and care must be taken not to direct too much heat on it.

4. Weld from one side only and fill the seam in the first pass. See Fig. 2. Refrain as much as possible from going back over a weld. Success in welding stainless steel depends on keeping the heat to a minimum. Retracting a hot weld produces excessive heat, which is likely to increase the loss of the corrosion-resistant elements in the metal.

Points to Remember

1. Whenever possible, use copper backing strips to weld stainless steel.

2. Clamp the pieces to reduce distortion and warpage.

3. Use a tip that is one or two times smaller than for welding mild steel.

4. Be sure the flame is fully neutral or slightly reducing.

5. Use columbium treated 18-8 filler rods.

6. Always use a flux especially designed for stainless steel.

7. On thin sheet use the forehand welding technique. Use either the forehand or backhand method on heavy plate.

8. Incline the pieces slightly downward in the direction of the weld.

9. Withdraw the rod completely from the flame when it is not being dipped into the puddle.

10. Complete the weld in one pass.

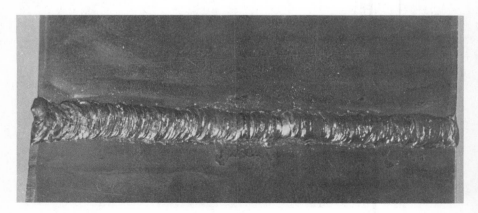

Fig. 2. A weld on stainless steel should look like this.

QUESTIONS FOR STUDY AND DISCUSSION

1. Why is the gas-shielded arc more adaptable for welding stainless steel?

2. How should the edges be prepared on stainless steel pieces to be welded?

3. Why should greater precautions be taken on stainless steel to avoid distortion and warping?

4. What kind of filler rod is needed to weld stainless steel?

5. Why is a flux required to weld stainless steel?

6. Where and how should the flux be applied?

7. How should the torch be held when welding stainless steel?

8. How should the filler rod be applied?

9. Why should the weld be completed in one pass?

10. Why should the pieces be inclined slightly downward in the direction of the welding?

WELDING ASSIGNMENTS

1. Weld a butt joint using light stainless steel sheet.

2. Weld a lap and T-joint using heavy stainless steel plate.

CHAPTER 28

Oxy-Acetylene Welding

Bronze Welding

~~~~~~

Bronze welding is often referred to as brazing, but in the true sense of the word it is not an actual brazing process. According to the American Welding Society, *brazing* is defined as a group of welding processes wherein coalescence (forming together in one mass) is produced by heating the metal to suitable temperatures above 800° F and by using a non-ferrous filler metal having a melting point below that of the base metals. The filler metal is distributed between the closely fitted surfaces of the joint by capillary attraction (power of a heated surface to draw and spread molten metal). Silver soldering is a typical example of such a brazing operation. The strength of a brazed joint depends entirely upon the uniform flow of a thin layer of filler material between the closely fitted surfaces of the metal.

Bronze welding, on the other hand, is carried out much as in fusion welding except that the base metal is not melted. The base metal is simply brought up to what is known as a *tinning temperature* (dull red color) and a bead deposited over the seam with a bronze filler rod. Although the base metal is never actually melted, the unique characteristics of the bond formed by the bronze rod are such that the results are often comparable to those secured through fusion welding.

Bronze welding is particularly adaptable for joining or repairing such metals as cast iron, malleable iron, copper, brass, and various dissimilar metals (cast iron and steel, etc.). See Fig. 1. *The one precaution that must be considered in bronze welding is not to weld a metal that will be subjected to a high temperature later,* since bronze loses its strength when heated to 500° F or more. Also, bronze weld-

Fig. 1. Building up a missing gear tooth with a bronze weld. (Linde Co.)

ing should not be used on steel parts that must withstand unusually high stresses.

Advantages of Bronze Welding

Since the metal does not have to be heated to a molten condition in bronze welding, there is less possibility of destroying the main characteristics of the base metal. Thus in repairing malleable castings the danger of jeopardizing its ductility properties is minimized.

Equally important is the elimination of stored-up stresses which are often present in fusion welding. This is especially critical in repairing castings. The low degree of heat in bronze welding reduces to a minimum these expansion and contraction forces.

With bronze welding there is less need for extensive preheating. On thick sections where some preheating may be desirable the temperature is only brought up to a black heat.

Characteristics of the Filler Rod

The main elements of a bronze filler rod used in bronze welding are copper and zinc, which produce high tensile strength and ductility. In addition, it contains small quantities of tin, iron, manganese, and silicon. These elements help to de-oxidize the weld metal, decrease the tendency to fume, and increase the free-flowing action of the molten metal.

Using Flux

An essential factor for bronze welding is a clean metal surface. If the bronze is to provide a strong bond, it must flow smoothly and evenly over the entire weld area. Adhesion of the molten bronze to the base metal will take place only if the surface is chemically clean. The flow action of the bronze over a surface is much like the flow of water over a piece of glass. If the glass is perfectly clean, the water will spread out into a thin, even film, whereas if the glass is dirty the water tends to gather into tiny drops and roll off.

Even after a surface has been thoroughly cleaned by mechanical means, certain oxides may still be present on the metal surfaces. These oxides can only be removed by means of a good flux. There are many satisfactory fluxes on the market.

The flux is applied by dipping the heated rod into the powdered flux. The flux adheres to the surface of the rod and thus can be transferred to the weld. Another method is to dissolve the flux in boiling water and brush it on the rod before welding is started.

Welding Procedure

1. Clean the surfaces thoroughly with a stiff wire brush. Remove all scale, dirt, or grease; otherwise the bronze will not stick. If a surface has

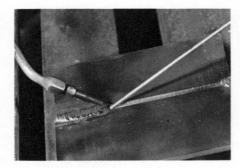

Fig. 2. Arrange the work so the weld travels upward on an incline.

oil or grease on it, remove these substances by heating the area to a bright red color and thus burning them off.

2. On thick sections, especially in repairing castings, bevel the edges to form a 90° vee-groove. This can be done by chipping, machining, filing, or grinding.

3. Arrange the work so the weld travels upward on an incline. In this position the molten bronze cannot flow ahead of the heated welding area and the surface in front of the weld is left open to heating. See Fig. 2.

4. Adjust the flame so it is slightly oxidizing. Then gently heat the surfaces of the weld area.

5. Heat the bronzing rod and dip it in the flux. (This step is not necessary if the rods have been prefluxed.) In heating the rod, do not apply the inner cone of the flame directly to the rod.

6. Concentrate the flame on the starting end until the metal begins to turn red. Melt a little bronze rod onto the surface and allow it to spread along the entire seam. The flow of this thin film of bronze is known as the *tinning* operation. Unless the surfaces

are tinned properly the bronzing procedure to follow cannot be carried out successfully. You will find that if the base metal is too hot, the bronze will tend to bubble or run around like drops of water on a warm stove. If the bronze forms into balls which tend to roll off just as water would if placed on a greasy surface, then the base metal is not hot enough. When the metal is at the proper temperature the bronze spreads out evenly over the metal.

7. Once the base metal is tinned sufficiently, start depositing the proper size beads over the seam. Use a slight circular torch motion and run the beads as in regular fusion welding with a filler rod. Keep dipping the rod in the flux as the weld progresses forward. Be sure that the base metal is never permitted to get too hot. See Fig. 3.

8. If the pieces to be welded are grooved, use several passes to fill the vee. On the first pass make certain that the tinning action takes place along the entire bottom surface of the vee and about half way up on each side. The number of passes to be made will depend on the depth of the vee. When depositing several layers of beads be sure that each layer is fused into the previous one.

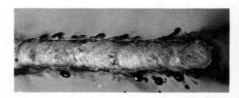

Fig. 3. Here is an example of a properly deposited layer of bronze. (Linde Co.)

Fig. 4. When making a bronze weld in a vertical or semivertical position, first build up a shelf at the bottom. (Linde Co.)

9. When making a bronze weld with the work in a vertical position, first build up a slight shelf at the bottom. The shelf then acts as a support for further bronze. As the weld is carried upward, swing the flame from side to side to maintain uniform tinning and to produce even beads. See Fig. 4.

Points to Remember

1. Do not bronze weld a metal that is to be subjected to high temperatures or high stresses.

2. If some preheating is necessary, bring the temperature up to only a black heat.

3. Use only regularly approved rods for bronze welding operations.

4. Use a special bronzing flux for all bronze welding jobs.

5. Clean surfaces thoroughly before applying the bronze.

6. Arrange the work so the weld progresses upward at a slight angle.

7. Use a slightly oxidizing flame.

8. Be sure the surfaces are properly tinned before depositing beads.

9. Do not melt the surfaces to be welded; heat them to a dull red only.

10. Use a circular torch motion.

QUESTIONS FOR STUDY AND DISCUSSION

1. What is the difference between bronze welding and brazing?

2. What are some of the advantages of bronze welding?

3. When should a part not be bronze welded?

4. What kind of rod is needed for bronze welding?

5. What is the function of the flux in bronze welding?

6. How should the flux be applied?

7. Why should the piece to be bronze welded be placed on a slight incline?

8. What kind of a flame is recommended for bronze welding?

9. What is meant by tinning?

10. How can you tell when the surface is hot enough for bronze welding?

WELDING ASSIGNMENTS

1. Bronze weld a butt joint on ¼″ steel plates.

2. Bronze weld a lap or T-joint on ¼″ steel plates.

3. Bronze weld a casting.

CHAPTER 29

Oxy-Acetylene Welding

Gray Cast Iron

~~~~~~

Gray cast iron may be fusion welded, except that greater precautions must be taken to offset expansion and contraction forces than if it were bronze welded. Since gray cast iron is unusually brittle, it is very susceptible to temperature changes. Consequently, more preheating is necessary and considerably more care is required to cool the parts after welding.

To maintain the gray iron structure throughout the weld area, the weld has to be made with the correct filler rod and the parts cooled slowly. If the casting is cooled rapidly, the weld area is likely to turn into white cast iron, thereby making the weld section not only extremely brittle but so hard that machining might be impossible.

Preparing the Edges

The edges of the casting should be beveled to have a 90° included angle, but the vee should extend only to $\frac{1}{8}''$ from the bottom of the break. Beveling in this manner makes it easier to build up a sound weld near the bottom and lessen the danger of melting through. Placing carbon backup blocks underneath the joint also helps to prevent the molten cast iron from running out the seam.

The same precautions as in bronze welding must be taken in cleaning the surfaces of the joint. The weld area should be cleaned at least one inch on both sides of the vee as shown in Fig. 1. Improperly cleaned surfaces will result in porous spots and blowholes in the weld, even though sufficient flux is used.

Preheating the Cast Iron

One important rule that you must

Fig. 1. Clean the surface around the seam to be welded.

follow for successful fusion welding of cast iron is to preheat the entire casting to a dull red. Uniform preheating will equalize the expansion and contraction forces and thus minimize the possibility of cracks developing. On a small section, the preheating can be carried out by playing the flame over the casting. A large casting may have to be placed in a preheating furnace. The temperature has to be watched very carefully on a heavy casting, especially if it has thin members. The thin members will heat more rapidly, so care must be taken not to get them too hot.

It is also a good practice to bring the entire casting up to a uniform temperature again after the welding is completed. Then the casting can be covered with asbestos paper so it will cool slowly.

Using Filler Rod and Flux

A special cast iron filler rod having the same composition as the base metal is needed to weld cast iron. It is impor-

tant that the rod contain the correct amount of silicon. During the welding process, the silicon in the weld area has a tendency to burn away. Hence if the rod has sufficient silicon, there will be a proper amount of this element in the weld area after the welding is completed.

A flux is essential in welding cast iron to keep the molten puddle fluid. Otherwise, infusible slag mixes with the iron oxide that forms on the puddle. When this happens, the weld will contain inclusions and blowholes.

Welding Procedure

1. Prepare the edges to be welded. Bevel the joint if necessary and remove all foreign matter from the surface.

2. Slowly heat the entire metal to a dull red.

3. Concentrate the flame near the starting point of the weld until the metal begins to melt. Keep the torch in the same position as in welding mild steel with the inner cone of the flame about $1/8''$ to $1/4''$ from the seam.

4. When the bottom of the vee is thoroughly fused, move the flame from side to side, melting down the sides so the molten metal runs down and combines with the fluid metal in the bottom of the vee. Rotate the torch in a circular motion to keep the sides and bottom of the vee in a molten condition. If the metal gets too hot and tends to run away, raise the torch slightly.

5. Once you have a molten puddle, bring the filler rod into the outer envelope of the flame and keep it there until the rod is fairly hot. Then dip it

into the flux. Now insert the fluxed end of the rod into the molten puddle. The heat of the puddle will melt the rod. Never keep dipping the rod in and out of the puddle. As the rod melts, the molten metal will rise in the groove. When it has been built up slightly above the top surface move the puddle forward about one inch and repeat the operation. Be sure not to move the puddle before the sides of the vee have been broken down, as this will force the molten puddle ahead on the cold metal. See Fig. 2.

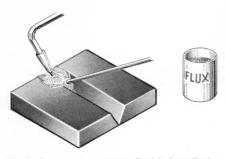

Fig. 2. Be sure the metal is fluid before dipping in the rod.

6. When gas bubbles or white spots appear in the puddle or at the edges of the seam, add more flux and play the flame around the specks until the impurities float to the top. Skim these impurities off the puddle with the rod. By tapping the rod against the bench the impurities can be removed.

7. After the weld is completed, reheat the entire piece to a dull red. Then cover the metal with asbestos paper and allow it to cool slowly. A proper cast iron weld should look like the specimen shown in Fig. 3.

8. To test your weld sample, place it in a vise with the weld flush with the top of the jaws. Strike the upper end with a heavy hammer until the piece breaks. If the metal has been welded properly, the break should not occur along the fused line but in the base metal.

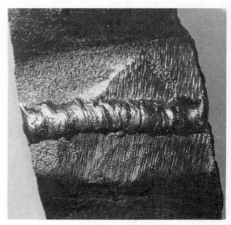

Fig. 3. Appearance of properly welded cast iron.

Points to Remember

1. If possible, use carbon backup blocks when welding cast iron.

2. Clean the surfaces at least one inch around the seam which is to be welded.

3. Preheat the cast iron to a dull red before welding.

4. Use a good grade of cast iron filler rod.

5. Apply flux to the molten metal as the weld is being made.

6. Keep the torch moving in a circular motion to distribute the heat evenly.

7. Reheat the entire piece after the weld is completed and then cover it with asbestos paper so the weld will cool slowly.

QUESTIONS FOR STUDY AND DISCUSSION

1. Why should a rod having the same properties as the base metal be used for this type of welding?

2. Why should cast iron pieces be preheated before welding?

3. How can you tell when a casting has been preheated enough to weld satisfactorily?

4. Why should welded cast iron pieces be cooled slowly?

5. How should the joint of castings be prepared for welding?

6. Why is a flux necessary in welding cast iron?

7. How is the flux deposited in the weld?

8. How should the rod be introduced into the puddle?

9. What precaution should be taken in moving the puddle forward?

10. If the metal has been properly welded, where should the break occur when tested?

WELDING ASSIGNMENT

Weld a piece of cracked cast iron.

CHAPTER 30

Oxy-Acetylene Welding

Aluminum

〜〜〜〜〜〜〜〜〜〜〜〜〜〜〜〜〜〜〜〜〜〜〜

Although the gas shielded-arc processes are generally the most practical for welding most types of commercially pure aluminum, there are occasions when oxy-acetylene welding is still used (See Fig. 1, and Chapters 14, 15, and 16).

Fig. 1. Fusion welding with a gas torch flame is sometimes used in welding aluminum. (Aluminum Company of America)

Welding Characteristics of Aluminum

The following are some of the characteristics which must be kept in mind when welding aluminum with a gas flame:

1. Aluminum has a relatively low melting point compared to other metals that are welded. Pure aluminum melts at 1220° F.

2. The thermal conductivity of aluminum is exceptionally high, being almost four times that of steel.

3. Due to its light color, there is practically no indication when the melting point is reached, for when the metal begins to melt it collapses suddenly.

4. Molten aluminum oxidizes very rapidly, forming a heavy coating on the surface of the seam, which necessitates the use of a good flux.

5. Aluminum when hot is very flimsy and weak, and care must be taken to support it adequately during the welding operation.

Choosing the Correct Joint Design

In general, the same principles of joint design for welding steel apply to aluminum. On thin material up to about $\frac{1}{16}''$ thick, the edges should be formed to a 90° flange at a height equal to the thickness of the material. Flanges will prevent excessive warping and buckling and also serve as filler metal when the flange is melted in the welding operation. Usually no additional filler rod is necessary.

Aluminum from $\frac{1}{16}''$ to $\frac{3}{16}''$ in thickness can be butt welded, providing the edges are notched with a saw or cold chisel. See Fig. 2. Notching minimizes the possibility of burning holes through the joint, permits full penetration, and prevents local distortion.

As a rule the lap joint is not recommended for welding aluminum because of the danger of flux and oxide being trapped between the surfaces of the joint. When this happens the aluminum is likely to corrode.

For welding heavy aluminum plate $\frac{3}{16}''$ or more in thickness, the edges should be beveled to form a 90° to 120° vee. It is usually better to allow a $\frac{1}{16}''$ to $\frac{1}{8}''$ root at the base. This shoulder should be notched as shown in Fig. 3.

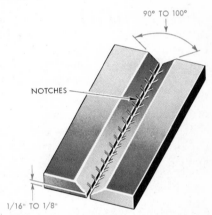

Fig. 3. For welding aluminum plate $\frac{3}{16}''$ to $\frac{3}{8}''$ in thickness, the edges should be beveled and the base notched.

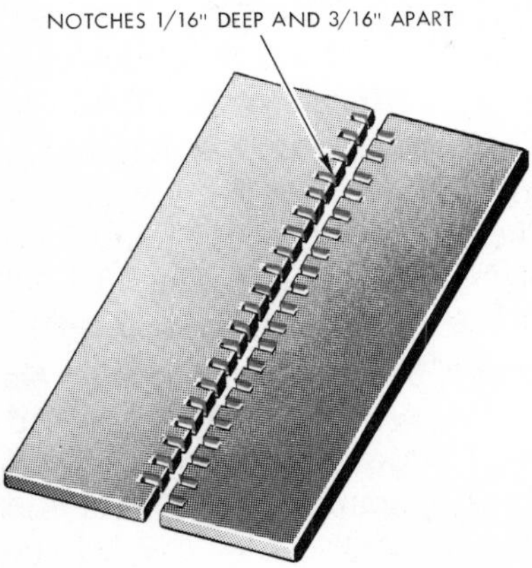

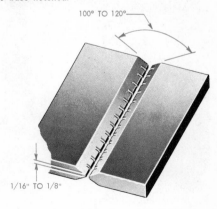

Fig. 4. Use a double-vee on aluminum plate greater than $\frac{3}{8}''$ in thickness.

NOTCHES 1/16" DEEP AND 3/16" APART

Fig. 2. Unbeveled butt joints on $\frac{1}{16}''$ to $\frac{3}{16}''$ aluminum should be notched.

Aluminum that is greater than ⅜″ in thickness should have a double-vee with the center shoulder notched as illustrated in Fig. 4.

Using Flux

The most important step in welding aluminur.1 is to clean the edges to be joined thoroughly. All grease, oil, and dirt must be removed either with gasoline, naphtha, carbon-tetrachloride, or by rubbing the surface with steel wool or a wire brush. See Fig. 5.

Since all aluminum oxidizes very rapidly, a layer of flux must be used to ensure a sound weld. The flux is sold as a powder, which is usually mixed with water to a consistency of a thin paste (approximately two parts of flux to one part of water).

If the welding does not require the addition of any filler rod, the flux is applied to the joint by means of a

Fig. 6. Flux should be applied to the rod (top) and the metal (bottom) when welding heavy aluminum sheets.

Fig. 5. Be sure to clean the edges before welding aluminum.

brush. When a filler rod is used, the rod also is coated with flux. On heavy sections it is advisable to coat the metal as well as the rod for greater ease in securing better fusion. See Fig. 6.

When the welding has been completed, it is very important that all traces of the flux be washed away. Otherwise, the remaining flux will subsequently cause corrosion. The flux is removed by washing the piece in hot water or by immersing the weld in a 10 per cent cold solution of sulphuric acid, followed by rinsing in hot or cold water.

Selecting the Filler Rod

As in welding other metals, the proper selection of a filler rod is important for welding aluminum. The composition of the rod should compare to that of the metal to be welded. The three most common rods for welding non-heat-treatable aluminum are 1100, 4043, and 5356. The 4043 and 5356 rods are recommended when greater strength is required.

Welding rods are obtainable in sizes of $\frac{1}{16}''$, $\frac{1}{8}''$, $\frac{3}{16}''$, and $\frac{1}{4}''$ diameter. As a rule, a rod whose diameter equals the thickness of the metal should be used.

Preheating Aluminum

All aluminum to be welded, including thin sheet, should be preheated as this will decrease the effects of expan-sion and minimize cracks. Aluminum plate $\frac{1}{4}''$ or more in thickness should be preheated to a temperature of 300°-500° F. Preheating to these temperatures can usually be done by playing the flame of the oxyacetylene torch over the work. For large or complicated parts, the preheating is done in a furnace.

It is very important that the preheating temperature does not exceed 500° F. If the temperature goes beyond this point, the alloy may be weakened or parts of the aluminum may collapse under its own weight.

The correct preheating temperature may be determined by the following three methods:

1. If a mark is made on the metal with a carpenter's blue chalk, it will turn white.

2. If a pine stick is rubbed on the metal, a char mark will be left on it.

TABLE I
Torch Welding Data for Aluminum of Various Thicknesses

Aluminum Thickness (inch)	Oxyacetylene		Oxyhydrogen*		
	Oxygen Pressure PSI	Tip Orifice Diameter (inch)	Acetylene Pressure PSI	Tip Orifice Diameter (inch)	Hydrogen Pressure PSI
1/16	1 +	.021 - .031	1	.031 - .0465	1-3
1/8	1-2	.025 - .038	1-2	.038 - .055	2-4
3/16	1-3	.031 - .0465	1-3	.0465- .067	3-5
1/4	2-4	.038 - .055	2-4	.055 - .076	4-6
3/8	5-7	.067 - .086	5-7	.086 - .110	7-9
1/2	6-8	.076 - .098	6-8	.098 - .1285	8-10

(Reynolds Metals Co.)

*Hydrogen may be burned with oxygen in the same tips used with acetylene. However, since the flame temperature is lower, larger tip sizes, as indicated, are necessary. Exact oxygen pressures for oxyhydrogen welding are not given for the reason that, first, a wider range of adjustment is possible and, second, it is common practice to use slightly reducing flames with hydrogen, the exact adjustment of which is largely a matter of experience. Theoretically, two volumes of hydrogen are required to burn one of oxygen; in actual welding practice, at least 2½ volumes are used, and under some circumstances as much as three or four volumes may be employed. Obviously, with such wide discrepancies as encountered in actual practice, a reasonable table of pressures cannot be given.

3. If the metal is struck with a hammer, no metallic ring will be heard.

Selecting the Correct Tip Size

Since aluminum has such a high thermal conductivity, it is necessary to use a tip slightly larger than the one ordinarily used for steel of the same thickness. Table I shows the recommended sizes and gas pressures to use for welding aluminum of varying thicknesses.

Adjusting the Flame

Many operators use hydrogen instead of acetylene for welding aluminum, and this in many cases is more desirable, especially for welding light gage material. In either case, the torch should be adjusted so it will have a neutral flame. Some authorities recommend a slightly reducing flame, but usually a neutral flame will be found to be very satisfactory in producing a clean, sound weld. Whether using acetylene or hydrogen, the flame should be adjusted to a low gas velocity to permit a soft and not a "blowy" flame.

Welding Technique[1]

After the pieces to be welded have been properly prepared and fluxed, the flame is passed in ever smaller circles over the starting point until the flux melts. Then the rod should be scraped over the surface at about 3 or 4 second intervals permitting the rod to come clear of the flame each time, otherwise the rod will melt before the parent metal and it will be hard to note when the welding should start. The scraping action will reveal when welding can be started without over-heating the aluminum. The same cycle should be maintained throughout the course of welding except for allowing the rod to remain under the flame long enough to melt the amount of metal needed. The movement of the rod can easily be mastered with little practice. One of the difficulties sometimes experienced in aluminum welding is failure of the deposited metal to adhere. This is generally caused by attempts to deposit the weld metal on cold base metal. After the flux melts, the base metal must be melted before the rod is applied. Or the metal and the filler metal may be brought to the molten state simultaneously.

Forehand welding is generally considered best for the welding of aluminum since the flame points away from the completed weld and thus preheats the edges to be welded. Too rapid melting is also prevented. The torch should be held at a low angle (less than 30° above horizontal) when welding thin material. For thicknesses $3/16''$ and above, the angle of the torch should be increased to nearer the vertical. Changing the angle of the torch to accord with the thickness minimizes the likelihood of burning through the sheet during welding.

In welding aluminum, there is little need to impart any motion to the torch other than moving it forward. On flanged material, care should be taken to break the oxide film as the

Fig. 7. Appearance of a properly made aluminum weld.

angle of the torch has much to do with welding speed. Instead of lifting the flame from time to time in order to avoid melting holes in the metal, it will be found advantageous to hold the welding torch at a flatter angle, thus increasing the speed. The speed of welding should also be increased as the edge of the sheet is approached. The flame should never be permitted to come in contact with the molten metal. Also hold it no greater distance away from the material than 1 inch. See Fig. 7 for appearance of a good aluminum weld.

Welding Aluminum-Alloy Castings

In general, the welding of aluminum-alloy castings requires techniques similar to those used on aluminum sheet and other wrought sections. However, the susceptibility of many castings to thermal strains and cracks, because of their intricate design and varying section thickness, should be carefully considered. In addition, many castings in highly stressed structures depend upon heat treatment for their strength, and welding tends to destroy the effect of such initial heat treatments. If satisfactory facilities for re-heat treatment are not available, the welding of such heat-treated castings is not recommended.

When a broken aluminum casting is to be welded, it is first cleaned carefully with a wire brush and gasoline to remove every trace of oil, grease, and dirt. Unless the casting has a very heavy cross section, it is not necessary to tool the crack or cut out a vee, as this can be accomplished by means of

flange melts down. This task may be accomplished by stirring the melted flange with a puddling rod.

With aluminum above $\frac{3}{16}''$ thick, the torch should be given a uniform (but not unduly) lateral motion in order to distribute the weld metal over the entire width of the weld. A slight back and forth motion will assist the flux in its removal of oxides. The rod should be dipped into the weld puddle periodically and withdrawn from the puddle with a forward motion. This method of withdrawal closes the puddle, prevents porosity, and assists the flux to remove the oxide film.

Aluminum welds should be made in a single pass as far as possible. This is especially true of alloys other than 1100 and 3003.

It must be remembered that the

---

[1]Reproduced through the courtesy of Reynolds Metals Co.

the torch and puddling iron. (A puddling iron is a piece of low-carbon stainless steel rod with a flattened end.) It is necessary, however, that the stock surrounding the defect be completely melted or cut away before proceeding with the weld. If a piece is broken out, hold it in the correct position by light iron bars and appropriate clamps. The clamps should be so attached that the casting will not be stressed during heating.

If the casting is large or one with intricate sections, it should be preheated slowly and uniformly in a suitable furnace prior to welding. If the casting is small, or if the weld is near the edge and in a thin-walled section, the casting may be preheated in the region of the weld by means of a torch flame. Cast aluminum should be heated slowly to avoid cracking in the section of the casting nearest the flame.

Broken pieces are tack welded into place as soon as the casting has been preheated. The actual welding of the piece should commence at the middle of the break, and should be continued toward the ends. The welding rod must be melted by the torch, as the heat of the molten metal is not sufficient to melt it. When the weld is finished, the excess molten metal is scraped off with a puddling iron, and the casting allowed to cool slowly.

Holes in castings are welded in much the same manner as are cracked and broken castings. But it is necessary to melt away or cut away the sides of the hole in order to remove all pockets and to permit proper manipulation of the torch.

For welding ordinary castings, an aluminum-silicon or aluminum-copper-silicon welding rod is necessary. A flux must also be used. Puddling alone will merely break up the oxide film and leave it incorporated in the weld, while fluxing will cause the oxide particles to rise to the surface, resulting in a clean, sound weld. It is important that the added metal be completely melted and the molten metal thoroughly turned with the end of the welding rod or with a puddling iron. Thus the flux and oxide are worked to the surface of the molten metal, and there is very little danger of the finished weld becoming contaminated with particles of flux or other foreign material.

Points to Remember

1. Always use a flux to weld aluminum.

2. Use a 1100, 4043, or 5356 rod for welding aluminum.

3. Preheat the work before welding.

4. Never allow the preheat to exceed 500° F.

5. Rub a pine stick or blue chalk on the aluminum to determine the correct preheating temperature.

6. Use a slightly larger tip than for welding steel.

7. Use a neutral or slightly reducing flame for all aluminum welding.

8. Hold the torch at an angle of 30° or less when welding thin material.

9. For thicknesses $3/16''$ and above,

increase the torch angle to nearer the vertical.

10. Clean the surfaces thoroughly before starting the welding operation.

QUESTIONS FOR STUDY AND DISCUSSION

1. What are some of the characteristics that must be taken into consideration when welding aluminum?

2. How can you determine when aluminum has reached its preheating temperature?

3. Why must flux be used to weld aluminum?

4. How is this flux applied?

5. What type of welding rod is recommended for welding aluminum?

6. At what angle is the torch inclined when welding aluminum? Why?

7. Why should the rod be held in the flame and not away from it as in welding steel?

8. Why are the edges of the joint notched?

WELDING ASSIGNMENTS

1. Weld a flange joint on light gage aluminum.

2. Weld a butt joint on heavy gage aluminum.

CHAPTER 31

Oxy-Acetylene Welding

Pipe Welding

~~~~~~

Although the shielded metal-arc welding process described in Chapter 14 is used more extensively today in joining pipe, there are still occasions when some welding is done with the oxy-acetylene torch. The same type of pipe joints are employed for welding with gas as in welding with the electric arc. The specific instructions needed to carry out pipe welding operations with gas torch are described in this chapter.

Beveling the Pipe

Ordinarily, most pipe will have the ends already beveled in preparation for the standard form of butt weld. However, some sections of pipe will need to be cut into odd lengths, and where these odd lengths are cut, beveling will be necessary. Beveling will also be required whenever angle connections and special fittings, branches, or bends, are made on the job. The most economical way to do this beveling and cutting is with the oxyacetylene cutting torch. See Chapter 32.

Expansion and Alignment

Every operator of gas welding equipment will remember that his first practice welding exercises acquainted him with the phenomena of expansion and contraction — how they caused pieces to separate and then draw together while being welded—and what precautions are necessary to prevent the metal in the vicinity of the weld from becoming warped or buckled. You must bear in mind that expansion also occurs in welding pipe and some difficulties can be expected unless the following precautions are taken:

1. Spacing the pipes — On small sizes of pipe, that is, up to 2″, the amount of metal involved is so small and the pipe wall is so light that only a small separation is necessary — in fact, just enough to make sure that fusion can be secured all the way to the inside wall of the pipe. In these small sizes, the pipe is often welded without beveling. For 3″ pipe, however, leave a space of about $\frac{3}{32}$″ between the butted ends of the pipe. When diameters of from 4″ to 6″ are involved, the spacing should be about $\frac{1}{8}$″; and for everything over 6″, increase the space to $\frac{3}{16}$″ between the edges.

2. *Clamping the pipes* — A special clamp is used to hold the two lengths of pipe in perfect alignment and to keep them properly spaced just as in arc welding. After they are tacked firmly into position, there is no further need of the clamp, so it is removed in order that it will not interfere with the proper manipulation of the rod and torch while the weld is being made.

3. *Tacking the pipes* — For small pipe, three tacks are usually sufficient, and for medium sizes, four or five will be ample. On very large pipes, that is, 12″ in diameter and over, use enough tack welds so they are not spaced more than 7″ or 8″ apart.

The tack welds need be only about 1″ long and should not be reinforced. As the joint is welded, remember to weld completely through each tack instead of just running the weld over it.

Welding Procedure

The two general methods for welding pipe with an oxy-acetylene torch are the same as in arc welding; that is, roll and position welding. In roll welding the torch is started approximately

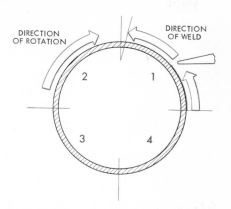

Fig. 1. In roll pipe welding with a gas torch, follow the sequence illustrated here.

one-quarter of the way down from the top of the pipe. The torch is held with the tip pointing upward (as in vertical welding) so that the flame is nearly in a direct line with the pipe. The weld is carried up on the pipe to a point slightly below the top center. When this point is reached, the pipe is given one-quarter turn and the weld begun where it was left off. This procedure is carried out until the joint is completed. See Fig. 1.

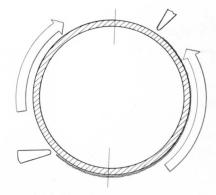

Fig. 2. For fixed-position pipe welding with a gas torch follow this procedure.

In the fixed-position weld, the welding is started at the bottom of the pipe and carried up one side until the top is reached. The weld is then again started at the bottom and carried up the opposite side to complete the joint. See Fig. 2.

Points to Remember

1. The butt weld with the edges of the pipe beveled is usually the most satisfactory joint.

2. When beveling pipe, leave a shoulder at the bottom of the vee.

3. Provide a space between pipes to compensate for expansion forces.

4. Tack the pipes in position before welding.

5. In roll welding, start the weld one-quarter of the way down from the top of the pipe, and carry the weld to a point slightly below the top. Then turn the pipe and proceed in the same manner.

6. For making a fixed position weld, start the welding at the bottom of the pipe and proceed upward.

QUESTIONS FOR STUDY AND DISCUSSION

1. What advantages do welded pipe joints offer over screw joints?

2. Why is the butt joint the most satisfactory for welding pipe?

3. When should the edges of the pipe be beveled before welding?

4. Why should the pipes be spaced apart for welding?

5. What is the general practice for space allowance on pipe?

6. Why are clamps essential for welding long sections of pipe?

7. Why are pipes tacked before the welding is started?

8. Describe two methods that may be used in welding pipes.

9. How should the torch be held for pipe welding?

WELDING ASSIGNMENTS

Obtain several short lengths of pipe and practice:

1. Roll welding.
2. Fixed position welding.

CHAPTER 32

Oxy-Acetylene Welding

Flame Cutting

～～～～～～～～～～～～～～～～～～～～～～～～～～～～～～～～

Cutting metal by the oxy-acetylene process is widely used in many industrial fields. The cutting may be done by means of a simple, hand cutting torch or by a more complicated, automatically controlled cutting machine as shown in Fig. 1.

Severing metal by this process is made possible by the fact that ferrous metals are subject to oxidation. When a piece of wrought iron or steel is left exposed to various atmospheric conditions, a reaction known as rusting begins to take place. This rusting is simply the result of the oxygen in the air uniting with the metal, causing it gradually to decompose and wear away. Naturally this action is very slow but, if the metal is heated and permitted to cool, heavy scales form on the surfaces, showing that the iron oxidizes much faster when subjected to heat. Now, if a piece of steel were to be heated red hot and dropped in a vessel containing oxygen, a burning action would immediately take place, reducing the metal to an iron oxide commonly known as slag.

In order to make possible the rapid cutting of metal, it is necessary to have an implement that will heat the iron or steel to a certain temperature and then throw a blast of oxygen on the heated section. The cutting torch, whether operated manually or by machine, functions in just such a manner. See Fig. 2.

The Cutting Torch

The cutting torch varies from the regular welding blowpipe in that it has an additional lever for the control of the oxygen used to burn the metal. It is possible to convert the welding torch into a cutting torch by replacing the mixing head with a cutting attachment.

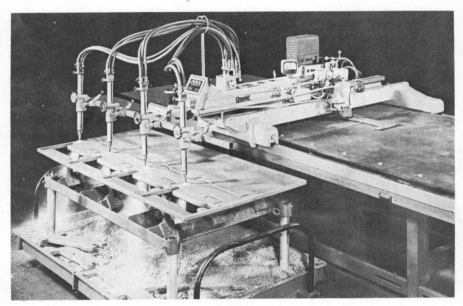

Fig. 1. An automatic flame-cutting machine. (Linde Co.)

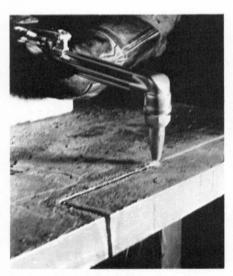

Fig. 2. Little metal is actually removed when severing this 1½" plate by oxygen cutting. (Linde Co.)

It will be noticed from Fig. 3 that the torch has the conventional oxygen and acetylene needle valves. These are used to control the passage of oxygen and acetylene when heating the metal. Many cutting torches have two oxygen needle valves for securing a finer adjustment of the neutral flame. The cutting tip is made with an orifice in the center surrounded by several smaller ones. The center opening permits the flow of the cutting oxygen and the smaller holes are for the heating flame. See Fig. 4. Usually four different tip sizes are provided for cutting metals of varying thicknesses. In addition, special tips are made for other purposes, such as for cleaning metal, cutting rusty, scaly or painted surfaces, rivet washing, etc.

Determining Pressure

The pressure of oxygen and acetylene needed will depend upon the size tip used, which in turn is governed by the thickness of the metal to be cut. Table I points out the approximate

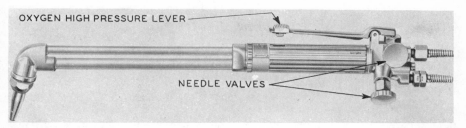

Fig. 3. A flame-cutting torch with one oxygen needle valve (top) and one acetylene needle valve (bottom). (Linde Co.)

pressure for various tip sizes for a particular type of cutting torch.

Always consult the manufacturer's recommendations for your particular torch as to the proper oxygen and acetylene pressure. The given oxygen pressure cannot always be strictly followed because, for example, steels may have an exceptionally heavy coating of rust or scale and, if so, will require a somewhat greater oxygen pressure to make the oxygen burn entirely through the metal.

Lighting the Torch

1. Turn on the acetylene needle valve and light the gas as if for welding.

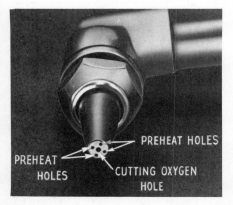

Fig. 4. The cutting tip for a flame-cutting torch. (Linde Co.)

TABLE I

Cutting Pressure

Tip No.	Thickness of Metal (inches)	Acetylene Pressure (pounds)	Oxygen Pressure (pounds)
0	1/4	3	30
1	3/8	3	30
1	1/2	3	40
2	3/4	3	40
2	1	3	50
3	1 1/2	3	45
4	2	3	50
5	3	4	45
5	4	4	60
6	5	5	50
6	6	5	55
7	8	6	60
7	10	6	70

(Air Reduction Co.)

2. Turn on the oxygen valve and adjust it for a neutral flame. This flame is the one used to bring the metal to a kindling temperature which, for example in the case of plain carbon steel, is 1400° F to 1600° F.

3. Observe the nature of the cutting flame by pressing down the oxygen control lever. When the oxygen pressure lever is turned on it may be necessary to make an additional adjustment to keep the preheating cones burning with a neutral flame.

Cutting Steel

1. It is well for the beginner to practice making straight cuts. To aid

in keeping the cut in a horizontal line, rule a chalk line about ¾″ from one edge of the plate.

2. Place the plate so this line clears the edge of the welding bench as shown in Fig. 5.

3. With the torch adjusted to a neutral flame, grasp the blowpipe handle with the right hand in such a position as to permit instant access to the oxygen control lever. The valve is usually operated either with the thumb or forefinger.

4. The knack of making a clean, straight cut depends on how steady you hold the torch. Naturally, when the tip wavers from side to side, a wide kerf (cutting slit) will result, which means a rough cut, slower speed, and greater oxygen consumption. To help keep the blowpipe steady, hold the elbow or forearm on some convenient support.

5. Start the cut at the edge of the plate. Hold the torch with the tip vertical to the surface of the metal, with the inner cone of the heating flame approximately ⅟₁₆″ above the chalk line. Keep the torch in this position until a spot in the metal has been heated to a bright red heat.

Fig. 6. This is how a correct cut appears. The shower of sparks under the cut shows complete penetration. (Linde Co.)

6. Gradually press down the oxygen pressure lever and move the torch forward slowly along the chalk line. See Fig. 6. The movement of the torch should be just rapid enough to ensure a fast but continuous cut. A shower of sparks will be seen to fall from the underside, indicating that the penetration is complete and the cut is proceeding correctly.

7. If the cut does not seem to go through the metal, close the oxygen pressure lever and reheat the metal until it is a bright red again. If the edges of the cut appear to melt and have a very ragged appearance, the metal is not burning through and the torch is being moved too slowly.

8. When an exceptionally straight cut is desired, clamp a bar across the plate alongside the cutting line to act as a guide for the torch to follow.

9. At the start, the pieces may stick together even when the cut has penetrated through. This is due to the slag, produced by the cutting, flowing across the metal pieces. However, this is not serious, as the slag is quite brittle and a slight blow with a hammer will separate the two sections.

Fig. 5. Starting the cut. (Linde Co.)

10. It may be necessary sometimes to start the cut in from the edge of the plate. In such a case, hold the pre-heating flame a little longer on the metal; then raise the cutting nozzle about ½″ and pull the oxygen lever. When a hole is cut through, lower the torch to its normal position and proceed with the cut in the usual manner.

Cutting Round-Bar Steel

1. To sever round stock, start the cut about 90° from the top edge as shown in Fig. 7.

Fig. 8. Beveling with a cutting torch.

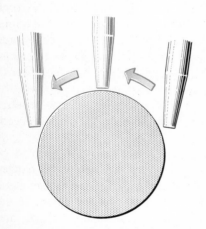

Fig. 7. When cutting round stock start 90° from the top, as shown by the torch position at the right, and follow around the bar, as indicated by the arrow.

2. Keep the torch in a perpendicular position and gradually lift it to follow the circular outline of the bar. Maintain this position of the blowpipe while ascending as well as descending on the opposite side.

Beveling

To make a bevel cut on a steel plate,

incline the head of the torch to the desired angle instead of holding it vertically. An even bevel may be made by resting the edge of the nozzle on the work as a support, as shown in Fig. 8, or be guided by means of a piece of angle iron clamped across the plate.

Piercing Holes

1. Hold the torch over the spot where the hole is to be cut until the flame has heated a small, round spot.

2. Gradually pull the oxygen lever and at the same time raise the nozzle slightly. In this manner a small, round hole can be pierced quickly through the metal.

3. When larger holes are required, trace the shape of the openings with a piece of chalk. If the holes are located away from the edge of the plate, first pierce a small hole, and then start the cut from this point, gradually working to the chalk line and continuing around the outline. For holes near the

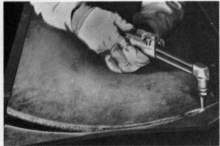

Fig. 9. Cutting holes (top) and large curves (bottom). (Linde Co.)

outer edge of the plate, proceed as shown in Fig. 9.

Cutting Cast Iron[1]

To describe this process intelligently, we must first consider the nature of cast iron from two angles. Since it has such a wide range of use, it is natural that we may expect a wide difference in quality or chemical composition and a corresponding difference in ease of cutting. The better grades of castings are more easily cut, and those of random grades of scrap, such as counterweights, gratebars, floorplates, etc., present greater difficulty, requiring more gas, a wider kerf,

---

[1]Reproduced through the courtesy of the Modern Engineering Co.

and a corresponding slower rate of cutting speed.

Preparation. There is a rule for heavy steel cutting which certainly applies in every way to cast-iron cutting, and that is, *DO NOT START THE CUT UNTIL YOU ARE CERTAIN THAT YOU CAN COMPLETE IT*. It is obvious that, if the cut is stopped on a heavy section, it is extremely difficult to start it again, and may doubly increase the cost as well as the annoyance. Considerably more heat, as well as sparks and slag, is generated in cast iron, so that proper protection to the body, face, and limbs is necessary. Asbestos gloves are essential, and a fire brick or suitable torch rest is desirable.

Cutting procedure. 1. For cutting the better grades of cast or gray iron, set the regulator to deliver the proper pressure as indicated in Table II. The regulator adjustment, of course, is made with the high-pressure cutting valve open to compensate for the customary drop in pressure when the gas is released.

TABLE II
Pressure Table for Cutting Cast Iron

Size of Tip	Thickness of Metal (inches)	Oxygen Pressure (pounds)	Acetylene Pressure (pounds)
L–3	1/2	40	7 to 8
	3/4	45	
	1	50	
	1 1/2	60	
	2	70	
L–4	3	80	8 to 10
	4	90	
	6	110	
	8	120	
	10	150	
	12	170	

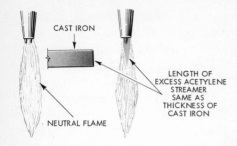

Fig. 10. For cutting cast iron use a flame with an excess of acetylene.

2. Next, light the torch and adjust the preheating flame so that it will show an excess of acetylene. This is done preferably with the high-pressure valve wide open to avoid any change in the character of the flame during the actual cutting operation. This is important! The excess acetylene, as indicated by the length of the white cone, must be varied to best suit the grade and thickness of the material cut. Experience is naturally the best guide on this point. However, it will generally vary from little or no excess of acetylene for the extremely light sections to an excess indicated by a one to two inch white cone for the heavier sections cut. See Fig. 10.

3. Bring the tip of the torch to the top or starting point as indicated in Fig. 11. Hold the torch on an angle of approximately 40° to 50° and heat a spot about ½″ in diameter to a molten condition.

4. With the end of the shorter, preheating cone about ³⁄₁₆″ from the metal, start to move the torch with a swinging motion, as shown in Fig. 12, and open the high pressure cutting valve.

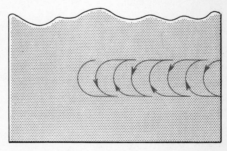

Fig. 12. Movement of the torch for cutting cast iron.

5. Gradually bring the torch along the line of the cut, continuing the swinging motion. As the cut progresses, gradually straighten the torch to an angle of 65° to 70°, as shown

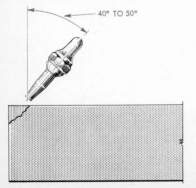

Fig. 11. Position of the torch to start cutting cast iron.

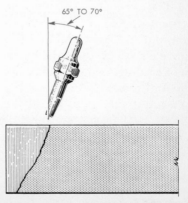

Fig. 13. Advanced position in cutting cast iron.

in Fig. 13, which will help to facilitate the penetration.

6. The same swinging movement is continued throughout the entire length of the cut. As you gain experience and confidence, you will be able to reduce somewhat the length of the arc of this swinging motion, thereby reducing the width of the kerf and the corresponding amount of gas consumed.

7. On the heavier sections, sufficient heat is usually developed to allow the cut to proceed without interruption. On the lighter sections, however, more difficulty is experienced. The operator is frequently bothered with losing his cut; in other words, the surface of the metal cools too rapidly and only a slight groove is made in it by the flame. Start over again by heating a small circle as previously described, but gradually raise the torch and incline it so as to cut away the lower portion of the section. Then proceed as before. As long as the exposed side of the cutting groove appears bright, continue the cut until it is completed.

Powder Cutting

The regular oxygen cutting process is ineffective for cutting metals that form refractory oxides such as aluminum, bronzes, and high-nickel alloys. To cut these metals an iron powder is fed into the oxygen stream. A mixture of iron powder and aluminum powder is sometimes used for cutting brass, copper, and high-nickel alloys. The aluminum releases more heat than just the iron powder alone. Iron powder also produces a rapid cutting action on stainless steels and is very effective in getting smoother cuts in cast iron.

Powder cutting is done with a special powder-cutting torch as shown in Fig. 14. The torch is equipped with a powder tube, nozzle, and powder valve. The powder is stored in a dispenser and is carried to the powder valve by compressed air or nitrogen where it is fed to the flame. In operation the powder valve is opened first and then the oxygen valve.

Points to Remember

1. Use the correct size cutting tip.
2. Light the cutting torch the same way you would a welding torch.
3. To start a cut, hold the tip in a vertical position with the inner cone of the heating flame $\frac{1}{16}''$ above the metal.

Fig. 14. Powder-cutting torch. (Linde Co.)

4. Heat the metal to a bright red before pressing the oxygen high pressure lever.

5. If the cut is proceeding correctly, a shower of sparks will be seen to fall from the underside of the plate.

6. If the edges of the cut appear to be too ragged, the torch is being moved too slowly.

7. To cut round stock, start the cut about 90° from the top and move the torch upward.

8. To bevel stock, hold the torch at the desired angle and proceed as in making a straight cut.

9. To cut large holes, draw the shape of the opening required and proceed as in making a straight cut.

10. When cutting cast iron, adjust the heating flame so it shows an excess of acetylene.

11. For cast iron cutting, hold the torch at an angle of 40° to 50° and heat a spot ½″ in diameter to a molten condition.

12. Use a swinging motion to cut cast iron.

13. After the cut is begun on cast iron, raise the torch to an angle of 65° to 70°

QUESTIONS FOR STUDY AND DISCUSSION

1. What causes metal to rust?

2. What principle makes possible the cutting of metal by means of oxygen and acetylene?

3. Describe the process for lighting and adjusting the flame for a cutting torch.

4. What is the function of the high-pressure oxygen valve?

5. How does the cutting tip differ from the welding tip?

6. What governs the pressure of oxygen and acetylene that must be used for cutting.

7. As a general rule where should the cut be started? Why?

8. What aids may be used to facilitate an even cut?

9. How can one determine whether the cut is penetrating through the metal?

10. What happens when the cutting torch is moved too slowly?

11. What is the position of the torch when cutting round material?

12. How is it possible to make a bevel cut with a cutting torch?

13. Describe the operation followed in piercing small holes with a cutting torch.

14. What type of flame is used for cutting cast iron?

15. How is the torch held when cutting cast iron?

16. What torch motion is used for cutting cast iron?

CUTTING ASSIGNMENTS

1. Obtain a piece of ¼″, ⅜″, or ½″ steel plate and rule off chalk lines ¾″

apart. Fit the proper size cutting tip and proceed to cut these strips.

2. Obtain pieces of round stock of different diameters. Mark these into $\frac{3}{4}''$ pieces and proceed to cut them.

3. Obtain a piece of steel $3'' \times 4''$, $\frac{1}{4}''$ or greater in thickness. Draw a $\frac{3}{8}''$ line around the inside of the four edges. With the correct cutting tip, bevel these four edges.

4. Obtain a piece of steel $3'' \times 5''$ of any desired thickness. Draw a $2\frac{1}{2}''$ opening and cut.

5. Obtain a number of pieces of scrap iron and practice cutting them.

CHAPTER 33

Oxy-Acetylene Welding

Airplane Tubing

The oxy-acetylene welding process is used a great deal in the fabrication and repair of airplanes. Most aircraft designs employ an alloy steel tubing in the fuselage, tail assembly, or landing gear. The best method of joining the tubing is by oxy-acetylene welding.

Aircraft welding is a specialized field of its own, and although an individual may be an expert in other types of welding, this does not necessarily mean that he can satisfactorily weld airplane tubing. This type of welding involves more precision, better technique in handling the torch in various positions, and far greater responsibilities.

Preparation for Welding

Considerable attention must be given to the clearance between the joints to provide for proper expansion of the metal. A space ranging from $\frac{1}{32}''$ to $\frac{1}{16}''$ or more, depending on the thickness of the tubing, is required.

The pieces to be welded should be held in suitable jigs to keep them in perfect alignment and to prevent any distortion caused by the expansion and contraction forces generated during the welding operation.

Before any welding is begun, the pieces must be thoroughly cleaned by brushing the area to be joined with a wire brush or sandpaper. When a wire brush is used, care should be taken never to use a brush of a dissimilar metal; for example, brass or bronze. The small deposit left by a brass or bronze brush will materially weaken the weld and may cause cracking and subsequent failure of the weld. In case members were metallized, the surface metal may be removed by careful

sandblasting followed by a light buff-
ing with emery cloth.

Selecting the Correct Tip

A soft neutral flame must be used
for successfully welding aircraft tubing. The size of the tip is governed
by the thickness of the metal. Care
must be taken to use a tip that will permit a rapid weld and at the same time
will not produce a flame so hot that it
will burn the metal, thereby weakening the joint or the tube. This point is
very important and must be kept constantly in mind when learning to weld
tubing, because any slight defect in
any section of an airplane is liable to
cause a structural failure that may
have disastrous results.

Using the Proper Welding Rod

A low-carbon steel rod is used for
welding chrome-molybdenum tubing.
Although attempts have been made to
use an alloy rod, experiments have
shown that these rods do not offer
enough advantages to offset the difficulty in using them. A low-carbon rod
flows smoothly, making a clean, sound,
uniform weld.

Conditions of a Completed Weld

The finished weld should have the
following characteristics:

1. The bead should be smooth and
of uniform thickness.

2. The weld metal should taper off
smoothly into the base metal.

3. No oxide should be formed on
the base metal at a distance of more
than one-half inch from the weld.

4. The weld should show no signs
of blow holes, porosity, or projecting
globules.

5. The base metal should show no
signs of pitting, burning, cracking, or
distortion.

6. The depth of penetration should
be sufficient to ensure fusion of the
base metal and filler rod.

7. Welding scale should be removed by wire brushing or sandblasting.

Guarding Against Poor Practices

No welds should be filed in an effort
to make a smooth appearing job, as
such a treatment causes a loss in
strength. Welds should not be filled
with solder, brazing metal, or any
other filler. When it is necessary to
reweld a joint, all old weld material
should be thoroughly removed before
rewelding. Never weld over a previous
weld if it can be avoided because con-
tinual reheating may cause the material to lose its strength and become
brittle. Never weld a joint which has
been previously brazed.

Employing Rosette Welds

Rosette welds are generally employed to fuse an inner reinforcing
tube (liner) with an outer member as
shown in Fig. 1. Where a rosette weld
is used, the hole should be made in the
outside tube only and be of a sufficient
size to ensure fusion on the inner tube.
A hole diameter of approximately one-
fourth the tube diameter of the outer

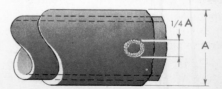

Fig. 1. A rosette weld is used to fuse two tubes
together.

tube has been found to serve adequately for this purpose. In cases of tightly fitting sleeves, or inner liners, the rosettes may be omitted.

Repair of Tubular Members[1]

Inspection—Prior to repairing tubular members, the structure surrounding any visible damage should be carefully examined to ensure that no secondary damage remains undetected. Secondary damage may be produced in some structure remote from the location of the primary damage by the transmission of the damaging load along the tube. Damage of this nature usually occurs where the most abrupt change in direction of load travel is experienced. If this damage remains undetected, loads applied in the normal course of operation may cause failure of the part.

Location and Alignment of Welds

Unless otherwise noted, welded steel tubing may be spliced or repaired at any joint along the length of the tube. Particular attention should be paid to proper fit and alignment to avoid eccentricities.

Repairing Members Dented at a Cluster

Dents at a steel tube cluster joint may be repaired by welding a specially formed steel patch plate over the dented area and surrounding tubes as shown in Fig. 2. To prepare the patch plate, cut a section of steel sheet of the same material and thickness as the heaviest tube damaged. Trim the reinforcing plate so that the fingers

[1]Federal Aviation Agency
Advisory Circular 43.13-1

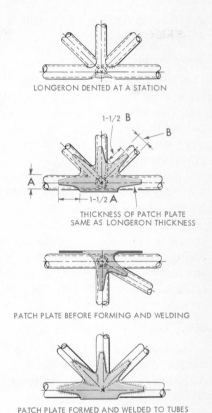

LONGERON DENTED AT A STATION

THICKNESS OF PATCH PLATE
SAME AS LONGERON THICKNESS

PATCH PLATE BEFORE FORMING AND WELDING

PATCH PLATE FORMED AND WELDED TO TUBES

Fig. 2. Repairing members dented at a cluster.

extend over the tubes a minimum of 1.5 times the respective tube diameter as shown in the figure. Remove all the existing finish on the damaged cluster joint area to be covered by the reinforcing plate. The reinforcing plate may be formed before any welding is attempted, or it may be cut and tack-welded to one or more of the tubes in the cluster joint, then heated and formed around the joint to produce a smooth contour. Apply sufficient heat to the plate while forming so that there is generally a gap of no more than

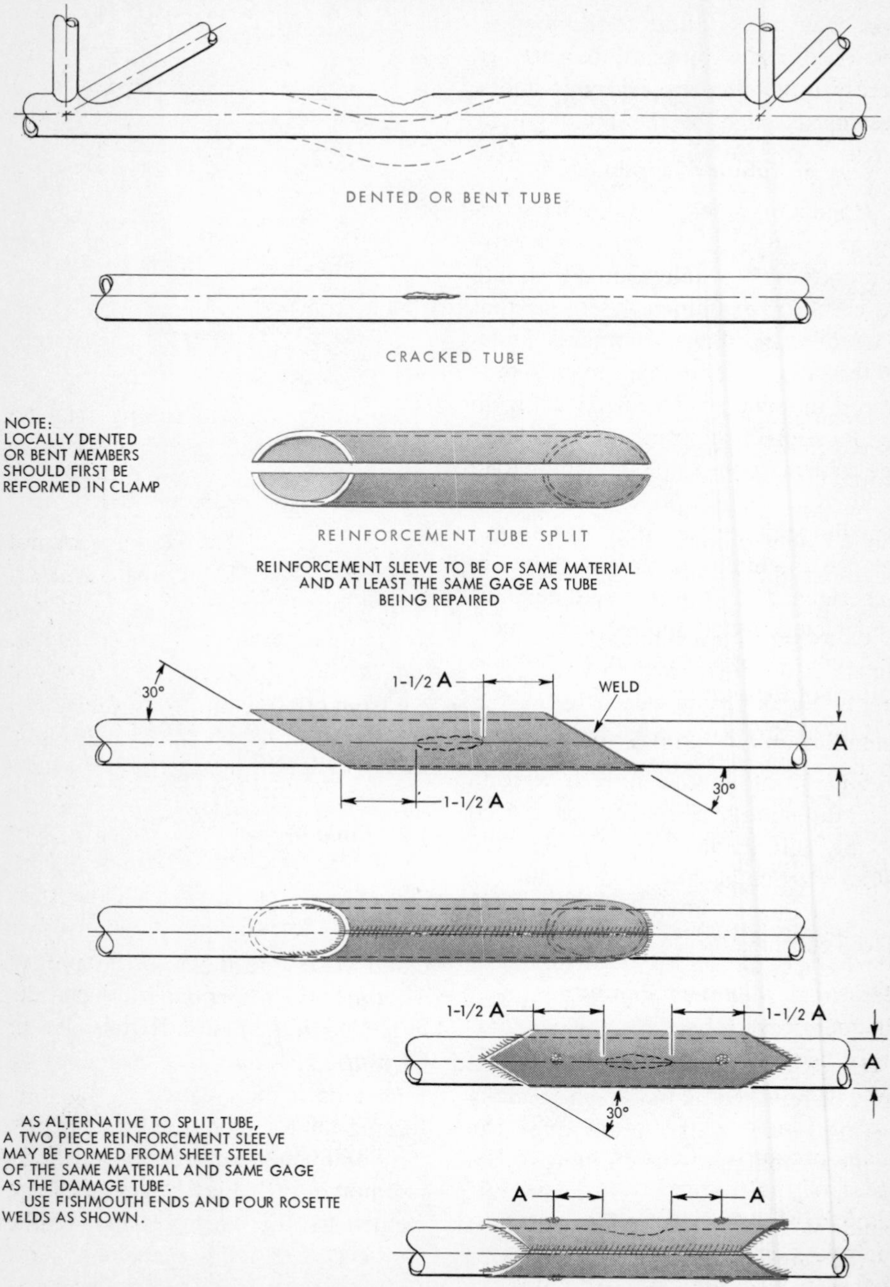

DENTED OR BENT TUBE

CRACKED TUBE

NOTE:
LOCALLY DENTED
OR BENT MEMBERS
SHOULD FIRST BE
REFORMED IN CLAMP

REINFORCEMENT TUBE SPLIT

REINFORCEMENT SLEEVE TO BE OF SAME MATERIAL
AND AT LEAST THE SAME GAGE AS TUBE
BEING REPAIRED

30°   1-1/2 A   WELD   A

1-1/2 A   30°

1-1/2 A   1-1/2 A   A

30°

A   A

AS ALTERNATIVE TO SPLIT TUBE,
A TWO PIECE REINFORCEMENT SLEEVE
MAY BE FORMED FROM SHEET STEEL
OF THE SAME MATERIAL AND SAME GAGE
AS THE DAMAGE TUBE.
USE FISHMOUTH ENDS AND FOUR ROSETTE
WELDS AS SHOWN.

Fig. 3. When members are dented in a bay, repair them with a welded sleeve.

$\frac{1}{16}''$ from the contour of the joint to the plate. In this operation avoid unnecessary heating and exercise care to prevent damage at the apex of the angle formed by any two adjacent fingers of the plate. After the plate is formed and tack-welded to the cluster joint, weld all the plate edges to the cluster joint.

Repairing Members Dented in a Bay

Dented, bent, cracked, or otherwise damaged tubular members may be repaired by using a split sleeve reinforcement, after first carefully straightening the damaged member and, in the case of cracks, drilling No. 40 (0.098) stop holes at the ends of the crack.

Repair with a welded sleeve. This repair is outlined in Fig. 3. Select a length of steel tube sleeve having an inside diameter approximately equal to the outside diameter of the damaged tube and of the same material and at least the same wall thickness. Diagonally cut the sleeve reinforcement at a 30° angle on both ends so that the minimum distance of the sleeve from the edge of the crack or dent is not less than $1\frac{1}{2}$ times the diameter of the damaged tube. Cut through the entire length of the reinforcing sleeve and separate the half sections of the sleeve. Clamp the two sleeve sections to the proper positions on the affected areas of the original tube. Weld the reinforcing sleeve along the length of the two sides, and weld both ends of the sleeve to the damaged tube as shown in Fig. 3. Filling dents or cracks with a welding rod in place of reinforcing the member is not acceptable.

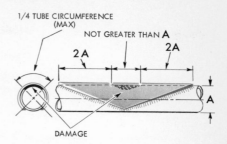

Fig. 4. Welded-patch repair.

Welded-Patch Repair

Dents or holes in tubing may be repaired by a welded patch of the same material and one gage thicker, as shown in Fig. 4, provided:

1. Dented tubing. (a) Dents are not deeper than $\frac{1}{10}$ of the tube diameter, do not involve more than $\frac{1}{4}$ of the tube circumference, and are not longer than the tube diameter. (b) Dents are free from cracks, abrasions, and sharp corners. (c) The dented tubing can be substantially re-formed without cracking before application of the patch.

2. Punctured tubing. Holes are not longer than the tube diameter and involve not more than $\frac{1}{4}$ of the tube circumference.

3. Location of the patch. No part of the patch is permitted in the middle third of the tube. The patch should not overlap a tube joint.

Splicing by the Inner Sleeve Method

If the damage to a structural tube is such that a partial replacement of the tube is necessary, the inner sleeve splice shown in Fig. 5 is recommended, especially if a smooth tube surface is desired. Diagonally cut out the damaged portion of the tube, and remove the burr from the edges of the cut by

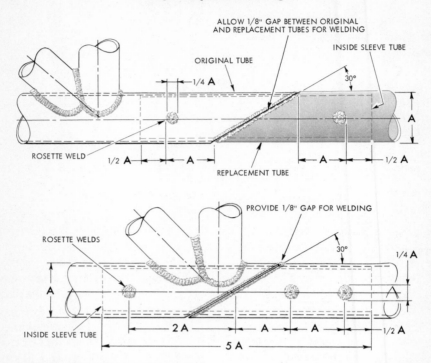

Fig. 5. Splicing by the inner sleeve method.

filing or other means. Diagonally cut a replacement steel tube of the same material and diameter and at least the same wall thickness to match the length of the removed portion of the damaged tube. At each end of the replacement tube allow a $\frac{1}{8}''$ gap from the diagonal cuts to the stubs of the original tube. Select a length of steel tubing of the same material and at least the same wall thickness and of an outside diameter approximately equal to the inside diameter of the damaged tube. This inner sleeve tube material should fit snugly within the original tube, with a maximum diameter difference of $\frac{1}{16}''$. From this inner sleeve tube material, cut two sections

of tubing, each of such a length that the ends of the inner sleeve will be a minimum distance of $1\frac{1}{2}$ tube diameters from the nearest end of the diagonal cut.

If the inner sleeve fits very tightly in the replacement tube, chill the sleeve with dry ice or in cold water. If this is insufficient, polish down the diameter of the sleeve with emery cloth. Weld the inner sleeve to the tube stubs through the $\frac{1}{8}''$ gap between the stubs, completely filling the gap and forming a weld bead over it.

Splicing by the Outer Sleeve Method

If partial replacement of a tube is necessary, an outer sleeve splice using

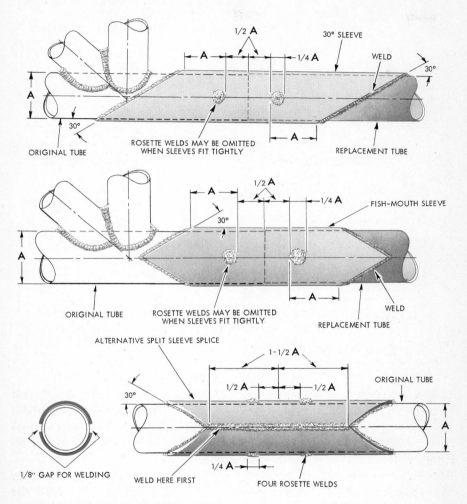

1/2 A

30° SLEEVE

A

1/4 A

WELD

30°

A

30°

ORIGINAL TUBE

ROSETTE WELDS MAY BE OMITTED
WHEN SLEEVES FIT TIGHTLY

A

REPLACEMENT TUBE

1/2 A

A

1/4 A

FISH-MOUTH SLEEVE

30°

A

A

ORIGINAL TUBE

ROSETTE WELDS MAY BE OMITTED
WHEN SLEEVES FIT TIGHTLY

WELD

REPLACEMENT TUBE

ALTERNATIVE SPLIT SLEEVE SPLICE

1-1/2 A

1/2 A

1/2 A

ORIGINAL TUBE

30°

A

1/8" GAP FOR WELDING

WELD HERE FIRST

1/4 A

FOUR ROSETTE WELDS

SPLITE SLEEVE MADE FROM STEEL TUBE OR SHEET
WHEN OUTSIDE DIA OF ORIGINAL TUBE IS LESS THAN 1"
USE SHEET STEEL FOR ORIGINAL TUBES 1" OD AND OVER.
USE SAME MATERIAL AND AT LEAST THE SAME GAGE.

Fig. 6. When splicing by the outer sleeve method, replace with a welded outside sleeve.

a replacement tube of the same diameter may be made. However, the outer sleeve splice requires the greatest amount of welding and, therefore, should be used only if the other splicing methods are not suitable. Information on the replacement by use of the welded outside sleeve method is given in Figs. 6 and 7.

Squarely cut out the damaged section of the tube. Cut a replacement steel tube of the same material and

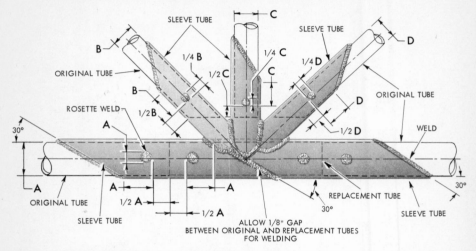

Fig. 7. Tube replacement at a station by a welded outer sleeve.

diameter and at least the same wall thickness to match the length of the removed portion of the damaged tube. This replacement tube must bear against the stubs of the original tube with a total tolerance not to exceed $\frac{1}{32}''$.

Select a length of steel tubing of an inside diameter approximately equal to the outside diameter of the damaged tube, of the same material, and of at least the same wall thickness. This outer sleeve tube material should fit snugly about the original tube with a maximum diameter difference of $\frac{1}{16}''$.

From this outer sleeve tube material, cut two sections of tubing diagonally or fishmouth, each of such a length that the nearest ends of the outer sleeve are a minimum distance of $1\frac{1}{2}$ tube diameters from the ends

of the cut on the original tube. Use a fishmouth-cut sleeve wherever possible.

Remove the burr from all the edges of the sleeves, replacement tube, and original tube stubs. Slip the two sleeves over the replacement tube, line up the replacement tube with the original tube stubs, and slip the sleeves out over the center of each joint.

Adjust the sleeves to suit the area and to provide maximum reinforcement. Tack weld the two sleeves to the replacement tube in two places before welding. Apply a uniform weld around both ends of one of the reinforcing sleeves and allow the weld to cool. Then weld around both ends of the remaining reinforcing tube.

Allow one sleeve weld to cool before welding the remaining tube in order to prevent undue warping.

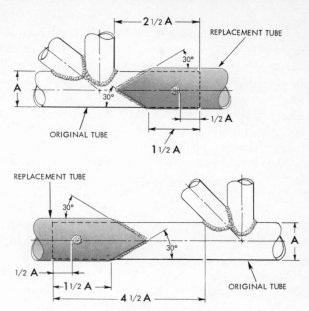

Fig. 8. Splicing with a larger diameter replacement tube.

Splicing Using Larger-Diameter Replacement Tubes

This method of splicing structural tubes, shown in Fig. 8, requires the least amount of cutting and welding. However, it cannot be used if the damaged tube is cut too near the adjacent cluster joints or if bracket mounting provisions make it necessary to maintain the same replacement tube diameter as the original. As an aid in installing the replacement tube, squarely cut the original damaged tube, leaving a minimum short stub equal to 2½ tube diameters on one end and a minimum long stub equal to 4½ tube diameters on the other end.

Select a length of steel tube of the same material and at least the same wall thickness, having an inside diameter approximately equal to the outside diameter of the damaged tube. This replacement tube material should fit snugly about the original tube with a maximum diameter difference of $\frac{1}{16}''$. From this replacement tube material, cut a section of tubing diagonally, or fishmouth, of such a length that each end of the tube is a minimum distance of 1½ tube diameters from the end of the cut on the original tube.

Use a fishmouth-cut replacement tube wherever possible. Remove the burr from the edges of the replacement tube and the original tube stubs. If a fishmouth cut is used, file out the sharp radius of the cut with a small, round file. Spring the long stub of the original tube from the normal position; slip the replacement tube over the long stub, then back over the short stub.

Center the replacement tube between the stubs of the original tube. At several places, tack weld one end of the replacement tube; then weld completely around the end. In order to prevent distortion, allow the weld to cool completely; then weld the remaining end of the replacement tube to the original tube.

Points to Remember

1. Provide a space between tubular joints for expansion.

2. Clean tubular joints before welding.

3. When making a rosette weld, drill a hole in the outside tubing only.

4. A bead made on tubing must be smooth and uniform in thickness.

5. Do not file or grind welds on tubing.

6. When re-welding a tubular joint be sure all old weld material is removed.

7. Never weld over a weld on tubing.

8. Use a soft neutral flame for welding tubing.

9. Use the correct size tip.

10. Weld tubular joints with a low carbon steel filler rod.

11. Follow all FAA specifications when making tubular repairs on aircraft structures.

QUESTIONS FOR STUDY AND DISCUSSION

1. How far apart should tubular pieces be spaced for welding?

2. How should tubular members be cleaned prior to welding?

3. What must be taken into consideration in selecting the tip for welding?

4. What kind of filler rod is used to weld chrome-molybdenum tubing?

5. What are some of the characteristics which finished welds on tubing must have?

6. What are some of the practices which must be guarded against in welding tubing?

7. What is a rosette weld?

8. How is a tube cluster joint repaired?

9. When is an outer sleeve used to repair tubing?

10. What is the procedure in repairing dents or holes in tubing?

11. What are the restrictions concerning the location of patches?

12. When is an inner sleeve used to repair tubing?

WELDING ASSIGNMENTS

Practice Weld No. 1—Butt Joint.
Cut two pieces of tubing and tack-weld them in two places. Practice

welding this joint first with the tubes in a horizontal and then in a vertical position. Frequently test the welded

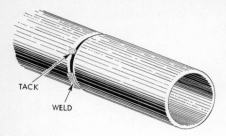

Fig. 9. Butt weld.

joint by cutting the tubing through the center, straightening it, and then bending it in the usual manner. See Fig. 9.

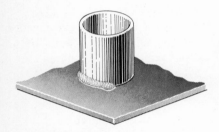

Fig. 10. Butt weld on a flat plate.

Practice Weld No. 2—Butt Weld on a Flat Plate.
Weld a short section of a piece of tubing on a flat plate. See Fig. 10.

Fig. 11. Tee weld.

Practice Weld No. 3—Tee Weld.
Shape the vertical member to fit over the bottom piece. Tack the weld in place and weld around the joint without moving the tubing. See Fig. 11.

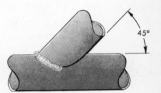

Fig. 12. Angular weld.

Practice Weld No. 4 — Angular Joint.
Shape an angular piece to some desired angle, tack the two pieces together, and weld around the joint. See Fig. 12.

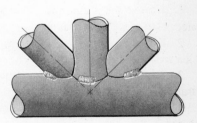

Fig. 13. Cluster weld.

Practice Weld No. 5—Cluster Weld.
Shape three pieces of tubing so that their centerlines will meet at one point. Tack them in place and weld around each tube. See Fig. 13.

Practice Weld No. 6.
Weld the various types of tubular repairs illustrated in Figs. 2 to 8.

CHAPTER 34

Supplementary Welding Data

Testing Welds

In the fabrication of any welded product, tests are generally employed to determine the soundness of welds. The nature of the test is governed to a great extent by the service requirements of the finished product.

Various types of tests have been devised, each for a specific purpose. These tests may be broadly classified as visual, destructive, and nondestructive.

overlaps, and crater deficiencies. Very often weld gages are used to check for proper weld bead size and contour.

The limitation of any visual examination is that there is no way of knowing if internal defects exist in the welded area. The outer appearance of a weld may be satisfactory, yet cracks, porosity, slag inclusions, or excessive grain growth can be present which are not externally apparent.

Visual Examination

Visual examination consists of looking at a weld with the naked eye or through a magnifying glass. A thorough examination of the weldment may disclose such surface defects as cracks, shrinkage cavities, undercuts, inadequate penetration, lack of fusion,

Destructive Testing

Destructive testing involves the use of sample portions of a welded structure and subjecting them to loads until they fail. The most common types of destructive tests are known as tensile, shearing, weld uniformity, etching, and impact.

Fig. 1. A specimen being tested in a universal testing machine.

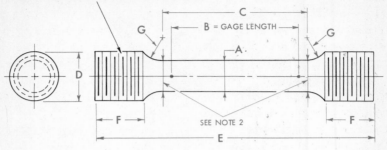

AMERICAN STANDARD COARSE THREAD — CLASS 2 FIT

SPECIMEN	DIMENSIONS OF SPECIMEN						
	A INCHES	B INCHES	C INCHES	D INCHES	E INCHES	F INCHES	G INCHES MIN
C-1	0.500 ± 0.01	2	2 1/4	3/4	4 1/4	3/4	3/8
C-2	0.437 ± 0.01	1 3/4	2	5/8	4	3/4	3/8
C-3	0.357 ± 0.007	1.4	1 3/4	1/2	3 1/2	5/8	3/8
C-4	0.252 ± 0.005	1.0	1 1/4	3/8	2 1/2	1/2	1/4
C-5	0.126 ± 0.003	0.5	3/4	1/4	1 3/4	3/8	1/8

NOTE 1: DIMENSION A, B AND C SHALL BE AS SHOWN, BUT ALTERNATE SHAPES OF ENDS MAY BE USED AS ALLOWED BY ASTM SPECIFICATION E-8.

NOTE 2: IT IS DESIRABLE TO HAVE THE DIAMETER OF THE SPECIMEN WITHIN THE GAGE LENGTH SLIGHTLY SMALLER AT THE CENTER THAN AT THE ENDS. THE DIFFERENCE SHALL NOT EXCEED 1 PERCENT OF THE DIAMETER.

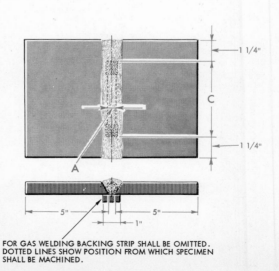

FOR GAS WELDING BACKING STRIP SHALL BE OMITTED. DOTTED LINES SHOW POSITION FROM WHICH SPECIMEN SHALL BE MACHINED.

Fig. 2. Tensile specimen for all weld metal.

Tensile Testing

Tensile testing involves the placement of a weld specimen in a tensile testing machine, as shown in Fig. 1 and pulling the piece until it breaks. The specimen is cut either from an all weld metal area or from a welded butt joint for plate and pipe.

The specimen for an all weld metal area should conform to dimensions shown in Fig. 2. It should be cut from the welded section so its reduced area contains only weld metal.

For a plate and pipe welded butt joint, the specimen should be similar to the ones illustrated in Figs. 3 and 4.

Before the specimen is placed in the tensile testing machine an accurate measurement should be taken of the gage length so the per cent of elongation can be determined.

The actual tensile strength is found by dividing the maximum load needed to break the piece by the cross-sectional area of the specimen. The cross-sectional area is determined by multiplying the width of the bar by its thickness. For example, assume that the specimen is 1½" wide and ¼" thick. The computation is carried out as follows:

Cross-sectional area = 1½ × ¼ = ⅜ sq. in.

Pull to break the bar = 24,500 lbs.

Tensile strength = 24,500 ÷ ⅜ = 65,333 lbs. per sq. in.

The per cent of elongation is found by fitting the broken ends of the two pieces and measuring the new gage length. The per cent of elongation is a good indicator of the plasticity of the weld and is calculated with this formula:

$$\frac{FGL - OGL}{OGL} \times 100$$

where: FGL = Final gage length

OGL = Original gage length

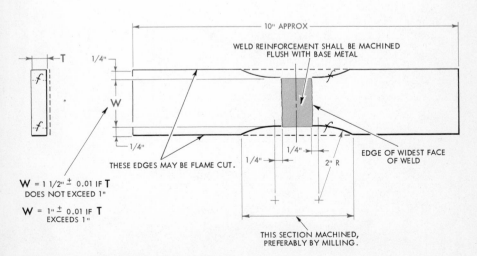

Fig. 3. Tensile specimen for flat plate butt weld.

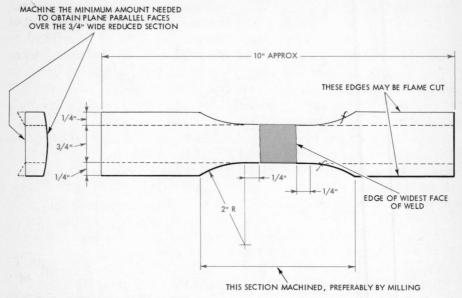

MACHINE THE MINIMUM AMOUNT NEEDED
TO OBTAIN PLANE PARALLEL FACES
OVER THE 3/4" WIDE REDUCED SECTION

10" APPROX

THESE EDGES MAY BE FLAME CUT

1/4"

3/4"

1/4"

1/4"

1/4"

2" R

EDGE OF WIDEST FACE
OF WELD

THIS SECTION MACHINED, PREFERABLY BY MILLING

Fig. 4. Tensile specimen for pipe butt weld.

Shearing Strength

The shearing strength of a weld can apply either to a transverse or a longitudinal weld.

Transverse Shearing Strength. To check the shearing strength of a transverse weld, a specimen is prepared similar to the one shown in Fig. 5. The specimen is then placed in a tensile

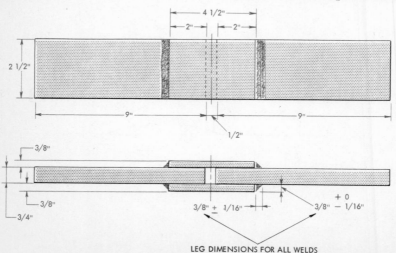

4 1/2"

2"   2"

2 1/2"

9"   9"

1/2"

3/8"

3/8"

3/4"

3/8" + 1/16"

3/8" − 1/16" + 0

LEG DIMENSIONS FOR ALL WELDS

Fig. 5. Specimen for determining the shearing strength of a transverse weld.

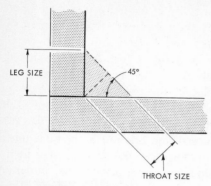

Fig. 6. Fillet weld throat and leg.

testing machine and pulled until it breaks. Dividing the maximum load in pounds by twice the width of the specimen will indicate the shearing strength in pounds per linear inch. If the shearing strength in pounds per square inch (psi) is desired, the shear-

ing strength in pounds per linear inch is divided by the throat dimension of the weld. See Fig. 6. Expressed as formulas, these relationships are shown as:

Shearing Strength (lb/in.) =

$$\frac{\text{Maximum Load}}{2 \times \text{Width of Specimen}}$$

or

Shearing Strength (psi) =

$$\frac{\text{Shearing Strength (lb/in.)}}{\text{Throat Dimension of Weld}}$$

Longitudinal Shearing Strength. To determine the shearing strength of a longitudinal weld, a specimen as shown in Fig 7 is prepared. The length of

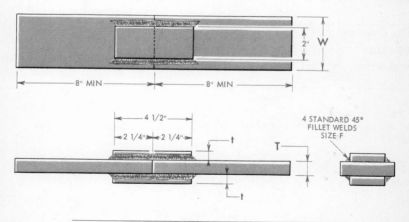

DIMENSIONS			
SIZE OF WELD **F**, INCHES	1/8	1/2	1/4
THICKNESS **T**, INCHES MIN	3/8	1/2	1
THICKNESS **T**, INCHES MIN	3/8	3/4	1 1/4
WIDTH **W**, INCHES	3	3	3 1/2

LONGITUDINAL FILLET-WELD SHEARING SPECIMEN AFTER WELDING

Fig. 7. Specimen for determining the shearing strength of a longitudinal weld.

each weld is then measured and the piece fractured in a tensile testing machine. The shearing strength in pounds per linear inch is found by dividing the maximum load by the length of the ruptured weld. Expressed as a formula:

Shearing Strength (lb/linear inch) =

$$\frac{\text{Maximum Load}}{\text{Length of Ruptured Weld}}$$

Weld Uniformity Test

The soundness or uniformity and ductility of a weld can be ascertained by the nick-break test, the free-bend test, and the guided-bend test.

Nick-break Test. A test specimen as illustrated in Fig. 8 is prepared and placed on supporting members as shown in Fig. 9. A load is applied on this specimen until it breaks. The surface of the fracture is then examined for porosity, gas pockets, slag inclusions, overlaps, penetration, and grain size. For a more accurate check of the weld, the fractured pieces should be subjected to an etch test as described in the paragraph on etching testing.

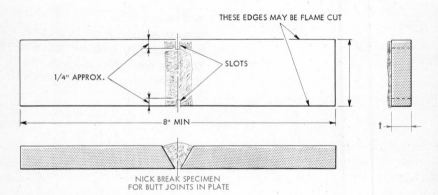

THESE EDGES MAY BE FLAME CUT

SLOTS

1/4" APPROX.

8" MIN

t

NICK BREAK SPECIMEN
FOR BUTT JOINTS IN PLATE

Fig. 8. Specimen for a nick-break test.

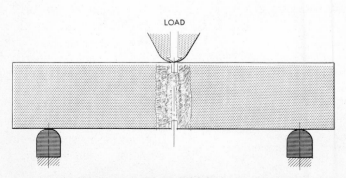

LOAD

Fig. 9. Method of rupturing a nick-break specimen.

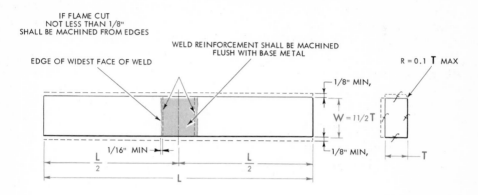

IF FLAME CUT
NOT LESS THAN 1/8"
SHALL BE MACHINED FROM EDGES

WELD REINFORCEMENT SHALL BE MACHINED
FLUSH WITH BASE METAL

EDGE OF WIDEST FACE OF WELD

R = 0.1 T MAX

1/8" MIN,

$W = 1 1/2 T$

1/16" MIN

1/8" MIN,

$\frac{L}{2}$

$\frac{L}{2}$

L

T

T, INCHES	1/4	3/8	1/2	5/8	3/4	1	1 1/4	1 1/2	2	2 1/2
W, INCHES	3/8	9/16	3/4	15/16	1 1/8	1 1/2	1 7/8	2 1/4	3	3 3/4
L MIN, INCHES	6	8	9	10	11	12	13 1/2	15	18	21
B*MIN, INCHES	1 1/4	1 1/4	1 1/4	2	2	2	2	2	2	3

* SEE FIG 13

NOTE — THE LENGTH L IS SUGGESTIVE ONLY, NOT MANDATORY

Fig. 10. Specimen for a free-bend test. (American Welding Society)

Free-bend Test. The free-bend test is used to determine the ductility of the welded specimen. For this test, cut the test piece from the plate so as to include the weld as shown in Fig. 10. Grind or machine the top of the weld so it is flush with the base metal sur-

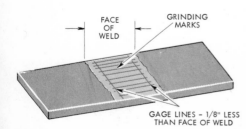

FACE OF WELD

GRINDING MARKS

GAGE LINES - 1/8" LESS THAN FACE OF WELD

Fig. 11. How gage marks are located on the weld face.

face. The scratches produced by grinding should run across the weld in the direction of the bend as illustrated in Fig. 11. If the scratches extend along the weld they might cause premature failure and give incorrect results.

Now measure the distance across the weld and mark it with prickpunch marks. The measured length (between gage lines) must be about ⅛″ less than the width of the face of the weld as shown in Fig. 11.

Bend the specimen by a steady force, with the face containing the gage lines on the outside of the bend. Start the initial bend by placing the piece in a vise as shown in Fig. 12, or by using a device as illustrated in Fig.

Fig. 12. This is one way the initial bend can be made.

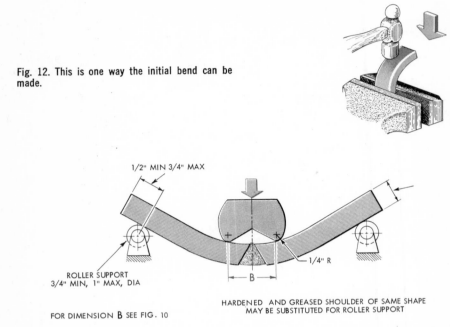

ROLLER SUPPORT
3/4" MIN, 1" MAX, DIA

FOR DIMENSION B SEE FIG. 10

HARDENED AND GREASED SHOULDER OF SAME SHAPE
MAY BE SUBSTITUTED FOR ROLLER SUPPORT

Fig. 13. Here is another device that can be used to make the initial bend. (American Welding Society)

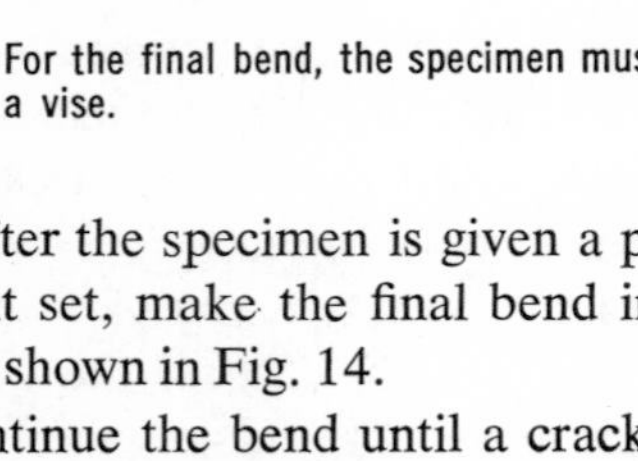

Fig. 14. For the final bend, the specimen must be bent in a vise.

13. After the specimen is given a permanent set, make the final bend in a vise as shown in Fig. 14.

Continue the bend until a crack or depression appears, and then immediately remove the load. Measure the distance between the prick-punch marks or gage lines with a flexible rule graduated in hundredths of an inch. This elongation is measured between the gage lines along the convex surface of the weld to the nearest 0.01 in. The per cent of elongation is obtained by dividing the elongation by the initial gage length and multiplying by 100. For example, suppose the initial gage lines measure 2″, and after the bend the elongation measured 2.5″. The calculation then would be:

Increase in elongation = 2.5″ — 2″ = 0.5″

Per cent elongation = 0.5 ÷ 2 × 100 = 25

The ductility of this specimen is therefore considered to be 25% in 2″.

Guided-bend Test. For this test, two specimens, as shown in Fig. 15, are required. One piece referred to as the *face-bend specimen* is used to check

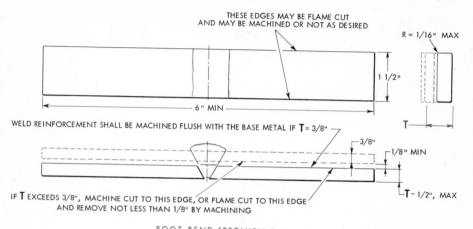

THESE EDGES MAY BE FLAME CUT
AND MAY BE MACHINED OR NOT AS DESIRED

R = 1/16" MAX

1 1/2"

6" MIN

T

WELD REINFORCEMENT SHALL BE MACHINED FLUSH WITH THE BASE METAL IF T = 3/8"

3/8"

1/8" MIN

T - 1/2", MAX

IF T EXCEEDS 3/8", MACHINE CUT TO THIS EDGE, OR FLAME CUT TO THIS EDGE
AND REMOVE NOT LESS THAN 1/8" BY MACHINING

ROOT-BEND SPECIMEN F-1

NOTE
THE FACE BEND AND ROOT BEND TEST ARE NOT APPLICABLE IF THE PLATE THICKNESS T IS LESS THAN 3/8"

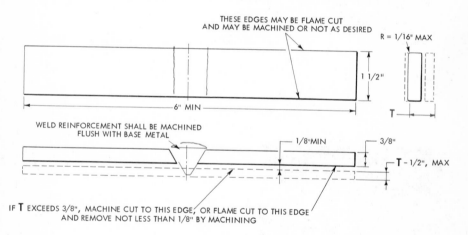

THESE EDGES MAY BE FLAME CUT
AND MAY BE MACHINED OR NOT AS DESIRED

R = 1/16" MAX

1 1/2"

6" MIN

T

WELD REINFORCEMENT SHALL BE MACHINED
FLUSH WITH BASE METAL

1/8"MIN

3/8"

T - 1/2", MAX

IF T EXCEEDS 3/8", MACHINE CUT TO THIS EDGE, OR FLAME CUT TO THIS EDGE
AND REMOVE NOT LESS THAN 1/8" BY MACHINING

FACE-BEND SPECIMEN E-1

Fig. 15. Specimen for a guided-bend test. (American Welding Society)

the quality of fusion; that is, whether the weld is free of defects such as porosity, inclusions, etc. The second piece, referred to as the *root-bend specimen,* is used to check the degree of weld penetration.

To perform the face-bend test, place the specimen in the guided-bend jig face down and depress the plunger until the piece becomes **U**-shaped in the die. See Fig. 16. If upon examination, cracks greater than 1/8" appear in any direction, the weld is considered to have failed.

In the root-bend test, place the specimen in the jig with the root down

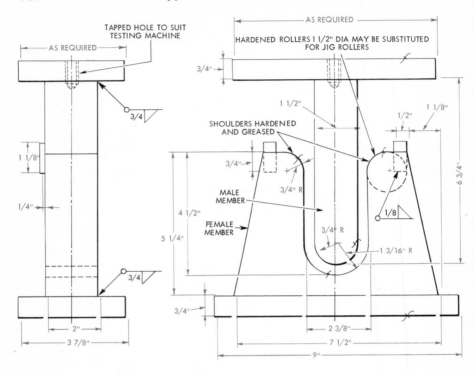

TAPPED HOLE TO SUIT
TESTING MACHINE

AS REQUIRED

3/4

AS REQUIRED

HARDENED ROLLERS 1 1/2" DIA MAY BE SUBSTITUTED
FOR JIG ROLLERS

3/4"

1 1/2"

1/2"   1 1/8"

SHOULDERS HARDENED
AND GREASED

1 1/8"

3/4"

3/4" R

MALE
MEMBER

1/4"

4 1/2"

5 1/4"

FEMALE
MEMBER

1/8

3/4" R

1 3/16" R

6 3/4"

3/4

3/4"

2"

3 7/8"

2 3/8"

7 1/2"

9"

Fig. 16. The above view shows a detail working
drawing of a jig for a guided-bent test. The view
at the left shows the jig being used to perform
the test.

or in just the reverse position of the face-bend piece. The results must also show no cracks to be acceptable.

Fillet Welded Joint Test

This test is used to ascertain the soundness of fillet welds. *Soundness* refers to the degree of freedom a weld has from defects discernable by visual inspection of any exposed surface of weld metal. These defects include penetrations, inclusions, and gas pockets. For such a test, prepare a specimen as in Fig. 17. Then apply force on point *A,* as shown in Fig. 18, until a rupture of the specimen occurs. The force may be applied by a press, a testing machine, or hammer blows.

In addition to checking the fractured weld for soundness, this weld

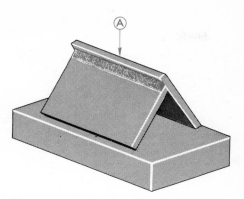

Fig. 18. Method of rupturing fillet weld specimen. (American Welding Society)

specimen should be subjected to the etching test so that the transverse section of the weld can also be examined for soundness.

Etching Tests

The etching test is used to determine the soundness of a weld and to make visible the boundary between the weld metal and the base metal.

To make such a test, cut a specimen from the welded joint so it displays a complete transverse section of the weld. The piece may be cut either by sawing or flame cutting. File the face of the cut and polish it with grade 00 abrasive cloth. Then place the specimen in one of the following etching solutions:

1. Hydrochloric acid — This solution should contain equal parts by volume of concentrated hydrochloric (muriatic) acid and water. Immerse the weld in this reagent at or near the boiling point. Hydrochloric acid will etch satisfactorily on unpolished surfaces. It will usually enlarge gas pock-

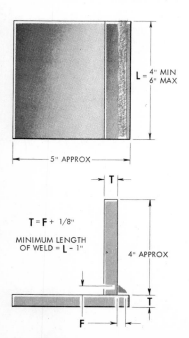

Fig. 17. Specimen for fillet weld test. (American Welding Society)

ets and dissolve slag inclusions, enlarging the resulting cavities.

2. Ammonium persulphate — Mix
one part of ammonium persulphate
(solid) to nine parts of water by
weight. Vigorously rub the surface of
the weld with cotton saturated with
this reagent at room temperature.

3. Iodine and potassium iodide—
This solution is obtained by mixing
one part of powdered iodine (solid)
to twelve parts of a solution of potassium iodide by weight. The latter solution should consist of one part potassium iodide to five parts water by
weight. Brush the surface of the weld
with this reagent at room temperature.

4. Nitric acid — Mix one part of
concentrated nitric acid to three parts
of water by volume. *Always pour the
acid into the water when diluting.
Nitric acid causes bad stains and severe burns.*

Either apply this reagent to the surface of the weld with a glass stirring
rod at room temperature, or immerse
the weld in a boiling reagent provided
the room is well ventilated. Nitric acid
etches rapidly. It should be used on
polished surfaces only, and will show
the refined zone as well as the metal
zone.

After etching, wash the weld immediately in clear water, preferably hot
water; remove the excess water; immerse the etched surface in ethyl alcohol; and then remove and dry, preferably in a warm air blast.

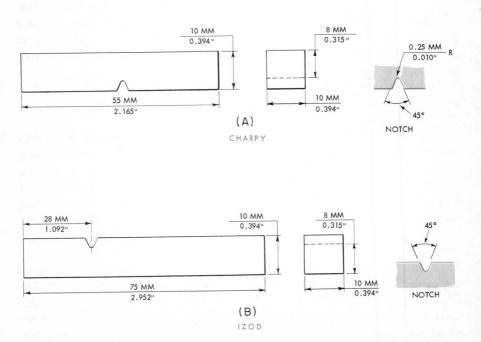

Fig. 19. Specimens for impact testing.

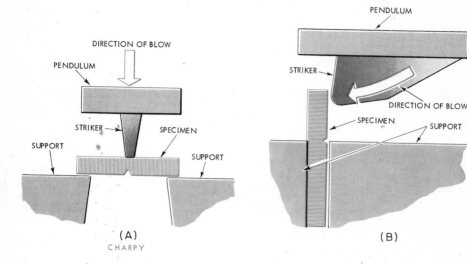

Fig. 20. Performing impact tests.

Impact Testing

Impact testing is concerned with the ability of a weld to absorb energy under impact without fracturing. This is a dynamic test in which a specimen is broken by a single blow and the energy absorbed in breaking the piece is measured in foot pounds. The purpose of the test is to compare the toughness of the weld metal with the base metal. It is especially significant in finding if any of the mechanical properties of the base metal have been destroyed due to welding.

The two types of specimens used for impact testing are known as Charpy and Izod. See Fig. 19. Both specimens are broken in an impact testing machine. The difference is simply in the manner in which the specimens are anchored. The Charpy piece is supported horizontally between two anvils and

the pendulum allowed to strike opposite the notch as shown in Fig. 20A. The Izod specimen is supported as a vertical cantilever beam and struck on the free end projecting above the holding vise. See Fig. 20B.

Nondestructive Testing

Nondestructive testing is used to evaluate a structure without destroying it or impairing its actual usefulness. Tests of this nature will disclose all of the common surface and internal defects that normally occur with improper welding procedures or practices.

Currently a variety of testing devices are available which do provide effective data concerning the reliability of a weldment. These devices are often more convenient to use than other regular destructive testing techniques particularly on large and costly welded units.

Magnetic Particle Inspection

The magnetic particle inspection method uses a strong magnetizing current and a finely divided powder suspended in a liquid to detect lack of fusion, very fine cracks, and inclusions or internal flaws which are slightly below the surface in weldments.

In this test the piece to be examined is subjected to a very strong magnetizing current and the areas of inspection are covered with the suspended power. Any impurities or discontinuities in the magnetized material will interrupt the lines of magnetic force causing the particles of suspended powder to concentrate at the defect showing its size, shape, and location. Surface cracks of all kinds are detected by this method. It is one of the most reliable techniques for nondestructive testing. See Fig. 21.

Dye Penetrant Inspection

In dye penetrant inspection, surface defects are found by means of proprietary dyes suspended in liquids having high fluidity. These liquids are readily drawn into all surface defects

Fig. 21. Magnetic particle inspection.

Fig. 22. Dye penetrant inspection.

by capillary action. Application of a suitable developer brings out the dye and outlines the defect.

In this test, the surface of the weldment, which must be clean and dry, is coated with a thin film of a penetrant. After allowing a small amount of time for the penetrant to flow into the defects, the part is wiped clean. Only the penetrant in the defects remains. An absorbent material, called a developer, is put on the weldment and allowed to remain until the liquid from the imperfection flows into the developer. The dye now clearly outlines the defects.

Some of the penetrants used contain a fluorescent dye. The method of applying and developing are the same as for the previously mentioned dye penetrants, however the fluorescent penetrant must be viewed under ultraviolet light, commonly referred to as "black light." This light causes the penetrants to fluoresce to a yellow-green color which is more clearly defined than regular dye penetrants. The dye penetrant methods are particularly useful for bringing out defects in nonferrous materials such as aluminum. These materials are nonmagnetic so magnetic particle tests can not be used on them. See Fig. 22.

Eddy Current Testing

Eddy current testing uses electromagnetic energy to detect discontinuities in weld deposits and is effective in

Fig. 23. Eddy current testing.

testing both ferrous and nonferrous materials for porosity, slag inclusions, internal cracks, external cracks, and lack of fusion.

Whenever a coil carrying a high frequency alternating current is brought close to a metal, it produces a current in the metal by induction. The induced current is called an eddy current.

The part to be tested is subjected to electromagnetic energy by being placed in or near high frequency alternating current coils. Discontinuities in the weld deposit change the impedance of the coil. The change in impedance is indicated on electronic measuring instruments, and the size of the defect is shown by the amount of this change. See Fig. 23.

Radiographic Inspection

Radiographic inspection is a method of determining the soundness of a

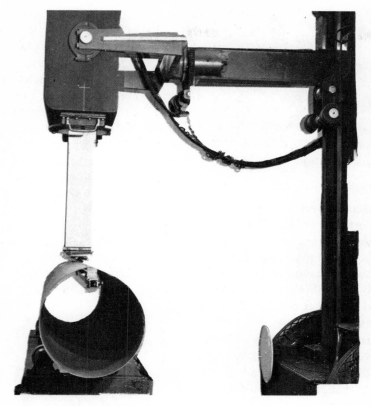

Fig. 24. Radiographic inspection.

weldment by means of rays which are capable of penetrating through the entire weldment. X-Rays and Gamma Rays are two types of electro-magnetic waves used to penetrate opaque materials. A permanent record of the internal structure is obtained by placing a sensitized film in direct contact with the back of the weldment. When these rays pass through a weldment of uniform thickness and structure, they impinge upon the sensitized film and produce a negative of uniform density. If the weldment contains gas pockets, slag inclusions, cracks, or lacks penetration, more rays will pass through the less dense areas and will register on the film as dark areas, clearly outlining the defects and showing their size, shape and location.

X-Rays are produced by electrons traveling at high speed which are suddenly stopped by impact with a tungsten anode. Gamma Rays are given off when radium or its salts decompose. Gamma Rays are of shorter wave length than X-Rays. See Fig. 24.

Ultrasonic Testing

In ultrasonic testing, high frequency vibrations or waves are used to locate

Fig. 25. Ultrasonic testing.

and measure defects in both ferrous and nonferrous materials. This method is very sensitive, and is capable of locating very fine surface and subsurface cracks, as well as other internal defects. All types of joints can be evaluated and the exact size and location of defects measured.

Ultrasonic testing utilizes high frequency vibratory impulses to ascertain the soundness of a weld. If a high frequency vibration is sent through a sound piece of metal, a signal will travel through it to the other side of the metal and be reflected back and shown on a calibrated screen of an oscilloscope. Discontinuities interrupt the signal and reflect it back sooner than the signal of the sound material. This interruption is shown as a shorter line on the oscilloscope screen and indicates the depth of the defect. Only one side of the weldment needs to be exposed for testing purposes. See Fig. 25.

Hardness Testing

Hardness testing is often used in preference to the more expensive ten-

sile testing methods since comparable results are obtained.

Hardness tests are effective in determining the relative hardness of the weld area as compared with the base metal. This hardness is indicated by values obtained from various hardness testing machines. Hardness numbers represent the resistance offered by the metal to the penetration of an indentor. The standard hardness machines are known as Brinell and Rockwell. See Fig. 26.

In the Brinell test, a 10 mm diameter ball is forced into the surface of a metal by a load of 3000 kg. The load must remain on the specimen 15 seconds for ferrous materials and 30 sec-

Fig. 26. Hardness testing.

onds for nonferrous materials. Sufficient time is required for adequate flow of the material being tested otherwise the readings will be in error. Brinell hardness numbers are calculated by dividing the applied load by the area of the surface indentation. The diameter of the indentation is read from a calibrated microscope and this number is then converted to a Brinell hardness number from a chart.

The Rockwell hardness tester employs a variety of loads and indentors, consequently different scales can be used. These scales are designated by letters. For example, R_c 60 represents a Rockwell scale with a diamond penetrator and a 150 kg load. Since hardness numbers give relative or comparative hardness values of materials, the scale must always be specified.

QUESTIONS FOR STUDY AND DISCUSSION

1. What is the limitation of any visual inspection method for testing a weld?

2. What is the difference between destructive and nondestructive testing methods?

3. What will a tensile test of a weldment show?

4. In conducting a tensile test, what is the value of finding the per cent of elongation?

5. What is the function of a shearing strength test?

6. What is meant by a longitudinal and transverse weld?

7. What is the function of a nick-break test?

8. When is a free-bent test used?

9. How is a guided-bent test conducted?

10. How can the soundness of fillet welds be determined?

11. What will etching tests disclose?

12. What precautions must be taken using nitric acid?

13. Of what value is impact testing?

14. Why are nondestructive tests often more valuable than destructive tests?

15. What is the basic principle of magnetic particle testing?

16. How are dye penetrants used for inspection purposes?

17. What is the basic principle of eddy-current testing?

18. What is radiographic inspection?

19. What is ultrasonic testing?

20. Of what value are hardness tests?

TESTING ASSIGNMENTS

1. Prepare specimen as described in this chapter and perform one or more of these tests:
   a. Tensile strength
   b. Free-bend
   c. Guided-bend
   d. Fillet weld
   e. Etching

CHAPTER 35

Supplementary Welding Data
Reading Weld Symbols

In the fabrication of metal products, the welder usually has to work from a print which shows in detail exactly how the structure is to be made. He will find on the print not only where the welds are to be located but also the type of joint to be used as well as the correct size and amount of weld to be deposited at the designated seams. This information is indicated by a set of symbols which have been standardized by the American Welding Society (AWS). Some of the more common symbols for welding are reproduced in

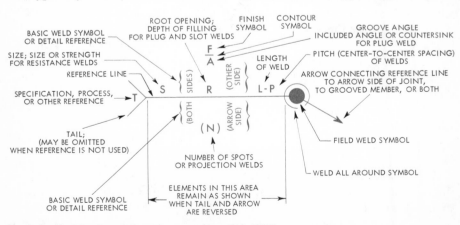

Fig. 1. Standard location of elements on a weld symbol. (AWS)

this chapter. A more complete treatment of symbols as they apply to all forms of manual and automatic machine welding will be found in the pamphlet *Welding Symbols,* published by the American Welding Society.

Base of Weld Symbol

The main foundation of the weld symbol is a reference line with an arrow at one end. See Fig. 1. The other data reflecting various characteristics of the weld are shown by abbrevia-

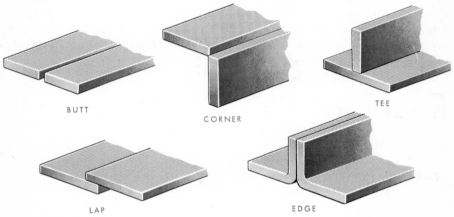

Fig. 2. Common types of weld joints.

FILLET	PLUG OR SLOT	SPOT OR PROJECTION	SEAM		BACK OR BACKING	MELT THRU	SURFACING	FLANGE	
								EDGE	CORNER

BASIC ARC AND GAS WELD SYMBOLS

	GROOVE					
SQUARE	V	BEVEL	U	J	FLARE-V	FLARE-BEVEL

BASIC ARC AND GAS WELD SYMBOLS

WELD ALL AROUND	FIELD WELD	CONTOUR		
		FLUSH	CONVEX	CONCAVE

SUPPLEMENTARY SYMBOLS

Fig. 3. Weld symbols. (AWS)

tions, figures, and other line arrangements placed around the reference line.

Designating Types of Welds

The first important factor in understanding weld symbols is recognizing the representations used for different types of welds. These welds are used on five basic kinds of joints: butt, corner, lap, tee, and edge. See Fig. 2.

Welds are classified as fillet, plug or slot, spot, seam, and groove. Groove welds are further divided according to the particular shape of the grooved joint.

Each type of weld has its own specific symbol. For example, a fillet weld is designated by a right triangle, and a plug weld by a rectangle. All of the basic weld symbols are included in Fig. 3.

Location of Welds

Another requirement in understanding weld symbols is the method which is used to specify on what side of a joint a weld is to be made. A weld is said to be either on the arrow or other side of a joint. The arrow side is the surface that is in direct line of vision,

while the other side is the opposite surface of the joint. See Fig. 4.

Weld location is designated by running the arrowhead of the reference line to the joint. The direction of the arrow is not important, that is, it can run on either side of a joint and extend upward or downward. See Fig. 5. If the weld is to be made on the arrow side, the appropriate weld symbol is

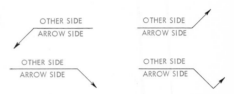

Fig. 5. The arrow may run in any direction.

placed below the reference line. If the weld is to be located on the other side of the joint, the weld symbol is placed above the reference line. When both sides of the joint are to be welded, the same weld symbol appears above and below the reference line. See Fig. 6.

The only exception to this practice of indicating weld location is in seam and spot welding. With seam or spot welds, the arrowhead is simply run to the centerline of the weld seam and the appropriate weld symbol centered above the reference line. See Fig. 6.

Information on weld symbols is placed to read from left to right along the reference line in accordance with the usual conventions of drafting.

Fillet, bevel and J-groove, flare-bevel groove, and corner-flange weld symbols are shown with the *perpendicular leg* always to the left.

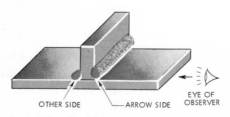

Fig. 4. Sides of a joint.

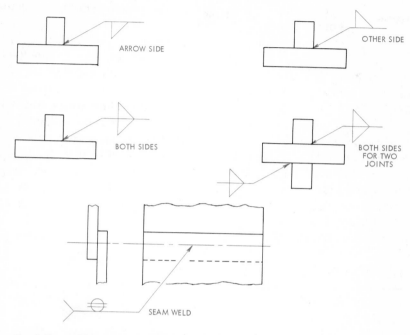

Fig. 6. How weld locations are designated. (AWS)

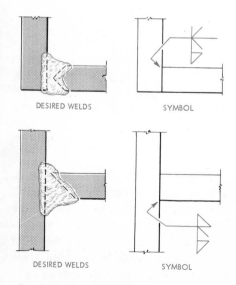

Fig. 7. Combined weld symbols.

Combined Weld Symbols

In the fabrication of a product, there are occasions when more than one type of weld is to be made on a joint. Thus a joint may require both a fillet and double-bevel groove weld. When this happens, a symbol is shown for each weld. See Fig. 7.

Size of Welds

Fillet welds. The width of a fillet weld is shown to the left of the weld symbol and is expressed in fractions with or without the inch mark. When both sides of a fillet are to be welded and both welds have the same dimensions, one or both may be dimensioned. If the welds differ in dimensions, both are dimensioned. Where a

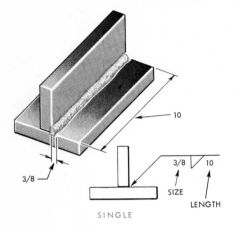

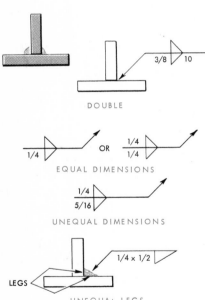

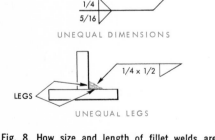

Fig. 8. How size and length of fillet welds are indicated.

values representing the actual required length.

When a fillet weld with unequal legs is required, the size of the legs is placed in parentheses as shown in Fig. 8.

Intermittent fillet welds. The length and pitch increments of intermittent welds are shown to the right of the weld symbol. The first figure represents the length of the weld section and the second figure the length of spacing between welds. See Fig. 9.

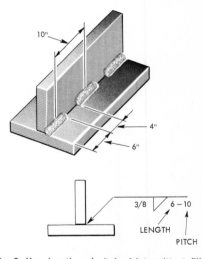

Fig. 9. How length and pitch of intermittent fillet welds are indicated.

note appears on a drawing that governs the size of a fillet weld, no dimensions are usually shown on the symbol. The length of the weld is shown to the right of the weld symbol by numerical

Plug welds. The size of plug welds is shown to the left of the weld symbol, the depth when less than full on the inside of the weld symbol, the center-to-center spacing (pitch) to the right of the symbol, and the included angle of countersink below the symbol. See Fig. 10.

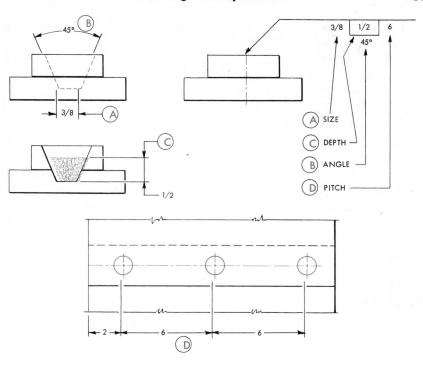

Fig. 10. How dimensions apply to plug welds.

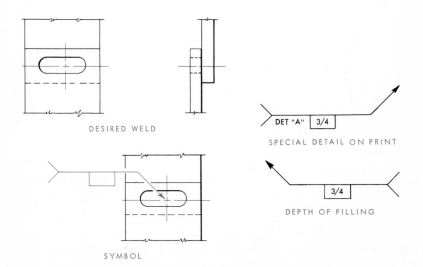

Fig. 11. How slot welds are indicated.

Slot welds. Length, width, spacing, angle of countersink, and location of slot welds are not shown on the weld symbol because it is too cumbersome. This data is included by showing a special detail on the print. If the slots are only partially filled, then the depth of filling is shown inside the weld symbol. See Fig. 11.

Spot welds. Spot welds are dimensioned either by size or strength. Size is designated as the diameter of the weld expressed in fractions, or decimally in hundreths of an inch, and placed to the left of the symbol. The strength is also placed to the left of the symbol and expresses the required minimum shear strength in pounds per spot. The spacing of spot welds is shown to the right of the symbol. When a definite number of spot welds are needed in a joint, this number is indicated in parentheses either above or below the weld symbol. See Fig. 12.

Seam welds. Seam welds are dimensioned either by size or strength. Size is designated as the width of the weld in fractions, or decimally in hundreths of an inch, and shown to the left of the weld symbol. The length of the weld seam is placed to the right of the weld symbol. The pitch of intermittent seam welds is shown to the

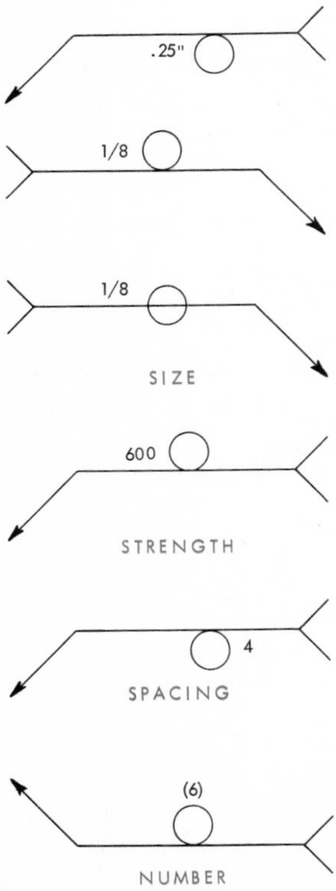

.25"

1/8

1/8

SIZE

600

STRENGTH

4

SPACING

(6)

NUMBER

Fig. 12. Method of designating spot welds.

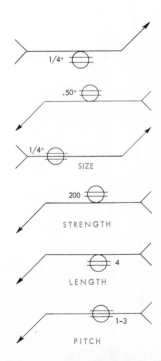

1/4"

.50"

1/4"   SIZE

200   STRENGTH

4   LENGTH

1-3   PITCH

Fig. 13. Method of designating seam welds.

right of the length dimension. See Fig. 13. The strength of the weld, when used, is located to the left of the symbol, and is expressed as the minimum acceptable shear strength in pounds per linear inch.

Groove welds. There are several types of groove welds. Their sizes are shown as follows:

1. For single-groove and symmetrical double-groove welds which extend completely through the members being joined, no size is included on the weld symbol. See Fig. 14.

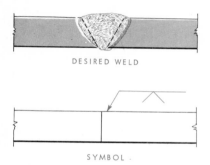

DESIRED WELD

SYMBOL .

Fig. 14. Size is not shown for single and symmetrical double-groove welds with complete penetration. (AWS)

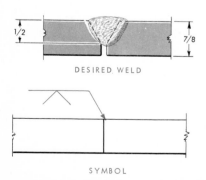

DESIRED WELD

SYMBOL

Fig. 15. How size is shown on grooved welds with partial penetration. (AWS)

2. For groove welds which extend only partly through the members being joined, the weld size is included on the left of the weld symbol. See Fig. 15.

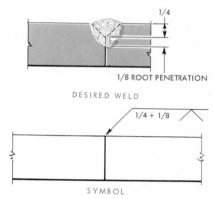

1/4

1/8 ROOT PENETRATION

DESIRED WELD

1/4 + 1/8

SYMBOL

Fig. 16. How dimensions are used to show size and root penetration of grooved welds. (AWS)

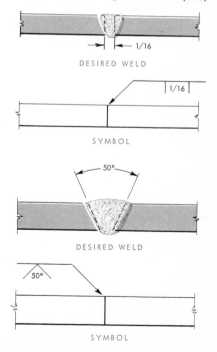

1/16

DESIRED WELD

1/16

SYMBOL

50°

DESIRED WELD

50°

SYMBOL

Fig. 17. How root opening and included angle are shown for groove welds. (AWS)

3. If grooved welds require certain root penetration, this size is indicated by showing the depth of chamfering and the root penetration, separated by a plus mark, and placed to the left of the weld symbol. See Fig. 16.

4. Root opening and included angle of groove welds are shown inside the weld symbol. See Fig. 17.

5. The size of flare-groove welds is considered as extending only to the tangent points as indicated by dimensional lines. See Fig. 18.

Flange welds. The radius and height of the flange is separated by a plus mark and placed to the left of the weld symbol. The size of the weld is shown by a dimension located outward of the flange dimensions. See Fig. 19.

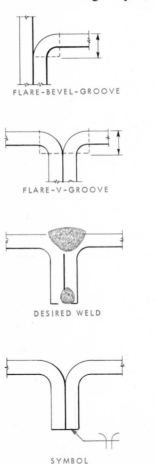

FLARE-BEVEL-GROOVE

FLARE-V-GROOVE

DESIRED WELD

SYMBOL

Fig. 18. How size of flare-grooved welds are indicated. (AWS)

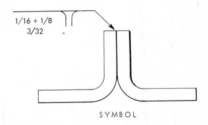

DESIRED WELD

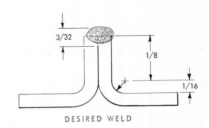

SYMBOL

Fig. 19. How dimensions apply to flange welds. (AWS)

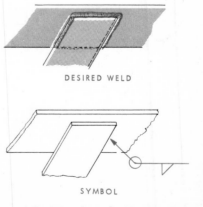

DESIRED WELD

SYMBOL

Fig. 20. Weld-all-around symbol. (AWS)

Weld-All-Around Symbol. When a weld is to extend completely around a joint, a small circle is placed where the arrow connects the reference line. See Fig. 20.

Field Weld Symbol. Welds that are to be made in the field (welds not made in a shop or at the place of initial construction), are indicated by a darkened circle. See Fig. 21.

Reference Tail. The tail is included only when some definite welding specification, procedure, reference, weld or cutting process needs to be called out, otherwise it is omitted. This data is often in the form of symbols and is

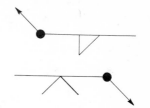

Fig. 21. Field weld symbol. (AWS)

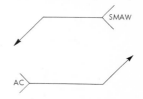

Fig. 22. The tail is used to indicate some specific detail or weld process. (AWS)

TABLE I
Designation of Welding Processes by Letters*

WELDING PROCESS		LETTER DESIGNATION
Brazing	Torch Brazing	TB
	Twin-Carbon-Arc Brazing	TCAB
	Furnace Brazing	FB
	Induction Brazing	IB
	Resistance Brazing	RB
	Dip Brazing	DB
	Block Brazing	BB
Flow Welding	Flow Brazing	FLB
Resistance Welding	Flow Welding	FLOW
	Flash Welding	FW
	Upset Welding	UW
	Percussion Welding	PEW
Induction Welding	Induction Welding	IW
Arc Welding	Bare Metal-Arc Welding	BMAW
	Stud Welding	SW
	Gas-Shielded Stud Welding	GSSW
	Submerged Arc Welding	SAW
	Gas Tungsten-Arc Welding	GTAW
	Gas Metal-Arc Welding	GMAW
	Atomic Hydrogen Welding	AHW
	Shielded Metal-Arc Welding	SMAW
	Twin-Carbon-Arc Welding	TCAW
	Carbon-Arc Welding	CAW
	Gas Carbon-Arc Welding	GCAW
	Shielded Carbon-Arc Welding	SCAW
Thermit Welding	Nonpressure Thermit Welding	NTW
	Pressure Thermit Welding	PTW
Gas Welding	Pressure Gas Welding	PGW
	Oxy-Hydrogen Welding	OHW
	Oxy-Acetylene Welding	OAW
	Air-Acetylene Welding	AAW
Forge Welding	Roll Welding	RW
	Die Welding	DW
	Hammer Welding	HW

Note: Letter designations have not been assigned to arc-spot, resistance-spot, arc-seam and resistance-seam welding or to projection welding since the weld symbols used are adequate.
*The following suffixes may be used if desired to indicate the method of applying the above processes:

Automatic Welding	—AU
Machine Welding	—ME
Manual Welding	—MA
Semi-Automatic Welding	—SA

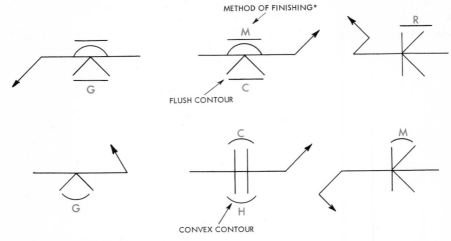

METHOD OF FINISHING*

FLUSH CONTOUR

CONVEX CONTOUR

*Finish symbols used herein indicate the method of finishing ("C" = chipping; "G" = grinding; "M" = machining; "R" = rolling; "H" = hammering) and not the degree of finish.

Fig. 23. Method of showing surface contour of welds. (AWS)

inserted in the tail. See Fig. 22 and Table I. Abbreviations in the tail may also call out some welding specifications which are included in more precise details on some other part of the print.

Surface Contour of Welds. When bead contour is important, a special flush, concave or convex contour symbol is added to the weld symbol. Welds that are to be mechanically finished also carry a finish symbol along with the contour symbols. See Fig. 23.

Back or Backing Welds. Back or backing welds refer to the weld made on the opposite side of the regular weld. Back welds are occasionally specified to insure adequate penetration and provide additional strength to a joint. This particular requirement is included opposite the weld symbol. No dimensions of back or backing welds except height of reinforcement

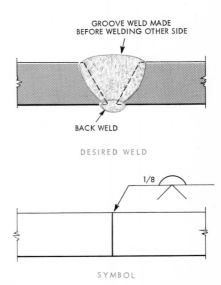

GROOVE WELD MADE BEFORE WELDING OTHER SIDE

BACK WELD

DESIRED WELD

1/8

SYMBOL

Fig. 24. Use of back weld symbol to indicate back weld. (AWS)

is shown on the weld symbol. See Fig. 24.

Melt-Thru Welds. When complete joint penetration of the weld through

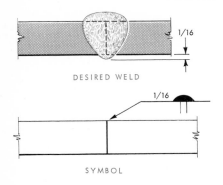

Fig. 25. Application of melt-thru symbol.

the material is required in welds made from one side only, a special melt-thru weld symbol is placed opposite the regular weld symbol. No dimension of melt-thru, except height of reinforcement, is shown on the weld symbol. See Fig. 25.

Surfacing Welds. Welds whose surfaces must be built up by single or multiple pass welding are provided with a surfacing weld symbol. The height of the built-up surface is indicated by a dimension placed to the left of the surfacing symbol. See Fig. 26.

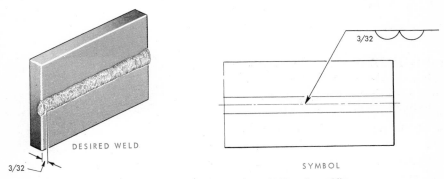

Fig. 26. Application of surfacing symbol to indicate surfaces built up by welding.

CHAPTER 36

Supplementary Welding Data

Underwater Cutting and Welding*

In principle, underwater cutting and welding is much the same as conventional cutting and welding in air, except that environmental conditions impose additional limitations on the operator. Diving apparel (Fig. 1), water depth, adverse currents, low temperatures, poor visibility, and unstable footing, are all factors which make underwater cutting and welding difficult. Since the diver can work only a short time on the bottom, particularly at lower depths, the use of correct techniques and equipment is extremely important.

Underwater Cutting—Principles of Operation

Metals may be cut or pierced underwater by any of three methods. The two most common methods are known

Fig. 1. Special equipment is used for underwater cutting and welding. (Craftsweld Equipment Corp.)

* Courtesy Craftsweld Equipment Corp. and U.S. Navy Dept.

as oxy-hydrogen and arc-oxygen and they depend on the oxidation of metals for cutting action. In these two processes, heat is applied to a spot on the metal. When the metal has reached the "kindling" temperature, pure oxygen is directed at the heated spot. This causes the metal to burn very rapidly. Both the oxy-hydrogen and arc-oxygen methods are limited to cutting plain carbon and low alloy steels.

The third method of cutting uses the metallic arc. Actually, this is more of a melting rather than a burning operation. The metallic arc cutting process is better for cutting corrosion resisting and austenitic steels or other metals which do not corrode readily.

Oxygen-Hydrogen Cutting

The oxy-hydrogen process of flame cutting underwater involves the use of compressed oxygen, compressed hydrogen, and air under pressure. The technique does not differ radically from open-air cutting practice, since the torch performs in much the same way as a standard torch being operated in air. One of the characteristics that set underwater cutting apart from ordinary cutting is that the former requires the operator to accustom himself to working with relatively high gas pressures. These pressures must of necessity increase with the water depth at which the work is being performed. Mechanically, underwater cutting is accomplished by the same means used topside, except that an additional hose is used to deliver compressed air to an air shield, or "skirt," that surrounds

the cutting tip and sheaths it with a bubble of air.

This shield is not necessary to keep the flame alight in that the fuel gas and oxygen support combustion even when the flame is immersed in water. The purpose of the shield is to stabilize the flame and hold the water away from the area of metal being heated. The higher pressures in underwater work are necessary to provide the required increase in flame intensity and to overcome the water pressure at whatever depth the torch is being operated. Hydrogen therefore, is the fuel gas used almost exclusively in this type of cutting, because it is generally unsafe to use acetylene at pressures higher than 15 pounds.

Equipment. The *underwater cutting torch* is made to operate with one hand, leaving the other hand free or for steadying the progress of the torch. It is generally manufactured with a 90° head, but may be special ordered with straight head, 75° or 45° specified. See Fig. 2. An *air shield,* or jacket, screws over the cutting tip with the front end extending about ⅛″ beyond the end of the tip.

The *oxygen and hydrogen regulators* are of the heavy-duty type equipped with adequate safety blow-off devices.

A special *electrical lighter* has been developed to ignite the torch underwater. This lighter is not designed for operation in the air. When used above water, the tips burn and have to be renewed. The lighter operates on 110-120 volts, and is controlled from the surface. It consists of an insulated han-

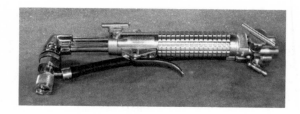

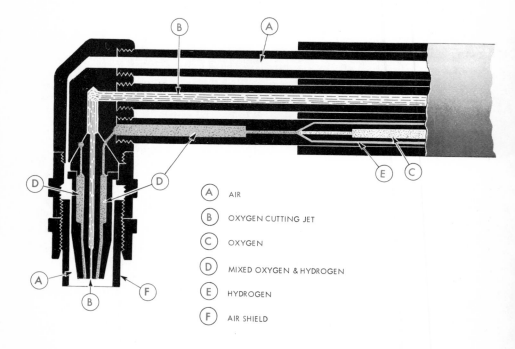

A   AIR

B   OXYGEN CUTTING JET

C   OXYGEN

D   MIXED OXYGEN & HYDROGEN

E   HYDROGEN

F   AIR SHIELD

Fig. 2. Underwater oxy-hydrogen cutting torch.   (U.S. Navy)

dle with two spring copper jaws terminating in carbon tips. See Fig. 3. The current is always turned off when the lighter is not in use.

Lighting the torch in air. The following procedure is to be used when lighting the oxy-hydrogen cutting torch in the air:

1. Open hydrogen cylinder valve

and adjust pressure regulator to 25 to 30 lbs., plus additional pressure to compensate for water depth where cutting is to be done and hose friction. Added pressure should be approximately 50 lbs. per 100 feet of water depth and 5 lbs. per 100 feet for hose friction. See Table I.

2. Open oxygen cylinder valve and

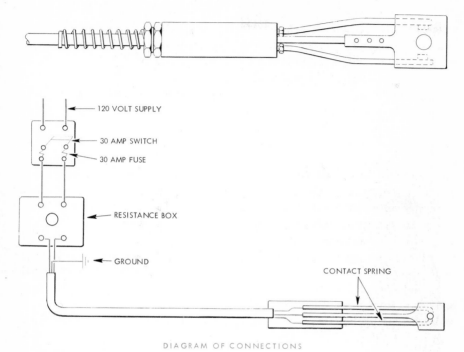

DIAGRAM OF CONNECTIONS

Fig. 3. Underwater torch lighter. (U.S. Navy)

TABLE I

Recommended Pressures (Gage Pressure at Surface) for Oxy-Hydrogen
Underwater Cutting Torch

WORKING DEPTH (FEET)	WATER PRESSURE (LBS. APPROX.)	LENGTH OF HOSE (FEET)	AIR	HYDROGEN	OXYGEN
			PRESSURE (LBS.)		
10	4	100	55	55	75
20	9	100	60	60	80
30	13	100	65	65	85
40	17	150	75	75	95
50	22	150	80	80	100
60	26	200	90	90	110
70	30	200	95	95	115
80	35	250	100	100	120
90	39	250	105	105	125
100	43	300	115	115	135
125	54	300	125	125	145
150	65	300	140	140	160
175	76	400	155	155	175
200	87	450	170	170	190
225	97	450	185	185	200

(U.S. Navy)

adjust pressure regulator. Oxygen pressure should be proportional to surface cutting, depending upon the thickness of metal, plus additional pressure to compensate for depth of water and hose friction.

3. Adjust the compressed air control valve to provide about 25 lbs. of pressure plus additional pressure to compensate for depth and hose friction. The compressed air is not a critical factor except if the pressure is too great it may affect vision because of the excessive flow of air bubbles.

4. Open the oxygen and hydrogen valves to clear the hose, and then shut them.

5. Now proceed to light the torch and adjust it with both the oxygen and hydrogen preheating valves as wide open as possible and still have long sharp cones in the flame. If you cannot see the cones in the sunlight, hold the torch in the shade against a dark object.

Testing flame. Before lowering the torch to the diver, the flame should be tested for stability underwater. This may be done as follows:

1. Hold the hose at a point 6 ft. or so back from the torch. Drop or throw the lighted torch into the water so that the flame is three feet or more underwater.

2. If close to the water level, the torch may be held in the hand and moved back and forth with the flame well underwater. The properly adjusted torch will not go out under these conditions.

3. The torch may be tested for cutting by making a short cut on a piece of scrap steel. A torch that will not cut in air can not be expected to cut underwater. Care should be taken not to foul the tip.

Lowering the torch. A lighted torch may be lowered underwater in one of three ways:

1. In moderate or shallow depths and easily accessible locations, the lighted torch may be carried below by hand. In such case, the diver should be prepared to make adjustments to the flame to compensate for increased pressure during descent.

2. In shallow depths and locations where it is absolutely certain that the flame can be kept clear of all hoses, lines, diver's suit, and helmet, etc., the lighted torch may be lowered directly to a point within reach of the diver. Never lower a lighted torch until it is certain that the diver is ready and watching for it and is in the clear in such a position that the torch flame cannot possibly strike his helmet, suit or air line.

3. The torch may be carried below by the diver or bent to a shackle and sent down on a finder-line.

Lighting torch underwater. The following procedure is to be used when lighting the oxy-hydrogen torch underwater:

1. Open the air valve until the bubble coming from the tip is 3″ long.

2. Open the hydrogen valve until the bubble from the torch tip is about 3″ long. Note the setting and close the valve.

3. Open the preheating oxygen valve until the bubble is about 2½″ long.

4. Reopen the air and hydrogen valves to the settings determined in steps 1 and 2.

5. Signal the tender to turn on the igniter.

6. Hold the torch horizontally with the tip pointing away from the lines, hose, and person.

7. Hold the igniter so that the gas from the torch tip blows through the hole in the igniter guard and past the igniter points.

8. Squeeze the igniter contacts together and then release. The spark formed as the igniter points spring apart will ignite the preheat flame, if adjustment of the torch valves is correct.

9. If the torch fails to ignite, open the hydrogen valve a little more and try again.

10. If the torch still fails to ignite, enrich the mixture by turning on a little more oxygen.

11. Adjustment may be continued, turning on first more hydrogen and then more oxygen, until it is certain that adjustment of the mixture is not at fault.

Cutting operation. Successful underwater cutting means the ability to adjust the torch for preheating in both fresh and salt water. Also necessary is the skill to recognize the action of the torch when it begins to cut and when the cutting stops. With proper flame, instantaneous preheat results and cutting is rapid and continuous in any position, even under poor visibility when guiding the torch by sound, glow, and feel.

The lighted torch underwater gives off a characteristic rumbling or bubbling sound. By listening to this sound, you can get an indication of the condition of the flame.

Here are some general conditions to watch for:

1. *Compressed air too high.* Cools metal too rapidly and excessive force is required to hold the torch head against the work.

2. *Compressed air too low.* Fails to displace water, causing the flame to flicker and sputter.

3. *Hydrogen too high.* This will "blast" or "flare" and may melt the torch tip.

4. *Hydrogen too low.* Will not maintain flame or may not light or may backfire into the tip. Flame will not cut.

5. *Oxygen too high.* Torch sputters and flares. Excessive force is required to hold torch to the work.

6. *Oxygen too low.* Preheat flame will not light or will pop out.

On the bottom, place yourself in a comfortable position with your eyes below the level of cutting whenever possible. Hold the preheating flame against the metal. If the flame is right, there should be a bright yellow glow. If not, readjust the valves until you get it, first the hydrogen and then the oxygen. Move the valves very little at a time and watch the results.

When the proper preheat is reached, squeeze the high pressure oxygen lever. Pull the trigger gradually rather than suddenly to avoid chilling the preheated spot. Hold the end of the air nozzle about ⅜″ away from the metal and point it slightly in the direction of the cut. Some divers hold the edge of the nozzle against the metal as a gage. Others use nozzles with prongs, and rest the prongs lightly on the metal. However, the skillful operator usually is able to hold the torch a uniform distance without any steadying devices. Occasionally, even the skillful operator will use prongs when cutting in muddy waters or in difficult positions.

Advance the cut by moving the torch at a steady, even rate of speed, along the line of cut, fast enough to keep tthe cut going, and slow enough to cut completely through the metal.

If the torch is advanced too slowly, the steel will cool below the ignition temperature and the cutting action will stop. You then will have "lost the cut" and will have to start over.

If the torch is advanced too rapidly, the metal will not be completely cut in two. The skipped spots will be very hard to cut out.

If the cut has been lost, it may be restarted by going back ½ to ¾ inch and starting on the side of the old cut. The purpose of this is to be sure that the cut is complete and no "holiday" left to give trouble.

After the cut is completed, close tightly all valves on the torch before returning to the surface to prevent clogging of passages. At the end of the day, blow out the torch, dry it and put it away with all valves open.

Arc-Oxygen Cutting

The Arc-Oxygen cutting process is in wide use throughout the world for both surface and underwater cutting because of the many advantages it offers. The principles of arc-oxygen cutting are very simple. An electric current is applied through a tubular steel electrode, creating an arc that heats the metal to be cut. Oxygen, delivered through the hollow core of the electrode directly to the point of reaction, serves as the cutting agent. The arc has sufficient heat to start melting the metal instantly, even underwater. And, in cutting mild steel for example, the application of oxygen to the molten metal results in the oxidation or combustion of the steel. The additional heat liberated by this oxidation "superheats" the arc and, as the cut proceeds, the steel is actually consumed by a self-sustaining process — not just melted away.

In application, arc-oxygen cutting is fast, easy, safe and economical. No pre-heating is required, and no previous skill or experience is needed. It can be used to cut metals of almost any thickness. An unskilled operator will cut a 1″ mild steel plate with arc-oxygen in less than half the time required for oxy-acetylene on the surface. The heat affected area of the cut metal is about the same as in arc welding, and since the heat penetration is quite shallow, there is practically no warpage of the cut metal, and therefore no attendant stresses.

For underwater, the process has all but replaced oxy-hydrogen because, with the "drag technique," arc-oxygen cutting can be accomplished in zero visibility at any practical depth, while oxy-hydrogen involves considerable skill, pre-heating, and the difficulty of maintaining proper flame, advance of cut, etc.

Equipment. Underwater cutting with arc-oxygen requires an oxygen supply, a 300 ampere Welding Machine (preferably DC) and a fully insulated torch. See Fig. 4. A double

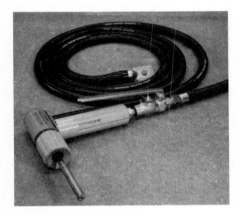

Fig. 4. Arc-oxygen underwater cutting torch. (Craftsweld Equipment Corp.)

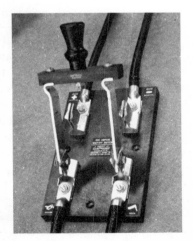

Fig. 5. 300-ampere shut-off switch shown installed along ground and torch cables. (Craftsweld Equipment Corp.)

pole single throw knife switch must be installed along the torch and ground welding cables at a point that is within easy reach of the diver's tender. See Fig. 5. The switch is turned on only when the diver is actually making a cut. At all other times, the switch must be kept in the off position.

Additional equipment includes a ground clamp designed for underwater service, a diver's flip-type eyeshield, diving outfit equipped with telephone, oxygen cylinder with pressure regulator, oxygen hose, and welding cables.

Cutting operation. DC current with straight polarity is recommended for underwater cutting. AC current is less desirable because it increases the electrical hazards to the diver and causes greater electrolytic damage to underwater equipment. The cutting arc is produced by special high speed $5/16''$ x $14''$ tubular steel waterproofed electrodes.

Arc oxygen cutting electrodes are manufactured to the highest commercial and military standards. They are recommended for use with a 300-ampere DC welding machine, but are almost equally as efficient with AC. These electrodes have a special extruded flux covering that makes some very important contributions to the cutting process. First, the flux burns at a rate slower than the consumable hollow steel core of the electrode, and thereby maintains an automatic arc gap at the cutting point. This makes it unnecessary for the operator to hold an arc (as he must do in conventional arc welding) and therefore the simple technique requires only that he *drag*

Fig. 6. Diver's flip-type eyeshield shown installed on helmet. (Craftsweld Equipment Corp.)

the electrode across the work. Second, the flux is an insulating medium, and eliminates all chance of arcing from the side of the electrode to any adjacent metal. Third, the flux performs the very special function of helping any non-oxidized metal or slag flow from the cut. In addition, the steel core of the electrode, by introducing molten steel into the reaction, makes it possible to cut "hard-to-cut" metals in a way much like the iron powder cutting process. (See Chapter 32) Thus, one electrode combines the qualities of flux-injection and iron powder

cutting without the need for special additional equipment.

All cable and connections must be in perfect condition. All connections should be insulated and made watertight by careful taping, especially those that will be submerged during operations.

The flip-type eyeshield should be attached to the outside of the diver's helmet faceplate (Fig. 6) with appropriate lenses as follows:

#4 lens for very muddy water

#6 lens for average conditions

For ease in handling, the power cable and oxygen hose should be taped together at intervals of 2 feet.

The diver should wear a watertight dress, dry rubber mittens and a "beany" that covers his ears. The helmet chin button is usually insulated with rubber tape or a baby bottle nipple.

The actual cutting operation should proceed in the following manner:

1. Start the welding machine and set for 300 amperes. Be sure the knife switch on the welding cable is open (off).

TABLE II
Arc-Oxygen Cutting Data
(Average Conditions for Mild Steel)

THICKNESS OF STEEL	¼"	½"	¾"	1"
Tubular Steel Electrodes Consumed per 100 ft. of cut	21 lbs. 70 pcs.	29 lbs. 100 pcs.	29 lbs. 100 pcs.	33 lbs. 100 pcs.
Oxygen Consumed per 100 ft. of cut	250 cu. ft.	300 cu. ft.	350 cu. ft.	400 cu. ft.
Oxygen Pressure*	20 psi	30 psi	40 psi	50 psi

*Add 5 psi for each 10 ft. depth of water plus 5 to 10 psi for each 100 ft. of hose used.
*Use additional 10 to 20 psi for cutting cast iron, stainless steel and nonferrous metals.

2. Set the oxygen regulator for the required pressure. See Table II.

3. When submerged to the proper cutting position, attach the ground clamp to a clean area on the work that will provide a good electrical connection. Locate the ground clamp so you always face it when the current is on. Cutting must be done when facing the ground connection to avoid serious electrolytic damage to the helmet. See Fig. 7.

4. Insert an electrode in the torch and lock it in position with a slight turn of the torch locknut. Close the eyeshield over the faceplate and crack open the oxygen valve on the torch by squeezing the lever slightly. Cracking the oxygen valve keeps the electrode from welding itself to the work when the arc is started.

5. Call to the surface for "Current On." This tells the tender to close the knife switch on the welding cables.

6. Place the tip of the electrode at right angles to the work and strike the arc. As soon as the arc is started, squeeze the oxygen lever all the way and then drag the electrode along the line of cut.

7. Bear down on the torch so as to keep pressing the electrode against the work. Move forward as fast as possible while maintaining full penetration of cut. Lack of penetration will be evident by the amount of "back spray." Always keep the electrode against the work while cutting.

8. When the electrode has been consumed, call to the surface for "Current Off." After the tender reports that the current is off, unscrew the torch locknut slightly and blow the electrode stub out of the torch by squeezing the oxygen lever. Then insert a new electrode and continue the cut.

Metallic Arc Underwater Cutting

The process of arc cutting is purely a method of applying the heat of the electric arc to melt the metal along a desired line of cut. In underwater cut-

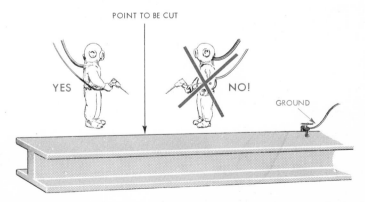

Fig. 7. Diver must always face the ground connection when the current is on. He should do all cutting between himself and the ground. To avoid serious damage to helmet, diver must never stand between torch and ground. (Craftsweld Equipment Corp.)

ting, this method may be used in situations in which no oxygen is available and when employing ordinary covered welding electrodes, provides a means for cutting both ferrous and nonferrous metals. This process, known as metallic arc cutting, is superior to those employing oxygen when cutting steel plate of thickness less than 1/4" as well as for nonferrous materials such as brass, copper, nickel-copper, and manganese bronze, regardless of thickness.

Equipment. The recommended power supply for metallic arc underwater cutting is a DC welding generator having a capacity of at least 400 amperes and connected for straight polarity. Satisfactory cutting can be done with a 300 ampere DC machine but the cutting rate will be slower. An alternating current power source is usually not recommended for underwater cutting because the heat produced is less and the hazard greater from a safety standpoint.

As in all underwater cutting operations involving an electrical circuit, it is important that a positive disconnecting switch be used in the circuit. This gives the diver full protection by having the current on only when he is actually cutting.

The electrode holder must be completely insulated and designed specifically for underwater cutting.

Special waterproof electrodes are available for cutting purposes. See Table III.

Operation. When employing 3/16" electrodes with a power source of 300 amperes at about 40 volts, steel plate up to 1/4" thickness can be cut by simply "dragging" the electrode along the the desired line of cut. The thickest plate which can be cut using this drag technique is about 1/4" where the capacity is 300 amperes, and about 3/8" where the amperage can be increased to 400. To cut thicker plate, a slow, short stroke, sawing motion must be used to push the molten metal out of the far side of the cut. Skillful application of this sawing technique makes the metallic arc-cutting process practical over a wide range of thicknesses even where the large electrodes and heavy currents recommended for use

TABLE III
Metallic Arc Underwater Cutting

ELECTRODE SIZE	UNIT	NO. OF ELECTRODES APPROX.	POWER SOURCE	STEEL PLATE CUT IN FT/BOX OF ELECTRODES		
				1/4" THICK	1/2" THICK	3/4" THICK
3/16"..........	50 lb. box	410	300 amps	185	102	—
3/16"..........		410	400 amps	307	135	58
1/4"..........		220	400 amps	176	77	44

(U.S. Navy)

Note: With 300 amperes available for underwater cutting, use 3/16" diameter electrodes; 5/32" may be used but the burnoff rate is very rapid.
With 400 amperes available, use 3/16" diameter or preferably 1/4" diameter electrodes.

with the drag technique are not available. Where large electrodes and heavy currents can be had, the drag technique has the advantages of speed and simplicity of operation. Mastery of the cutting technique will be aided by a thorough understanding on the part of the operator that the metal is merely melted, not oxidized or consumed in any way, and that if the molten metal does not run out of the cut by itself, it must be pushed out by manipulation of the electrode.

nature, it is generally advisable to make a test weld at the same water depth and working conditions. This test should then be brought to the surface for inspection and testing.

Equipment. The preferred power source for underwater welding is a 300 ampere DC generator connected for straight polarity. A positive operating safety switch must be installed in the welding circuit. See Fig. 8.

The electrode holder must be completely insulated, durable, and allow

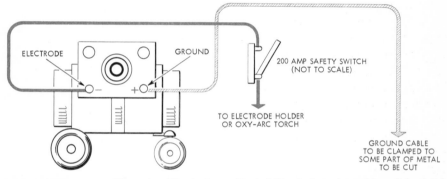

ELECTRODE · GROUND · 200 AMP SAFETY SWITCH (NOT TO SCALE) · TO ELECTRODE HOLDER OR OXY-ARC TORCH · GROUND CABLE TO BE CLAMPED TO SOME PART OF METAL TO BE CUT

Fig. 8. All underwater cutting and welding is done with straight polarity and a safety switch must be installed in the circuit. (U.S. Navy)

Underwater Welding

Underwater welding is done primarily on mild steel with special underwater welding electrodes. These electrodes will produce welds that develop 80 per cent of the tensile strength and 50 per cent of the ductility of similar welds made on the surface. The reduced ductility and strength is the result of the quenching action of the water.

If a weld to be made is of a critical

Fig. 9. Underwater welding electrode holder. (Craftsweld Equipment Corp.)

for easy changing of electrodes. Holders with metallic jaws as used for welding in air are not generally recommended even if they are fully insulated. A specially designed plastic holder for underwater welding is shown in Fig. 9.

Operation. Welding is done either with $3/16''$ or $5/32''$ diameter electrodes. No specifically designed electrodes have been developed for use in underwater welding. The two commercial brands of electrodes which have given satisfactory performance in underwater welding test are Westinghouse "Flexarc SW" and Lincoln "Fleetweld 37." These are designated for all-position welding. Since all electrode coatings deteriorate when immersed in water, it is a good idea to waterproof the covering by dipping the electrode in some waterproofing solution. Several solutions are commercially available. However, waterproofing is not entirely necessary if the electrodes are used within a short time after immersion. This can be achieved by sending the diver a few electrodes at a time. If the electrodes are waterproofed, care must be taken to clean off the tips so enough of the bare wire is exposed for easy starting of the arc.

The actual welding procedure underwater should be carried out as follows:

1. With $3/16''$ electrodes, set the welding machine for 225 to 280 amperes at water depths up to 50 feet. The correct amount of current should result in consuming one electrode in 49 to 55 seconds. If the electrode is not consumed in this time, proper current is not reaching the work due to long cables, poor connections, or improper setting of the welding machine. The $5/32''$ electrodes require somewhat less current and are consumed in a slightly shorter time.

2. Because of poor visibility under water, fillet welds should be used wherever possible, in order to provide an edge that the diver can use as a guide. The work must be clean of rust, paint and marine growth at all times.

3. Attach the ground clamp as close as possible to the section to be welded. It must be located so you always face the ground clamp when the current is on. See Fig. 7.

4. In making a *horizontal weld,* place the end of the electrode against the left end of the work at an angle of about 15° to 45° (right-hand operator) and call for "Current On." The arc should start as soon as the tender closes the knife switch. It may be necessary to scrape or tap the electrode against the work in order to start the arc.

When the arc has started, press the electrode against the work so that it consumes itself, and move the electrode along the line of weld at an even speed. Generally, 10″ of electrode will deposit about 8″ of weld.

Do not hold or space the arc the way welding is done in air when welding underwater, just keep holding the electrode against the work at the same angle that was used when starting the weld. After the electrode has burned down to the stub, call for "Current Off."

5. Before starting with another elec-

trode, clean the end of the previous deposit and then make a slight overlap when the weld is resumed. When making multiple passes, the entire weld must be thoroughly cleaned before the next pass is made.

6. Use the same technique for *vertical welds,* starting from the top down, with the electrode pointing upward.

7. *Overhead welds* require greater skill and more exact manipulation but can be made successfully. Increasing the angle of the electrode to the work up to 55° will help improve the contour of the weld.

Safety in Underwater Cutting and Welding

In underwater cutting and welding, no matter what procedure is used, the importance of safety must be constantly emphasized. In underwater operations, the life and safety of the divers are ever dependent upon the strict observance of safety regulations. The use of electric power in underwater cutting and welding can be very hazardous. This is especially true in sea water which is an excellent conductor of electricity. With the proper safeguards and reasonable care, underwater cutting and welding can be accomplished with comparative safety if the basic protective measures which follow in this section are strictly observed. Furthermore, personnel engaged in welding or cutting operations should exercise their imagination to insure that no hazard not specifically mentioned herein, but caused by a pe-

culiar combination of unusual circumstances, exists without all possible steps being taken to eliminate it or to provide emergency controls.

1. Only a qualified diver, assisted by an experienced tender, should use underwater equipment.

2. The diver should practice cutting or welding above water before attempting underwater work.

3. Detailed operating instructions should be obtained from the equipment manufacturer and followed carefully.

4. The oxygen regulator used should be adequate for delivery of the required volume without freezing up. Be sure oxygen regulator, hose, fittings and torch are all clean and free of oil. Never use oil, grease or any other combustible lubricant on equipment that uses oxygen.

5. The diver must be attired so that his body is fully insulated from the work, torch, and water. Precautions must be taken to insulate the diver's head from the helmet by wearing a skull cap.

6. The current should be off at all times except when the diver is actually cutting or welding.

7. After inserting the electrode in the holder, the diver should place the electrode against the work before signalling for "Current On." The tender, after closing the switch, should immediately confirm this action by repeating "Current On."

8. When the electrode is consumed, the diver should not attempt to remove the stub until he has signalled for "Current Off" and then he

must wait until the request is confirmed.

9. A careful examination should always be made before starting a cut to prevent the piece that is cut away from falling or rolling over and pinning the diver down or fouling his lines.

10. The cable and torch insulation, and all joints in electrical circuit, should be checked for current leakage at frequent intervals. All underwater cable connections should be fully insulated and watertight.

11. No work of any kind should ever be permitted on the surface over the area in which the diver will be working within a radius of at least equal to the depth of underwater operations.

12. The diving gear should be in good condition, and equipped with a reliable loudspeaker telephone. The diver should always wear dry rubber mittens.

13. Before starting any cutting or welding, be sure there are no highly combustible or explosive materials (whether gases, liquids or solids) close to the point to be cut or welded, or within a radius of at least 50 feet. Sparks have been known to travel that far, especially upwards (and in other directions through existing channels).

14. Because difficult footing and poor visibility generally prevail underwater, the diver should handle torch or welding holder with care, staying completely clear of all hoses, and avoiding too much slack in his lines. Keep all hoses and lines away from the cutting or welding operation. Diver must also be careful not to get himself into any position where something might fall on him or his lines.

15. The diver should not permit any part of his body or gear to become a part of the electric circuit.

16. If AC current must be used for cutting, the resulting shock can be more severe if the diver's body or gear accidentally "enters the circuit." (AC current is not recommended for welding.)

17. The diver should always telephone the tender to shut off current before changing electrodes, and keep it shut off except when actually cutting or welding. Be sure to close eyeshield (with proper lens) before striking an arc. Always remove the electrode before taking torch or welding holder underwater or returning it to the surface.

18. The diver should inspect his helmet and all other metallic parts of his grear regularly for signs of deterioration resulting from electrolysis. He should make his ground connection at a point with reference to his welding or cutting position that will reduce electrolysis to a minimum. He should never turn his back on the ground connection.

19. After each day's use, the torch or welding holder should be thoroughly rinsed in fresh water, and then dried, to help maintain proper operating efficiency.

20. All Arc-Oxygen Cutting Torches are equipped with a removable Flash Arrester Cartridge containing a monel screen. This screen is very

inexpensive and easy to replace. If the screen gets clogged with dirt or slag, or burns out, it should be replaced. Operating the torch without flash arrester or screen could be a safety hazard. (Frequent clogging or burning out of the screen may occur if too little oxygen pressure reaches the electrode or if you attempt to burn the electrode down to the very last.)

QUESTIONS FOR STUDY AND DISCUSSION

1. Why is hydrogen rather than acetylene used as a fuel in underwater cutting?

2. How does an underwater cutting torch differ from a cutting torch used in open air?

3. Approximately how much additional hydrogen pressure must be provided to compensate for water depth and hose friction?

4. Why is excessive compressed air pressure undesirable?

5. How should a flame be tested before lowering the torch to the diver?

6. In what ways can a lighted torch be lowered underwater?

7. How should a torch be lighted underwater?

8. How is it possible to tell underwater if a torch flame is correctly adjusted?

9. What happens when the compressed air is too high or too low?

10. What is likely to occur if the hydrogen pressure is too high or too low?

11. What occurs when the oxygen pressure is too high or too low?

12. Why is the proper speed at which a torch is advanced so important in making a clean cut?

13. What is the basic principle of the arc-oxygen cutting process?

14. In the arc-oxygen system, why must a switch be installed on the surface along the torch and ground welding cables?

15. Why is DC current preferable for underwater cutting?

16. What type of electrodes are used for underwater cutting in the arc-oxygen process?

17. What is meant by the "drag technique" in underwater cutting?

18. When cutting with arc-oxygen, why should the operator always face the ground connection?

19. When is the metallic arc process used in underwater cutting?

20. Why is an AC machine not recommended for underwater cutting?

21. What type of motion is used to cut light materials with the metallic arc?

22. Why do welds made underwater have less ductility than those made on the surface?

23. What type of electrodes are used for underwater cutting?

24. Why are fillet welds most often recommended for all underwater welding?

INDEX

[Text references are shown in standard type; page numbers of additional illustrations which may be helpful are shown in italics.]

INDEX

INDEX

Edge joint, inert-gas-
    shielded arc, 162
Elastic limit, 10
Elasticity, 10
    modulus of, 10
Electrical terms, 32-35
Electrode
    for AC arc welders, 49
    for arc welders, 45, 49-51
    backed carbon, 216
    carbon arc, 216
    cast iron, 104-105
    characteristics, 55
    color code, 51-53
    conservation, 57
    definition, 49
        cast iron, 49-54
        high carbon steel, 49-54
        mild steel, 49-54
        non-ferrous, 49-54
        shape, *216*
        special alloy steel, 49-54
    diameter, 54-56
    Ferroweld, 104
    hardfacing
        chromium, 225
        moderate abrasion and
            impact resistant,
            225-227
        severe abrasion resist-
            ant, 225
        severe impact and
            moderately severe
            abrasion resistant,
            227
        stainless steel, 227
        tungsten, 225
    holder, arc welding, 5,
        215-216
        gripping, 63
    holding, 85-86
    identification, 51-53
    machinable, 104-105
    non-machinable, 104
    pure graphite, 216
    selecting, 57-60
    Softcast, 104
    Softweld, 104
    stainless steel, 122-123
    special, 60
    storage, 57
    Strongcast, 104
    tnngsten, 156-158
Electron beam, 267-272
    advantages, 268-269

controls, 271-272
equipment, 272
gun, *268*
limitations, 269
machine, *269*
pumping system, 271
vacuum chamber, *271*
Equal pressure blowpipe, 291
Etching tests, 383-384
Etching solutions
    ammonium persulphate,
        384
    hydrochloric acid, 383-384
    nitric acid, 60
Eutectic electrodes, 60
Expansion, 23-25
Expansion and alignment of
    pipe
    clamping, 349
    spacing, 348-349
    tacking, 349

F

Face centered cube, 16
Fatigue, 11
Ferrite, 18
Ferritic stainless steel, 120
Ferroweld, 104
Filler rod
    for carbon arc, 217
    characteristics in bronze
        welding, 333
    selecting for stainless
        steel, 329
    for Tig welding, 160
    use with gray cast iron,
        337
Fillet weld
    welded joint test, 283
    welding symbols, 395-396
Fixtures, 27
Flame
    adjustment,
        for aluminum, 344
        oxyacetylene, 303-304
        for stainless steel,
            328-329
    characteristics, 305
    control, 305-306
    cutting, 4
        beveling, 355
        cast iron, 356-358

determining pressure
    352-353
    lighting torch, 353
    piercing holes, 355
    round bar steel, 355
    steel, 353-355
    torch, 351-352
testing, 304-305
types
    carbonizing, 305,
        328-329
    neutral, 305, 328-329
    oxidizing, 305,
        328-329
Flange joint, oxy welding,
    315
Flashback, 306
Flash welding, 261-263
Flat position welding
    arc, 75
    butt joints, 312-314
    carrying puddle, 308-310
    corner joints, 315
    flange joints, 315
    lap joints, 315-316
    laying beads, 310-312
    oxyacetylene, 308
    T-joint, 316-317
Flux
    with aluminum, 342
    for bronze, 333
    for giay cast iron, 337
    for stainless steel, 329
Free-bend test, 379-380

G

Gamma iron, 18
Gas
    application, 5
    bubbles, 338
    welding, 3-4
Gas-shielded arc, 142
    processes, 143
Generator
    acetylene, 290
    high-pressure, 289
    low-pressure, 289
Gloves, *41-42*
Goggles, *41,* 296-297
Grain growth, 22
Gray cast iron, 100-101
    appearance of weld, *338*

INDEX

Pure graphite electrode, 216

INDEX